Annotated Texts for Translation
English–German

Karen Seago

TOPICS IN TRANSLATION
Series Editors:
Susan Bassnett, *University of Warwick, UK*
and Edwin Gentzler, *University of Massachusetts, Amherst, USA*
Editor for Translation in the Commercial Environment:
Geoffrey Samuelsson-Brown, *University of Surrey, UK*

Other Books in the Series
Annotated Texts for Translation: French – English
   Beverly Adab
Annotated Texts for Translation: English – French
   Beverly Adab
'Behind Inverted Commas': Translation and Anglo-German Cultural Relations in the
Nineteenth Century
   Susanne Stark
Constructing Cultures: Essays on Literary Translation
   Susan Bassnett and André Lefevere
Culture Bumps: An Empirical Approach to the Translation of Allusions
   Ritva Leppihalme
Practical Guide for Translators
   Geoffrey Samuelsson-Brown
The Coming Industry of Teletranslation
   Minako O'Hagan
The Interpreter's Resource
   Mary Phelan
The Pragmatics of Translation
   Leo Hickey (ed.)
The Rewriting of Njáls Saga: Translation, Ideology, and Icelandic Sagas
   Jón Karl Helgason
Translation, Power, Subversion
   Román Álvarez and M. Carmen-África Vidal (eds)
Translation and Nation: A Cultural Politics of Englishness
   Roger Ellis and Liz Oakley-Brown (eds)
Time Sharing on Stage: Drama Translation in Theatre and Society
   Sirkku Aaltonen
Words, Words, Words: The Translator and the Language Learner
   Gunilla Anderman and Margaret Rogers
Written in the Language of the Scottish Nation
   John Corbett

Please contact us for the latest book information:
Multilingual Matters, Frankfurt Lodge, Clevedon Hall,
Victoria Road, Clevedon, BS21 7HH, England
http://www.multilingual-matters.com

TOPICS IN TRANSLATION 20
Series Editors: Susan Bassnett, *University of Warwick*
and Edwin Gentzler, *University of Massachusetts, Amherst*

Annotated Texts for Translation: English–German

Functionalist Approaches Illustrated

Christina Schäffner

with Uwe Wiesemann

MULTILINGUAL MATTERS LTD
Clevedon • Buffalo • Toronto • Sydney

Library of Congress Cataloging in Publication Data
Schäffner, Christina
Annotated Texts for Translation: English–German: Functionalist Approaches
Illustrated/Christina Schäffner, Uwe Wiesemann
Topics in Translation: 20
Includes bibliographical references.
1. English language–Translating into German–Problems, exercises, etc. 2. Translating
and interpreting–Problems, exercises, etc. I. Wiesemann, Uwe. II. Title. III. Series.
PE1498.2.G47 S32 2001
438'.0221–dc21   00-068235

British Library Cataloguing in Publication Data
A catalogue entry for this book is available from the British Library.

ISBN 1-85359-407-5 (hbk)
ISBN 1-85359-406-7 (pbk)

Multilingual Matters Ltd
UK: Frankfurt Lodge, Clevedon Hall, Victoria Road, Clevedon BS21 7HH.
USA: UTP, 2250 Military Road, Tonawanda, NY 14150, USA.
Canada: UTP, 5201 Dufferin Street, North York, Ontario M3H 5T8, Canada.
Australia: Footprint Books, Unit 4/92a Mona Vale Road, Mona Vale, NSW 2103, Australia.

Typeset by Archetype-IT Ltd (http://www.archetype-it.com).
Printed and bound in Great Britain by the Cromwell Press Ltd.

Contents

Acknowledgements vii

Introduction: Aims of the Book 1
Developing Translation Competence within the Framework
of a Functionalist Approach 4

User Information, User Manuals: Introductory Comments 49

Sample Text 1:
Source Text: Hoover Ecologic, Washer dryer, Users Manual:
Step-by-step Guide 55
Target Text: Hoover Ecologic: Bedienungsschritte 59
Annotations 63

Sample Text 2:
Source Text: Community Information. How to Make an
Emergency '999' Call 79
Target Text: Community Information. Hinweise zum
Notruf 999 81
Annotations 83

Popular-scientific Texts in the Media: Introductory Comments

Sample Text 3:
Source Text: Infuriatingly Misleading Forecasts 95
Target Text: Irreführende Prognosen. 98
Annotations 102

Sample Text 4:
Source Text: Proof Against Heart Attacks 120
Target Text: Promille für das Herz 121
Annotations 122

Political Texts: Introductory Comments 133

Sample Text 5:
Source Text: Bad Faith and Dishonesty 137

Target Text: Mißtrauen und Unehrlichkeit 141
Annotations 146

Sample Text 6:
Source Text: John Major, Address spoken on the Occasion
of the Warsaw Uprising, 50th Anniversary Commemoration,
Warsaw, 1 August 1994 166
Target Text: Ansprache von John Major 169
Annotations 172

Reviews: Introductory Comments 184

Sample Text 7:
Source Text: German Media Moguls. Soul-searching 187
Target Text: Auf der Suche nach Herz – Deutschlands
Medienmagnaten 189
Annotations 191

Promotional Texts: Introductory Comments 200

Sample Text 8:
Source Text: Birmingham. Europe's Meeting Place 204
Target Text: Birmingham 208
Annotations 213
Target Text: Birmingham (Alternative Solution) 243

Legal Texts: Introductory Comments 248

Sample Text 9:
Source Text: Association of Independent Railways and
Preservation Societies Ltd. 252
Target Text: Satzung der Association of Independent
Railways and Preservation Societies Ltd. 257
Annotations 263

References 286

Acknowledgements

Acknowledgement is made to the Hoover European Appliance Group, the West Midlands Fire Service, Time Inc. (27 December 1993), Gerry Adams MP, John Major MP, *The Economist* (23 April 1994), *The Economist* (3 February 1996), Birmingham Marketing Partnership, and the Association of Independent Railways and Preservation Societies Ltd. for permission to reprint the English texts used in this volume.

The authors would like to express their gratitude for the support, comments and valuable advice received from friends and colleagues, in particular Albrecht Neubert (Hartenstein), Paul Kussmaul (Germersheim), Beate Herting (Leipzig), Sabine Buchröder-Brotherton (Birmingham), Andrew Chesterman (Helsinki) and Dariusz Galasinski (Wolverhampton). Thanks are also due to Final Year students in the School of Languages and European Studies, Aston University Birmingham, who helped in testing the approach to translating as illustrated in this book.

Introduction: Aims of the Book

The processes of globalisation and internationalisation of political, economic, educational, and cultural communicative practices are accompanied by increasing demands for translations, in particular for translations from English (see the statistics in Venuti, 1995: 12ff.). These translations are expected to be of high quality and available to clients and/or addressees very quickly. That is, cost-effect calculations apply to the translation industry as well. Professional translators are expected to produce target texts (*products*) that are appropriate for their purpose in an efficient and effective way (*process*). In order to fulfil these expectations and requirements, translators need to be highly qualified; in other words, they need to have developed a specific translation competence.

Despite advances in machine translation, it is generally recognised that such systems can (at present) only cope successfully in a limited way; for example, if the texts are highly conventionalised in their structure, or if only a 'rough' translation is required. Translation is not a mechanical process but rather a complex social and cognitive activity which requires decision-making. Moreover, it is the professional expertise of human translators and translation scholars that is a condition for the further development of machine translation and machine-assisted translation. As a consequence, practising translators can increasingly benefit from software that has been provided to make their daily work more efficient, effective, and reliable (e.g. translation memory systems).

The complex activity of translation as a human activity involves the production of a text by translators as experts in interlingual and intercultural communication. This activity involves informed decision-making, i.e. informed on the basis of translation competence. Translation competence is itself a complex notion; it includes, at least, linguistic, cultural, and subject competence, as well as procedural competence (e.g. efficient research on necessary background information about the topic, the subject domain, or genre conventions). Translator-training programmes aim at developing translation competence, and they do this partly by providing a theoretical framework. There is increasing agreement within the discipline of Translation Studies that translators need to be aware of the nature of their professional activity. More specifically, they need to be, or need to be trained to become aware of translation as a social and cognitive activity. They need to understand that all activities are determined by a specific purpose and aim to achieve some goal; to understand that translators work in specific socio-cultural conditions, that decision-making involves reflecting about these conditions, etc. A functionalist approach to translation is particularly well suited as a framework for performing actual translation assignments and for commenting on the decisions made. Working within this specific framework is also very useful for students of translation and novices in the field, to help them develop their translation competence.

The aim of this book is to present a specific framework for dealing with recurring translation problems in a number of genres that are frequently translated. The translation direction is from English into German, and the framework with its methodology and concepts is provided by functionalist approaches to translation. On the basis of illustrative sample texts, we comment on the decisions taken in our production of the target texts in view of the specified translation assignments. This means, taking into consideration the social contexts in which the target texts have to function, their addressees, genre conventions, linguistic constraints, etc. We have opted for rather lengthy annotations in order to provide a detailed account of the relevant translation decision-making processes, thus making our decisions transparent to the readers.

The addressees of this book are primarily students of translation and novices in the field. They may use the English source texts and produce (independently or in teamwork) their own target texts and then compare them to the target texts provided by us. Reading our extensive and detailed comments in the annotations can help them develop, or enhance, their translation competence. We do not claim that our target texts are the only possible solutions. However, we wish to maintain that they are highly appropriate for the specified purposes. In this respect, the texts, and in particular the annotations, may also be used by translator trainers in classroom situations, e.g. to discuss whether our arguments are convincing and to assess the appropriateness of alternative solutions in comparison to those suggested by us. Practising translators who wish to learn more about a functionalist approach, or who are preparing to sit translation examinations, may also find this book helpful.

Although our primary addressees are students, the book is not intended to be a textbook to be worked through from beginning to end. That is, the texts are not arranged according to a didactic scaling, taking students from simple to complex tasks. We have instead grouped the texts according to types and genres, with each group preceded by some general comments about recurring translation problems and potential translation strategies that can be applied. We are concerned with professional translation, and not with using translation exercises for language learning purposes. Therefore, we have provided a translation brief for each of the sample texts (including deadlines), and in the annotations, we have also commented on requirements for layout and (re)search procedures. The introductory chapter presents a brief survey of the discipline of Translation Studies and a detailed account of the framework used for the sample texts, so that the book will also be useful for students and/or translators who do not have a thorough grounding in translation theory.

By focusing on recurring translation problems and illustrating the translation strategies applied, we want to demonstrate that critical reflection on a translation assignment will help translators to make informed decisions, to comment on them, and defend them, if required.

Developing Translation Competence within the Framework of a Functionalist Approach

The Increasing Need for Translation, Translators and Translator Training

Translation plays an increasingly important role in and for society. To cope with this demand, more and more highly qualified translators are needed. Translators gain a professional qualification by a variety of methods, e.g. in specifically designed university programmes at undergraduate level or at postgraduate level, by passing specific examinations (such as the Institute of Linguists' examination for the Diploma in Translation in the UK), by attending workshops organised by professional bodies. There is widespread agreement among translation scholars and translator trainers that knowledge of two languages is not enough for performing the task of translation up to a professional standard. What is required is a specific translation competence, which, however, takes time to develop. Moreover, the actual activities performed by translators are constantly changing in view of new requirements, i.e. they go beyond what is traditionally understood by the term 'translation' (on the job profiles of translators see Snell-Hornby, 1999; Schmitt, 1998b). For example, their work may also include technical writing (see Göpferich, 1998a), pre- and post-editing, desktop publishing, etc. As Pavlovich (1999: 37) argues: 'Nowadays clients expect and demand finished products complete, with RAM-eating graphics on self-opening disks in addition to electronic transfers.'

The growing need for translations and thus for qualified professional translators has gone hand in hand with the emergence of Translation Studies as an academic discipline in its own right. Within the discipline, there has been a development from a more traditional view of translation as reproduction of a text to more dynamic approaches which focus on the purposes and functions of texts in communicative settings which, in turn, are determined by socio-historical conditions. Theoretical reflections about translation have largely been motivated by practical needs. In other words, it has often been an aim of translation scholars to transform theoretical insights into guidelines for practical application and/or into methodologies for teaching and training. Performing the activity of translation within the framework of a theoretical approach allows translators to make informed decisions. Functionalist approaches, which view translation as professional text production for intercultural communication, as a social and cognitive activity performed by experts are very well suited to provide such a framework, as will be illustrated in this volume.

In the following sections, I will briefly discuss major approaches within the development of Translation Studies as a discipline, and some of the central concepts used, and then present in more detail the framework of a functionalist approach within which the sample texts in this volume have been translated and annotated.

The Discipline of Translation Studies: Approaches and Concepts

Translation as an activity has a tradition reaching far back to the beginnings of recorded history and beyond that to the oral tradition. Throughout history, translators have contributed to the development of alphabets and of national languages (for example, Bible translators played a decisive role in the development of the vernacular in their nations), to the development of national literatures, to the dissemination of knowledge and the advancement of science, to the transmission of cultural values (see Delisle & Woodsworth, 1995). The translation methods predominantly employed over the centuries were determined by the dominant philosophy of the time and / or underlying conceptions of the nature of translation and how the translated text would be used. There is a long tradition of thought and an enormous body of opinion about translation. There is evidence that translators argued about literal *versus* free translation, that they defended their translation solutions against criticism (e.g. Martin Luther on his translation of the Bible into German, see Störig, 1963), and that they questioned the very possibility of translation (Humboldt, 1963; Schleiermacher, 1963; Venuti, 1995: 99ff; Schäffner, 2000c). The vast body of theoretical and practical reflections on translation is well documented, for example, in the anthologies edited by Robinson (1997a) and Venuti (2000).

However, it can be argued that the views and / or doctrines expressed by translators in the past, i.e. mainly up till the middle of the 20th century, were not based on an elaborate theory of translation. For example, in the first half of the 19th century, Schleiermacher, from his considerations about translatability, called for a theory of translation; but it was not until the middle of the 20th century that such a theory began to emerge. This was related to the increasing need for translation and interpreting in a variety of new domains (mainly science and technology, politics and diplomacy), and to the beginning of systematic training for translators and interpreters in institutions. With the development of Translation Studies as an academic discipline in the second half of this century, theoretical principles have been formulated which are the basis for the description, observation, and teaching of translation. There is a vast body of data, and an ever increasing amount of specialist literature, but there is no unified theory of translation and no agreement on the central concepts of the discipline (incidentally, the more modest 'Translation Studies', introduced by Holmes (1988) to cover the whole domain of translation theory and practice, has largely replaced 'theory'). What we have instead is a multiplicity of different approaches, each of which focuses on specific aspects, looking at the product or the process of translation from a specific angle, and using or avoiding specific terminology (on surveys of modern translation theories see, for example, Stolze, 1994, 1997; Gentzler, 1993, and also the encyclopaedias and handbooks edited by Baker, 1998; Snell-Hornby et al., 1998; Frank et al., in press). Applying the concept of 'memes' (i.e. units of cultural transfer that spread and mutate like genes, from mind to mind, and from culture to culture), Chesterman (1997a) describes the current stage of the academic discipline of Translation Studies as a mixed bag of memes. He argues that focusing on hypotheses, which have been formulated over the years and which are a particular kind of memes, can be an important step in building a theory of translation.

Translation scholars and translator trainers are more and more in agreement that the complex activity of translation requires qualified practitioners, fully competent to perform their tasks. Such a translation competence involves expertise in a number of areas and skills, including an awareness of the theorectial aspects and concepts. The lack of a unified translation theory need not be considered a disadvantage in this respect. On the contrary, familiarising students with various definitions of translation, various approaches and controversial concepts, and encouraging critical reflection may actually help them to make informed decisions in producing target texts.

Linguistics-based approaches to translation

Translation Studies, although still a young discipline, has undergone considerable development. Originally, it had been understood as a sub-discipline of (applied) linguistics, and consequently the methods that were applied to the study of translation were those that had been developed in linguistics. Translation was understood as a linguistic phenomenon, as an operation performed on languages; or, more precisely, as a process of linguistic transcoding. Since the change in the language was considered to be the determining characteristic feature of translation, the aim of a *linguistic theory of translation* (e.g. Catford, 1965; Nida, 1964; Wilss, 1977; Koller, 1979) was to give a precise description of the systematic relations between the signs and combinations of signs in the two languages, i.e. the source language (SL) and the target language (TL). Any difference between SL and TL that became obvious in a translation was attributed to the differences in the two linguistic systems. In this way, translation problems were identified and explained from a linguistic perspective. Key concepts of linguistic approaches are reproduction of the SL-text, invariance of the message, faithfulness, equivalence. The following definition is a clear example of this view:

> Translation is the operation which consists in transferring from one language to another all the meaning elements of a text, and nothing but these elements, making sure that in the TL they preserve both their relative importance and also their tonality, and taking account of the differences between the cultures of the source and TLs. (Darbelnet, 1977, cited in Newmark, 1989: 133)

The relationship between the SL-text and the TL-text was defined as *equivalence*, and this term was equally applied to smaller units of the text, which were treated as the units of translation (the smallest possible segments of the SL-text for which equivalent segments could be substituted in the TL-text, e.g. morphemes, words, phrases, or even sentences). Types of (potential) equivalence relations were established at the lexical level. Kade (1968) lists total equivalence, diversification (i.e. one:many correspondence), neutralisation (i.e. many:one correspondence), approximative equivalence, and zero equivalence as, for example, in the case of culture-specific terms, so-called *realia*). Total equivalence and zero equivalence form the endpoints of the equivalence scale. Total correspondence, i.e. where one SL unit exactly corresponds to one TL unit, and these units being interchangeable in any context, is extremely rare (applicable to numbers: 'five – fünf', proper names: 'Switzerland – la Suisse – die Schweiz', or terminology). Similar types of equivalence (or paradigms) were set up for syntactic structures. For example, for English gerunds after a preposition (e.g. 'After divorcing his wife, he went abroad'), the following German structures were established as being equivalent:

(1) subordinate clause with indicative form of verb ('Nachdem er von seiner Frau geschieden wurde, ging er ins Ausland'); or
(2) a nominal structure ('Nach der Scheidung von seiner Frau ging er ins Ausland').

Linguistic-oriented translation studies in the 1960s/1970s were also concerned with setting up methods of translation, or translation procedures. Highly influential in this respect have been the seven methods of translation of the *Stylistique comparée* (Vinay & Darbelnet, 1958), set up on the basis of a comparison of the lexical and syntactic structures of English and French:

(1)   emprunt/borrowing,
(2)   calque/loan translation, calque,
(3)   traduction littérale/literal translation,
(4)   transposition/transposition, i.e. a change in word class,
(5)   modulation/modulation, i.e. a change in the point of view,
(6)   équivalence/equivalence, i.e. the same situation rendered by completely different stylistic and structural methods,
(7)   adaptation/adaptation, i.e. compensation of socio-cultural differences between SL and TL.

They group methods (1)–(3) under the heading 'traduction directe' (i.e. direct, or literal translation, substitution) and methods (4)–(7) under 'traduction oblique' (indirect translation or paraphrasing). These translation methods can be optional or obligatory. Newmark's (1988) seven translation procedures (transference, cultural equivalent, through translation, literal translation, functional equivalent, descriptive equivalent, translation couplet) and Friederich's (1969) translation techniques for several linguistic problems are other examples of attempts at defining systematic guidelines or rules for translators.

It is largely due to the fact that linguistic approaches to translation were often normative and prescriptive that the term 'equivalence' has become the most controversial term in Translation Studies (see Snell-Hornby, 1988: 13ff; Halverson, 1997; Hermans, 1998). It has been rejected by some translation scholars who argue that equivalence, as identity of meaning, can never be achieved. Linguistic approaches to translation are indeed concerned with transferring meanings, and they use the relation of equivalence to set translation apart from other forms of interlingual communication, based on the degree of meaning correspondence between the structures of SL-text and TL-text. Such differences are also reflected in the terminology, e.g. translation (proper) and adaptation (Koller, 1979, 1993), semantic translation and communicative translation (Newmark, 1981, 1989, 1991a), 'translation' and 'adaptation' (Jäger & Müller, 1982), overt and covert translation (House, 1977).

In the 1960s and 1970s, studies conducted within a linguistics-based approach to translation concentrated on the systematic relations between units of the language systems, but often abstracted from aspects of their contextual use. A chosen TL-form may well be correct according to the rules of the language system, but this does not necessarily mean that the text as a whole appropriately fulfils its communicative function in the TL situation and culture. Since we do not translate words or grammatical forms, but texts with a specific communicative function, the limitations of a narrow linguistic approach soon became obvious. Thus, a logical development was that from the 1970s, insights and approaches of new (sub-)disciplines from the area of (applied) linguistics were taken into translation studies, notably socio-linguistics, pragmatics (see also the contributions in Hickey 1998), text-linguistics, and discourse analysis. Already in the 1960s, Nida's definition of equivalence was influenced by cultural and social considerations. He had argued that the TL-text should have the same effect on its audience as the SL-text had on its audience, as reflected in the following definition:

> Translating consists in reproducing in the receptor language the closest natural equivalent of the source-language message. (Nida & Taber, 1969: 12)

Based on Bible translations into a number of 'exotic' languages and the comprehension problems caused by cultural barriers, he differentiated between formal equivalence and dynamic equivalence. Formal equivalence requires 'that the message in the receptor language should match as closely as possible the different elements in the SL'. In contrast, a 'translation of dynamic equivalence aims at complete naturalness of expression, and tries to relate the receptor to modes of behavior relevant within the context of his own culture; . . . ' (Nida, 1964: 159). For Bible translation, dynamic equivalence was advocated.

Koller, too, although representing a mainly linguistics-based approach to translation, had gone beyond a narrow conception of equivalence as sameness of meaning at the level of linguistic units. He defined the equivalence relationship between SL-text and TL-text in respect of

(1) extralinguistic facts / state of affairs (denotative equivalence),
(2) form of verbalisation, including connotations, style (connotative equivalence),
(3) text norms and language norms (text-normative equivalence),
(4) TL-text audience (pragmatic equivalence),
(5) specific aesthetic, formal, characteristic features of text (formal-aesthetic equivalence) (Koller, 1979: 215f).

Text-linguistic approaches to translation

As previously indicated, the relevance of the text had not been ignored in linguistic approaches. However, in listing 'potential equivalent relations' between units in the SL and TL, linguistic approaches could not provide criteria for a translator's decision as to the most appropriate TL-form, or they remained rather vague. *Text-linguistic approaches*, on the other hand, and also *pragmatic approaches*, described the text itself as the unit of translation, and defined translation primarily as retextualising the SL-text in a new environment. The focus changed from micro units (words, sentence structures) to macro units (the text as an organic whole), from reproducing meanings to producing texts. This is illustrated in Neubert's definition of translation as 'source-text induced target-text production' (Neubert, 1985: 18), and also in the following quote:

> With the global meaning of the original as the determining factor, the translation is reconstructed as a new semantic and pragmatic totality in the TL community. The surface structure of the reconstruction is not a sentence by sentence rendering of the original. It is a top-down recreation of the text through the purposeful selection of TL resources. (Neubert & Shreve, 1992: 23)

Notions of text-linguistics (such as 'textuality', 'macrostructure', 'superstructure', 'text schema', see de Beaugrande & Dressler, 1981; van Dijk, 1980) were applied to translation analysis, and more attention was paid to the fact that translators are always dealing with a text in a situation and in a culture, meant to fulfil a specific function. Based on regularities that are identified in texts, text-linguistic research also attempts to categorise texts into text types, genres, text classes.

One of the first translation scholars to point out the importance of a categorisation of texts for translation purposes was Reiss (1971, see also the English version of this book: Reiss, 2000). The aim of her translation-oriented text typology was to derive strictly objective criteria for assessing the quality of translations. Based on Bühler's three functions of language, 'Darstellung' (description, presentation), 'Ausdruck' (expression), and 'Appell' (appeal), Reiss derived three corresponding dimensions of language (logical, aesthetic, dialogical) and three corresponding text types (informative, expressive, appellative). These three text types were linked to translation methods. According to Reiss, for the informative text type (examples of which would be reports and textbooks) the aim is invariance of content, and the translation is successful when the information has been transmitted in full. In the case of the expressive text type (e.g. a novel, or poem), the aim is an analogy of the artistic form, and the translation method is called identifying. For the appellative or operative text type (e.g. advertising, propaganda leaflet), the aim is identity of the behavioural reactions, and the translation method is called adaptation. Reiss's text typology has often been criticised for being too rigid, and her translation methods for being too prescriptive, for example by Snell-Hornby (1988), who applies prototype theory to a text typology to demonstrate that text types do not display clear-cut features.

Instead of looking for the characteristic features of text types, scholars working within a text-linguistic (and/or functionalist, see later) approach to translation have been concerned with setting up prototypes of genres, or genre profiles ('Textsortenprofile' in Göpferich, 1995). Genres reflect the effective, conscious and situationally appropriate choice of linguistic means, and they may be, more or less, conventionalised (see Swales, 1990). Genre conventions are culture-specific and can change over time, which makes genres relevant for translation studies (see Schäffner, 2000a). Genre profiles can be determined on the basis of a systematic comparison of genre exemplars in the source culture and in the target culture, i.e. of 'parallel texts', which Neubert (1985: 75) defines as SL and TL 'texts of equal informativity which have been produced in more or less identical communicative situations'. Genre profiles can serve as models for the retextualisation of the SL-text according to the TL conventions. In other words, knowledge of cross-cultural similarities and/or differences regarding genres and genre conventions is crucial to the translator in order to produce appropriate TL-texts (see also Hatim & Mason, 1990, 1997, Göpferich, 1995; Stolze, 1999, and the contributions in Trosborg, 1997).

The point stressed by text-linguistic approaches, that translators always deal with a text in a situation and in a culture, was developed further with a specific focus on the purpose of the text, particularly by German translation scholars. These approaches have become known as *functionalist approaches* (see later). On the other hand, other views of translation have emerged from other disciplines, and Translation Studies has alternatively been understood as part of comparative literature (or even *vice versa*, comparative literature is defined as part of Translation Studies, see Lefevere & Bassnett, 1990: 12) or as a sub-discipline of Cultural Studies.

Descriptive Translation Studies and the Impact of Cultural Studies

In particular since the late 1980s, scholars have increasingly (and more and more forcefully) pointed out that authentic translations are not faithful and equivalent reproductions of the source texts (ST) as demanded by (normative) linguistics-based translation theories. These findings are related to the socio-historical constraints translators are faced with. Scholars working within *Descriptive Translation Studies* decribe translation as the result of a context-dependent activity and the resulting target texts (TT) are seen as facts of target systems (e.g. Toury, 1995; Hermans, 1999). They examine decision-making in translation, translational norms (see also Simeoni, 1998 on the notion of translator's habitus), the effects of translated texts on the target national literature, how TTs have been brought into line with the system of norms that govern the literary system in a culture (e.g. Hermans, 1998), how they succeeded (or not) in competing with original texts and genres for prestige and power in the target polysystem (see Even-Zohar, 1978). It is argued that, from the TT perspective, 'all translation implies a degree of manipulation of the ST for a certain purpose' (Hermans, 1985: 11 – hence the name 'Manipulation School', see Snell-Hornby, 1988). The term 'equivalence' is either rejected or redefined (on the controversy with respect to this term in general and also within the framework of Descriptive Translation Studies (see the two debates in *Current Issues in Language and Society* 5 (1, 2) 1998).

In common with descriptive approaches, more recent approaches to translation that are inspired by Cultural Studies argue that texts do not have any intrinsically stable meaning that could be repeated elsewhere. Since there is always some interference from the subjective translator, as well as constraints from cultural, historical, ideological, or political circumstances, the discipline of linguistics is dismissed as being too narrow for describing and explaining translations (for an overview see Arrojo 1998). Translation is defined as a form of regulated transformation, and a translation method is recommended which signifies difference (Venuti, 1995) and which allows the reader to discover the cultural other. Venuti calls this recommended translation method 'foreignisation' and sets it apart from 'domestication'. The translation strategies corresponding to these two methods are called resistancy and fluency, respectively. Venuti criticises the dominant Anglo-American tradition of fluency and transparency in translation as 'forcible replacement of the linguistic and cultural difference of the foreign text with a text that will be intelligible to the target-language reader' (Venuti, 1995: 18). In its place he argues for the development of a 'theory and practice of translation that resists dominant target-language cultural values so as to signify the linguistic and cultural difference of the foreign text' (Venuti, 1995: 23). Venuti's arguments for favouring foreignisation, which are reflected in the following quotation, are developed largely on the basis of literary texts:

> A translated text should be the site where a different culture emerges, where a reader gets a glimpse of a cultural other, and resistancy, a translation strategy based on an aesthetic of discontinuity, can best

preserve that difference, that otherness, by reminding the reader of the gains and losses in the translation process and the unbridgeable gaps between cultures. (Venuti, 1995: 306)

The forceful arguments of scholars inspired by Cultural Studies have resulted in a more extensive discussion of topics that were previously hardly raised, or considered to be outside the domain of Translation Studies. Such new areas are, for example, the study of translation and power (e.g. Álvarez & Vidal, 1996; the special issue of *The Translator* on '*Translation and Minority*,' 1998, edited by Venuti), translation and political engagement (e.g Venuti, 1998; Robinson, 1997b; Tymoczko, 2000a), or translation and gender (e.g. Simon, 1996). Within the discipline of Translation Studies, linguistic and cultural studies approaches have sometimes been presented as total opposites, one or the other being attributed exclusive validity. However, these approaches are not necessarily exclusive, but rather complementary, as also stressed, among others, by Baker (1996) and Tymoczko (2000b, see also Chesterman & Arrojo, 2000). This ties in with the view that Translation Studies, applying insights and methods from various disciplines, can be characterised as an independent discipline in its own right or, more precisely as an interdiscipline (see Snell-Hornby *et al.* 1992, in contrast to Gutt's (1991) extreme view that there is no need for a discipline of Translation Studies at all because it can be subsumed under relevance theory – but see counter-arguments by Hönig, 1997). Translations can be described in terms of their linguistic profile, segmenting the text into smaller and smaller units, applying concepts and methods of linguistics, text-linguistics, pragmatics. They can also be studied by linking them to the social context, discovering their causes and effects (see Chesterman, 1998b).

I would like to argue that *functionalist approaches* to translation work very well in describing and explaining translation processes and products. They are not based on an opposition between linguistic and cultural aspects. On the contrary, they allow an account of the systematic relationship between linguistic structures at the textual micro-level and social, cultural, historical conditions of text production and reception (both in the source and target cultures). They also accommodate Toury's differentiation between the act of translation and the translation event (e.g. Toury, 1995: 249ff.), i.e. the differentiation between the cognitive aspects of translation as a decision-making process and the social, historical, cultural, ideological, etc. context of situation in which the act is embedded. Functionalist approaches are, thus, also well suited to the systematic training of translators. However, whereas for Toury the TT is the starting point for his aim of identifying regularities in translators' behaviour and linking them to acts, events and determining norms, the TT is usually (but not exclusively) the end product when functionalist approaches are used for training purposes.

Since the illustration of translation strategies for the sample texts in this volume is based on functionalist approaches, they will be presented in more detail now, including a discussion of some of the objections that have been raised (for a more extensive account of functionalist approaches see Nord, 1997).

Functionalist approaches to translation

'Functionalist approaches' is a cover term for a number of theoretical reflections that were developed predominantly in Germany and Finland, and largely motivated by the needs of both practical translation activities and translator training (e.g. Vermeer, 1978, 1989, 1996; Reiss & Vermeer, 1984, 1991; Nord, 1988, 1991, 1993, 1997, Hönig & Kussmaul, 1982, 1991; Hönig, 1995, 1997; Kussmaul, 1995; Holz-Mänttäri, 1984, 1993). What they have in common with Descriptive Translation Studies and the Cultural Studies paradigm is the view that texts do not have any intrinsically stable meaning that could be extracted and repeated elsewhere. Therefore, the perception of translation as meaning transfer (as commonly found in linguistic approaches, and also repeatedly in text-linguistic approaches) is rejected as being too narrow. More precisely, meaning transfer is seen as one out of several possible aims of translation. The main argument of functionalist approaches is that texts are produced and received with a specific purpose, or function, in mind. The starting point for any translation is therefore not the linguistic surface structure of the ST, but the purpose of the TT. Scholars working within functionalist approaches prefer to speak of source text and target text, instead of source-language and target-language text, because they want to highlight that translation is not only, or exclusively, a linguistic activity, but rather a purposeful activity (Nord, 1997), embedded in and contributing to other purposeful activities. TTs are (meant to be) used in and for specific actions. The action of translating itself (both as act and event) is part of a sequence of actions; it may be a pre-condition for or a consequence of other actions.

Skopos theory

Functionalist approaches were initiated, in principle, by Vermeer in the late 1970s with his *Skopos theory* (derived from the Greek word 'skopós', which means purpose, aim, goal, objective – these terms are sometimes used interchangeably, but see Nord (1997: 27ff.) for a discussion and distinct definitions). Vermeer's general skopos theory was further developed and combined with Reiss's specific translation theory to arrive at a general translation theory (Reiss & Vermeer, 1984, 1991). This theory is presented as being sufficiently general to cover a multitude of individual cases, i.e. to be independent of individual languages, cultures, subject domains, text types and genres. The basic assumptions are as follows: translation is a specific kind of communicative action; each action has a specific purpose, and therefore, the most decisive criterion for any translation is its purpose (*skopos*). A text is information offered ('Informationsangebot') by the text producer to a text receiver. Subsequently, a translation, i.e. a TT, is information offered in a TL and culture about information offered in a SL and culture. This is succinctly reflected in the following definition:

> To translate means to produce a text in a target setting for a target purpose and target addressees in target circumstances. (Vermeer, 1987: 29)

Vermeer often refers to the product of translation as the *translatum* (Vermeer, 1996) or *translat* (Reiss & Vermeer, 1991). Since language and culture are interdependent, translation is transfer between cultures, i.e. it is a specific kind of culture-determined text production (see Vermeer, 1978, 1996; Reiss & Vermeer, 1991). The skopos of the ST and the skopos of the TT can be either identical or different. In cases where the skopos is the same for the two texts, we have 'Funktionskonstanz' (functional constancy), whereas cases in which the skopos differs between the two texts undergo 'Funktionsveränderung' (change of function – 'Funktionskonstanz' and 'Funktionsveränderung' are also used by Hönig & Kussmaul (1982); Nord (1997) uses the labels 'equifunctional and heterofunctional translation'). In each case, the TT has to be structured in such a way that it is appropriate, or adequate, to the requirements of the translation brief. Reiss and Vermeer (and similarly Hönig & Kussmaul) use 'adequacy' as a dynamic concept, related to the required standard and quality of the TT. That is, adequacy is a generic concept, in contrast to linguistic approaches that see the traditional concept of equivalence as a constitutive feature of (any) translation. Reiss and Vermeer (1991: 140) do use the label 'equivalence', however, in the sense of adequacy to a skopos that requires functional constancy (e.g. if the translation brief requires a faithful reproduction of the words and structures of the TT, as happens frequently in pedagogical situations). Non-functionalist approaches (predominantly linguistic-oriented ones) have normally assumed that all translations should preserve the function of the ST. Introducing a differentiation between

'Funktionskonstanz' and 'Funktionsveränderung', thus, also means that the longstanding debate about literal *versus* free translation, or translation *versus* adaptation, becomes superfluous, since all forms, whether literal translation, communicative translation, or adaptation, are all equally valid translational procedures, depending on the purpose of the TT.

Focusing on the (purpose of the) end product of the translation process, i.e. the TT, can be characterised as a prospective view. By adopting such a prospective view, translation scholars consciously set themselves apart from the more retrospective view of linguistic approaches with a focus on reproducing the ST. This changed perspective can be illustrated by the following definition:

> I understand translating roughly as a procedure initiated by a commission consisting of a set of (verbal and non-verbal) instructions (plus additional material) to prepare an (oral or written) 'target-text' for transcultural interacting on the basis of 'source-text' material. (Vermeer, 1996: 6)

As is obvious in this definition, the relationship between ST and TT is not an objectively given one, nor one of absolute identity concerning the linguistic make-up of ST and TT (in other words: not one of equivalence in the narrowly defined sense of identity of meaning). Instead, the exact relationship between ST and TT needs to be stipulated in each case depending on the skopos. Therefore, the relationship between ST and TT is not determined by the structure of the ST and / or its effects on the ST addressees, but by the intended purpose of the TT. Vermeer has expressed these aspects in a hierarchy of three rules as follows. The most general rule is the *skopos rule*, which states that translation, as a sub-category of human action, is determined by its purpose (skopos), that it is a function of its purpose. The two further rules are the coherence rule and the fidelity rule. The *coherence rule* stipulates that the TT must be sufficiently coherent in itself to allow the intended users to comprehend it, given their assumed background knowledge and situational circumstances. The *fidelity rule* concerns intertextual coherence between ST and TT and stipulates that some relationship must remain between the two once the overriding principle of skopos and the rule of intratextual coherence have been satisfied. A similar view is expressed by Nord:

> Translation is the production of a functional TT maintaining a relationship with a given ST that is specified according to the intended or demanded function of the TT (translation skopos). (Nord, 1991: 28)

Nord distinguishes two types of translation: documentary and instrumental translation. Since we will refer to these types in our sample texts, we will provide Nord's definitions here. Documentary translation is a

> type of translation process which aims at producing in the TL a kind of document of (certain aspects of) a communicative interaction in which a source-culture sender communicates with a source-culture audience via the ST under source-culture conditions. (Nord, 1997: 138)

Interlinear, literal, philological and exoticising translations belong to this type, depending on which aspects of the ST are reproduced in the TT. Instrumental translation, on the other hand, is a

> type of translation process which aims at producing in the TL an instrument for a new communicative interaction between the source-culture sender and a target-culture audience, using (certain aspects of) the ST as a model. (Nord, 1997: 139)

According to the degree of functional invariance, Nord further distinguishes between equifunctional translation (e.g. instructions for use), heterofunctional translation (e.g. *Gulliver's Travels* for children) and homologous translation (e.g. poetry translated by a poet) as forms of instrumental translation (see Nord, 1997: 47–52).

Objections to functionalist approaches and counter-arguments

The conception of the ST as an offer of information ('Informationsangebot') has met with criticism and objections mainly from linguistically oriented approaches which argue that the target-orientedness means a dethronement of the SL-text, a neglect of the richness of its meaning (e.g. Newmark, 1991b; Schreitmüller, 1994; Kohlmayer, 1988 – for a more detailed reflection on criticisms that have been raised against functionalist approaches see Vermeer, 1996; Nord, 1997: 109–22). These objections are linked to the very definition of translation. The argument is: if translation is defined as being based on 'source-text material' (Vermeer, 1996, see previous definition), or as 'using certain apects of the ST' (Nord's definitions above), then where is the difference between, for example, a translation of Shakespeare's *Hamlet* into German and an adaptation of the text for German-speaking children, or an adaptation to a fictional setting in the 21st century? Linguistic approaches argue that not just any TL-text that is based on a SL-text can be called a translation, and they have repeatedly stressed the necessity to deliminate translation clearly from other types of secondary text production (this is also reflected in terminological oppositions, e.g. translation proper and adaptation, see previous discussion). Vermeer's fidelity rule is considered to be too vague in this respect. To counter this criticism, functionalists argue that a narrow definition of translation would put constraints on the research from the very beginning. Since various forms of translational activity do occur in professional practice, all of them should be addressed by Translation Studies (this view is shared by Toury, 1995). Or in Nord's words:

> The functional approach offers the possibility of using one and the same theoretical model to account for both documentary and instrumental forms of translation, including, of course, any form of equivalent translation, whatever the specification of equivalence may be. (Nord, 1997: 114)

Translation scholars who argue that functionalist approaches do not respect the (richness of the) ST and its autonomy may themselves be 'accused' of isolating the text from its social embeddedness. In translation, we are always dealing with texts-in-situation-and-in-culture, texts are always produced and received, and their 'meanings' interpreted, in time and space by people with specific communicative purposes, knowledge, and expectations. There is never *the* ST which can be turned into *the* TT, which also accounts for the well-known fact that several TTs of the same ST may be possible (admittedly, more or less appropriate ones), and that some STs (especially literary texts) are translated again and again. The prospective view of functionalist approaches means that the linguistic structures of the ST are no longer seen as the only yardstick with which to judge the quality and appropriateness of the TT. The choice of the linguistic structures of the TT is not (exclusively and predominantly) determined by the linguistic structures of the ST but by the translation brief; i.e. consideration needs to be given to the intended purpose of the TT, its situation of use, its addressees with their knowledge and expectations, the relevance of genre conventions, etc. In other words, the linguistic structure of the ST is only one factor in the network of factors determining TT production. Thus, functionalist approaches do not 'dethrone' the ST, but they require the translator to carry out a thorough ST analysis (as a text in a situation in a source culture) in order to determine the translation strategies by which the translation brief can be fulfilled most appropriately.

The focus on the 'translation brief' and on translations being 'commissioned' by clients, with the commission consisting of a set of 'instructions' (see the earlier definition by Vermeer, 1996: 6) has led some scholars to argue that functionalism turns translators into mercenaries who simply do what their clients want them to do. Vermeer's skopos rule, as the most prominent of his three rules, allows for the interpretation that any end (the purpose as specified by clients) justifies the means (the choice of linguistic structures). Would skopos theory therefore justify translations that are incompatible with the ST author's intentions? This point links with ethical issues and the question of how it can be ensured that translators base their decisions on intersubjectively valid criteria. Kadric and Kaindl (1997) argue for the inclusion of ethical aspects into skopos theory in order to avoid misinterpretation of the skopos rule for unethical purposes. Nord has introduced the concept of loyalty to highlight the 'responsibility translators have toward their partners in translational interaction' (Nord, 1997: 125). Whereas concepts such as faithfulness or fidelity usually refer to relationships between the texts themselves, loyalty stresses the translator's responsibilities towards people, i.e. not only with regard to clients and users of their translations, but also with regard to the author(s) of the ST. Chesterman (1997a, b) bases his considerations on translation ethics on values which, in turn, govern fundamental norms: the value of clarity governing expectancy norms (i.e. readership expectations about the translation product), truth governing the relation norm (i.e. an appropriate relation between ST and TT), trust governing the accountability norm (i.e. the translator's accountability to all parties involved), and the value of understanding governing the communication norm (i.e. the translator's task to ensure communication between partners as required). Neither authors nor clients are usually in a position to check whether translators work in accordance with these norms. As Hönig (1997: 12) argues:

> [...] a loyal translator [...] will not consciously violate these norms and traditions without informing the author(s). In other words: the *skopos* of the translation must be compatible with the intentions of the ST author(s). If they are not, it is the translator's duty to inform his/her client accordingly.

Theory of translatorial action

Many of the basic assumptions of skopos theory are shared by another functionalist approach, i.e. the *theory of translatorial action* ('translatorisches Handeln'), developed by Justa Holz-Mänttäri (1984), a German scholar working in Finland. This theory is based on principles of action theory (e.g. making use of key concepts such as division of labour, cooperation, roles of participants) and goes slightly further than skopos theory. Holz-Mänttäri defines translation as a complex action designed to achieve a particular purpose, an action that is realised by an expert in a network of translatorial actions involving the initiator, the client and the translator. She introduces a specific terminology (in German), for example, 'Botschaftsträger' ('message transmitter') instead of text, 'Botschaftsträgerproduktion' ('production of message transmitters') instead of text production, 'translatorisches Handeln' ('translational' or 'translatorial action') instead of translating. She argues that the verb 'translate' requires a grammatical object, a reference to the 'what' that is (to be) translated, thus orienting the attention in a retrospective way and giving prominence to the ST. Her own prospective view is summarised in the following definition:

> Translational action is the process of producing a message transmitter of a certain kind, designed to be employed in superordinate action systems in order to coordinate actional and communicative cooperation (quoted in Nord, 1997: 13; original German definition in Holz-Mänttäri, 1984: 17)

Holz-Mänttäri highlights the professionality of translation. That is, in translatorial action, a text is professionally produced for a specific purpose in a specific situation. This text is required by a client (who has a specific purpose in mind), and therefore, all specifications for the text production ('Bedarfserfassung', 'Produktspezifikation') have to be negotiated between client and text producer (i.e. translator), with these negotiations including deadlines, fees, potentially necessary contact addresses, etc. The translator is characterised as an expert for the production of transcultural message carriers ('Experte für die Produktion von transkulturellen Botschaftsträgern'), which are used by the clients in their communicative actions in order to achieve some aim in their communicative interactions. Since Holz-Mänttäri has published predominantly in German and since her terminology has not been widely accepted, her very important ideas have unfortunately not seen the reception they deserve beyond German-speaking functionalists.

The didactic value of functionalist approaches

With their focus on translation as a purposeful activity which is embedded in and determined by other activities, functionalist approaches also stress the role of translators as experts, i.e. as experts in text production for interlingual and intercultural communication. Expertise requires knowledge and skills, in short, competence. Translation competence is a complex notion which involves an awareness of and conscious reflection on all the relevant factors for the production of a TT that appropriately fulfils its specified function for its target addressees. Such a complex notion of translation competence can be broken down into a number of more specific sub-competences, for example:

(1)   *linguistic competence* of the languages concerned;
(2)   *cultural competence,* i.e. general knowledge about historical, political, economic, cultural, etc. aspects in the respective countries;
(3)   *textual competence,* i.e. knowledge of regularities and conventions of texts, genres, text types;
(4)   *domain/subject-specific competence,* i.e. knowledge of the relevant subject, the area of expertise;
(5)   *(re)search competence,* i.e. a general strategic competence whose aim is the ability to resolve problems specific to the cross-cultural transfer of texts;
(6)   *transfer competence,* i.e. ability to produce TTs that satisfy the demands of the translation task (see Schäffner, 2000b; Neubert, 2000; Wilss, 1996).

It is generally accepted that nobody is a born translator; as in any other field, in order to become an expert, competence has to be acquired in the training process (on stages in the development of translation competence see Chesterman, 1997a, 2000). In view of the listed sub-competences, it can be stated that translator training is not merely a skill-producing activity but one that needs a theoretical framework and foundation. The didactic value of functionalist approaches lies in the fact that they support translators' decision-making strategies in producing TTs (see also the textbook by Hönig & Kussmaul, 1982, 1991). In the lengthy annotations which are provided in this volume, we try to make the decisions we took in the production of the relevant TTs transparent. In doing so, we illustrate the reasoning behind our decisions, taken within the framework of a functionalist approach, and thus help readers recognise (and, hopefully, acknowledge) the merits of the translation strategies chosen.

Functionalist approaches give translators guidelines (and not fixed rules) for their decisions. They stress the complexity of the activity, i.e. the need to link decisions at the micro level to macro aspects (the immediate context, the larger context, the function of the ST, the skopos of the TT, etc.). In this way, they put more emphasis on the expertise of the translator and his/her responsibility for the end product (i.e. a TT that is appropriate for its specified purpose). At the same time, they give translators more freedom, release them from the limitations and restrictions imposed by narrowly defined concepts of equivalence and faithfulness to the ST alone.

A Framework for Translating

The conception of translation as purposeful activity, as text production for intercultural communication, allows for the identification of steps (or stages) in dealing with translation assignments. As stressed by functionalist approaches, for each translation, there is a specific assignment or translation brief ('Übersetzungsauftrag'). The first step of any translation is therefore the analysis of this assignment; in other words, the specification of the purpose (skopos) of the TT (cf. skopos rule: the most decisive criterion for any translation is its purpose). Analysing the translation assignment means establishing why a translation has been commissioned and by whom, what the clients need, when and where and why the TT will be used, who the TT addressees are, what background knowledge they have with regard to the topic and/or subject area, etc. Based on these considerations, initial decisions can be taken as to a TT specification, the type of translation (documentary or instrumental translation) and the form of translation (equifunctional or heterofunctional). Toury (1980: 53ff.) discusses such considerations with reference to what he calls preliminary norms, which decide the overall translation strategy and the choice of texts to be translated; and initial norms, which govern the translator's decision to adhere primarily to the ST or to the target culture. Each decision leads on to further decisions, from more general to more specific issues. For example, in the case of instrumental translation, the consideration of text typological and/or genre conventions may become relevant.

As a second step, a translation-oriented analysis of the ST is carried out, i.e. an analysis of the ST as a text-in-situation-in-culture against the background of the translation assignment (see Nord, 1988, 1991; Erdmann *et al.*, 1994). The aim of such a pre-translation ST analysis is to identify specific translation problems, on the basis of which decisions about the most appropriate translation strategies can be taken (for more details on these topics see later). Another part of this analysis is a reflection about the research that may become necessary in carrying out the task, such as finding parallel texts, consulting background literature about the subject domain, consulting experts and/or native speakers. Translators cannot be experts in all subject domains, but it is part of their translation competence to know how and where to get the required (linguistic, cultural, textual, subject-specific) knowledge if they do not have it (this is what is meant by (re)search competence). Sources for doing such research are manifold, and they include mono- and bi-lingual dictionaries, special dictionaries (e.g. etymological dictionaries, terminological dictionaries and glossaries, slang dictionaries, dictionaries of quotations), reference works (e.g. *Encyclopaedia Britannica*, handbooks), background and parallel texts, IT facilities (e.g. dictionaries on CD-ROM, on-line terminology systems, translation memory systems), and human sources (e.g. clients and commissioners, experts and subject specialists, fellow translators, native speakers). (NB: The rapidly changing challenges of the market make it necessary for professional translators to be equipped with suitable technological skills, which involves updating IT hardware and software. The most recent software includes highly relevant tools for translators, such as multilingual concordance systems and translation memory systems. On developments in machine translation and machine-assisted translation see Freigang (1998), Somers (1998), Schmidt (1998), also Sager (1994) for a survey of the extensive use of computers in today's translation industry.)

Such (re)search activities will also be necessary during the actual production of the TT. This phase is not a linear process, starting with the first sentence and ending with the last one. On the contrary, decisions made at the beginning of the text (e.g. a decision on a specific lexical unit or on a certain syntactic structure) may have to be revised later on in the text (for example, if it is realised that the TL word chosen does not contribute most appropriately to the style of the text as a whole or if research into parallel texts has revealed that another syntactic structure is required for the TT to conform to the genre conventions of the target culture). Substantial insights into what actually happens in the heads of translators while they are performing their task have been gained by studies of the translation process, the most frequently used research method being the analysis of think-aloud protocols (TAPs). That is, while translating a text, translators (individual translators or teams of translators) are asked to verbalise their actions and thoughts. On the basis of the transcribed recordings (mainly tape-recordings, but more recently also combined with video taping), translation scholars can analyse the strategies employed (at both the macro- and micro-level), set up types of strategies and discover differences in the use of these strategies between professional translators and students of translation, i.e. between experts and novices (e.g. Krings, 1986; Lörscher, 1991; Séguinot, 1989; Kussmaul, 1997; the contributions in Danks *et al.*, 1997).

The aim of translation is the production of a TT which is functionally appropriate and communicatively acceptable. As previously stated, the textual make-up of the TT is determined by the purpose of the TT, and not exclusively or predominantly by the textual make-up of the ST. Decisions at the textual micro-level will therefore have to be made against the background of the translation brief, knowledge of the addressees, situational considerations, genre conventions, etc. This can be linked to Nord's concept of a vertical unit of translation (see Nord, 1997: 68ff.). That is, whereas linguistic approaches to translation treated the unit of translation as the smallest possible segment in the ST for which an equivalent segment could be substituted in the TT (see Kade, 1968: 90), i.e. as a horizontal segment, Nord's view is influenced by functionalist criteria. In this way, a specific textual function (e.g. the evaluative function of a specific ST) which is realised in a variety of textual segments (e.g. evaluative adjectives, metaphors, metacommunicative sentences, ironic undertones) can be seen as a unit of translation. In Toury's norm-based approach, operational norms control the actual decisions made during the act of translation (Toury, 1980).

Functionalist approaches usually refer to *strategies* of translation, and not to rules, techniques, or principles. As already stressed, informed decisions have to be made in the process of translation, and the discipline of Translation Studies can provide support for these decision-making strategies, but it cannot (and must not) establish rules or ready-made solutions. With a didactic aim in mind, translation scholars have set up typologies of translation problems and translation strategies which are meant as guidelines for translators, and which can be used equally by students of translation, translator trainers, professional translators, or translation critics to comment on translation processes and products. The typology we are using throughout this volume has mainly been inspired by Nord (1988, 1991, 1993, 1997), Hönig and Kussmaul (1982, 1991), and Chesterman (1997a). In the following sections, types of translation problems and translation strategies will be presented in more detail with illustrative examples, thereby providing explanations for the terms used in the annotations to the sample texts.

Types of translation problems and translation strategies
Translation problems are objective problems which can be identified in a ST before the actual production of the TT starts. They must not be confused with subjective difficulties a translator may have due to deficient translation competence. For didactic purposes, Nord classified translation problems into four main types: pragmatic, intercultural, interlingual (or linguistic), and text-specific translation problems.

Pragmatic translation problems result from the contrast between the two communicative situations (ST situation and TT situation) in which the texts are used and relate, in particular, to place, time, and addressees.

Examples are culture-bound terms, references to place and time, indication of the relationship between communicative partners. Intercultural translation problems arise from differences in the conventions between the two cultures involved, such as measuring conventions, formal conventions, text-type and genre conventions, conventional forms of address, salutation formulas. Interlingual translation problems result from structural differences in vocabulary, syntax, and suprasegmental features of the two languages; and text-specific translation problems are those problems which arise in the translation of one specific text and cannot be generalised, for example, puns, rhetorical figures, alliteration, rhyme.

In translation we are always dealing with texts, which have been defined as communicative occurrences characterised by seven standards of textuality, i.e. situationality, intentionality, acceptability, informativity, intertextuality, coherence and cohesion (see de Beaugrande & Dressler (1981), and adapted to the translation situation by Neubert (1985), and Neubert & Shreve (1992)). In the identification of the translation problems in a translation-oriented ST analysis, we have to be aware that we are dealing with a ST, i.e. a text that has (normally) fulfilled its intended purpose and function in the source culture (in the primary communicative situation). More specifically, we are analysing a ST that was produced and received at a specific place and time in the source culture (situationality), produced for source culture addressees and with a specific purpose in mind (intentionality), with text author and addreesees (usually) sharing culture-specific and domain-specific (background) knowledge (which accounts for the degree of informativity), the ST being an exemplar of a genre (intertextuality), and accepted as a coherent and cohesive unit (acceptability) in a communicative situation. The majority of texts to be translated have not been produced primarily in order to be translated (see Neubert's (1968) four types:

(1)   exclusively source culture addressed, e.g. legal texts with only locally relevant information;
(2)   primarily source culture addressed, but potential addressees in target cultures, e.g. scientific reports in journals;
(3)   originally source culture addressed, but addressees principally not limited, e.g. novels;
(4)   primarily target culture addressed, e.g. information for foreign countries).

Whenever there is a need for a TT (this need, and subsequently the translation commission, originating either in the source culture or in the target culture), the TT will (have to) function in a secondary communicative situation, as an independent communicative occurrence displaying the seven standards of textuality in its respective way. In other words, the TT will address a new audience in the new target community, at a different time and place (Neubert, 1985: 71 speaks of *displaced situationality*). The purpose and function of the TT may be the same as that of the ST or it may be different (see *Funktionskonstanz* versus *Funktionsveränderung*), the subject knowledge of the TT addressees may be more or less the same as that of the ST addressees, and depending on the particular text type and genre, there may be more or less conventionalised structures. The TT is, thus, in a double intertexuality relationship, i.e. it is related to the ST (see Neubert's (1985: 18) definition of translation as ST induced TT production) and, depending on the skopos, its structure will be influenced by the genre conventions of the target culture (Neubert (1985: 115) speaks of *mediated intertextuality*).

As Nord (1991: 28) states

[t]ranslation allows a communicative act to take place which, because of existing linguistic and cultural barriers would not have been possible without it.

But in order to allow this communicative act to take place, the TT has to be appropriately structured for its specified purpose. Therefore, translators need to decide on the translation strategies once the translation problems have been identified. A strategy is a general procedure or approach for the accomplishment of a task or for the solution of a problem. A translation strategy is defined by Lörscher (1991) as 'a potentially conscious procedure for the solution of a problem which an individual is faced with when translating a text segment from one language into another' (cited in Chesterman, 1993: 13). And Chesterman (2000: 82) comments that

[s]trategies represent well-tried, standard types of solution to a lack of fit between goals and means; they are used when the means that first appear to be at hand seem to be inadequate to allow the translator to reach a given goal.

It is in this sense of 'well-tried, standard types of solution' that we will use 'translation strategies' and for which some illustrations are given later. As translation strategies are potentially conscious, translators should be in a position to reflect about them and subsequently comment on them. This is what we have attempted to do in the annotations to the sample texts in this volume.

In functionalist approaches, the process and the product of translation are seen as parts of a more general goal-oriented action in which the goals and sub-goals of the action are usually set by somebody else than the translator (see Holz-Mänttäri, 1984: 65–66, 111–13). This perception has consequences for the notion of strategies, i.e. strategies will play a role for each of the goals and sub-goals of the general action. Also for the process of translation as a purposeful activity, we can make a difference between macro- and micro-strategies. Macro-strategies concern the decision about an appropriate type of translation, for example, the decision that the translation brief requires a documentary translation. However, in this respect, notions such as type of translation, translation method, or translation procedure are more commonly used (although there is no general agreement as to the terminology used within the discipline of Translation Studies). Micro-strategies concern the lexical and syntactic levels of the text, but bearing in mind that the solutions to the identified translation problems are always relative to the translation skopos, text function, genre conventions, addressee specifications, etc. Another differentiation can be made between comprehension strategies (concerning the analysis of the ST and the translation brief) and production strategies (concerning the production of an appropriate TT, see Gile, 1995; Chesterman, 1997a). In the following discussion and also in the annotations to the sample texts we are predominantly concerned with production strategies. More specifically, the translation strategies we illustrate are mainly of a linguistic and text-linguistic nature, but they are applied within a functionalist approach. (Note that functionalist approaches do not totally reject insights of the more traditional linguistic, text-linguistic and socio-linguistic approaches; they often use the same or similar concepts and methods, but argue about their values in respect to the purpose of the translation.)

In speaking about strategies, the labels originally introduced by Vinay and Darbelnet, Newmark (see above) and others, can be made use of (although there is again a different terminology in that Vinay and Darbelnet speak of methods of translation, and Newmark of translation procedures; see also Schreiber (1997) on a classification of translation procedures for didactic purposes). Chesterman's (1997a) classification of translation strategies comprises three primary groups:

(1)   mainly syntactic/grammatical,
(2)   mainly semantic, and
(3)   mainly pragmatic translation strategies,

with these groups overlapping to some extent (see Chesterman (1997a: 92–116) for a more extensive discussion). I will give Chesterman's complete list of strategies, but comment only briefly on them (also indicating which labels will come up in the annotations in this volume).

Syntactic translation strategies

Syntactic strategies have effects on the form of the text, that is, looked at from the point of view of comparing the ST and the TT, they indicate a change in the grammatical form. Chesterman lists the following forms.

(1) Literal translation (i.e. the TT is maximally close to the ST and grammatically correct according to the TL norms. This strategy was considered to be the norm by many scholars working within a linguistic approach to translation. From a functionalist perspective, it may be the most appropriate strategy if the skopos requires an interlinear version of the ST, e.g. for language learning purposes.).

(2) Loan, *calque* (i.e. the borrowing of SL lexical units and / or the substitution of morphemes. For Vinay and Darbelnet (1958) these are two separate procedures, labeled *emprunt* and *calque*, in German often called 'Lehnwort' and 'Lehnübersetzung').

(3) Transposition (This term taken is from Vinay and Darbelnet (1958) and indicates any change in the word class, i.e. the replacement of one word class with another one without changing the meaning of the message).

(4) Unit shift (These are shifts between the units – morpheme, word, phrase, clause, sentence, paragraph, e.g. a ST clause corresponds to a TT sentence, or a ST word to a TT phrase).

(5) Phrase structure change (e.g. changes in number, definiteness, tense, mood).

(6) Clause structure change (e.g. a ST active intransitive structure into a TT passive voice, or a semantically locative item appearing as subject in the ST and as an adverbial in the TT).

(7) Sentence structure change (e.g. changes between main clause and subordinate clause, or changes of sub-clause types).

(8) Cohesion change (i.e. a change that affects intratextual reference, ellipsis, substitution, etc., for example making an implicit connection explicit in the TT by adding a connector).

(9) Level shift (i.e. a shift in the mode of expression from one level to another, e.g. a polite request is expressed by a lexical unit in the ST and by a combination of lexical and syntactic means in the TT, see 'please' – 'wir ersuchen Sie + infinitive').

(10) Scheme change (i.e. changes in dealing with rhetorical schemes, e.g. parallelism, repetition, alliteration, rhyme, rhythm).

In Vinay and Darbelnet's classification, several of the strategies listed by Chesterman in this group would have fallen under the label 'transposition'. Following Vinay and Darbelnet's book, scholars working within a linguistic approach to translation have done detailed analyses into translation procedures for specific linguistic structures. As a consequence, more detailed sub-procedures were set up for transpositions (and also for modulations, see later). For example, Friederich (1969: 91ff.) lists eight possible solutions for translating the German 'es' into English, all of them based on syntactic criteria. Looking at translation journals, especially in the 1970s, we see a large number of articles dealing with establishing translation procedures and strategies for specific phenomena (see the following titles, taken at random from the German journal *Fremdsprachen*: 'Der deutsche Konditional und seine Übersetzung ins Russische' (3/1972), 'Die Substitution der Wortarten in der Sprachmittlung zwischen Englisch und Deutsch' (4/1974), 'German Pre-Nominal Extended Attributes Translated into English' (1/1978), 'Adjektive und Adverbien bei der Translation' (3/1980); for sub-procedures see also Wotjak 1985).

Semantic translation strategies

Semantic translation strategies in Chesterman's classification are those that change or modify the meaning of the text, a sentence, or a clause. Such changes are grouped under the label 'modulation' by Vinay and Darbelnet, and again, other translation scholars have set up sub-procedures on the basis of a detailed comparison of the semantic structures of the lexical units involved (thereby often working within a linguistic approach to translation and applying more traditional methods of lexical semantics, such as semantic feature analysis, see, for example, Doherty and Angermüller, 1983). Chesterman (1997a) lists the following semantic strategies:

(1) synonymy (i.e. use of a synonym in the TT instead of a more immediately available unit);
(2) antonymy (i.e. use of the negated opposite);
(3) hyponomy (i.e. changes between superordinates and hyponyms);
(4) converses (i.e. ST and TT express the same state of affairs from opposing points of view);
(5) abstraction change (i.e. changes between abstract and concrete terms; sometimes 'specification' and 'generalisation' are listed as

separate translation strategies; these two terms will also be used in the annotations);

(6) distribution change (i.e. a change in the distribution of the same semantic elements over more or fewer lexical items; here again, 'expansion' and 'compression' are sometimes used as separate translation strategies; with these terms being used in the annotations);

(7) emphasis change (adding to, reducing or altering the emphasis or focus);

(8) paraphrase (i.e. TT is looser than ST);

(9) trope change (strategies used in dealing with rhetorical tropes, i.e. figurative expressions; other labels used in the literature in this respect are 'metaphorisation', 'demetaphorisation', 'remetaphorisation');

(10) other semantic changes (i.e. modulations of various kinds which do not fall under the previous strategies).

Pragmatic translation strategies

Chesterman's *pragmatic translation strategies* are those which

primarily have to do with the selection of information in the TT, a selection that is governed by the translator's knowledge of the prospective readership of the translation [. . .] These strategies are often the result of a translator's global decisions concerning the appropriate way to translate the text as a whole. (Chesterman, 1997: 107)

These strategies can be compared to what I have previously called macro-strategies, and what Nord (1997) refers to as choice for documentary or instrumental translation, also to Toury's (1995) concept of initial norms. Pragmatic strategies, thus, concern the message of the text itself, and they typically incorporate syntactic and semantic strategies. Chesterman lists the following ones.

(1) cultural filtering (i.e. adaptation of, in particular, source culture-specific terms – *realia* – to target culture norms and expectations, with exoticisation as the opposite procedure; comparable to Venuti's concepts of 'domestication' and 'foreignisation'; see also House (1997) for a more detailed discussion of the concept of a cultural filter);

(2) explicitness change (i.e. making information more explicit or more implicit in the TT, depending on readers' knowledge; again here, 'explicitation' and 'implicitation' are sometimes listed as separate translation strategies; these terms are also used in the annotations);

(3) information change (i.e. addition of new, relevant, and non-inferrable, information or omission of irrelevant information;

with 'addition' and 'omission' often listed as separate translation strategies in the literature and used in the annotations);

(4) interpersonal change (changes at the level of formality, reflected, for example, in forms of address, choice of technical terms);

(5) illocutionary change (changes of speech acts);

(6) coherence change (concerning the logical arrangement of the information in the text: the translation strategy of 'relocation', or 'dislocation' ('Disloziierung') which is found in the literature and which denotes a rearrangement of information at various levels could also be added here);

(7) partial translation (e.g. summary translation, gist translation);

(8) visibility change (i.e. concerning the author's or translator's presence; e.g. translator's notes, footnotes, comments in brackets; on the notion of 'visibility' see also Venuti, 1995);

(9) transediting (i.e. re-editing by translators, e.g. in the case of deficient STs);

(10) other pragmatic changes (e.g. layout).

There is no direct relation between the four types of translation problems mentioned here and the translation strategies; that is, the strategies can be applied for all types of problems, which is what Chesterman means by saying that the three groups of strategies overlap. However, there may be differences in the frequency of specific strategies as related to a specific problem type, or preferences in the use of strategies; for example, pragmatic strategies may apply predominantly to pragmatic translation problems, but further analyses would be required to establish such preferences. Chesterman himself presents his strategies as hypotheses whose validity would need to be tested on the basis of empirical data (i.e. actual translations) in order to find out which of them are actually used and in which conditions, whether the list is sufficient, whether the labels are appropriate, etc. In a similar way, Nord's types of translation problems can also be described as hypotheses. In other words, neither Nord's translation problems nor Chesterman's translation strategies have (or claim to have) the status of generally recognised concepts. However, I have arranged the annotations in this volume with reference to these typologies because they allow a consistent illustration of the sample texts and are, thus, pedagogically useful.

In the following section, I will only give some illustrations for possible translation strategies as applied to the four types of translation problems, always bearing in mind that the choice of a strategy is determined first of all by the translation skopos and not primarily by the specific problem type (I realise that this statement is itself a hypothesis). The discussion in the annotations can therefore also be seen as a way of testing the validity of such typologies of problems and strategies as presented by Nord and Chesterman (the proof of the pudding is in the eating . . .).

Examples of Potential Translation Strategies for Recurring Translation Problems

In using Nord's four types of translation problems for the annotations to the sample texts, it turned out that it is not always possible to assign an identified problem in a specific ST easily and exclusively to one specific problem type. Frequently, overlaps and interrelationships occur. We have briefly commented on such cases in the respective annotations. Despite such overlaps, the following illustrative examples can be provided as general guidelines.

Pragmatic translation problems

As stated earlier, these result from the contrast between the ST situation and the TT communicative situation. Culture-bound terms, references to place and time, proper names, addressee specifications, are examples of this problem type. The pragmatic translation strategy of cultural filtering is relevant in all of these cases.

References to time and place

Such references in a ST, e.g. 'today', 'last week', 'here', 'in our country', usually refer to the communicative situation and to the culture of the ST, i.e. they are indicative of the conditions of the production and reception of the ST. In the production of the TT, such references often have to be changed for the TT to fulfil its purpose most appropriately (see Neubert's (1985) concept of 'displaced situationality'), unless the skopos demands otherwise. For example, temporal references to a publication date in journalistic texts often have to be adapted to the publication date of the TT (e.g. 'Last week a report in the *New England Journal of Medicine* . . . ' – 'Im *New England Journal of Medicine* wurden kürzlich . . .' or 'Das *New England Journal of Medicine* berichtete vor zwei Wochen . . .', see Sample Text 4). On the other hand, in speeches by politicians, references to, for example, 'our country' will be kept in the TT ('unser Land', see Sample Texts 5 and 6).

Culture-bound or culture-specific phenomena and terms

Culture-bound, or culture-specific, terms are labels used for phenomena (i.e. objects, situations, events, etc.) that exist only in one of the two cultures that are compared in the translation process (i.e. they may be exclusive to this one culture, but not necessarily so; what is important here is that they are specific to one of the two cultures, usually the source culture). The label *realia* is often used to denote such phenomena (see Markstein, 1994, 1998), covering geographical, ethnographical, folk-loric, socio-historical, and also everyday aspects. In more traditional approaches they were often characterised as untranslatable (i.e. in the narrow sense of seeing translation as substitution of SL units by equivalent TL units).

Culture-specific terms frequently pose translation problems since the target readers cannot (always) be supposed to be fully familiar with the source culture. The choice of the most appropriate translation strategy in each case is largely determined by an awareness of a kind of addressees' profile (as part of the analysis of the translation brief). Therefore it is important for translators to know for whom they are producing the TT. Possible strategies are:

(1) the use of a loanword (this is how, for example, *glasnost* and *peres-troika* came into the English language, and also into the German language, with spelling, pronunciation and grammatical gender adopted to the rules and patterns of the TLs; this is what Newmark (1988) calls 'transference');
(2) calque (e.g. 'Hinterbänkler' as a loan translation of 'backbencher');
(3) substitution of the analogous term of the target culture (e.g. 'A level' – 'Abitur', Newmark calls this procedure 'cultural equivalent');
(4) an explanation (or, in Newmark's classification, use of either a 'functional equivalent', e.g. 'le baccalauréat – the French secondary school leaving examination', or of a 'descriptive equivalent', e.g. 'le baccalauréat – the French secondary school leaving examination in which candidates take 8–10 subjects and which is necessary to gain admission to higher education', examples taken from Newmark, 1998). These procedures can also be combined (Newmark refers to this by the label 'translation couplet', e.g. 'le baccalauréat – the 'baccalauréat', the French secondary school leaving examination').

Based on the translation skopos, translators will have to decide whether a loanword alone will be sufficient (which may be the case if the brief requires the TT to reflect a local, historical, or exotic flavour). A sub-stitution of the analogous term of the target culture may not be an appropriate solution if the ST is clearly about the source culture (e.g. substituting 'Abitur' for 'A level' may result in the TT readers assuming that the two examinations, and subsequently the education systems in the two cultures, have a lot in common, which, however, is not the case).

Therefore, combinations are frequently 'safer' solutions, e.g. loanword with added explanation, loanword with an added culturally neutral TL term to define the source culture specific term. Explanations can be added either within the sentence, i.e. immediately following the loanword, or added in brackets, or as a footnote (all of them examples of visibility change as a pragmatic translation strategy in Chesterman's classification, combined with strategies of information change, i.e. additions). Combining the SL term with an explanation at the first textual occurrence also has the advantage that the concept is introduced to the TT addressees, so that in subsequent textual occurrences the loanword alone can be used.

If the translator herself or himself is not familiar with a specific culture-bound reference in the ST, consulting bilingual dictionaries will often not be sufficient, since they may not list the term at all (e.g. 'Balti restaurants' in Sample Text 8). Specialist dictionaries (e.g. *Longman's Dictionary of English Language and Culture*), and other reference works are more useful (see [re]search competence).

Proper names

Practically the same strategies listed for culture-specific terms can be applied to proper names, depending also on the type of the proper name (i.e. people, countries, or institutions). Proper names for people are normally taken over into the TT as they are, although there are a few exceptions (e.g. the name of the Pope is adapted: 'John Paul' – 'Johannes Paul'; spelling variation often applies with reference to names from languages which use different writing systems, e.g. in Russian: 'Yeltsin' – 'Jelzin', 'Gorbachev' – 'Gorbatschow'). If names are meant to tell us something about the character (descriptive names, 'sprechende Namen'), a literal translation or calque may be required (e.g. in fiction 'Snow White' – 'Schneewittchen'). For proper names of countries and towns, there are mostly standard terms in the TL (e.g. 'Köln' – 'Cologne').

For proper names of institutions in the widest sense, loan, calque, explanations (i.e. functional and descriptive equivalents) are characteristically used translation strategies, again often in combination. For example, in the case of names for newspapers or magazines, the proper name alone can be used if the paper is well known to the TT addressees or in the target culture in general (e.g. '*The Times* reported' – '*The Times* berichtete'). If it can be assumed that the publication is not so well known, the proper name can be combined with a generic label ('die Tageszeitung *The Times*') or with a more detailed description ('die britische konservative Tageszeitung *The Times'*, see also Sample Texts 4 and 7). Similar arguments apply with reference to names of political parties (see Sample Text 5). For national and international institutions, there are frequently established standard terms in the target culture. For such names, abbreviations often exist, which can be different in source culture and target culture (see 'International Monetary Fund, IMF' – 'Internationaler Währungsfond, IWF' in Sample Text 3). In the case of some international bodies, the abbreviation formed on the basis of the SL (often English) has become established in the target culture too, although a TL version of the full name exists (e.g. the abbreviation 'WHO' for 'World Health Organisation' is commonly used in German alongside the full name 'Weltgesundheitsorganisation'). The substitution of the analogous term of the target culture for a source culture proper name is not so frequent since it can result in misinterpretation (e.g. 'Bundestag' cannot be substituted for 'House of Commons' in political texts).

The decision on the most appropriate translation strategy in the case of the pragmatic translation problems previously mentioned (and additional ones) depends on the purpose of the TT (e.g. Is a documentary or an instrumental translation necessary? Is the text to convey an 'exotic' flavour of the source culture?), the knowledge of the addressees (e.g. Are the addressees familiar with the source culture or not?); and the situational aspects (i.e. When and where will the TT be used? For example, it will be important to know if the addressees will receive the TT in the target culture or in the source culture – see Sample Texts 2 and 8). I only want to mention in this respect that the notions of source culture and target culture themselves are relative terms; that is, with increasing globalisation and supra-national cooperation, cultural boundaries are changing and becoming blurred (see Lambert, 1994, and on aspects of culture in relation to translations in the European Union see Koskinen, 2000; Schäffner, 1997a). The relevance of a specific term for a concrete text, the genre and the length of a text are other considerations to be taken into account when deciding on translation strategies.

One more useful concept in deciding on the most appropriate translation strategies is the principle of the necessary degree of precision or necessary degree of differentiation ('Prinzip des notwendigen Differenzierungsgrads') which was proposed as a guideline by Hönig and Kussmaul (1982). What is 'necessary' always depends on the purpose of the TT, that is, the word 'necessary' emphasises the fact that in functionalist approaches there can never be absolutes. The authors illustrate this principle particularly with reference to lexical–semantic aspects of the text. For example, the culture-specific term 'Eton' will be differently treated in the following two sentences:

In Parliament he fought for equality, but he sent his son to Eton. – Im Parlament kämpfte er für Chancengleichheit, aber seinen eigenen Sohn schickte er auf eine der *englischen Eliteschulen* (one of the English elite schools).

When his father died his mother could not afford to sent him to Eton any more. – Als sein Vater starb, konnte seine Mutter es sich nicht mehr leisten, ihn auf eine der *teuren Privatschulen* zu schicken (one of the expensive private schools).

The TTs are considered to be sufficiently detailed. As Hönig (1997: 11) argues:

Of course, there is more factual knowledge implied in the terms 'Eton' or 'public school' than expressed in the translation, but the translation mentions everything that is important within the context of the sentence, in other words, the translation is semantically precise enough.

Based on Chesterman's (1997a) classification, we can say that a distribution change was applied as a semantic translation strategy, but for a pragmatic reason.

Intercultural translation problems

These arise from the differences in conventions between the two cultures involved, and therefore cultural filtering will apply as well. Examples are measuring conventions, forms of address, and text-typological and genre conventions, the last one being most important with reference to the sample texts in this volume.

Measuring conventions

Depending on the translation brief, it may become necessary to convert references to measurements (e.g. inches into centimetres, miles per hour into Kilometer pro Stunde, see Schmitt, 1999 and the Appendix in Snell-Hornby *et al.*, 1998: 401ff.).

Conventional forms of address and salutation formulas

Forms of address often differ in source culture and target culture, also depending on the genre (e.g. 'Dear Sir' in official letters would correspond to 'Sehr geehrter Herr', often followed by the name; or, recently more frequently with regard to political correctness, 'Sehr geehrte Damen und Herren', see 'Dear Sir/Madam'). The relationhip between communicative partners as expressed in German in 'Du' compared with

'Sie' can also become a translation problem, for example in literary texts (e.g. at which point in the progression of a personal relationship can the 'Sie' be replaced by 'Du' in the text?) and in advertising (e.g. advertisements addressed to young people may use the more informal 'Du' – 'young', however, is a relative concept).

Text-typological conventions

In translation, we are always dealing with texts, and they are exemplars of text types and of genres (see the earlier discussion on text-linguistic approaches to translation and on Reiss's text typology). The notion of genre emphasises that texts which perform a common function typically share specific structural characteristics (for example, letters need opening and closing formulas). In other words, although each individual text may be unique in its precise form, it usually fits a given pattern (or 'template'), which can be more or less conventionalised. The term 'genre' is frequently used to denote such patterns. The corresponding German term is 'Textsorte', which, however, is sometimes rendered as 'text type' in English (see Schäffner 2000a), as in the following definition:

> A traditional text type is what a given speech community, at a given time and over a considerable period of time, accepts as a traditional, conventional and in some specific way linguistically standardised textual model to be constantly re-used for specific communicative purposes. (Suter, 1993: 48)

We will use 'genre' to denote what Suter defines as 'text type'. Examples of genres are the business letter, weather report, joke, newspaper editorial, instruction manual, user manual, etc. The term 'text type' will be used to refer to functional characteristics of a text (e.g. informative, expressive, argumentative, persuasive, etc., see also Hatim & Mason (1997) who differentiate argumentation, exposition, and instruction as three major text types).

Genre conventions are culture-specific and can change over time, which makes genres relevant for translation (studies). Genre conventions concern both macrostructural aspects (i.e. information units and their typical arrangement in the genre, resulting in the specific pattern, or schema, of the genre; on the notions of 'macrostructure' to denote global semantic units and 'super-structure' to denote global functional units (see van Dijk, 1980) and applied to the news genre (van Dijk, 1985)). For example, English instruction manuals for electrical appliances normally have one macro-structural component 'How to fit a plug', which is not a characteristic textual building block of the German genre. For translation from English into German, thus, there is no need to account for this information unit (unless the skopos demands otherwise). At the level of the micro-structures, i.e. lexical and grammatical choices, we find the following syntactic conventions in instruction manuals: imperatives are preferentially used in English texts to express the directive speech act instructing, compared to infinitives in the German genre. The concept 'speech act' refers to the (intended) illocutionary force of an utterance, e.g. issue a command, request information, offer an apology, make an assertion, make a promise. Speech acts can be classified as representatives, directives, commissives, expressives, declaratives (for more detailed discussions see Austin, 1962; Searle, 1969). There is usually a systematic relationship between preferred forms and structures at the micro-level and the macro-structural component in which they are used (see, for example, Kussmaul (1997: 77) on the variety of forms to express instructions in German user manuals). Another example of a specific speech act being expressed differently in different cultures can be found with orders and instructions in legal texts, where English texts often use modal verbs compared to passive infinitives in German texts (e.g. 'Applications shall be submitted by . . . ' – 'Anträge sind bis . . . einzureichen'; see also Göpferich, 1995; Schäffner, 2000a; and Sample Text 9).

Parallel texts (see Neubert (1985) and the earlier definition) are useful for assessing how identical communicative functions are expressed in specific genres, in other words, to identify genre conventions in source and target culture. Parallel texts are also particularly useful for translators (see research competence), because very often typical structures and formulations found in target culture exemplars can be taken over into the TT (see Schäffner, 1998c). Both in the introductory comments to groups of texts and in the annotations I have tried to provide evidence of the practical use of parallel texts for making informed decisions in the choice of translation strategies.

Interlingual translation problems

These result from structural differences in the vocabulary and syntax of the two languages, i.e. they are more specifically related to the linguistic systems of SL and TL. These contrasts were mainly (or exclusively) focused on when Translation Studies began to develop as a sub-discipline of (applied) linguistics (as characteristically reflected in Vinay & Darbelnet (1958), and Friederich (1969) among others). Functionalist approaches, however, stress that no clear line can be drawn between language and culture. Translation means crossing cultural boundaries, not only language boundaries. Knowledge of the linguistic structures of the two languages is obviously highly relevant for translators (see linguistic competence), but it is not sufficient to carry out the task of translation. In other words, the concrete linguistic structure in the ST needs to be analysed against the background of the translation brief in order to decide about the most appropriate structure of the TT. That is, functionalist approaches do not ask 'Has the translator succeeded in reproducing a specific ST lexical feature in the TT?' or 'Why has an ST word not been rendered in the TT?' or 'How has the translator coped with a gerund in the ST?'. The relevance of such linguistically oriented questions with a focus on the ST surface structure is questionable from a functionalist point of view. The dominant question here would be 'Does the TT display a linguistic structure which is most appropriate to the intended purpose of the text for its addressees in the target culture?' (which may, of course, include questions such as those mentioned earlier, but the answers to them will have to be judged against the skopos).

Linguistic similarities and differences in a narrow sense are also being studied by contrastive/comparative linguistics, and a variety of publications can help translators to solve interlingual translation problems (see the numerous articles in journals with a more practical orientation, such as *Lebende Sprachen*, *Babel*, *The Linguist*, see also Chesterman, 1998a).

Only a few examples of interlingual translation problems in the language pair English and German will be mentioned here, both at the lexical and at the grammatical level. For example, English infinitive structures and -ing structures (e.g. gerunds, present participles) frequently pose translation problems since in the German linguistic system they may not be used in the same positions, or may not exist at all (more detailed explanations for the choice of specific solutions can be found in the annotations to the sample texts).

Dialect (regional variation) and sociolect (social variation)

Words and other features indicating the local origin of the ST (e.g. UK or USA as source culture, see Sample Text 4), a more specific regional origin (e.g. a particular part of a country), or a sociolect, may add a specific meaning or connotation to the text and thus achieve a specific effect for the ST readers. The skopos may require the translator to recreate this effect. For example, in the case of *My Fair Lady*, the English sociolect – Cockney – was replaced in the German translation by a local dialect, the Berlin dialect. The effect was somewhat distorted, since the Berlin dialect is not socially marked, but the musical was a success nevertheless (see Holz-Mänttäri's (1984) hierarchy of goals, i.e. the goal of producing a TT is subordinate to the goal of performing a musical, as in the case of *My Fair Lady*; on the semiotic aspects of translation if music is involved see, for example, Kaindl (1995, 1997); Gorlee (1997)).

Reported speech, abstract agents

There are specific grammatical rules and textual conventions to express reported speech in German (any German grammar book provides a detailed account). Reported speech in German is often, but not exclusively, indicated by subjunctive verb forms. Indicative verb forms for reported speech are also very common in German, especially when there is a verb of speaking/reporting (such as 'betonen, äußern'). In English texts, ongoing reported speech may be signalled by a verb in the past tense, without additional explicit indicators. This makes it sometimes difficult to decide whether a given sentence is indeed a continuation of reported speech or a factual statement. Textual and contextual information will provide the answer in most cases. In addition to this grammatical feature, English texts indicate direct and reported speech predominantly by adding the verb 'say'. In German texts, however, there is more lexical variation, e.g. verbs ('sagen, meinen, hinzufügen, . . . '), nominal structures (e.g. 'nach Meinung von'), or a preposition ('laut').

Differences may also concern the selection of elements (of some state of affairs) that become explicitly codified. For example, 'the meeting held in London' can be rendered as 'das Treffen in London', i.e. the element of 'holding' can be inferred by the readers (on inference and implicature see also Grice, 1975). This would be an example of the semantic translation strategy distribution change (here: compression; see also Schmidt, 1977). Syntactic positions can also be determined by the language systems, such as abstract agents taking subject position in English texts (e.g. 'The study suggests that . . . '). In German texts, prepositional phrases are more common (e.g. 'In dem Bericht wird die Vermutung geäußert, daß . . . '; i.e. syntactic translation strategy: clause structure change). However, since such structures often occur in news reports, reviews, or in journalistic texts more generally, they might be considered to be a genre convention (and would fall under intercultural translation problems; see also the annotations for Sample Texts 3, 4, 8).

Theme–rheme structure

A related point is the theme–rheme structure of a sentence (also refered to in the literature as functional sentence perspective, topic and focus, foregrounding and backgrounding), concerning the information focus. The theme is the old and/or known information, and the rheme the new information; this new information being the focus of the message, and normally taking the end position in a sentence. For example, in a written text on Shakespeare, in the sentence 'Shakespeare wrote *Hamlet*', 'Shakespeare' is the theme, and '*Hamlet*' the rheme (and correspondingly in German: 'Shakespeare schrieb *Hamlet*'). If, depending on text and context, 'Shakespeare' is to be the rheme (e.g. in a quiz or to correct a wrong statement), the German sentence could be '*Hamlet* schrieb Shakespeare'. That is, because of the (relatively) free word order in German, such a change of the position of words is possible (in spoken language this would, in addition, be indicated by the stress on 'Shakespeare'). Because English has a more fixed word order, making 'Shakespeare' the rheme of the sentence would require a different syntactic structure, for example, a passive structure ('*Hamlet* was written by Shakespeare') or a cleft sentence ('It was Shakespeare who wrote *Hamlet*'; see also Doherty, 1999).

There may be theme patterns that are more characteristic and/or more frequent in a particular language (or in a particular genre), but more research into this issue is needed before the consequences for translation can be discussed in more detail. Research methods in the field of corpus studies, i.e. the recently growing number of analyses of large corpora, will be very useful in this respect (see Baker, 1995; Laviosa 1997).

Text-specific translation problems

Nord refers to all those problems which arise in the translation of one specific text and which cannot be generalised as text-specific problems. As examples she gives metaphors, puns, neologisms, rhetorical figures, alliteration, rhyme, etc. A decision as to the most appropriate translation strategy will have to be based on a consideration of their relevance for the text, potential genre conventions, and, of course, the purpose of the TT.

Alliteration, puns, and similar rhetorical figures

Rhetorical figures are often very important for the effect of the text (and may be characteristic of a genre, e.g. advertising texts). However, since some of these figures are based on linguistic systems (e.g. an alliteration, or a pun due to polysemy), a reproduction of the same feature in the same position in the TT may not be possible, even if this is the aim in view of the skopos. Translators can act creatively (on creativity see

Kussmaul, 1998a, b, 2000), for example, (re)creating a specific effect somewhere else in the text (translation strategy 'Disloziierung'; and an example of Nord's notion of a vertical unit of translation mentioned earlier; see also Sample Text 8 for relocation, and Sample Text 4 for puns and allusions).

Word systems/lexical-semantic fields in a text, frames

   In the annotations to the sample texts in this volume, we have listed word systems and/or lexical-semantic field under text-specific translation problems. The motivation for this decision has been to emphasise that the texts deal with a specific topic, and that the lexical structures used contribute to the intratextual coherence. The concepts of frames and scenes, scripts, scenarios, and schemata can be introduced in this respect. These terms stress the cognitive nature of text production and reception, but they are used with slightly different definitions in the literature (of linguistics, cognitive linguistics, psycholinguistics, artificial intelligence; for an overview, see, for example, Tannen, 1993: 14–21). What they mainly have in common is an assumption that knowledge and experience is structured in the human mind, which results in structured expectations in communicative interaction. In other words, human beings experience the physical and social world in their given culture, and, based on this experience, they organize their knowledge about the world in their minds. This knowledge is organized in specific cognitive structures (which are called frames, schemata, etc.) and it is used, or activated, in order to interpret (new) information.

   Fillmore (1975, 1976, 1985) uses *frame* and *scene* to link linguistic and cognitive structures, arguing that people associate certain scenes with certain linguistic frames. He uses *scene* for 'any kind of coherent segment of human beliefs, actions, experiences or imaginings' and *frame* 'for any system of linguistic choices . . . that can get associated with prototypical instances of scenes' (Fillmore, 1975: 124). The organisational structures of knowledge provide the conceptual basis for lexical material, and *vice versa*, lexical structures encountered in a text evoke knowledge structures, i.e. cognitive frames. Frames are shared by a group of people or by a whole speech community, depending on their social experience, including experience with texts. This also means that frames may be culture-specific, or alternatively, they may be fairly similiar or identical between two cultures, but the actual arrangement at the textual surface may still be different. The relevance of the frame concept for translation (studies) should thus be obvious. For example, owing to the presence of a specific frame in a text, the actual lexical structures chosen for the TT may be more or less specific than those in the ST (translation strategies: abstraction change, distribution change, explicitness change; see, e.g. the frame-determined lexical choices 'Krieg' for 'battles' in Sample Text 4, 'Waffen' for 'guns of war' in Sample Text 5; for the application of frame and scene semantics to translation see also Vannerem & Snell-Hornby, 1986, Kussmaul, 1995: 91ff.).

Metaphors

Nord (1997) lists metaphors as text-specific translation problems. I want to use this phenomenon to discuss the difficulty of assigning a specific translation problem to one of the four types. In the literature on translation (studies), metaphor has traditionally been defined as a figure of speech, as a linguistic expression which is substituted for another expression (with a literal meaning), and whose main function is the stylistic embellishment of the text. The two main issues discussed are the translatability of metaphors (for linguistic and / or cultural reasons), and the potential translation procedures. Newmark (1981) lists seven translation procedures:

(1)   reproducing the same image in the TL;
(2)   replacing the image in the SL with a standard TL image;
(3)   translation of metaphor by simile; retaining the image;
(4)   translation of metaphor (or simile) by simile plus sense;
(5)   conversion of metaphor to sense;
(6)   deletion; and
(7)   same metaphor combined with sense.

From a target perspective, Toury (1995: 81ff.) identifies two additional cases:

(1)   non-metaphor into metaphor; and
(2)   the addition of a metaphor in the TT without any linguistic motivation in the ST (zero into metaphor).

He views metaphor not only as a translation problem (of the ST, i.e. as a horizontal unit of translation), but also as a translation solution. Chesterman (1997a) deals with metaphors with reference to the semantic translation strategy trope change.

More recently, a cognitive approach to metaphor (initiated by Lakoff & Johnson, 1980) is increasingly being applied to Translation Studies as well (see Stienstra, 1993; Schäffner 1997b, in press). The main argument for a cognitive approach is that metaphors are not just decorative elements, but rather basic resources for thought processes in human society. Metaphors are a means to understand one domain of experience (a target domain) in terms of another one (a source domain). The source domain is mapped onto the target domain, whereby the structural components of the base conceptual schema are transferred to the target domain, thus also allowing for knowledge-based inferences and entailments. Such models are largely encoded and understood in linguistic terms. In cognitive linguistics the term 'metaphor' is used to refer to the conceptual mapping (e.g. ANGER IS THE HEAT OF A FLUID IN A CONTAINER); and the term 'metaphorical expression' is used to refer to an individual linguistic expression that is based on a conceptualisation and as such sanctioned by a mapping (e.g. 'I gave vent to my anger' – 'Ich kochte vor Wut').

With respect to translation, the same conceptual metaphor may exist in source and target culture with identical (or similar) metaphorical expressions, with different metaphorical expressions, or a conceptual metaphor may be specific (or exclusive) to one culture. Metaphors can also be more or less specific and/or can be subsumed under a more general conceptual metaphor. For example, both in English and in German, development may be conceptualised either as construction (DEVELOPMENT IS A BUILDING PROCESS) or as movement (DEVELOPMENT IS MOVEMENT ALONG A PATH). Potential translation strategies can therefore be changes of the conceptual metaphor (e.g. 'rebuild the peace process' – 'den Friedensprozeß wieder in Gang setzen'), changes of the metaphorical expressions (e.g. 'issues at the heart of a conflict' – 'Probleme, die dem Konflikt zugrundeliegen', both in Sample Text 5, see the more detailed discussions there). It is for these reasons that in the annotations, metaphors (as conceptual metaphors) are usually discussed under the heading of intercultural translation problems, and not as text-specific ones, as suggested by Nord.

At the end of this section, I want to give just one more example which will also be evidence that the assignment of a specific translation problem to one of the four types is not a straightforward affair. The example is the scene 'accidents'. Elements of the scene are the following: the actual type of accident, the cause of the accident, victims, place and time. These elements are linguistically represented by a frame, but the frame elements are distributed differently in the genre short news items in English and German mass media. English texts show the following characteristic (prototypical) structure: victims (in a verbal style), cause (in a verbal style), place and/or time, background information; whereas the typical structure of German texts is: cause (in a nominal style, often a prepositional phrase), place and/or time, victims (often nominal style), background information. The position of place and/or time may vary. An identical state of affairs (scene), i.e. identical propositions, could therefore be verbalised (framed), for example, as:

Twenty die in tragedy at sea
All twenty Polish crew members of a Greek freighter died when their
ship sank in six metre waves, about forty miles west of Stavanger off
Norway's south-west coast.

compared to

Schiffsunglück in Norwegen
Beim Untergang eines griechischen Frachters vor der Südwestküste
Norwegens kamen alle 20 polnischen Besatzungsmitglieder ums
Leben. Das Schiff sank bei 6m hohem Wellengang ca. 40 Seemeilen
westlich von Stavanger.

Additional references to the source of the information (e.g. the news
agency) may be placed either at the beginning or the end of the text
(newspapers normally have their conventional in-house style). With
respect to such texts, it could be argued that we have text-specific translation problems as far as the choice of frame-related lexical units is
concerned, e.g. 'die'. The decision to use a nominal structure ('ums
Leben kommen') instead of a verbal one ('sterben'), however, is determined by genre conventions (intercultural translation problems).
Moreover, in-house styles may have an effect on the actual structure of
an individual text, as there may be specific intentions to foreground a
particular element (e.g. if the place is meant to be the rheme, the text
could start with 'Unmittelbar vor der Südwestküste Norwegens kamen
beim . . .'; if the focus is on the victims, e.g. if their nationality is relevant,
the text could start with 'Alle 20 polnischen Besatzungsmitglieder . . .').
Whether such variations are considered under the heading intercultural
translation problems (e.g. as deviations from the prototypical structure)
or under text-specific translation problems can be open to discussion.

Any translation task can be approached within a functionalist framework, i.e. identifying specific translation problems as belonging to a
problem type, and deciding on the most appropriate translation strategies on the basis of an analysis of the translation assignment. This is
illustrated in this volume. Although there is no clear correlation between
Nord's problem types and the translation strategy used, the classification of problem types is a useful pedagogical device for arguing about
the reasons for the choice of a particular strategy.

Outline of the Book
Nine texts have been chosen to illustrate a functionalist approach to
translation. These texts represent a variety of kinds, text types and
genres, and deal with several topics. We have arranged them into the following six categories:

(1)   user information, user manuals,
(2)   popular-scientific texts in the media,
(3)   political texts,
(4)   reviews,
(5)   promotional texts, and
(6)   legal texts.

For each category, short introductory comments are provided, summarising some translation problems that are typically posed by texts in that category. Since the book is not meant to be a textbook in the sense that the texts can be 'worked through' from the first to the last, we have not opted for an arrangement according to degrees of difficulty. The discussion of each sample text follows the same pattern: the ST is provided with a specified translation assignment. Then a sample TT is presented, followed by lengthy annotations. The annotations include the following points: a repetition of the translation assignment at the very beginning (i.e. specification of the purpose); then a ST characterisation (i.e. brief comments on the ST as a text-in-situation-in-culture, see translation-oriented ST analysis); then a TT specification (i.e. brief comments on the required profile of the TT as a text-in-situation-in-culture). The following detailed annotations are arranged on the basis of the four types of translation problems illustrated above.

All STs are authentic texts, presented and translated in full (except Sample Text 1), with their exact sources provided (i.e. information about when and where the ST was published). In the selection of the text categories and genres we have paid attention to the requirements of the translation industry and translator training. All genres represented in the book are of practical relevance, although the actual proportion of those genres in the translation industry is continuously changing, depending mainly on economic factors. With respect to the UK, Germany and France are the largest non-English-speaking export markets (see Hagen, 1998), and the largest share of translation production is technical and scientific (see the statistics in Sager, 1994: 297ff.; Laviosa, 1997: 316). With respect to the translation market in Germany, English is the most prominent SL and also the most frequent TL. The most dominant genres are business correspondence, user information, scientific-technical articles, contracts and treaties, technical specifications, popular-scientific texts, promotional texts (see the statistics in Schmitt, 1990, 1998a; Stoll, 2000).

All STs were published between 1992 and 1998 (with the translation assignments including realistically corresponding deadlines), which raises the issue of 'dated' texts. However, the aim of this book is to illustrate a functionalist approach, for which 'newness' of the topic is not an absolute requirement. Each text is full of translation problems on the basis of which more general conclusions can be drawn for translating similar texts of the same genre or on a similar topic.

Authentic translation assignments existed for some of the texts (Sample Texts 2 and 8), the others were translated specifically for inclusion in this book, i.e. with a pedagogical purpose in mind (however, a realistic assignment could well have been possible). All texts were translated by us (either jointly or individually), with the exception of Sample Text 8, for which a German TT already existed. Since this text displayed some deficiencies, we produced another TT which is added after the annotations. It needs to be stressed that all our TTs are *sample translations*, i.e. alternative solutions are always possible (in the annotations, alternative versions for sentences or clauses have sometimes been provided). However, we wish to argue that our TTs are sufficiently appropriate for their specified purposes. With reference to translation quality assessment, this means that they satisfy the specifications (the skopos). Functionalist approaches emphasise that quality can only be assessed against a set of specifications and requirements, including the terms and conditions of the assignment, the intrinsic quality of the TT and its presentation form (on quality assessment and quality standards see also House, 1977, 1997; Hönig, 1997; Muzii, 1998; Schmitt, 1998d; of particular relevance for the translation industry in Germany, Austria and Switzerland is DIN 2345, the result of an agreement between translator-training institutions, professional translator organizations, and clients, and introduced in 1996 as a guideline to customers and translators for organising translation projects).

In producing the German TTs, we have used the traditional spelling rules. The new rules, introduced in 1999 as a result of the spelling reform which the German-speaking countries had agreed on, are meant to be phased in over the coming years, but in view of ongoing debates about inconsistencies, additional changes and revisions are likely. (NB: In the case of literary translations, publishing companies in Germany nowadays often request the TT to follow the new rules; specifications are part of translation contracts; see also *Der Spiegel*, 3 April 2000, p. 244.)

In the annotations, we comment in depth on how we arrived at our solutions and why a particular choice was made (often backed up by additional evidence, e.g. examples from parallel texts). In other words, in the annotations we illustrate our decision-making processes. That is, we do not discuss individual translation problems by reference to texts and/or genres in which those problems may occur, as is done in other books of a similar nature (e.g. Hervey *et al.*, 1995; Hohenadl & Will, 1994). In our comments, we make use of some of the labels for the translation strategies presented here (often using only the more general labels 'modulation' and 'transposition'), but we do not aim at completeness. We do not list each individual case of, for example, unit shift, phrase structure change, hyponomy, illocutionary change, for each individual text, but instead, we try to explain what we have done and why, with reference to the skopos, the addressees, the communicative situation, genre conventions, etc. By doing so, we hope that it will be easier for readers to understand our argumentation and our decisions for the TT profiles.

I have already pointed out that the assignment of a specific translation problem to one of the four problem types is not always easy, and that sometimes there are overlaps. In such cases (e.g. titles, reported speech, abstract agents, metaphors, as translation problems), pragmatic and genre criteria have been taken into account for the decisions on where to discuss them. There is also some repetition of information, that is, arguments and comments made in this introductory chapter may be taken up again in the introductory comments and in the actual annotations. This will make it possible for readers to focus on (an) individual text(s). Cross-references have been provided where appropriate.

In sum, the book is intended to illustrate how an awareness of translation problems and potential translation strategies will result in appropriate TTs.

User Information, User Manuals:
Introductory Comments

Texts that can be grouped under the heading *user information* account for a large percentage of texts that are translated in a professional environment (see the statistical data in Schmitt, 1998a: 10). More specifically, the label 'user information' covers installation manuals (predominantly for experts), operating leaflets (both for experts and laypeople), user manuals (predominantly for laypeople), and similar genres. What they all have in common is that their main function is to provide information and to give instructions about specific procedures, actions and behaviour.

In her translation-oriented text typology, Reiss (1971) had assigned such texts to the informative text type, related to description as the dominant function of language and to the logical dimension of language. For Reiss, the invariance of the content was the main criterion for translating such texts. As has repeatedly been argued, Reiss's typology is rather rigid, and genres she would describe as informative often also show expressive and/or appellative elements. In more detailed studies of text types and genres, informative and instructive texts are frequently set apart as distinctive types. For example, Rolf (1993) characterises texts such as user manuals as belonging to the 'directive' text type, i.e. the text addressees are expected (or directed, instructed) to do something. In other words, without fulfilling the instructions of the text, an intended state of affairs or action cannot be brought about. Providing information about the product (or the service) is an integral part of the message, indeed a prerequisite for a successful operation. The texts, thus, function in a larger communicative setting and contribute to achieving a specific goal (e.g. use a washing machine to do one's laundry).

Göpferich (1995) bases her text classification on the parameters of the interactional setting and proposes 'human/technology-interaction-oriented texts' as a superordinate category (which, however, excludes cooking recipes and patient information leaflets as other examples of genres with information combined with instruction as predominant text functions). In her detailed study, Göpferich analysed genre-specific features (on the basis of German and English texts) of 'user manuals', i.e. in her understanding texts as documents about products, intended to acquaint the user of the product with its use ('Gebrauch'), operation ('Bedienung'), maintenance ('Wartung'), and/or repair ('Reparatur').

Depending on the (legal) status of the text sender and the corresponding degree of authority, there is usually a difference in the German culture between 'Anweisung' (i.e. the sender is authorised to give instructions; for example, the sender is the manufacturer and the manual is for experts who do the installation work, see 'Gebrauchsanweisung, Bedienungsanweisung') and 'Anleitung' (i.e. the sender is not authorised to give instructions; for example, manuals for laypeople who use the product in their daily lives, see 'Gebrauchsanleitung, Bedienungsanleitung').

Unless the skopos demands otherwise, user manuals and user information serve identical purposes and fulfil identical functions for their respective addressees in the source culture and target culture (equifunctional translation). Target readers, thus, usually expect the texts to correspond to the genre conventions with which they are familiar. It is therefore important for translators to be aware of the genre conventions in the target culture or to find out about such conventions by checking parallel texts. The following aspects can be seen as generally relevant for the translation of user information and user manuals.

Macro-structure/Super-structure

User manuals and instruction leaflets often follow a specific pattern in the arrangement of the textual building blocks (the textual superstructure). At the beginning there is information about the product itself (name of the product, name of the producer, description of the product, technical features), followed by textual building blocks accounting for the instructive function, i.e. general and specific instructions about the use and/or operation of the product (safety instructions, detailed instructions for use). At the end of the text, there is usually information about care and maintenance, service information, warranty. This structure is relatively fixed, and it corresponds to a logical order in the actual operation of the products. In other words, the superstructure of such genres is conventionalised. For the translation of such texts, the textual building blocks are usually kept in the same order.

In the case of electrical appliances, the English instruction manuals normally have one category in the superstructure which concerns wiring instructions. This information part is culture specific and is not a conventional element of the genre in Germany. This difference is due to the different practice in the UK and in Germany: whereas electrical appliances have always come with the plug fitted in Germany, this was only introduced in the UK in the early 1990s. If German texts of this genre refer to different types of plugs and sockets (e.g. in user information for hairdryers or electric irons) they have an explicit sentence to this effect, such as the following: 'Hinweis: Für einige Reiseländer mit anderen Steckersystemen sind spezielle Steckeradepter im Fachhandel erhältlich.' For translating user manuals from English into German, there is normally no need to account for the textual information about wiring instructions (unless the translation brief, the skopos, requires it).

Micro-structure

A characteristic feature of user manuals is that the instructions themselves are typically expressed by imperative structures in English and by infinitive (or imperative structures) in German. This applies particularly to cases where the instructions are arranged in a sequence to indicate the individual steps of the action (see also Kussmaul, 1990). Illustrative examples from a German and English instruction leaflet for hairdryers and for a radio, respectively, are 'Check the position of the voltage selector switch before use' compared to 'Darauf achten, daß die eingestellte Spannung mit der Netzspannung übereinstimmt', and 'Gerät einschalten und Lautstärke einstellen' compared to 'Switch on the radio and adjust volume'.

As Schmitt (1998c) and Göpferich (1995) have shown on the basis of comparative text analyses, imperative structures seem to be more frequent if the text addressees are laypeople who want to use the product, whereas infinitive structures are more common if the addressees are experts who are, for example, installing the product to be subsequently used by laypeople. The difference in imperative *versus* infinitive structures also means a difference in the ordering of the syntactic elements: in English texts, the object follows the verb ('Push the button', 'Keep away from direct sunlight'), whereas in German the object takes initial position ('Taste drücken', 'vor direkter Sonneneinstrahlung schützen'). Any additional information, such as adverbs or prepositional phrases follow the object in English texts, whereas they are placed between the object and the infinitive in German texts (e.g. in cooking instructions 'cook in salted water', 'season to taste', 'Mischung langsam erhitzen', 'Suppe unter ständigem Rühren zum Kochen bringen' – for the translation of cooking recipes see Colina, 1997).

Modal verbs are not too frequent in user manuals, but they can be found in the textual building blocks dealing with the use of the product ('Your hair should be dry before ...'), with information about repair ('Elektrogeräte dürfen nur durch Elektro-Fachkräfte repariert werden'), and wiring instructions in the English texts ('If the mains plug contains a fuse, this should have a value of 5A').

Also in negated form, to express prohibitions and warnings, imperatives are characteristic of English texts and infinitive structures of German texts (e.g. 'Do not remove any fixed cover', 'Gehäuse nicht beschädigen'). Frequently, such warnings are preceded by an explicit lexical expression. As Schmitt (1996) has shown, different expressions are used depending on the effects for humans ('Danger! or Warning:' – 'Vorsicht!') and / or objects ('Caution' – 'Achtung'); and with reference to potential operating problems which might cause harm ('Important:' – 'Wichtig:'). Exclamation marks are typically used in German, in contrast to colons in English texts.

Another characteristic feature at the lexical level is that German texts show a preference for a more general noun (especially 'Gerät', e.g. 'Gerät ausschalten' is more common than 'Fön ausschalten'), whereas English texts typically use the more concrete name for the respective product, combined with a more personal style (e.g. 'your hair styler').

Extra-linguistic Information

User information often combines verbal text with pictorial illustrations, drawings, photos, etc. Their function is to support and ease the comprehension process (on problems with comprehending user information texts see Liebert & Schmitt, 1998). Some of the drawings may be culture specific, some may be combined with textual information. In such cases, it is advisable for the translator to consult the client to negotiate the most appropriate translation solution.

Culture-specific Aspects

Schmitt (1998c: 209f.) refers to product documentation in the context of corporate identity. That is, if a company wishes to promote a product internationally, it is often the case that the accompanying documentation (e.g. instruction manuals) will look identical in all languages in which the texts have been produced (including layout, fonts, colour). Depending on the culture of the addressees, there are several other aspects of user information texts that are of relevance for translation. I have already mentioned that the wiring instructions which are typical of English texts need not be accounted for in a German TT. Another example are obligatory standard formulations, for instance, information regarding compliance with EU directives. In these cases, there are culture-specific standard formulations which can be used by the translator (again in consultation with the client, if appropriate), e.g. 'Funkentstört nach der Richtlinie 87/308 EWG', 'Dieses Produkt entspricht den Funkentstörvorschriften der Richtlinie des Rates 87/303/EWG', compared to 'Suppressed against radio and TV interference to EEC directive no 82/499', 'This unit is produced to comply with Directives 76/8809 EEC, 82/499/EEC and Standard IEC Publ. 65'. Measurement systems, too, are often culture-specific and may need to be adapted to the conventions of the target culture (e.g. converting ounces into grammes for recipes).

Culture-specific aspects may also be reflected in the textual microstructure. For example, a comparative analysis of exemplars of German and English patient information leaflets has shown, that with reference to storage, the English and German texts typically refer to the maximum temperature from a different perspective ('Keep X in a dry place below 25°C (77°F)' compared to 'Tube nicht über 25°C aufbewahren' – see the semantic translation strategy 'converses' in Chesterman's (1997a) classification).

The term 'localisation' has become a commonly used label to denote the process of adapting a product (and subsequently the accompanying product documentation) to the specific requirements and conventions of the target culture (primarily for marketing purposes, i.e. in order to sell a product in another culture). In the literature, 'localisation' is predominantly used with reference to the adaptation of computer hardware and software, concerning the layout of the keyboard, the layout of the user information on the monitor, the structure of help menus, etc. (see the contributions in Schmitz & Wahle, 2000). In a wider sense, localisation also applies to providing relevant contact addresses for after-sale service and/or maintenance and repair (see also Snell-Hornby, 1999: 112ff.). These aspects need to be taken into account when translating the accompanying documentation as well.

Sample Texts

The two sample texts we have chosen are an extract from a user manual for a washer/dryer and an information/instruction leaflet for a specific service (how to make an emergency telephone call, see also Schäffner, 1995a). The macro- and microstructure aspects mentioned earlier apply to these two texts, with the problem of a logical arrangement of the textual building blocks being of specific importance in the telephone text. Extra-textual information is of relevance in the washer/dryer text, which includes a number of drawings which illustrate the various steps of operation. In this respect, localisation will apply, since adaptation to the German-speaking market will be required. Culture-specific aspects are also related to the specific communicative settings of the two texts: the washer/dryer text is intended to be used in German-speaking countries; the emergency call text, on the other hand, is intended to be used by German speakers who live in the source culture, the UK. These settings influence the choice of translation strategies. Thus, the two sample texts may be seen as representing different degrees of conventionality of user information: the washer/dryer user manual is a genre exemplar which is highly characteristic of the genre (in other words, it is a good, almost prototypical exemplar of the category). Information gained from parallel texts is therefore very useful for producing the TT. The emergency call text, on the other hand, is more on the periphery of the genre category user information, in particular due to its specific pragmatic parameters. Parallel texts are useful to a certain degree for producing the TT, but genre conventions are subordinate to pragmatic aspects in this particular case.

Step-by-step guide

Use this washer dryer for washing only, tumble drying only or a combination of washing and tumble drying.

For continuous washing and tumble drying proceed through steps 1 to 12, but remember not to exceed the maximum recommended Tumble drying load.

If you are washing only or tumble drying only, not all stages need to be followed.

1 Sort the laundry

Sort articles into groups according to the wash care labels.

Remove everything from the pockets and folds of clothes.

Close all zips.

Shake out items as much as possible instead of leaving them crumpled.

2 Choose the programme

Choose the programme from the Programme Guide on the machine or the 'Programmes' section in this manual.

For mixed loads select the programme which corresponds to the lowest wash temperature and least vigorous wash and spin action as shown by the wash care labels on the garments.

3 Load the machine

Turn programme selector to the 'T' position.

Press button and open the door.

Put the laundry into the machine.

Refer to the 'Programmes' section and do not put into the machine more than the maximum recommended wash load.

Close the door ensuring that it latches correctly.

4 Add detergent and fabric conditioner

Press the drawer open button, pull out drawer and add right amount of powder and fabric conditioner.

For a normal, full wash load Hoover recommend using 1½ cups (cup size: 150 grams) of conventional automatic washing powder.

In soft water areas 1 cup should be sufficient.

Gently close the drawer.

Concentrated powder and liquid detergent

Fill the dispensing device with the correct amount of powder or liquid as recommended by the manufacturer.

Place the dispensing device upwards on top the laundry in the drum.

5 Set up the programme

Turn the programme selector until the letter corresponding to the chosen wash programme appears in the programme window.

For tumble drying turn the selector to position 'T'.

6 Press function buttons

Refer to the 'Programmes' section in this book to see which functions must be selected and which are optional.

7 Set the drying time
(not required for washing only)

Turn the selector to the required drying time.

Suggested drying times are given in the 'Programmes' section.

If more heat is required for drying cotton and linen, press the 'Cotton dry' function button.

8 Start the programme

Turn on the water supplies.

Plug into the electricity supply and switch on.

Press the start/stop button to start the programme.

If the wrong programme is selected, press and release the start/stop button to switch off the machine before re-selecting.

9 The wash cycle

If the programme incorporates 'Creaseguard' the machine will stop during the final rinse. Press the 'Creaseguard' button to continue the programme.

At the end of a washing only cycle the machine will switch off automatically.

On a continuous washing and tumble drying programme the machine will proceed to dry the load for the time selected.

10 The tumble drying cycle

IMPORTANT: Dispensers used for concentrated powder and liquid detergent must be removed from the drum before tumble drying.

The load is dried by tumbling in the thermostatically controlled warm air.

The drum changes direction during the cycle to prevent tangling and produce even drying.

Cool air is used during the last 12 minutes of the drying cycle to minimise creasing.

REMEMBER: The time needed for drying will depend on the materials in the load, how damp they are when put in and how dry they are required.

To stop tumble drying, press and release start/stop button.

Wait for the door interlock to release before opening the door.

To start tumble drying again, close the door and press the start/stop button.

11 Remove the load

When the programme has finished the machine will stop automatically.

Press and release the start/stop button to switch the machine off.

Wait for approximately 90 seconds after the programme has finished before opening the door. It may be necessary to set the programme selector in the 'T' position.

12 Switching off

Turn off the water supplies.

Switch off and remove the plug from the electricity supply.

These are safety measures to ensure that no harm can occur electrically or by water leakage.

Translation Assignment
Hoover want to sell their electrical household appliances in Germany and, therefore, have asked for a translation of their users manual for one of their washer/dryers. (Only a part of it is reproduced, translated, and discussed here.)

HOOVER ECOLOGIC
Bedienungsschritte

Anmerkung des Übersetzers: Bei verschiedenen Bedienungsschritten wird auf die Beschriftung der Funktionstasten Bezug genommen. Gegebenenfalls ist hier eine Anpassung der Übersetzung an die tatsächlichen Benennungen erforderlich.

Der *Hoover Ecologic* kann entweder ausschließlich als Waschmaschine bzw. Trockner oder als Vollwaschtrockner benutzt werden.

Für das Waschen mit anschließendem Trocknen gelten die Schritte 1 bis 12, wobei die empfohlene Trocknerhöchstlast nicht überschritten werden darf.

Wird das Gerät ausschließlich zum Waschen oder zum Trocknen eingesetzt, entfallen einige der angegebenen Schritte.

1 Sortieren der Wäsche

Sortieren Sie die Wäsche nach den Pflegesymbolen auf den Etiketten.

Leeren Sie die Taschen der Kleidungsstücke, entfernen Sie Fremdkörper aus der Wäsche, und bürsten Sie Taschen und Umschläge aus.

Schließen Sie alle Reißverschlüsse.

Legen Sie die Wäsche auseinandergefaltet und locker in die Trommel. Schütteln Sie die Stücke, wenn nötig, vorher gut aus.

2 Programmwahl

Wählen Sie das gewünschte Programm laut Programmanzeige des Geräts oder anhand der Programmtabelle in der Bedienungsanleitung.

Wählen Sie bei Mischladungen anhand der Pflegesymbole das Programm für die niedrigste Temperaturstufe und den schonendsten Wasch- und Schleudergang.

3 Einlegen der Wäsche

Stellen Sie den Programmwähler auf 'T'.

Öffnen Sie die Tür durch Knopfdruck.

Legen Sie die Wäsche ein.

Beachten Sie die Angaben zur maximalen Beladungsmenge in der Programmtabelle der Bedienungsanleitung. Waschmaschine nicht überladen.

Beim Schließen der Tür auf ordnungsgemäßes Einrasten achten.

4 Zugabe von Waschmittel und Weichspüler

Waschmittelfach per Knopfdruck öffnen, herausziehen und die benötigten Mengen Waschmittel und Weichspüler einfüllen.

Bei normal verschmutzter Wäsche reicht für eine volle Trommelladung 1½ Meßbecher (1 Meßbecher = 150 g) handelsübliches Waschpulver.

Bei weichem Wasser genügt in der Regel 1 Meßbecher.

Schließen Sie das Waschmittelfach vorsichtig.

Waschpulverkonzentrate und Flüssigwaschmittel

Geben Sie die vom Hersteller angegebene Menge Pulver oder Flüssigwaschmittel in den dafür vorgesehenen Dosierbehälter.

Stellen Sie den Dosierbehälter mit der Öffnung nach oben auf die Wäsche in der Trommel.

5 Einstellen des Programms

Die Programme werden mit dem Programmwähler eingestellt. Drehen Sie den Programmwähler so lange, bis der Buchstabe des gewünschten Waschprogramms im Programmfenster angezeigt wird.

Zum Trocknen den Programmwähler auf 'T' stellen.

6 Wahl der Zusatzfunktionen

Bei Bedarf können Zusatzfunktionen durch Drücken der entsprechenden Tasten gewählt werden. Welche dieser Funktionen obligatorisch sind, können Sie dem Abschnitt 'Programme' der Bedienungsanleitung entnehmen.

7 Einstellen der Trocknungszeit

(Entfällt, wenn das Gerät ausschließlich zum Waschen benutzt wird.)

Stellen Sie die gewünschte Trocknungszeit ein.

Die empfohlenen Trocknungszeiten können Sie dem Abschnitt 'Programme' entnehmen.

Mit der Funktionstaste 'Baumwolle trocknen' läßt sich die Wärmezufuhr erhöhen (für Baumwolle und Leinen).

8 Programmstart

Wasserhahn aufdrehen.

Gerät ans Netz anschließen.

Drücken Sie die Taste Start/Stop zum Starten des Programms.

Programmänderung: Wenn ein Programm irrtümlich eingestellt und gestartet wurde, drücken Sie die Start/Stop-Taste erneut, um das Gerät auszuschalten. Wählen Sie dann das Programm neu.

9 Waschgang

Ist die Zusatzfunktion 'Spülstop' bereits automatisch im Programm enthalten, so wird der letzte Spülgang unterbrochen. Durch erneutes Drücken der Funktionstaste 'Spülstop' wird das Programm fortgesetzt.

Bei Programmen ohne Trockengang schaltet sich das Gerät nach dem Waschen automatisch aus.

Bei kombinierten Wasch-/Trockenprogrammen folgt nach dem Waschgang non-stop der Trockengang. Seine Dauer richtet sich nach der eingestellten Trocknungszeit.

10 Trockengang

BITTE BEACHTEN: Der Dosierbehälter für Waschpulverkonzentrat und Flüssigwaschmittel ist vor dem Trockengang aus der Trommel zu entfernen.

Die Wäschetrocknung erfolgt durch Warmluftzufuhr, die von einem Thermostat geregelt wird.

Die Trommel ändert während des Trockengangs ihre Drehrichtung, um ein Verknoten der Wäsche zu verhindern und ein gleichmäßiges Trocknen zu gewährleisten.

Während der letzten 12 Minuten des Trockengangs wird Kaltluft zugeführt, um die Knittergefahr zu reduzieren.

HINWEIS: Die Trocknungszeit richtet sich nach der Gewebeart, dem

Feuchtigkeitsgrad der eingelegten Wäsche und der gewünschten Trockenstufe.

Um den **Trockner anzuhalten**, drücken Sie die Start/Stop-Taste.

Tür erst nach dem automatischen Entriegeln öffnen.

Zur Fortsetzung des Trockengangs schließen Sie die Tür und drücken Sie die Start/Stop-Taste erneut.

11 Entnahme der Wäsche

Der Vollwaschtrockner hält nach dem Programmende automatisch an.

Drücken Sie die Start/Stop-Taste, um das Gerät auszuschalten.

Die Tür läßt sich erst ungefähr 90 Sekunden nach Programmende öffnen. Im Bedarfsfall den Programmwähler erneut auf 'T' stellen.

12 Gerät abschalten

Wasserhahn schließen.

Netzstecker ziehen.

Diese Sicherheitsmaßnahmen verhindern das Auftreten von Schäden durch Strom oder Leitungswasser.

Annotations

Translation Assignment

Hoover want to sell their electrical household appliances in Germany and, therefore, have asked for a translation of their users manual for one of their washer/dryers. (Only a part of it is reproduced, translated, and discussed here.)

ST Characterisation

The text is part of the users' manual published by Hoover Ltd. The entire manual has the form of a brochure, and is divided into several chapters describing technical features, safety reminders, service and guarantee hints etc., and contains a number of illustrations to ease comprehension. The part discussed here is one of the core elements of the brochure, i.e. a 'Step-by-step guide', explaining how to operate the machine correctly. There are also cross-references to other sections of the manual (e.g. 'Choose the programme from . . . the 'Programmes' section in this manual.').

The part of the ST discussed here is an instructive sequence of the actions to be carried out for washing and/or drying. The text follows a clearly marked sequential structure: The main steps are numbered, bold-faced, and printed in a larger font or a different colour. We have reproduced the capital letters and the bold-faced information in our version of the ST, but not the different size and colour. The sentences are often short, containing only one step (one proposition). Important hints are typed in bold face, and are sometimes stressed by the use of markers, such as 'IMPORTANT' or 'REMEMBER' (or 'DO NOT' in another section of the manual).

The text addresses the general public, and this step-by-step guide, which is intended to be read while carrying out the instructions, does not contain any specialised terminology.

TT Specification

The TT addresses potential buyers of the washer/dryer in German-speaking countries. Its content does not present any major (culture-specific) differences between the ST and the TT communities because both of them are accustomed to the use of such appliances. The TT addressees will use the text for the same purpose and in the same situation as the ST addressees will use the ST, in other words, we have a case of identical function. In order for the TT to fulfil its function appropriately, it is important that it conforms to the text-typological conventions in German, including such formal aspects as font size and type (we have used bold face in the TT for the same information for which bold face was used in the ST; other decisions will be taken by the publishers of the manual). In addition, the labels in the text and on the control panel of the washer dryer (e.g. the function buttons) need to be identical. The main translation problems are pragmatic and intercultural ones.

Annotations

Pragmatic translation problems

(i) Verbal information and non-verbal information
In order to make the text easily understandable, a number of drawings have been added which illustrate the various steps of operation or there are icons representing the buttons on the control panel of the machine. The cross-references between the icons and the text result in pragmatic translation problems. Some of the icons contain the actual indicators given on the control panel or on the function buttons of the washer/dryer. Since the ultimate purpose is to sell the washer/dryer to German-speaking buyers, the manufacturer will probably choose German labels for the German control panel. It is generally advisable for the translation of users manuals which will accompany a machine, or an appliance, etc., to consult the clients in order to find out whether they have already defined the respective TL terms and adopt them in the translation, thus assuring terminological consistency. Since in our case a decision had not yet been taken by the manufacturer, we decided to add a translator's note at the very beginning of the TT (the TT has been requested by the company, so it can be assumed that they will make the respective changes if necessary).

For the various programmes, letters have been used. For example, the letter 'T' corresponds to the tumble-drying programme (but in general, the letters do not coincide with the initial letter of the respective word, for example, 'C' is used for the programmes 'Whites economy', 'D' for 'Fast coloureds'). In fact, 'T' stands for two functions: for opening the door (see Step 3) and for the tumble-drying programme (see Step 5):

Step 3:
Turn the programme selector to the 'T' position. – Stellen Sie den Programm-wähler auf 'T'.

Step 5:
For tumble drying turn the selector to position 'T'. – Zum Trocknen den Programmwähler auf 'T' stellen.

It is mere coincidence, that in the TT, the 'T' is also the initial letter of both the German noun 'Tür' and the verb 'trocknen'.

In the case of entire words, such as 'cotton dry' (in Step 7) and 'creaseguard' (in Step 9), the choice of the TT equivalent depends on the labels chosen by the manufacturers (see previous discussion as to our decision to add a translator's note for the client's attention).

Step 7:
. . . the 'Cotton dry' function button. – . . . Funktionstaste 'Baumwolle trocknen' . . .

Step 9:
If the programme incorporates 'Creaseguard' . . . Press the 'Creaseguard' button . . . – Ist die Zusatzfunktion 'Spülstop' bereits automatisch im Programm enthalten, . . . Durch erneutes Drücken der Funktionstaste 'Spülstop' . . .

We have opted for 'Spülstop' because this is the label frequently found on a function button on German washing machines (checking parallel texts is also helpful in this respect since German user manuals too, often include drawings and icons). 'Spülstop' actually describes what will happen in the washing cycle, whereas 'creaseguard' explicitly denotes the purpose of stopping the washing cycle. Alternatively, both of these aspects could have been stated in the TT: 'Ist die Zusatzfunktion 'Spülstop' zur Faserschonung bereits automatisch im Programm enthalten, . . . '. With the continuous development of washing machines and washer dryers it may well be that new labels will be chosen for the function buttons (e.g. 'Knitterschutz').

The other function buttons are 'econ wash' and 'half load', given in the drawing which accompanies Step 6. Similar decisions will have to be made for the production of the German user manual.

In the case of the main button, which is labelled 'start/stop button' in the ST (see Steps 8, 10, 11), we have opted for 'Start/Stop-Taste'. Both 'Start' and 'Stop' exist as nouns in the German language. The label frequently found on products (and also in user manuals) is 'Ein/Aus', as a systematic search in parallel texts has revealed. Since 'Ein' and 'Aus' are normally used for switching the machine on and off, but the start/stop button of the washer dryer fulfils different functions as well (e.g. interrupting a programme), we have decided against 'Ein/Aus'.

(ii) Proper names

The only proper name in the text is the name of the company:

Step 4: Hoover recommend using 1½ cups . . . – . . . reicht . . . 1½ Meßbecher . . .

It is treated as a collective noun in the ST with the verb used in the plural form. For the TT we have opted for omitting this reference to the manufacturer and use a more impersonal structure, as found to be characteristic of German parallel texts. In other words, German user manuals normally avoid the names of manufacturers or trademarks in the actual instruction section.

The brand name of the machine itself is used sparingly in the ST, we mainly find 'this machine'. In the TT, we use mainly 'Gerät' (see *(i) Text typological conventions.*

However, we have decided to reintroduce the proper name, i.e. the brand name, of the washer/dryer at the very beginning of the step-by-step guide:

Use this washer dryer . . . – Der *Hoover Ecologic* kann . . . benutzt werden.

The reason for this decision is that the first three paragraphs provide an introduction to the subsequent instructions (i.e. the twelve steps), and it reminds the user of the various operations of the machine in front of her/him (see the demonstrative pronoun 'this washer dryer'). Although the ST is written in an instructive mode here (i.e. imperatives, see *(i) Text typological conventions* under *Intercultural translation problems*), the function of the paragraphs is mainly to provide information and guidance as to the following message. We have therefore used descriptive sentences in the TT and mentioned the name of the washer/dryer once again. An alternative solution could have been: 'Dieses Gerät kann . . . benutzt werden.'

Intercultural translation problems

(i) Text typological conventions

(a) Speech act 'instruction'
The text is an instruction, i.e. it is meant to give clear and precise orders, advice, and recommendations for the safe operation of the washer dryer. User manuals as instruction texts (or, as belonging to the operative text type, see Reiss (1976) and the introductory comments) are characterised by specific conventions. As far as German and English are concerned, there are some differences in these text-typological conventions. One of those differences refers to the grammatical structures used to express the dominant speech acts of order, recommendation, and warning. English instruction manuals typically address the reader by using imperatives, whereas in the German ones we find more variation, i.e. infinitive constructions, imperatives, modal verbs, passive structures, impersonal structures (see introductory comments).

In the ST the instructions almost exclusively take the form of imperatives. Based on a survey of parallel texts and bearing in mind the findings of other scholars' analyses, we have opted for a combination of structures in the TT. We use imperatives for individual steps, i.e. whenever there are clear instructions given as to what to do and in which sequence (in other words, when we have a kind of dialogue with the user). Due to linguistic conventions, in the ST the imperative verb form is always in the front position, followed by an object and then maybe a prepositional phrase to indicate the semantic relations of location, direction, or instrument. In the case of imperatives in German, the verb also takes the front position, followed by the object. In Step 4, the adverb is put before the verb in the ST, but after the verb in the TT. We have also changed the semantic roles in the second extract from Step 4 where 'dispensing device' functions as patient in the ST but as locative in the TT, and 'the correct amount of powder' functions as instrument in the ST but as patient in the TT. This change was motivated by the formulations found in parallel texts (see the following formulations from parallel texts: 'Wasch- oder Pflegemittel in Kammer I einfüllen', or 'Füllen Sie das Spülmittel in die linke Kammer'). A few examples for imperatives in the TT:

Step 1:
Sort articles into groups . . . – Sortieren Sie die Wäsche . . .
Close all zips. – Schließen Sie alle Reißverschlüsse.

Step 4:
Gently close the drawer. – Schließen Sie das Waschmittelfach vorsichtig.
Fill the dispensing device with the correct amount of powder . . . – Geben Sie die vom Hersteller angegebene Menge Pulver . . . in den dafür vorgesehenen Dosierbehälter.

Place the dispensing device upwards on top the laundry in the drum. – Stellen Sie den Dosierbehälter mit der Öffnung nach oben auf die Wäsche in der Trommel.

Step 7:
Turn the selector to the required drying time. – Stellen Sie die gewünschte Trocknungszeit ein.

Step 8:
Press the start/stop button to start the programme.- Drücken Sie die Taste Start/Stop zum Starten des Programms.

We have opted to use infinitives for more general instructions (and recommendations), again based on an analysis of parallel texts (see 'Das Gerät entsprechend der Aufstellanleitung installieren.', 'Deckel schließen'), e.g.:

Step 3:
Close the door ensuring that it latches correctly. – Beim Schließen der Tür auf ordnungsgemäßes Einrasten achten.

Step 8:
Turn on the water supplies. – Wasserhahn aufdrehen.

Step 10:
Wait for the door interlock to release before opening the door. – Tür erst nach dem automatischen Entriegeln öffnen.

Step 12:
Turn off the water supplies. – Wasserhahn schließen.

Notice here that the phrasal verb is placed before the object in the ST, i.e. verb and preposition are not split.

Very strong instructions are sometimes signalled by the modal verb 'must' and an additional explicit signal, e.g. 'important', 'remember', often highlighted by different font or size (see Step 10). This is related to functional parameters, i.e. the fact that important hints or safety recommendations are often needed in 'panic' situations. Therefore, these formulations are short and eye-catching. In German user manuals, impersonal infinitive structures are frequently found in these cases. The additional signal in the German genre is typically 'Bitte beachten'. Some German parallel texts use some kind of typographical signal, e.g. an exclamation mark at the beginning of the line (see Schmitt 1996 and our introductory comments):

Step 10:
IMPORTANT: Dispensers used for concentrated powder and liquid detergent must be removed from the drum before tumble drying. – BITTE BEACHTEN: Der Dosierbehälter für Waschpulverkonzentrat und Flüssigwaschmittel ist vor dem Trockengang aus der Trommel zu entfernen.

The steps have to be followed exactly as instructed, i.e. in a sequence. The individual programmes, too, follow a sequence. We have made this sequence of actions sometimes more explicit in the TT by adding a preposition ('nach' in Step 9) or an adverb which implies a temporal sequence ('erneut' in Steps 8, 9, 10, 11).

Step 9:
On a continuous washing and tumble-drying programme . . . – Bei

kombinierten Wasch-/Trockenprogrammen folgt nach dem Waschgang
non-stop der Trockengang.

Step 8:
. . . press and release the start/stop button . . . – . . . drücken Sie die
Start/Stop-Taste erneut,

Step 9:
Press the 'Creaseguard' button to continue the programme. – Durch erneutes
Drücken der Funktionstaste 'Spülstop' wird das Programm fortgesetzt.

Step 10:
To start tumble drying again, close the door and press the start/stop button. –
Zur Fortsetzung des Trockengangs schließen Sie die Tür und drücken Sie die
Start/Stop-Taste erneut.

Step 11:
It may be necessary to set the programme selector in the 'T' position. – Im
Bedarfsfall den Programmwähler erneut auf 'T' stellen.

(b) Speech acts 'warnings', 'prohibitions', and 'advice'
In negated sentences, i.e. expressing warnings, strong advice (as in the first
example below) or prohibitions (as in Step 3), the ST again uses imperatives in
the front position. In Step 3, the directional aspect (expressed by the prepositional phrase) is placed before the object. In the TT, we have opted for a passive
structure with a modal verb for the strong advice, and for a negated infinitive to
express the prohibition. These solutions conform to German genre conventions
(see the formulation in a parallel text: 'Die Waschtrommel nicht an der gelochten
Mantelfläche drehen.').
. . . remember not to exceed the maximum recommended Tumble drying
load. – . . . wobei die empfohlene Trocknerhöchstlast nicht überschritten
werden darf.

Step 3:
do not put into the machine more than the maximum recommended wash
load. – Beachten Sie die Angaben zur maximalen Beladungsmenge . . .
Waschmaschine nicht überladen.
In some cases, modal verbs are used in the ST, mainly to express the speech acts
'recommendation' and 'advice'. Modal verbs are sometimes combined with
passive structures (see later comments). These speech acts are expressed in
German user manuals by modal verbs, impersonal structures, or infinitives:

Step 4:
In soft water areas 1 cup should be sufficient. – Bei weichem Wasser genügt in
der Regel 1 Meßbecher.
The recommendation (or suggestion) is conveyed (maybe more implicitly) by 'in
der Regel':

Step 6:
... to see which functions must be selected and which are optional. – Welche dieser Funktionen obligatorisch sind können Sie dem Abschnitt 'Programme' der Bedienungsanleitung entnehmen.

Step 11:
It may be necessary to set the programme selector in the 'T' position. – Im Bedarfsfall den Programmwähler erneut auf 'T' stellen.

The recommendation is obvious in the nominal structure 'im Bedarfsfall'.

Step 7 can be interpreted as giving information, or as an implicit recommendation to read (i.e. a reference to another section of the user manual). This aspect has motivated us to use a more personal structure and a modal verb in the TT:

Step 7:
Suggested drying times are given in the 'Programmes' section. – Die empfohlenen Trocknungszeiten können Sie dem Abschnitt 'Programme' entnehmen.

In Step 10, we have another case where an explicit signal ('remember') has been added to the advice (or a reminder). In German texts the corresponding signal is typically 'Hinweis', see:

Step 10:
REMEMBER: The time needed for drying will depend on the materials in the load, how damp they are when put in and how dry they are required. – HINWEIS: Die Trocknungszeit richtet sich nach der Gewebeart, dem Feuchtigkeitsgrad der eingelegten Wäsche und der gewünschten Trockenstufe.

(c) The washer/dryer as agent
There are a number of cases in the ST where the machine itself, or a part of it, functions in the semantic role of agent and takes the subject position in the sentence (frequently combined with future tense). For the TT we have opted for an identical structure (i.e. using 'Gerät' as agent in subject position, for the choice of 'Gerät' see below, *(e) Lexical choice*) or for a passive structure (first example in Step 9). The fact that the machine is treated as the actual agent of some action or process is probably related to the technical development and the idea of 'intelligent programmes' (see an example from a German parallel text: 'Die Waschmaschine wählt programmabhängig für jede Wäsche die richtige Drehzahl'). The grammatical tense in German texts is typically present tense, see:

Step 9:
... the machine will stop during the final rinse. – so wird der letzte Spülgang unterbrochen.
... the machine will switch off automatically. – schaltet sich das Gerät nach dem Waschen automatisch aus.
... the machine will proceed to dry the load ... – folgt nach dem Waschgang non-stop der Trockengang

Step 10:
The drum changes direction during the cycle . . . – Die Trommel ändert
während des Trockengangs ihre Drehrichtung, . . .

Step 11:
. . . the machine will stop automatically. – Der Vollwaschtrockner hält . . .
automatisch an.

(d) Headings
Imperatives dominate in the headings to the individual steps in the ST. We have
opted for nominal structures in the TT, in some cases verbal nouns, and only in
the last step for an infinitive structure. This choice has again been motivated by
an analysis of German parallel texts which has shown that nouns and to a lesser
degree infinitives are the preferred structures for headings (see examples from
parallel texts: 'Gerät kennenlernen', 'Wäsche vorbereiten', 'Zugabe des Spül-
mittels', 'Erste Inbetriebnahme', 'Programm ändern', 'Programmende'):

(1)   Sort the laundry – Sortieren der Wäsche
(2)   Choose the programme – Programmwahl
(3)   Load the machine – Einlegen der Wäsche
(4)   Add detergent and fabric conditioner – Zugabe von Waschmittel und
       Weichspüler
(5)   Set up the programme – Einstellen des Programms
(6)   Press function buttons – Wahl der Zusatzfunktionen
(7)   Set the drying time – Einstellen der Trocknungszeit
(8)   Start the programme – Programmstart
(9)   The wash cycle – Waschgang
(10)   The tumble drying cycle – Trockengang
(11)   Remove the load – Entnahme der Wäsche
(12)   Switching off – Gerät abschalten

(e) Lexical choice
In the ST, the name for the type of the appliance (i.e. washer dryer) is only used at
the beginning of the step-by-step guide. In the majority of cases, the more
general 'machine' is used (and in other sections of the user manual). In other
English user manuals, i.e. for other appliances, we noticed that it is often the
cover term of the product which is used (e.g. 'this hairdryer'). A more general
term is the characteristic convention in German texts, and the most frequently
used word is 'Gerät', which we have chosen in the TT as well (see Steps 2, 8, 9, 11).
In two cases we have opted for a more specific label:

Step 3:
Refer to the 'Programmes' section and do not put into the machine more than
the maximum recommended wash load. – Beachten Sie die Angaben zur
maximalen Beladungsmenge in der Programmtabelle der Bedienungsanleitung. Waschmaschine nicht überladen.

This choice has been motivated by the fact that the laundry is actually put into a more specific part of the machine, i.e. the drum. An alternative solution for the TT could have been '(Wasch)Trommel nicht überladen'.

In the next case, 'machine' is used in two immediately related sentences. The choice of the more specific 'Vollwaschtrockner' in the first sentence, followed by the more general 'Gerät' in the next one is due to stylistic considerations (i.e. avoiding immediate lexical repetition):

Step 11:
... the machine will stop automatically. ... to switch the machine off. – Der Vollwaschtrockner hält ... automatisch an. ... um das Gerät auszuschalten.

(f) Compact information

User manuals will typically be consulted when the respective machine is being operated. In order to fulfil this purpose most appropriately and efficiently, the information needs to be easily accessible and comprehensible. Therefore, short and compact sentences are used which give short and unambiguous instructions. These sentences are sometimes grammatically incomplete and list-like (although this is not the case in this ST, but see Sample Text 2, the 999 call text in this volume). Typographic variation and drawings/icons contribute to this function of the text.

For the TT, this purpose of providing clear and compact information has resulted in the omission of 'redundant' information or condensation of information. In other words, the translation strategies applied can be characterised as modulations, more specifically, mainly as compression or implication, which are normally accompanied by omission. The following examples are given as illustration:

Step 1:
Sort articles into groups ... – Sortieren Sie die Wäsche ...

Implication: 'sortieren' implies the grouping together of things with similar features.

Step 2:
For mixed loads select the programme which corresponds to the lowest wash temperature and least vigorous wash and spin action as shown by the wash care labels on the garments. – Wählen Sie bei Mischladungen anhand der Pflegesymbole das Programm für die niedrigste Temperaturstufe und den schonendsten Wasch- und Schleudergang.

Compression and implication: the preposition ('für') implies the 'correspondence' relationship expressed by the relative clause in the ST, and 'anhand' implies the location aspect of 'as shown by'. 'On the garments' can be considered redundant here since the more explicit 'Pflegesymbole auf den Etiketten' has already been introduced in Step 1.

Step 3:
Press button and open the door. – Öffnen Sie die Tür durch Knopfdruck.
Put the laundry into the machine. – Legen Sie die Wäsche ein.

Compression: two actions in the ST are combined into method of action in the TT. And implication: it is clear from the sequence of activities, and from the TT verb 'einlegen' that the laundry is put into the machine.

Step 7:
Turn the selector to the required drying time. – Stellen Sie die gewünschte Trocknungszeit ein.

Implication: Part of the ST information ('turn the selector') can be considered redundant because the action can be implied.

Step 8:
. . . press and release the start/stop button . . . – drücken Sie die Start/ Stop-Taste . . .

Implication: pressing and releasing are not actually two separate actions the user has to fulfil, but the button will be released when it is pressed. This information can therefore be implied (equally in Steps 10 and 11).

Step 10:
The load is dried by tumbling in the thermostatically controlled warm air. – Die Wäschetrocknung erfolgt durch Warmluftzufuhr, die von einem Thermostat geregelt wird.

Compression: the means of drying ('durch Warmluftzufuhr') is the focus, with the method ('tumbling') implied (see also the next sentence).

Step 10:
The time needed for drying will depend on the materials in the load – Die Trocknungszeit richtet sich nach der Gewebeart

Implication: It can be logically concluded from the context that the TT refers to the materials in the load.

Step 12:
These are safety measures to ensure that no harm can occur electrically or by water leakage. – Diese Sicherheitsmaßnahmen verhindern das Auftreten von Schäden durch Strom oder Leitungswasser.

Implication: that water may be leaking can be implied by the TT reader. In addition, it is common in German texts of this genre to use the 'official' insurance/warranty terms regardless of how the damage actually occurred.

In several other cases, the TT may be considered to be more explicit than the ST (i.e. translation strategies of explication and/or addition have been applied). We would argue that this decision has equally been motivated by the purpose of the text and that, as a result of these strategies, the TT information is equally clear and unambiguous for the TT readers as the ST information is for the ST readers:

Step 1:
Remove everything from the pockets and folds of clothes. – Leeren Sie die Taschen der Kleidungsstücke, entfernen Sie Fremdkörper aus der Wäsche, und bürsten Sie Taschen und Umschläge aus.
Shake out items as much as possible instead of leaving them crumpled. – Legen Sie die Wäsche auseinandergefaltet und locker in die Trommel. Schütteln Sie die Stücke, wenn nötig, vorher gut aus.

The more explicit information and the additions in the TT version have been decided upon after consulting parallel texts.

Step 5:
Turn the programme selector until the letter corresponding to the chosen wash programme appears in the programme window. – Die Programme werden mit dem Programmwähler eingestellt. Drehen Sie den Programmwähler so lange, bis der Buchstabe des gewünschten Waschprogramms im Programmfenster angezeigt wird.

The addition of one sentence in the TT has also been motivated by parallel texts where a more descriptive sentence often precedes the instruction (e.g. 'Das Programm ist beendet, wenn alle Lampen der Ablaufanzeige erloschen sind. Drücken Sie die Taste 'Deckel öffnen'.').

Step 8:
If the wrong programme is selected, press and release the start/stop button to switch off the machine before re-selecting. – Programmänderung: Wenn ein Programm irrtümlich eingestellt und gestartet wurde, drücken Sie die Start/Stop-Taste erneut, um das Gerät auszuschalten. Wählen Sie dann das Programm neu.

Again in conformity with target culture genre conventions, we have started by describing the situation and then separated the instructions also syntactically. The noun 'Programmänderung' has been added at the beginning, in order to catch the user's attention quickly in case of need.

Step 9:
On a continuous washing and tumble-drying programme the machine will proceed to dry the load for the time selected. – Bei kombinierten Wasch-/Trockenprogrammen folgt nach dem Waschgang non-stop der Trockengang. Seine Dauer richtet sich nach der eingestellten Trocknungszeit.

The choice of two sentences has been motivated mainly by stylistic reasons in this case. 'Non-stop' has been found in parallel texts.

(ii) Culture-specific conventions
Due to differences in the sockets in the UK and Germany, it is assumed that the device will be supplied with a plug that fulfils the technical standards in the target communities (a discussion with the manufacturer will be helpful in case of doubt). The sockets in Germany (and in other German-speaking countries as well) do not have an extra power switch. These differences have resulted in the TT formulations in Steps 8 and 12, i.e. 'switch on' and 'switch off' are superfluous for the TT instruction:

Step 8:
Plug into the electricity supply and switch on. – Gerät ans Netz anschließen.

Step 12:
Switch off and remove the plug from the electricity supply. – Netzstecker ziehen.

'Switch off' is used for two different functions in the ST: in Steps 8, 9 and 11 it denotes the end or interruption of a programme, whereas in Step 12 it denotes disconnection from the electricity supply. We use two different verbs in the TT, i.e. 'ausschalten' and 'abschalten', respectively:

Step 8:
press and release the start/stop button to switch off the machine ... – drücken Sie die Start/Stop-Taste erneut, um das Gerät auszuschalten.

Step 9:
At the end of a washing only cycle the machine will switch off automatically. – Bei Programmen ohne Trockengang schaltet sich das Gerät nach dem Waschen automatisch aus.

Step 11:
Press and release the start/stop button to switch the machine off. – Drücken Sie die Start/Stop-Taste, um das Gerät auszuschalten.

Step 12:
Switching off – Gerät abschalten

The water supply may also be regulated differently in the source culture and the target culture. In the target culture – Germany – the water supply is normally provided by linking the washing machine to the tap. This fact has motivated the formulation in the TT (if in doubt, the manufacturer can be contacted):

Step 8:
Turn on the water supplies – Wasserhahn aufdrehen

Or, alternatively, 'Wasserhahn öffnen';

Step 12:
Turn off the water supplies. – Wasserhahn schließen.

Interlingual translation problems
Interlingual translation problems are linked to specific grammatical structures which do not exist in the German linguistic system, or which are not equally frequently used. We have dealt with these problems in various ways.

(i) -ing structures

(a) Gerund after preposition

Step 1:
Shake out items as much as possible instead of leaving them crumpled. – Legen Sie die Wäsche auseinandergefaltet und locker in die Trommel. Schütteln Sie die Stücke, wenn nötig, vorher gut aus.

Here, we have opted for a formulation, which makes the instruction about what to do explicit. An alternative solution could have been: 'Wäsche nach Möglichkeit gut ausschütteln, um die Knitterbildung zu vermeiden.' In this solution, the potential effect of not following the instruction, which is given in the first part of the sentence, has been made explicit.

In the following case, the TT version has been chosen in order to avoid the repetition of 'trocknen' (drying), mainly for stylistic reasons:

Step 7:
If more heat is required for drying cotton and linen . . . – Mit der Funktionstaste 'Baumwolle trocknen' läßt sich die Wärmezufuhr erhöhen (für Baumwolle und Leinen).

In the next case, the proposition expressed by the gerund in the ST is conveyed by a separate sentence:

Step 8:
. . . press and release the start/stop button to switch off the machine before re-selecting. – . . . drücken Sie die Start/Stop-Taste erneut, um das Gerät auszuschalten. Wählen Sie dann das Programm neu.

For the two gerunds after preposition in Step 10, we have used a noun in the first case, i.e.:

Step 10:
. . . before tumble drying – . . . vor dem Trockengang . . .

and omitted this information in the second case:

The load is dried by tumbling in the thermostatically controlled warm air. – Die Wäschetrocknung erfolgt durch Warmluftzufuhr, die von einem Thermostat geregelt wird.

The focus is on the means of the drying process ('durch Warmluftzufuhr'), which is the most important information (see also, (f) *Compact information* under *Intercultural translation problems*).

In Steps 10 and 11, we have opted for antonymic structures ('erst nach'), the waiting instruction is thus implied in the TT:

Step 10:
Wait for the door interlock to release before opening the door. – Tür erst nach dem automatischen Entriegeln öffnen.

Step 11:
Wait for approximately 90 seconds after the programme has finished before opening the door. – Die Tür läßt sich erst ungefähr 90 Sekunden nach Programmende öffnen.

(b) Verbal nouns
For verbal nouns ending in -ing, we have used nouns in the TT:

Step 10:
. . . to prevent tangling and produce even drying . . . to minimise creasing . . . The time needed for drying . . . – . . . um ein Verknoten der Wäsche zu verhindern und ein gleichmäßiges Trocknen zu gewährleisten. . . . um die Knittergefahr zu reduzieren. . . . Die Trocknungszeit . . .

(c) Present participle

In Step 3, the present participle indicates attendant circumstances, i.e. expressing one action which simultaneously accompanies another one. In the TT, the aspect of simultaneity is expressed by a prepositional phrase ('beim' plus verbal noun 'Schließen'):

Step 3:
Close the door ensuring that it latches correctly. – Beim Schließen der Tür auf ordnungsgemäßes Einrasten achten.

In Step 5, the present participle functions as attribute after the noun. In the TT, the genitive structure expresses this 'correspondence' relation, thus contributing to the textual feature of compact information structure (see also above, *(f) Compact information* under *Intercultural translation problems*):

Step 5:
. . . the letter corresponding to the chosen wash programme – . . . der Buchstabe des gewünschten Waschprogramms . . .

(ii) Infinitive structures

(a) Infinitive after noun, expressing a semantic relation of intention or of consequence

In these cases, infinitive structures are common in German texts as well ('um . . . zu . . . '), a solution applied in Steps 8, 10, 11. See Step 8 as illustration:

Step 8:
. . . press and release the start/stop button to switch off the machine . . . – drücken Sie die Start/Stop-Taste erneut, um das Gerät auszuschalten....

Alternatively, nominal structures can be used, e.g.:

Step 8:
Press the start/stop button to start the programme.... – Drücken Sie die Taste Start/Stop zum Starten des Programms. . . .

Step 9:
Press the 'Creaseguard' button to continue the programme. – Durch erneutes Drücken der Funktionstaste 'Spülstop' wird das Programm fortgesetzt.

(b) Accusative with infinitive (i.e. for object plus infinitive)

In Step 10, the object (i.e. 'door') functions as the agent of the infinitive construction. In the TT, we have opted for a nominal structure:

Step 10:
Wait for the door interlock to release before opening the door. – Tür erst nach dem automatischen Entriegeln öffnen.

The waiting aspect is implied in the TT (see also the previous comments in *(i) -ing structures*), the most essential information being that the user cannot open the door immediately after the end of a programme. An alternative solution, albeit a slightly clumsy one, could have been 'Mit dem Öffnen der Tür bis zur Freigabe der Türverriegelung warten.'

(iii) Past participles

(a) Past participle as attribute after noun
In this function, the participle corresponds to a relative clause in the passive voice. For the TT, we have opted for compressions:

Step 10:
Dispensers used for concentrated powder and liquid detergent . . . The time needed for drying . . . – Der Dosierbehälter für Waschpulverkonzentrat und Flüssigwaschmittel . . . Die Trocknungszeit . . .

(b) Past participle as addition to the object
This structure is found in Step 1:

Shake out items as much as possible instead of leaving them crumpled.

We have already commented (see *(f) Compact information*) on the reasons for our choice of the TT structure.

Text-specific translation problems
The dominant lexical-semantic fields in the text relate to household appliances and textile care. The use of parallel texts is extremely useful in this respect to find the appropriate German expressions. We have already commented on the use of 'Gerät' for 'machine' (see *(e) Lexical choice*). For the items on the machine, especially buttons, the accompanying drawings in the user manual can be helpful for the choice of a TL expression. In some cases, it might be advisable to look at the actual machine or to consult the manufacturer. For example, a 'dispensing device' is mentioned in Step 4, which in Step 10 is only referred to as a 'dispenser'. These devices come in different shapes. For the TT, we have consistently opted for 'Dosierbehälter'. An alternative solution could have been 'Dosierungskugel', a term we came across by looking at the devices in shops in Germany. We have opted for the more general German term precisely because the actual shape of the device cannot be predicted (the accompanying leaflet shows two differently shaped devices, only one of them being round like a ball).

We only want to comment on one lexical problem here. In the ST, 'button' and 'selector' are used to indicate items, which the user must operate. There is one programme selector (see Steps 3, 5, 11), which is sometimes referred to only as selector (see Steps 5, 7, i.e. the shorter form is possible once the full name has been introduced). Then there are a number of buttons: there is a button to open the door (see Step 3) and another one to open the drawer for the detergent (see Step 4). There is also the start/stop button (see Steps 8, 10, 11) and the function buttons (see Steps 6, 7, 9). We have decided on the labels for the TT by looking at the verbs, which are used in connection with these nouns. The selector is turned (see Steps 3, 5, 7) or set in a position (see Step 11), and therefore we have opted for 'Programmwähler' and as verbs for 'stellen (auf)' or 'einstellen'. 'Einstellen' makes the use of 'Programmwähler' redundant in Step 7 (more specifically, it can be contextually implied in the TT: 'Stellen Sie die gewünschte Trocknerzeit ein.'). Buttons are pressed (see Steps 7, 8, 9, 10) and the start/stop button is sometimes also pressed and released (see Steps 8, 10, 11). Here we have opted for different labels, i.e. 'Knopf' for the buttons which open the door of the washer/dryer (see Step 3) and the drawer for the detergent, respectively (see

Step 4). We use 'Taste' for the start / stop button (see also the previous comments, *(i) Verbal information and non-verbal information*) and also for the function buttons. Consistency in the use of these labels is important in order not to confuse the user.

Community Information –
How to Make an Emergency '999' Call

[1]

If you have an emergency you will need to telephone for the emergency services by dialling '999', there is no charge for this call, if using a public telephone you do not need any money or a phone card.

[2]

Your call will be first answered by the British Telecom Operator who will ask you:

1. 'Which service do you require?'

Emergency services include:	Police
	Fire
	Ambulance
in coastal areas:	Coast Guard
in mountainous areas:	Mountain Rescue
in certain areas:	Cave Rescue.

If you are unsure which service you need, explain to the Operator why you require the emergency services, they will help you.

2. The British Telecom Operator will then ask you to give the telephone number of the telephone you are using.
3. The Operator will then pass you to the emergency service you require.

[3]

Let us imagine you have telephoned for the Fire Service; you will be connected to the Control Room of your local Fire Service, who will ask you for some of the following information.

[4]

ALL INFORMATION MUST BE GIVEN IN ENGLISH

1. Type of emergency (fire, road accident, etc.).
2. Number of the house or name of the property.
3. Name of the road or street.

LEARN HOW TO SPELL YOUR ROAD OR STREET IN ENGLISH, IN CASE YOU ARE ASKED.

4. Name of a nearby road or a large property or landmark.
5. District and/or town.
6. The telephone number from which you are calling.

[5]
REMEMBER – do not panic, speak slowly in English. If you do not speak English very well, practise your address in case you need to make a call.

Translation Assignment
This text was a real translation assignment from the Ethnic Relations Department from the West Midlands Fire Service. The original assignment was rather general and vague, though. It only said:

> with the possibility of a greater number of foreign visitors and workers coming into the West Midlands from Europe in the future, it would be of great benefit if we have details of how the emergency services can be contacted and the telephone number to use, available in as many European languages as possible.

After clarification talks, the assignment was specified as follows: production of a German text to be published in the form of a small information leaflet to be distributed among native-speakers of German living and working in the West Midlands, or on a longer-term visit in the area.

The original time of TT production was 1993, but it was intended to use the text for some more years to come.

Community Information
Hinweise zum Notruf 999

[1]

Im Notfall wählen Sie die Nummer 999. Diese Nummer gilt für Notrufe jeglicher Art. Notrufe sind gebührenfrei. Bei der Benutzung öffentlicher Fernsprecher benötigen Sie weder Münzen noch Telefonkarte.

[2]

Ihr Anruf wird zunächst von der Vermittlung entgegengenommen (*Operator*). Man wird Ihnen einige Fragen stellen.
Achtung: Alle Informationen müssen auf Englisch gegeben werden!

1. Eine erste Frage betrifft den von Ihnen benötigten Notdienst (*'What service do you require?'*). Zu den Notdiensten zählen:

	Polizei (*Police*)
	Feuerwehr (*Fire service*)
	Notarzt (*Ambulance*)
in Küstengebieten:	Küstenrettungsdienst (*Coast Guard*)
im Gebirge:	Bergrettungsdienst (*Mountain Rescue*)
in einigen Gebieten:	Höhlenrettungsdienst (*Cave Rescue*)

Wenn Sie nicht sicher sind, welchen Notdienst Sie benötigen, schildern Sie die Umstände Ihres konkreten Falles. Die Mitarbeiter der Vermittlung werden Ihnen behilflich sein.
2. Die nächste Frage ist die nach der Nummer des von Ihnen benutzten Telefons (*'What is your telephone number?'*). Bei öffentlichen Fernsprechern finden Sie die Nummer auf dem Apparat selbst oder auf einem neben dem Apparat befindlichen Informationsblatt. Geben Sie bei der Nennung Ihrer Telefonnummer am besten jede Zahl einzeln an.
3. Nun werden Sie mit dem von Ihnen benötigten Notdienst verbunden.

[3]

Beispiel: Sie haben 999 gewählt und die Feuerwehr verlangt. Die Vermittlung verbindet Sie mit der Zentrale der örtlichen Feuerwehr.
Der mit Ihnen verbundene Notdienst wird um folgende weitere Auskünfte bitten:

[4]

1. Art des Notfalls (Feuer [*fire*], Verkehrsunfall [*road accident*], usw.)
2. Angaben zum Notfallort: Hausnummer bzw. Grundstücks- oder Gebäudebezeichnung

3. Straßenname (Üben Sie für den Bedarfsfall, Straßennamen auf Englisch zu buchstabieren.)

4. Name der nächstgelegenen Straße, ein großes Gebäude oder ein anderes auffälliges Objekt in Ihrer Umgebung

5. Stadtteil und / oder Stadt

6. Nummer des von Ihnen benutzten Telefons

[5]

Beachten Sie bitte: Bleiben Sie ruhig! Sprechen Sie langsam und auf Englisch. Sollten Sie über geringe Englischkenntnisse verfügen, dann prägen Sie sich zumindest Ihre Adresse für den Fall eines Notrufes gut ein.

Annotations

Translation Assignment

This text was a real translation assignment from the Ethnic Relations Department from the West Midlands Fire Service. The original assignment was rather general and vague, though. It only said:

> with the possibility of a greater number of foreign visitors and workers coming into the West Midlands from Europe in the future, it would be of great benefit if we have details of how the emergency services can be contacted and the telephone number to use, available in as many European languages as possible.

After clarification talks, the assignment was specified as follows: production of a German text to be published in the form of a small information leaflet to be distributed among native-speakers of German living and working in the West Midlands, or on a longer-term visit in the area.

The original time of TT production was 1993, but it was intended to use the text for some more years to come.

ST Characterisation

The ST is one of a number of similar texts produced by the West Midlands Fire Service to provide information on how to act in cases of emergency and how to prevent such emergencies from arising in the first place. Similar leaflets had been produced on topics such as Smoke Detection; Fire Safety; How to Call the Fire Service; After the Fire Advice. However, the English ST functions mainly as a basis for producing TTs. In other words, the English texts are written to be translated, they often do not have an actual audience of their own (although in some of these leaflets the English text stands beside the respective TT). It can be assumed that the members of the source culture have learnt the required rules of behaviour in various situations, whereas it is considered more important to inform newcomers to the country of what to do. Traditionally, these information leaflets have been produced in the languages of the ethnic minorities living in Great Britain (e.g. Hindi, Chinese, Punjabi), but with increasing European integration there has been a perceived need to produce these leaflets in other European languages as well.

The ST is, above all, an instructive text, with informative elements at the beginning, i.e. it gives instructions of how to behave in a specific situation, what steps to follow (reflected in 'if–then' constructions), illustrated by an example. The information is arranged sequentially, following the logical sequence of the actions to take should the need arise (reflected in adverbs such as 'first, then, then').

The ST, having been produced to provide the required informative content for the TT, shows some 'deficiencies' as a result of neglecting the specific addressees of the TT. These deficiencies result in pragmatic and intercultural translation problems. They concern, in particular, the information arrangement and the important message that all information must be given in English.

The ST has been reproduced in the exact style and layout as it was sent from the clients.

TT Specification

The primary addressees of the TT are native-speakers of German who live (permanently or temporarily) in the ST culture, particularly those speakers who are not yet very familiar with the social life in Great Britain. They need to be informed how the emergency services can be contacted, which telephone number to use, and how to act in the respective circumstances. The information and instructions given are therefore very important. The leaflet with the TT is intended to be distributed among German speakers (e.g. in training programmes, in various courses) so that the readers can get the required information before they are actually in an emergency situation. The Fire Service is recommending that these leaflets should be kept close to a telephone so that they can be used as guidelines for action should the need arise.

The primary aim of the TT is to provide all the information the addressees need to know to (be prepared to) act appropriately in a specific source culture situation (of which they are a part), and where this situation is different to the one of their original home culture. In producing the TT, the (culture-specific) background knowledge of the TT addressees has been taken into consideration, as have text-typological conventions.

Annotations

Pragmatic translation problems

As stated earlier, the leaflet is meant to be used as a guide for action should the need arise. It is therefore important that the TT lists the individual steps in the correct sequence and that the information about the need to use the English language in the telephone conversation is given at the beginning. This need to communicate in English will also have to be accounted for in the TT, particularly by providing the English phrases and words that need to be used. In order to make the text more coherent and more effective for its addressees, ST propositions have been moved to other positions in the TT (i.e. based on the classification in Chesterman (1997a), a pragmatic translation strategy *coherence change* has been applied) and other information has been added or deleted.

(i) Changed position

All information must be given in English – Achtung: Alle Informationen müssen auf Englisch gegeben werden!

This proposition has been moved more to the beginning of the TT. 'Achtung' has been used in order to add emphasis, which is typical of German instruction texts (see Schmitt 1996 and the introductory comments to this genre).

(ii) Addition of information

This has been done first of all for the sake of the addressees, i.e. to account for differences in their background knowledge.

Paragraph 1:
If you have an emergency you will need to telephone for the emergency services by dialling '999' – Im Notfall wählen Sie die Nummer 999. Diese Nummer gilt für Notrufe jeglicher Art.

The addition of 'Diese Nummer gilt für Notrufe jeglicher Art' is motivated by the fact that there are different numbers for individual emergency services in Germany (110 for the police, 112 for the fire service; and there are different numbers in Austria too). Syntactically, this addition is linked to a deletion and compensation: 'you will need to telephone for the emergency services' has not been accounted for explicitly in the first sentence of the TT because it is semantically redundant. It is compensated in a sense by taking up 'Notrufe' again in the added sentence.

Paragraph 2 (point 2):
Bei öffentlichen Fernsprechern finden Sie die Nummer auf dem Apparat selbst oder auf einem neben dem Apparat befindlichen Informationsblatt. Geben Sie bei der Nennung Ihrer Telefonnummer am besten jede Zahl einzeln an.

The purpose of the addition here is to account for differences or lack in background knowledge and to give practical help to the TT addressees. For example, in contrast to Britain, telephone numbers are often given in pairs in German (e.g. one would say 30–26–78). To avoid misunderstandings and confusion in the case of emergency, this information has been added.

Paragraph 4 (point 2):
2. Number of the house or name of the property.
2. Angaben zum Notfallort: Hausnummer bzw. Grundstücks- oder Gebäudebezeichnung.

The addition 'Angaben zum Notfallort', which actually covers points 2 to 5, is in conformity with information found in public telephones in Germany. (In practice, it is not always possible for a translator to travel to the target culture to find out what the conventions are. It is also not necessary, since there are other ways of getting this kind of information if required, e.g. contacting friends or colleagues in the target culture, or – increasingly these days – search on the Internet).

(iii) German and English side by side
In Paragraphs 2 (points 1, 2) and 4, English and German phrases are set side by side, i.e. English phrases have been included or added in the TT, due to the need for communicating in English (see also the last sentence in the ST which explicitly refers to a lack of competence in English).

Paragraph 2 (point 1):
Your call will be first answered by the British Telecom Operator who will ask you:

1. 'Which service do you require?'
Emergency services include: –   Police
                                 Fire
                                 Ambulance
in coastal areas: –   Coast Guard
in mountainous areas: –   Mountain Rescue
in certain areas: –   Cave Rescue.

1. Eine erste Frage betrifft den von Ihnen benötigten Notdienst (*'What service do you require?'*). Zu den Notdiensten zählen:
                                 Polizei (*Police*)

                                   Feuerwehr (*Fire service*)
                                   Notarzt (*Ambulance*)
in Küstengebieten: Küstenrettungsdienst (*Coast Guard*)
im Gebirge: Bergrettungsdienst (*Mountain Rescue*)
in einigen Gebieten: Höhlenrettungsdienst (*Cave Rescue*)

Paragraph 2 (point 2):
2. The British Telecom Operator will then ask you to give the telephone number of the telephone you are using.
2. Die nächste Frage ist die nach der Nummer des von Ihnen benutzten Telefons (*'What is your telephone number?'*).

Paragraph 4:
1. Type of emergency (fire, road accident, etc.).
1. Art des Notfalls (Feuer [*fire*], Verkehrsunfall [*road accident*], usw.)

(iv) Culture-specific expressions
In addition, in Paragraph 2, we have a case of information deletion that is motivated by culture-specific aspects, e.g.:

> Your call will be first answered by the British Telecom Operator who will ask you:
> Ihr Anruf wird zunächst von der Vermittlung entgegengenommen (*Operator*).

'British Telecom' has been deleted because it is not really important (and because there are other telephone companies as well – actually, a more recent English text of a similar kind just said 'the first person you speak to is the telephone company operator', this is evidence of how text structures and content change according to changes in society). We have, however, included the English term 'Operator' in the TT for reasons of identification, i.e. the operator identifies herself/himself by using this word. Incidentally, 'Operator' has recently been introduced into the German language as a loanword from English and is used in the context of telephone-banking, telephone-marketing, or for registering votes or donations during TV-live events (e.g. 'Menschen, die den leukämiekranken Kindern mehr als 100 Mark zukommen lassen wollten, konnten bei 'Operatoren' der Telekom ihre Spende aufgeben.' in *Mitteldeutsche Allgemeine* 24 December 1995, p. 3; or 'Er steuert die Telefonanlage und disponiert, wie viele der insgesamt 240 Online-Operatorplätze auf der knapp 2000 Quadratmeter großen Etage besetzt sein müssen, um die Anfragen zu bewältigen.' in *Der Spiegel* 46 (1997: 132); and in a 1999 local telephone directory: 'vom Operator vermittelte Telefonverbindungen').

Moreover, the generalisation and de-personification in the TT ('Vermittlung') solves another translation problem, which is both a pragmatic and an interlingual one: the gender problem (but see Paragraph 2, point 2: 'explain to the Operator . . . they will help you. – . . . schildern Sie die Umstände Ihres konkreten Falles. Die Mitarbeiter der Vermittlung werden Ihnen behilflich sein.' – a de-personification would not work here because the prototypical agent of 'helfen' is a concrete person). The inconsistency in the number, i.e. 'Operator' in singular, but plural 'they' is also done away with as a result of these changes. Other strategies applied to solve this gender problem are nominalisation and passivisation:

Paragraph 2 (point 2):
The British Telecom Operator will then ask you to give the telephone number of the telephone you are using. – Die nächste Frage ist die nach der Nummer des von Ihnen benutzten Telefons.

Paragraph 2 (point 3):
The Operator will then pass you to the emergency service you require. – Nun werden Sie mit dem von Ihnen benötigten Notdienst verbunden.

It has become common practice in public German texts to avoid 'sexist' language use and give throughout the text either a combination of masculine and feminine forms (e.g. 'Telephonist oder Telephonistin', 'Telephonist(in)'; 'der/die TelephonistIn' – which might look a bit awkward in short instructive texts as is the case here) or find alternative forms (e.g. plural, generalisations), as we have done here.

Another pragmatic translation problem caused by a culture-specific expression is the title 'Community information'. This title is actually a label for the whole series of information leaflets produced by the West Midlands Fire Service. In each of these cases, 'community' refers to the specific ethnic community to which the text is addressed. This community is never identified by name but becomes clear only by the language that is used. 'Community information' was therefore kept in the TT, since, as stated earlier, the addressees form an ethnic community living in the culture of the ST.

Intercultural translation problems

(i) Genre conventions

(a) Title

We have already commented on the label 'Community information'. In conformity with conventions for headings of instructive texts, 'Hinweise zum Notruf 999' was chosen for 'How to Make an Emergency '999' Call'.

(b) Infinitives and imperatives

As has already been stressed, the procedures for getting into contact with emergency services are different in Great Britain and in Germany. A further consequence of this fact is that the genre of which the ST is an exemplar does not exist in Germany. The main reason for this is that in Germany one would call the respective emergency services directly, and there is no need for detailed instructions on how to communicate. Therefore, there is no 'proper' German parallel text that could serve as a model. However, some useful information can be gained both from information in German telephone directories or telephone boxes (where normally pictorial icons are used, e.g. a small car with the inscription 'Polizei' or 'Polizeinotruf' next to the telephone number) and from instruction texts in general.

The ST has been characterised as an instruction text, i.e. information and instructions for action. Instruction is the primary text function, whereas information is a secondary, subsidiary function. As a result of the translation, a new genre is produced in German, which, however, does not have to fulfil a function in a German-speaking country. For the instruction parts, this new genre could refer to the text-typological conventions of instruction texts, i.e. typically infinitives in German (but imperatives or modal verbs can also be found) in contrast to (almost exclusively) imperatives in English (see also the introductory comments). Since in this case the whole text is a kind of dialogue with the reader, imperatives have been preferred in the TT:

Paragraph 4 (point 3):
LEARN HOW TO SPELL YOUR ROAD OR STREET IN ENGLISH, IN CASE YOU ARE ASKED.
Üben Sie für den Bedarfsfall, Straßennamen auf Englisch zu buchstabieren.

Paragraph 5:
REMEMBER – do not panic, speak slowly in English. If you do not speak English very well, practice your address in case you need to make a call.
Beachten Sie bitte: Bleiben Sie ruhig! Sprechen Sie langsam und auf Englisch. Sollten Sie über geringe Englischkenntnisse verfügen, dann prägen Sie sich zumindest Ihre Adresse für den Fall eines Notrufes gut ein.

Some other structures, that are typical of German instruction texts, have been applied, e.g. the lexical structure 'Beachten Sie bitte' for 'Remember', and a nominal structure 'für den Bedarfsfall' for 'in case you need'. At the beginning of Paragraph 4, 'Beispiel' has been used, because in a German text of this kind a more informal structure like the English 'Let us imagine' would not be stylistically appropriate:

Paragraph 4:
Let us imagine you have telephoned for the Fire Service . . .
Beispiel: Sie haben 999 gewählt und die Feuerwehr verlangt.

(c) Tenses

Another aspect related to text-typological conventions is the use of tenses: for explaining the individual steps in the action sequence, the ST uses predominantly future tense. The typical tense in German instructive texts is present tense, sometimes used in combination with a passive sentence structure or imperatives. The future tense is sometimes used to put more emphasis on the sequence of the actions:

you will need to telephone – wählen Sie
Your call will be first answered – Ihr Anruf wird zunächst . . . entgegengenommen
who will ask you – Man wird Ihnen einige Fragen stellen.
they will help you – werden Ihnen behilflich sein
will then ask you – Die nächste Frage ist
The Operator will then pass you to – Nun werden Sie . . . verbunden.
you will be connected – Die Vermittlung verbindet Sie (addition of 'Vermittlung' for stylistic reasons)
who will ask you – wird um . . . bitten

(ii) Domain-specific lexical expressions

Checking German texts that deal with emergency services, with telephones and telephone calls, will provide German words and phrases that are typically used to refer to the objects and facts in question. Apart from the corresponding names for the individual emergency services, such phrases can be grouped according to the two dominant lexical-semantic fields in the text: (i) emergency services; and (ii) telephone calls. We have listed them here and not under text-specific translation problems since all the German expressions have been found in authentic German texts dealing with the topic in question (the main sources which we used to identify the relevant lexical expressions were German telephone books, and the motorist magazine *ADAC motorwelt*):

(i) Emergency services:
emergency service – Notdienst
Control Room – Zentrale
local Fire Service – örtliche Feuerwehr

(ii) Telephone calls:
there is no charge for this call – Notrufe sind gebührenfrei
public telephone – öffentlicher Fernsprecher
phone card – Telefonkarte

Interlingual translation problems

The ST poses a few syntactic and lexical problems that are determined by the differences in the two language systems (with overlaps to intercultural translation problems). Transpositions are required for the syntactic problems, and modulations for the lexical problems, although transpositions and modulations often go hand in hand.

(i) Gerund

The structure 'preposition plus gerund' does not exist in German and needs to be rendered by a structure which is appropriate both to the text-typological conventions and to the style of the text:

Paragraph 1:
you will need to telephone ... by dialling ... if using ... – wählen Sie ... Bei der Benutzung ...

In the first case, we have opted for a compression in the TT because a repetition would result in redundancy. In the second case, we used a nominal structure (preposition plus noun) as it is frequently an appropriate structure for instruction texts.

(ii) Relative clauses

There are some cases of relative clauses, with or without the relative pronoun, which consist just of a pronoun and a verb, or alternatively subject and predicate. In these cases, a passive structure, used as an adjectival phrase in front of the noun (i.e. pre-modification, 'von' plus personal pronoun plus past participle form of verb), is stylistically more appropriate (and also a more economical structure):

Paragraph 2:
the telephone number of the telephone you are using – Nummer des von

Ihnen benutzten Telefons
the emergency service you require – dem von Ihnen benötigten Notdienst

Paragraph 4:
The telephone number from which you are calling – Nummer des von Ihnen
benutzten Telefons

(iii) Lexical choices
Some lexical translation problems are related to culture-specific aspects of the
source culture (and could be discussed under the heading pragmatic translation
problems). These concern the listed facts in Paragraph 4:

Number of the house or name of the property – Hausnummer bzw.
Grundstücks- oder Gebäudebezeichnung
Name of the road or street – Straßenname
Name of a nearby road or a large property or landmark – Name der
nächstgelegenen Straße, ein großes Gebäude oder ein anderes auffälliges
Objekt in Ihrer Umgebung
District and / or town – Stadtteil und / oder Stadt

The problem here is again related to the fact that the TT has to function in the
source culture, and that the TT addressees have to act in the source culture. It is
therefore not possible to substitute words or phrases that are typically used for
geographical locations in the German culture. For example, in England it is
common that a house is referred to by the name that it was given. A 'large property
or landmark' can denote quite a number of concrete objects but the most important point is that they are easily identifiable for the police or the fire service.
Equally general expressions were chosen for the TT ('ein großes Gebäude oder ein
anderes auffälliges Objekt in Ihrer Umgebung'). The difference between 'road'
(outside city centre and / or small) and 'street' (within city centre and / or large),
however, is of no relevance for the specific function of the TT. In the German language, 'Straße' covers both 'road' and 'street' (alternative forms for small streets,
such as 'Gasse', 'Weg', or 'Landstraße' for a road outside a town would add information which would not be contextually and functionally appropriate).

Text-specific translation problems

Paragraph 3:
you have telephoned for the Fire Service – Sie haben 999 gewählt und die
Feuerwehr verlangt.

'Telephone for' is an economical structure for saying 'make a telephone call in
order to reach somebody'; it also implicitly says that the call was made to the
Operator. In the TT, this has been made explicit, there is no way of expressing
both propositions (i.e. (i) call the Operator and (ii) ask to be connected to the Fire
Service) in a similar short structure.
Other specific questions concern the layout of the text. Since the ST was submitted in the reproduced layout, the TT followed this layout more or less. Final
decisions as to the layout for the publication of the leaflet will be made by the
client.

Popular-scientific Texts in the Media: Introductory Comments

Texts from the field of science and technology in the widest sense constitute a large part of the translation business (see Schmitt, 1998a: 10), with such texts belonging to various genres. Lengthy specialist articles, research articles and academic papers are primarily translated for publication in specialist journals, addressed to other experts in the field (thus fulfilling a purpose in domain-internal communication, i.e. an expert writing for other experts in a specific academic field – on culture-specific discourse styles and problems for translation see, for example, Kussmaul, 1997: 72ff.; 1998c). In order to make new scientific discoveries and findings available to a wider public, magazines of a less specialist nature also publish articles on a variety of topics from science and technology, often written by experts (or journalists with some expertise in the field) for interested laypeople (thus fulfilling a purpose in domain-external communication). An example of this is the German version of the *National Geographic*, the official journal of the American National Geographic Society. The German edition with the name *National Geographic Deutschland* was launched in October 1999, and it consists of up to 80% of translations of the English texts, with some texts added specifically for the German-speaking market (for example advertising, readers' letters).

Daily and weekly newspapers and news magazines, too, regularly publish shorter articles about new developments in all fields of science and technology. These texts are addressed to laypeople, and are mostly written by journalists (with expertise in the subject field, the domain). These texts, which also contribute to domain-external communication (journalists as quasi-experts writing for laypeople) are normally referred to as 'popular-scientific texts'. Depending on the domain, there are also more specific labels such as 'financial reporting' or in German 'Wissenschaftsjournalismus' and 'Wirtschaftsjournalismus'. The translation practice in such cases is varied. Some newspapers employ their own in-house translators who translate, among other texts, news items as they arrive from international news agencies (for news translation in Finland see, for example, Vuorinen, 1996). STs that had been published somewhere else and for which a TT is required for publication may also be sent to translation agencies or to freelance translators. In all cases, the translation brief is often to produce the TT for the editors who may wish to use only parts of the text for actual publication (depending on available space, degree of newsworthiness, etc. – cf. partial translation as a pragmatic translation strategy in Chesterman's (1997a) classification).

Popular-scientific texts in newspapers and magazines share a number of characteristic features with other journalistic texts, although 'journalistic text' itself is not a genre (specific genres would be, among others, short news items, editorials, comments). Some of those features will be discussed briefly below since they are relevant for translation. One important point in this respect is the differentiation between more general features of journalistic texts (Hicks, 1999) and specific features of the texts of a particular newspaper (in-house style, see *The Economist Pocket Style Book* 1986; Sandford, 1976). Parallel texts, similar journalistic texts from the paper where the TT is to appear, and maybe even from other newspapers (if an in-house style is not relevant) can help the translator in the decision-making process. Such a search for parallel texts is increasingly being facilitated by the fact that many newspapers and journals are available on the Internet.

Titles, Headings, Sub-headings

There is usually some in-house style as far as the format of headings is concerned. Popular-scientific texts in British and American media have sometimes a title (as a main headline) and super- and/or sub-headlines (plus, depending on the overall length of the text, several internal sub-headlines). Different print fonts may set these heading types apart. The sub-headline (comparable to a 'lead') is often a summary of the most relevant content of the text. Semantically, the title of the text is often closely related to the lead. In some cases, the title may be a pun, or it may be ambiguous, which is related to the main function of titles, i.e. to attract the readers' attention. Popular-scientific texts in German media are typically characterised by a neutral style, which applies to the headings as well, but the translation brief and/or the in-house style may require a more eye-catching title (on the translation of titles see also Nord, 1993).

Direct and Indirect Quotations

In order to highlight their factual nature, popular-scientific texts, as belonging to the informative text type (Reiss, 1971), frequently make use of quotes. The sources that are quoted are typically scientists, professionals, authorities, i.e. sources that are usually regarded as respectable by society and, thus, as reliable. In the case of direct quotations, English texts use predominantly 'say'. Hicks (1999: 40) actually recommends to students of journalism to use 'say' for introducing and attributing quotes, and to 'always avoid variations'. In German texts, however, a variety in the use of explicit verbs of saying is highly common (e.g. 'bemerken, äußern, betonen'). In general, however, nominal expressions (e.g. 'nach Meinung von', 'nach Auskunft von') seem to be more conventional in German popular-scientific texts (as in journalistic texts in general). Indirect quotations, i.e. reported speech, is in German typically signalled by the verb in the subjunctive form (e.g. 'Wie er mitteilte, habe es 1996/97 ein enormes Überangebot an Monographien gegeben.')

Proper Names, Titles, Realia

Proper names of people and of institutions, titles, and other kinds of *realia* are another characteristic feature of popular-scientific texts. Depending on the knowledge of the addressees and the relevance of such information for the purpose of the text (i.e. the necessary degree of precision – see Hönig & Kussmaul, 1982), names of institutions may either be left in the original, or may be translated, or may be rendered by a combination of both (for example, 'Harvard Medical School' – 'Harvard Medical School', or 'Medizinische Fakultät der Harvard Universität', or simply 'Harvard Universität' – see Sample Text 4). In-house styles may also exist in those cases, and translators will have to take them into account (e.g. the use of 'Notenbankchef' in *Der Spiegel* – see Sample Text 3). Such in-house conventions may also involve formal aspects (e.g. italics, bold print). Proper names of institutions may be combined with abbreviations. In the case of well-known (e.g. international) institutions, a standard term, plus a standard abbreviation in the target culture (e.g. 'International Monetary Fund, IMF' – 'Internationaler Währungsfond, IWF') normally exists.

Terminology

Since popular-scientific texts are addressed to the general public and not to experts in the field, they do not normally show a high amount of terminology specific to the domain of expertise, although some terminology is required. Depending on the purpose of the text, the knowledge of the addressees, and the conventions of the newspaper, the translator will have to decide on the most appropriate solution (again, checking parallel and similar texts will be helpful; if necessary, editors may be consulted). For example, the convention in *Der Spiegel* seems to be to use the technical term in combination with an explanation (e.g. 'Schmerzen des Gesichtsnervs ('Trigeminusneuralgie')').

Argumentative Schemata and Style

Popular-scientific texts often belong to the argumentative text type, that is, they are structured around a problem–solution schema. Argumentation schemata may be culture-specific (see Hatim & Mason 1997 for English and Arabic), although for the language (and culture) pair English and German there are more similarities than differences. The function of argumentation may be systematically related to stylistic aspects of the text. One characteristic feature of German popular-scientific texts is that they frequently reflect a nominal style, in contrast to a more verbal style of the English texts (this difference seems to apply to journalistic texts in general). For translation this means that transpositions may often be applied as translation strategies, e.g. opting for nouns in the German TT where the English ST rendered a proposition in a verbal style. German texts of this genre also tend to be more neutral and impersonal in style compared to the English texts which may – depending on the subject area, the character of the publication, and the positioning of the text in the news magazine – include colloquialisms, puns, etc. In the process of translation from English into German, it may, thus, well be necessary to 'neutralise' (or even elevate) the style (unless the skopos demands otherwise).

Sample Texts

The two sample texts we have chosen here concern an economic issue (i.e. Sample Text 3 is an example of 'Wirtschaftsjournalismus') and a medical issue ('Wissenschaftsjournalismus' for Sample Text 4). For a number of translation problems we used parallel texts in the news magazines where the TTs are to be published (or in similar papers and magazines) to decide on the most appropriate translation strategies. These problems concern, above all, the various types of headings in the texts, proper names, terminology, and style. The translation strategies will be discussed with reference to the skopos, genre conventions, and in-house styles.

Infuriatingly Misleading Forecasts

Once again, the IMF is forecasting economic recovery in the rich industrial world. It may, fingers crossed, be right this time.

[1]
To give the world's finance ministers and central bankers something to read as they travel to Washington for the spring meetings of the International Monetary Fund and the World Bank, the IMF has published its *World Economic Outlook*, with its new forecasts for the world economy. The message – 'things are going to get better' – is the same one it has chanted, consistently but incorrectly, for the past three years.

[2]
The IMF considers itself on surer ground this time. The completion of the Uruguay round of world trade talks, lower interest rates in Western Europe, and fiscal stimulus in Japan, should, it says, boost economic activity in 1994 and 1995. The IMF forecasts that the world economy will grow by 3.0% this year (its fastest since 1989), and 3.7% in 1995. Developing countries will lead the way, with average growth of almost 6% this year and next. The rich industrial economies are expected to expand by a more modest 2.4% in 1994 and 2.6% in 1995.

[3]
This, however, still conceals big differences in the fortunes of individual economies. In contrast to the synchronised booms and busts of the 1970s and 1980s, the economies of the seven big industrial countries have been unusually out of step in recent years. America, Britain and Canada moved into recession in 1990, and started to move out of it in 1992, just as the economies of Japan and continental Europe went into a dive.

[4]
Last September the IMF expected growth of 2.6% in America in 1994. It is now forecasting a heady 3.9%. Almost everywhere else, however, growth forecasts have again been trimmed. Japan, for example, is now expected to grow by only 0.7% this year, down from the 2.0% pencilled in last September and an embarrassing 3,5% forecast a year ago. Western Germany is tipped to see growth of only 0.5% for the year as a whole. During 1994, however, growth is expected to speed up in Western Europe and Japan.

[5]
With America's recovery now established, the only worry is by how much policy-makers need to raise interest rates to prevent inflation from

accelerating. On April 18th the Federal Reserve raised its fed-funds rate for the third time this year, by another quarter point, to 3.75%.

[6]

America's growth this year has turned out far stronger than expected. During the first quarter, industrial production grew at an annual rate of 7.7%. Many economists expect that figures for total GDP, due on April 28th, will show annualised growth of almost 4%, despite the depressing impact of bad weather.

[7]

The IMF gives warning that America's spare capacity is likely to be fully absorbed during the course of the year. This is why, to slow the pace of growth, the Fed has been raising interest rates now, even though inflation is at present dormant. In theory, the rise in short-term rates should have reassured bond investors about inflation. Instead, long-term government bond yields have jumped sharply. This will also help to slow the economy. Fixed mortgage rates, for example, have jumped by more than 1.5 percentage points this year.

[8]

How much further should short-term interest rates rise? Alan Greenspan, the Fed's chairman, has been standing by his argument that, because real interest rates remain historically low, they are still giving an unwanted stimulus to the economy. His immediate aim is to move back towards a 'neutral' monetary policy. Over the past 30 years real short-term interest rates have averaged 2%. Given an inflation rate of 2.5%, most people have defined 'neutral' as a fed-funds rate of around 4.5%.

Europe's dilemma

[9]

For three reasons, recovery in continental Europe and Japan will not be as robust as in America, at least in the near future. Real interest rates have not been reduced by as much as they have in America; the need to trim budget deficits in Europe will act as a drag on growth; and high unemployment will continue to restrain consumer spending.

[10]

In 1995, the IMF expects unemployment to be almost 12% of the labour force in the European Union, double America's rate. It is striking that unemployment in the European Union has quadrupled since the 1960s, but has hardly risen at all in America and Japan. From this the IMF infers that, though some of Europe's unemployment can be blamed on the recent recession, the real cause is structural.

[11]
The IMF prescribes the usual remedies, notably making labour markets work better by removing distortions (e.g. rigid hiring and firing rules, minimum wages and over-generous unemployment benefits) that hamper job creation or the incentive to seek work. But it also questions the relevance of this American model in Europe, where some voters express different social preferences.

[12]
Wage differences are a handy example. Economic theory argues that unless wages reflect productivity and skill differences, firms will have little incentive to hire low-skilled workers, and workers will have little incentive to acquire more skills. Yet European countries that place a higher value on income equality feel queasy about wider pay differentials. This may dissuade European governments from swallowing the labour-market medicine the IMF prescribes.

[13]
That would be a pity. The IMF argues that there are better ways to achieve distribution objectives. One is to use the tax and benefit system instead of imposing minimum wages or centralised wage fixing, methods that can distort the functioning of labour markets. The IMF's forecasting records may be shaky, but this part of its economic advice deserves the full attention of governments.

Source: The Economist, 23 April 1994, p. 103

Translation Assignment
A German version of this text is to appear in May 1994 in *Wirtschaftswoche,* more specifically, in its section 'Konjunktur'. *Wirtschaftswoche* is a leading German magazine, published weekly and predominantly devoted to economic topics. Its readers are mainly managers and business people. The text is to be translated for the editors of the German magazine, who will then prepare the final version for the publication. The text has been requested for submission to the editors by the end of April 1994.

Irreführende Prognosen

Der IWF prophezeit erneut eine wirtschaftliche Gesundung in den reichen Industrieländern – diesmal hoffentlich zu Recht.

[1]

Gerade rechtzeitig vor ihrem Abflug zur Frühjahrstagung des Internationalen Währungsfonds (IWF) und der Weltbank in Washington erhielten die Finanzminister und Zentralbanker eine aktuelle Reiselektüre: den jüngsten Weltwirtschaftsausblick des IWF. Dessen Prognose lautet erneut 'die Lage wird sich bessern' – eine Prognose, die sich allerdings in den letzten drei Jahren immer wieder als falsch erwiesen hat.

[2]

Der IWF meint, diesmal auf sicherem Boden zu stehen. Da sind der Abschluß von Welthandelsgesprächen im Rahmen der Uruguay-Runde, geringere Zinssätze in Westeuropa und steuerliche Anreize in Japan, die seiner Meinung nach die Wirtschaft 1994 und 1995 ankurbeln müßten. Nach den Prognosen des IWF wird die Weltwirtschaft in diesem Jahr um 3% wachsen (die höchste Zuwachsrate seit 1989) und 1995 um 3,7%. Die höchste Steigerung mit durchschnittlich nahezu 6% wird in den nächsten zwei Jahren auf die Entwicklungsländer entfallen, im Vergleich zu bescheidenen 2,4% für 1994 und 2,6% für 1995 in den hochentwickelten Industrieländern.

[3]

Diese Zahlen verdecken allerdings noch erhebliche Unterschiede in der Wirtschaftsentwicklung der einzelnen Länder. Im Gegensatz zu den 70er und 80er Jahren, in denen Konjunktur- und Rezessionsphasen in den sieben führenden Industrieländern nahezu synchron verliefen, ist das in den letzten Jahren erstaunlicherweise nicht mehr der Fall. Die USA, Großbritannien und Kanada gerieten 1990 in eine Rezession, von der sie sich ab 1992 schrittweise wieder erholten, während sich zur selben Zeit in Japan und auf dem europäischen Festland ein wirtschaftlicher Niedergang abzeichnete.

[4]

Im September 1993 rechnete der IWF für das Jahr 1994 zunächst mit einem Wachstum von 2,6% in den USA, revidierte seine Prognose nun aber auf kräftige 3,9%. Für fast alle anderen Länder wurden die Prognosen jedoch wieder nach unten korrigiert. So wird in diesem Jahr zum Beispiel für Japan nur noch ein Wachstum von 0,7% veranschlagt, während im September noch mit 2,0% gerechnet wurde, und im Jahr zuvor sogar übertrieben optimistisch mit 3,5%. Für Deutschland (West) wird für das gesamte Jahr nur ein Wachstum von 0,5% angesetzt. Für 1994 gehen die Prognosen jedoch insgesamt wieder von einem beschleunigten Wachstum in Westeuropa und Japan aus.

[5]

Da die wirtschaftliche Gesundung der USA nunmehr als gesichert gilt, ist die einzige Sorge, um wieviel Prozent die Zinssätze erhöht werden müssen, um eine Beschleunigung der Inflation zu verhindern. Am 18. April 1994 hat die amerikanische Notenbank ihren Tagesgeldzinssatz in diesem Jahr zum dritten Male angehoben, und zwar um einen Viertelprozentpunkt auf 3,75%.

[6]

Das Wirtschaftswachstum der USA erweist sich in diesem Jahr als weitaus höher als erwartet. So ist die Industrieproduktion im ersten Quartal mit einer Jahresrate von 7,7% gewachsen. Viele Ökonomen rechnen damit, daß die für den 28. April angekündigten Zahlen für das gesamte BIP ein auf das Jahr hochgerechnetes Wachstum von fast 4% ausweisen werden, und dies trotz des schlechten Wetters.

[7]

Der IWF weist warnend darauf hin, daß es in den USA im Laufe des Jahres wahrscheinlich zu einer vollen Kapazitätsauslastung kommen wird. Deshalb hat die Notenbank jetzt zur Drosselung des Wirtschaftstempos die Zinssätze erhöht, obwohl es derzeit keine Hinweise auf eine Inflationsgefahr gibt. Theoretisch hätte die Anhebung der kurzfristigen Zinssätze den Besitzern von festverzinslichen Anleihen die Gewißheit geben sollen, daß keine Inflation bevorsteht. Andererseits sind die Rendite aus Staatsanleihen mit langen Laufzeiten sprunghaft angestiegen. Diese Entwicklung sollte jedoch ebenfalls zu einer Verlangsamung des Wirtschaftswachstums beitragen. Zum Beispiel haben sich die festverzinslichen Hypotheken in diesem Jahr um mehr als 1,5 Prozentpunkte deutlich erhöht.

[8]

Bis auf welche Höhe können kurzfristige Zinssätze noch steigen? Alan Greenspan, der Chef der amerikanischen Notenbank, hat wiederholt die Meinung vertreten, daß der Effektivzins schon zu lange auf einem historischen Tiefstand ist und deshalb die Wirtschaft noch immer auf unerwünschte Weise stimuliert wird. Greenspans unmittelbares Ziel ist die Rückkehr zu einer 'neutralen' Geldpolitik. In den letzten 30 Jahren betrugen die kurzfristigen Effektivzinsen im Durchschnitt 2%. Bei einer Inflationsrate von 2,5% glauben die meisten, daß 'neutral' einen Tagesgeldsatz von ca. 4,5% bedeutet.

Europas Dilemma

[9]

Aus drei Gründen wird die wirtschaftliche Gesundung auf dem europäischen Festland und in Japan schwächer ausfallen als in den USA, zumindest in naher Zukunft. Die Effektivzinsen sind nicht so stark gesenkt worden wie in den USA; die notwendige Begrenzung der Haushaltsdefizite in Europa hemmt das Wachstum; und die hohe Arbeitslosenrate läßt auch weiterhin keine Steigerung der Verbraucherausgaben erwarten.

[10]

Für 1995 erwartet der IWF eine Arbeitslosenrate von fast 12% in der Europäischen Union, doppelt so hoch wie die der USA. Es ist auffallend, daß sich die Arbeitslosenrate in der Europäischen Union seit 1960 vervierfacht hat, in den USA und Japan hingegen kaum gestiegen ist. Daraus schließt der IWF, daß – obwohl ein Teil der Arbeitslosigkeit in Europa der jüngsten Rezession geschuldet ist – die wahren Ursachen struktureller Art sind.

[11]

Der IWF verschreibt die üblichen Heilmittel, vor allem ein besseres Funktionieren des Arbeitsmarktes durch Beseitigung von Faktoren, die die Schaffung von Arbeitsplätzen behindern und auch keine Anreize zur Jobsuche bieten. Solche störenden Faktoren sind zum Beispiel die starren Regelungen für Einstellung und Entlassung von Arbeitnehmern, die Festlegung von Mindestlöhnen und das äußerst großzügige Arbeitslosengeld. Der IWF stellt aber auch die Übertragbarkeit des US-amerikanischen Modells auf Europa in Frage, wo Wähler unterschiedliche soziale Prioritäten setzen.

[12]

Lohnunterschiede sind ein anschauliches Beispiel dafür. Nach den Lehren der Ökonomie gilt das folgende Argument: solange nicht die Löhne die Unterschiede in der Produktivität und in den Fertigkeiten widerspiegeln, haben weder die Unternehmen einen Anreiz, gering qualifizierte Arbeitskräfte einzustellen, noch die Arbeitnehmer einen Anreiz, höhere Qualifikationen zu erwerben. Allerdings ruft der Gedanke an ein größeres Lohngefälle in den europäischen Ländern, die der Einkommensgleichheit einen hohen Stellenwert beimessen, ein ungutes Gefühl hervor. Das könnte europäische Regierungen davon abhalten, die vom IWF verschriebene Arbeitsmarktmedizin zu schlucken.

[13]

Das wäre jedoch schade. Nach Meinung des IWF gibt es bessere Mittel, um die Verteilungsziele zu erreichen. Eines davon ist die Nutzung des Systems der Steuer- und Sozialleistungen anstelle solcher Methoden wie der Vorgabe von Mindestlöhnen oder zentrale Lohnfestsetzungen, die das reibungslose Funktionieren des Arbeitsmarktes behindern. Auch wenn die Prognosen des IWF in der Vergangenheit mitunter ungenau waren, so verdient doch dieser Teil seiner Diagnose der Wirtschaftslage die volle Aufmerksamkeit der Regierungen.

Annotations

Translation Assignment
A German version of this text is to appear in May 1994 in *Wirtschaftswoche*, more specifically, in its section 'Konjunktur'. *Wirtschaftswoche* is a leading German magazine, published weekly and predominantly devoted to economic topics. Its readers are mainly managers and business people. The text is to be translated for the editors of the German magazine, who will then prepare the final version for the publication. The text has been requested for submission to the editors by the end of April 1994.

ST Characterisation
The text was published in the weekly *The Economist* on 23 April 1994, p. 103, in the journal's section on Business, and with an additional specification as 'Economics Focus' (which is a regular section in *The Economist*). As it is common practice for the magazine, no author is mentioned. The text is accompanied by a table showing some IMF forecasts for some of the data dealt with in the text (i.e. real GDP, consumer prices, and unemployment rate, for some countries or group of countries). This table will also be used for the TT (as is common practice in the section 'Konjunktur' of *Wirtschaftswoche*), but it has not been reproduced here, and we will not comment on it.

The text is a journalistic text on an economic topic. The immediate reason why this text was written was the publication of the IMF's *World Economic Outlook*. This publication was put on the market shortly before the meetings of the IMF and the World Bank, which were still to happen when the ST appeared. These facts/events are mentioned in the first paragraph of the article. The text is predominantly an argumentative text. Argumentative journalistic texts are not characterised by highly conventionalised text structures.

TT Specification
The *Wirtschaftswoche* is a journal read by people with respective interests and knowledge concerning questions of economy and finance. Therefore, it can safely be assumed that there will not be any comprehension problems as to the content and the argumentation in the ST. The organisations mentioned in the ST are international ones and therefore known to the TT addressees.

Since the text is to be translated for the editors, as specified in the translation assignment, it can be assumed that they will make minor modifications according to their in-house style (e.g. concerning formatting, font, temporal references).

The main translation problems this text poses are of a pragmatic nature.

Annotations

Pragmatic translation problems
(i) Situationality – references to time
According to the translation assignment, the TT is intended for publication in May 1994. Therefore, there is no need to adapt the temporal references in the text, i.e. the references to years have been kept (e.g.: Paragraph 2: 'in 1994 and 1995' –

'1994 und 1995'). For the same reason, all references to 'this year' (in Paragraphs 2, 4, 5, 6, 7), which is the year 1994, have been rendered as 'dieses Jahr'. In a few cases, slight modifications have been introduced, for reasons of economy of style:

Paragraph 2:
this year and next – in den nächsten zwei Jahren

(i.e. to avoid the repetition of the preposition which would have been required in the alternative version 'in diesem und im nächsten Jahr').

Respectively, modifications have also been introduced with regard to conventional structures, i.e. in the context of expectations concerning some future state of affairs, the preposition 'für' is typically used:

Paragraph 2:
The rich industrial economies are expected to expand by a more modest 2.4% in 1994 and 2.6% in 1995. – ... im Vergleich zu bescheidenen 2,4% für 1994 und 2,6% für 1995 in den hochentwickelten Industrieländern.

Paragraph 4:
Last September the IMF expected growth of 2.6% in America in 1994. – Im September 1993 rechnete der IWF für das Jahr 1994 zunächst mit einem Wachstum von 2,6% in den USA

Paragraph 10:
In 1995, the IMF expects unemployment to be almost 12% . . . – Für 1995 erwartet der IWF eine Arbeitslosenrate von fast 12% . . .

The additional specification in Paragraph 4 ('Last September' – 'Im September 1993') has been introduced to account for the fact that in German texts of this kind, exact dates are more common. Because of this specification, the next occurrence of 'last September' in the same paragraph has been rendered as 'im September', since the co-reference is obvious to the readers, due to the context. The preference for exact dates has also been the reason for the specification in Paragraph 5, with the subsequently shorter version in Paragraph 6:

Paragraph 5:
On April 18th . . . – Am 18. April 1994

Paragraph 6:
. . . figures for total GDP, due on April 28th, . . . – die für den 28. April angekündigten Zahlen

By the time the German text was to be published (May 1994), the figures will have been available. However, since the text was to be submitted to the editors of the German magazine by the end of April 1994 (as specified in the translation assignment), it could be assumed that they would make any changes they deemed necessary.

(ii) Proper names

The proper names refer mainly to national and international institutions and organisations, for most of which there are conventional proper names in German as well:

Paragraph 1:

International Monetary Fund and World Bank – Internationaler Währungsfond (IWF) und Weltbank

The standard abbreviations are 'IMF' and 'IWF', respectively. In the ST, the abbreviation 'IMF' is used in the sub-heading, the full name then in Paragraph 1, and then throughout the text we find only the abbreviation 'IMF'. In the TT we have opted for the strategy to put the abbreviation in brackets after the full name in Paragraph 1, as is usually the case in German journalistic texts for the first occurrence of a proper name for which a standard abbreviation exists. However, in this case, the first occurrence is in the sub-heading, and the decision to use the abbreviation 'IWF' there has been motivated by considerations for the style of headings (see also *(i) Headings and sub-headings*). The required gender for the abbreviation 'IWF' is masculine.

Paragraph 5:

the Federal Reserve – die amerikanische Notenbank

'Federal Reserve' is a shortened form of 'The Federal Reserve System' in the USA, responsible for financial affairs, and thus corresponding to the central bank of a country. The corresponding term, which is typically used in German texts, is 'Notenbank', often with the specification 'amerikanische Notenbank' or 'Notenbank der USA'. In the TT, 'amerikanische' could also have been omitted, since the paragraph reports about the USA. 'Fed' is the short form, frequently used in Anglo-American texts addressed to insiders, i.e. as a kind of jargon (see Paragraphs 5, 7, 8). Although the TT readers may be familiar with this jargon word, we have decided to use the full name 'Notenbank' consistently in the TT to conform to a coherent style (although 'die Fed' is sometimes used in short news items in *Wirtschaftswoche*). This applies equally to the title of the chairman:

Paragraph 8:

Alan Greenspan, the Fed's chairman – Alan Greenspan, der Chef der amerikanischen Notenbank

An alternative solution would be 'Notenbankchef'. In this case, it is advisable to check which term is normally used in the publication in which the TT will appear since there may be specific conventions. (A survey of *Wirtschaftswoche* showed that the term we have opted for and the versions 'Chef der US--Notenbank', or shorter 'Notenbankchef' / 'Notenbank-Chef', are typically used).

Another type of proper names is the title of the IMF report, *World Economic Outlook*. This is the name of a report which the IMF publishes regularly. It is published in English, but not in German (the IMF does not produce its official publications in German). For the specified purpose of the TT, the more general-ised and condensed version can be considered appropriate:

Paragraph 1:

the IMF has published its *World Economic Outlook*, – den jüngsten Weltwirtschaftsausblick des IWF

or, alternatively;

den jüngsten IWF-Bericht zur Lage und den Aussichten der Weltwirtschaft

In fact, 'new forecasts for the world economy' in the ST is synonymous to the title *World Economic Outlook*. The contrast between new and old (see 'new forecasts' and 'the message is the same') has been rendered in the TT by adjectives ('aktuelle', 'jüngsten') and adverbs ('allerdings', 'immer wieder').

In contexts where an exact reference might be required (e.g. in a translation for a government office), an alternative solution could be: 'IWF-Bericht *World Economic Outlook*', i.e. keeping the English title and adding a general label 'Bericht'.

Paragraph 2:
the Uruguay round of world trade talks – Welthandelsgespräche im Rahmen der Uruguay-Runde

'Uruguay-Runde' is the established term, and 'im Rahmen' indicates that these talks are institutionalised.

Some other proper names are *place names*. We want to comment only on the following examples: The ST uses always 'America' (Paragraphs 3, 4, 5, 6, 7, 9, 10, 11) to refer to the United States of America, as is clear from the context. For the TT, we have decided to use the more specific term 'USA'. For this specific text and its purpose, the abbreviation is appropriate, whereas in other contexts, the full name 'Vereinigte Staaten von Amerika' may be required (e.g. in legal texts).

Since the ST reports on economic developments at a more global level, i.e. with regard to economic areas and/or leading industrial countries, there is hardly a reference to individual European countries. They are normally grouped together under the labels 'Western Europe' (Paragraphs 2, 4), 'continental Europe' (Paragraphs 3, 9 – in these paragraphs, Britain is referred to separately, and we have opted for 'europäisches Festland' in the TT), 'the European Union' (twice in Paragraph 10), 'Europe' (Paragraphs 9, 10, 11, and in the collocations 'European countries', 'European governments' in Paragraph 12). In some cases, 'Europe' and 'European Union' are synonyms, which can be seen from the context. For example, 'Europe's unemployment' in Paragraph 10, refers only to the countries of the European Union (see the use of 'European Union' twice before in the same paragraph, and in addition, the table which accompanies the text – although not reproduced here – states in the column about the unemployment rate that the data are not available for Eastern Europe and the former Soviet Union).

In Paragraph 4, there is a reference to 'Western Germany', and also the data in the table are given for Western Germany only. The text comments on the situation four years after German unification, but due to the economic situation (i.e. there were still huge economic discrepancies between Eastern and Western Germany), the forecasts are only based on figures from Western Germany. In the German press (as e.g. in *Wirtschaftswoche*), 'Deutschland' was the commonly used term for the united country. However, if only the former East or West are referred to, more specific characterisations become necessary, e.g. adding 'Ost' or 'West' in brackets, especially in economic contexts, which is also the solution for which we have opted.

(iii) Culture-specific aspects of notions of banking
Several other terms, although not proper names, are related to the notion of banking and institutions:

Paragraph 1:
the world's finance ministers and central bankers – Finanzminister und Zentralbanker

Both 'finance ministers' and 'central bankers' are general umbrella terms for the two groups of people, with 'central banker' obviously denoting the heads of the respective national banks (this interpretation is based on – if necessary, the results of a search for – background information on the participants at such meetings). Often there are more specific titles in individual countries (e.g. 'Chancellor of the Exchequer' in the UK or 'Bundesbankpräsident' in Germany). We have opted for similar general cover terms in the TT (incidentally, since the early 1990s, 'Zentralbank' has largely replaced 'Nationalbank' as a cover term).

Paragraph 5 reports specifically about the USA:

Paragraph 5:
With America's recovery now established, the only worry is by how much policy-makers need to raise interest rates . . . the Federal Reserve raised its fed-funds rate . . . – Da die wirtschaftliche Gesundung der USA nunmehr als gesichert gilt, ist die einzige Sorge, um wieviel Prozent die Zinssätze erhöht werden müssen, . . . hat die amerikanische Notenbank ihren Tagesgeldzinssatz .. angehoben, . . .

There are different practices concerning the responsibility for monetary policy. In some countries interest rates are set by the government, in others by the central banks. In the USA, the Federal Reserve is responsible for the monetary policy, and 'policy-makers' refers to the Fed's board of governors. We have opted for a passive structure ('um wieviel Prozent die Zinssätze erhöht werden müssen') since the agent is explicitly mentioned in the following sentence and is also part of the background knowledge of the TT addressees. Alternative solutions could have been 'um wieviel Prozent die Notenbank-Gouverneure / die amerikanischen Währungshüter die Zinssätze erhöhen müssen'.

A systematic analysis of background texts in *Wirtschaftswoche* (i.e. texts reporting on economic and monetary developments in the USA) influenced our decision for 'Tagesgeldzinssatz', although the shorter 'Tagesgeldsatz' and the more explicit 'Zinssatz für kurzfristige Einlagen (Tagesgeld)' have also been found. Since the last one is an explanatory term, but the TT addressees are experts, we would consider it as providing redundant information in this case ('overtranslation'). For the second occurrence of 'fed-funds rate' in Paragraph 8, we have then opted for the shorter 'Tagesgeldsatz' since the whole paragraph reports on interest rates (although the repetition of 'Tagesgeldzinssatz' would have been equally appropriate).

Alternatively, or in the case of a different translation assignment (e.g. when the TT addressees are not experts in the field), another solution could be to use the more extensive 'Zinssatz für kurzfristige Einlagen (Tagesgeld)' for the first occurrence in Paragraph 5, and then later the shorter 'Tagesgeldzinssatz'. In Paragraphs 5–8, which all deal with the economy of the USA, 'fed-funds rate' and 'short-term (interest) rates' are used as synonyms. In the TT, 'kurzfristige Zinssätze' has been used as a synonym to 'Tagesgeldzinssatz'. It can be assumed that the TT addressees will be able to recognise these two expressions as synonyms.

Intercultural translation problems

The following text-typological and genre conventions are of relevance for the translation of this text:

(i) Headings and sub-headings

In English journalistic texts, the main title and the sub-heading often go together, with the sub-heading typically summarising the content of the text, whereas the function of the main title is to attract readers' attention. Texts in the section 'Konjunktur' in *Wirtschaftswoche* have one heading only. But since the text is to be translated for the editors of the German magazine, who will then prepare the final version for the publication, we have opted for a main title and a sub-heading. Incidentally, this is the convention too, for longer texts in *Wirtschaftswoche*. In these texts, the main title and the sub-heading together perform the summarising function. The sub-headings are almost regularly complete sentences (see the examples in issue 50/1998: 'Kühlschrank der Welt. Ausländische Firmen investieren massiv in die Landwirtschaft Argentiniens', p. 60; 'Allianz oder Mesalliance? Die Chemieindustrie liefert zahlreiche Lehrstücke zum Thema Fusionmanagement – leider sind sie oft abschreckend.' p. 140). In newspapers, sub-headings are sometimes incomplete sentences, e.g. articles are left out. We have opted for a complete sentence as common in *Wirtschaftswoche*:

Infuriatingly Misleading Forecasts
Once again, the IMF is forecasting economic recovery in the rich industrial world. It may, fingers crossed, be right this time.

Irreführende Prognosen
Der IWF prophezeit erneut eine wirtschaftliche Gesundung in den reichen Industrieländern – diesmal hoffentlich zu Recht.

Although the TT heading may be less dramatic than the English one (we have not accounted for the adverb 'infuriatingly'), it is in conformity with the general style and tone of *Wirtschaftswoche*.

For the other heading in the middle of the text ('Europe's dilemma'), we have opted for the same one in the TT ('Europas Dilemma') since Paragraphs 9–13 discuss the situation in Europe (whereas Paragraphs 5–8 focused on the USA).

(ii) Argumentative schema

Argumentative texts typically reflect a problem–solution schema as their macrostructure. Information units (propositions) are contrasted (as thesis – antithesis), which may also be reflected in the *theme–rheme arrangement*:

Paragraph 2:
Developing countries will lead the way, with average growth of almost 6% this year and next. The rich industrial economies are expected to expand by a more modest 2.4% in 1994 and 2.6% in 1995. – Die höchste Steigerung mit durchschnittlich nahezu 6% wird in den nächsten zwei Jahren auf die Entwicklungsländer entfallen, im Vergleich zu bescheidenen 2,4% für 1994 und 2,6% für 1995 in den hochentwickelten Industrieländern.

The change in the sequence of theme and rheme has been motivated by macro-propositional considerations: the dominant rheme of the whole para-graph (the macro-rheme) is 'there will be growth worldwide', with 'economic growth' introduced as rheme in the sentence before. The new information in the next two sentences (i.e. those quoted here) is the contrast of different growth rates in different areas. Therefore, we have decided to put 'growth' in the theme position at the front of the sentence (i.e. the propositions relating to growth are in the first part of the clauses), thus making the local specification the new rheme. In addition, we have included all propositions in one complex sentence, and have made the semantic relation of contrast, which is implicit in the ST, explicit in the TT by adding 'im Vergleich zu'.

Paragraph 4:
Last September the IMF expected growth of 2.6% in America in 1994. It is now forecasting a heady 3.9%. – Im September 1993 rechnete der IWF für das Jahr 1994 zunächst mit einem Wachstum von 2,6% in den USA, revidierte seine Prognose nun aber auf kräftige 3,9%.

The message here is a change of forecasts, contrasting two different times (1994 and now), and, more importantly, an originally slow growth rate with a more optimistic one. We have opted for combining the two propositions into one complex sentence in the TT and for placing the percentage to the end of each of the two propositions, thus putting more emphasis on the rheme. The change in the syntactic structure of the TT goes hand in hand with an explicitation of the coherence: adding a cohesive device (i.e. 'aber') has made the semantic relation of contrast more explicit (see Chesterman's (1997a) syntactic translation strategy of cohesion change).

In the following examples we have also made the semantic relation between propositions more explicit in the TT:

Paragraph 7:
Instead, long-term government bond yields have jumped sharply. This will also help to slow the economy. – Andererseits sind die Rendite aus Staatsanleihen mit langen Laufzeiten sprunghaft angestiegen. Diese Entwicklung sollte jedoch ebenfalls zu einer Verlangsamung des Wirtschaftswachstums beitragen.

In the ST, 'instead' expresses a contrast to the proposition in the previous sentence, i.e. on the one hand, one fact (raising interest rates) should have assured investors that there is no danger of inflation but, on the other hand, another fact (bond yields have jumped) means that the danger of inflation still exists. Based on knowledge about economic theory, especially the link between economic growth, bond yields, interest rates, and inflation, the ST reader will interpret this message as 'high yields mean high economic growth, continuing high growth may result in inflation, therefore something needs to be done to slow the pace of economic growth'. We have decided to add 'jedoch' in the TT to support the reasoning process.

Paragraph 12:
. . . unless wages reflect productivity and skill differences, firms will have little incentive to hire low-skilled workers, and workers will have little incentive to acquire more skills. – . . . solange nicht die Löhne die Unterschiede in der Produktivität und in den Fertigkeiten widerspiegeln, haben weder die Unternehmen einen Anreiz, gering qualifizierte Arbeitskräfte einzustellen, noch die Arbeitnehmer einen Anreiz, höhere Qualifikationen zu erwerben.

The addition of 'weder . . . noch' and 'andererseits' as cohesive devices makes the coherence (i.e. the semantic relation of contrast) more explicit.

Paragraph 13:
That would be a pity. – Das wäre jedoch schade.

Again, the addition of 'jedoch' establishes the link to the argumentation in the previous paragraph more explicitly.

As initial studies have proved, it seems to be more characteristic of German argumentative texts to have the semantic relations between propositions more explicitly indicated by cohesive devices (see e.g. Gommlich, 1985; Göpferich, 1995).

(iii) Style

Another characteristic feature of the ST concerns its style. Argumentative texts in *The Economist* are often characterised by a more informal style (however, this is *not* a text-typological feature that would apply to English argumentative texts in general), but this feature contributes to the characterisation of the text as a journalistic text rather than a technical text on an economic topic. German texts of this kind, i.e. journalistic texts on economic issues in German print media, on the other hand, are generally written in a more formal style. We have taken this aspect into account for producing the TT, e.g. we have opted for German expressions that can be characterised as stylistically neutral for the colloquial expressions in the English ST (which are often metaphorical expressions):

Paragraph 3:
booms and busts . . . just as the economies of Japan and continental Europe went into a dive. – Konjunktur- und Rezessionsphasen . . . während sich zur selben Zeit in Japan und auf dem europäischen Festland ein wirtschaftlicher Niedergang abzeichnete.

In German texts on economic issues we can also find 'Wirtschaftsboom' (see also the verbal expression 'die Wirtschaft brummt'), which we have not chosen here for stylistic reasons and for reasons of economy.

Paragraph 4:
growth forecasts have again been trimmed – . . . wurden die Prognosen jedoch wieder nach unten korrigiert.

Whereas the ST uses a metaphorical expression ('trimmed'), we have used a euphemism in the TT (i.e. a negative fact is hidden in a verb, 'korrigieren', which usually has a positive connotation, combined with an adverb expressing a downward direction, 'nach unten'). Such euphemisms are found relatively frequently in texts on economic issues. See also Paragraph 9: a more formal term is used in the TT, combined with nominal style:

the need to trim budget deficits – die notwendige Begrenzung der Haushaltsdefizite

Paragraph 7:
. . . long-term government bond yields have jumped sharply. . . . Fixed mortgages rates . . . have jumped by more than 1.5 percentage points – . . . sind die Rendite aus Staatsanleihen mit langen Laufzeiten sprunghaft angestiegen. . . . haben sich die festverzinslichen Hypotheken . . . um mehr als 1,5 Prozentpunkte deutlich erhöht.

The metaphorical expression in the TT ('sprunghaft angestiegen') is stylistically neutral, in the second occurrence we have decided not to repeat the metaphorical expression and have opted for a more neutral structure ('erhöht').

Paragraph 9:
. . . will act as a drag on growth – . . . hemmt das Wachstum

The choice of a verbal structure in the TT, with a more neutral verb, has again been determined by the stylistic conventions of journalistic texts, see also:

Paragraph 11:
hamper job creation – die Schaffung von Arbeitsplätzen behindern . . .

Paragraph 13:
The IMF's forecasting records may be shaky – Auch wenn die Prognosen des IWF in der Vergangenheit mitunter ungenau waren

(iv) Nominal style

Since nominal style is, in general, more characteristic of journalistic texts in German, we have opted for nominal style in the TT compared to verbal style in the ST:

Paragraph 1:
To give the world's finance ministers and central bankers something to read as they travel to Washington – Gerade rechtzeitig vor ihrem Abflug zur . . . in Washington erhielten die Finanzminister und Zentralbanker eine aktuelle Reiselektüre

The choice of nominal style has also been accompanied by some modulations: We have opted for a specification ('Abflug') since this is the most logical form of travel the ministers will choose. Moreover, the generalised noun 'Reise' usually denotes a longer period of travel (see 'Dienstreise, Urlaubsreise'). Alternatively, a verbal structure could have been used with a more general verb (for example: 'Wenn sich die Finanzminister und Zentralbanker zur Frühjahrstagung des Internationalen Währungsfonds (IWF) und der Weltbank nach Washington begeben, können sie sich einer aktuellen Reiselektüre widmen'). The aspect of the process of the travel, indicated by the conjunction 'as' in the ST ('as they travel') is conveyed by the compound 'Reiselektüre' in the TT. The semantic relation between the propositions 'to give . . . something to read' and 'publish' is one of enablement or of cause and effect, i.e. the fact that the report has been published makes it possible for the finance ministers and bankers to read it; with the timing of the publication coinciding with the spring meetings in Washington. In the TT, we have made this temporal relation more explicit by 'gerade rechtzeitig vor'.

Paragraph 7:
This is why, to slow the pace of growth, the Fed has been raising interest rates now, even though inflation is at present dormant. – Deshalb hat die Notenbank jetzt zur Drosselung des Wirtschaftstempos die Zinssätze erhöht, obwohl es derzeit keine Hinweise auf eine Inflationsgefahr gibt.

In the first case ('to slow the pace'), a verbal structure in the TT could have been an alternative solution: 'Deshalb hat die Notenbank jetzt die Zinssätze erhöht, um das Wirtschaftstempo zu drosseln' (for the second case, 'dormant', see *(vi) Abstract agents*).

Paragraph 8:
real interest rates remain historically low – daß der Effektivzins schon zu lange auf einem historischen Tiefstand ist
The nominal structure used in the TT is a collocation, which can typically be found in texts on economic topics and on forecasts, respectively.

In Paragraph 9 a nominal style has been combined with an antonymical translation:
high unemployment will continue to restrain consumer spending. – die hohe Arbeitslosenrate läßt auch weiterhin keine Steigerung der Verbraucherausgaben erwarten.

Paragraph 12:
Yet European countries . . . feel queasy about wider pay differentials. – Allerdings ruft der Gedanke an ein größeres Lohngefälle in den europäischen Ländern, . . . ein ungutes Gefühl hervor.

For this example, see also the later comments about abstract agents, i.e. the subject (agent) in the ST corresponds to a prepositional phrase in the TT, linked to a change from active into passive structure.

(v) Pre-modifications

Pre-modifications, too, are a characteristic feature of German journalistic texts, i.e. more characteristic than in English texts. We have opted for this structure in the TT in connection with dates:

Paragraph 6:
. . . figures for total GDP, due on April 28th, . . . – die für den 28. April angekündigten Zahlen
Possible synonyms to 'Zahlen' could be 'Statistiken' or 'Indikatoren'.

(vi) Abstract agents:

Paragraph 2:
The IMF . . . The completion of . . . should, it says, boost economic activity . . . Der IWF . . . die seiner Meinung nach die Wirtschaft . . . ankurbeln müßten. –

The 'it says' in the ST is no indication of direct speech, but a reference to some statement made by the IMF, therefore we have opted for a more indirect form ('seiner Meinung nach'). Throughout the text, we find expressions (mainly verbs) that indicate that the organisation IMF is conceptualised as a person (see Lakoff & Johnson, 1980, who provide evidence of the conceptual metaphor 'The State is a Person', a metaphor which can equally be applied to organisations). In the propositions, the IMF functions as the agent and, correspondingly, it often takes the subject position in a sentence. This conceptual metaphor exists in German too, and therefore we have used similar structures in most cases, i.e. 'IWF' in subject position and as agent of some action which is expressed by a verb:

sub-heading:
the IMF is forecasting – Der IWF prophezeit

Paragraph 2:
The IMF considers itself on surer ground this time. – Der IWF meint, diesmal auf sicherem Boden zu stehen.

For syntactic reasons, the verb of the idiomatic expression we have opted for ('auf sicherem Boden stehen') is required.

Paragraph 4:
the IMF expected growth – rechnete der IWF . . . mit einem Wachstum

Paragraph 7:
The IMF gives warning that – Der IWF weist warnend darauf hin, daß . . .

Paragraph 10:
the IMF expects unemployment to be . . . the IMF infers that . . . – erwartet der IWF eine Arbeitslosenrate . . . Daraus schließt der IWF, daß

Paragraph 11:
the IMF prescribes the usual remedies . . . it also questions . . . – Der IWF verschreibt die üblichen Heilmittel . . . Der IWF stellt . . . in Frage

In the case of more explicit verbs of saying, however, as in Paragraph 2 and in the following example, we have opted for a nominal structure. In German, verbs of perception and communication are normally combined with human agents and hardly with abstract concepts. Therefore, such textual expressions as 'nach Meinung von', 'nach Auskunft von', 'laut', seem to be more conventional in German journalistic texts, e.g.

Paragraph 13:
The IMF argues – Nach Meinung des IWF

Paragraph 2:
The IMF forecasts that – Nach den Prognosen des IWF . . .

In a few other cases, the decision to use a nominal structure in the TT has been motivated by stylistic considerations, e.g.

Paragraph 1 (no verb):
the IMF has published – den IWF-Bericht

Paragraph 1 (change of agent, i.e. agent IMF is implied by the genitive structure in the TT):
The message . . . is the same one it has chanted, – Dessen Prognose lautet erneut . . .

Paragraph 4 (see also previous comments on theme–rheme structure):
it is now forecasting . . . – revidierte seine Prognose

Treating abstract concepts as agents of some action and putting them in the subject position is, in general, a more characteristic feature of English texts (one which can be found in a number of genres). The corresponding German convention in this case would be to use a prepositional phrase (as in the case of

'European countries' in Paragraph 12, see previous comments on nominal style), substituting a concrete agent, or some other solution:

Paragraph 7:
. . . even though inflation is at present dormant. – . . . obwohl es derzeit keine Hinweise auf eine Inflationsgefahr gibt.

Due to the nominal style (see previous comments), inflation no longer functions as agent in the TT. In addition, a more general expression has been used instead of the metaphor ('dormant'), which in the ST is related to inflation being conceptualised as a person (translation strategy: de-metaphorisation). An alternative solution, equally de-metaphorical, but with the agent role kept in the TT, could be 'auch wenn die Inflation derzeit keine Anzeichen eines Anstiegs aufweist'.

Paragraph 12:
Economic theory argues that . . . – Nach den Lehren der Ökonomie gilt das folgende Argument: . . .

(vii) Other conventions

Several other conventions of a more general character become relevant in this text as well. They concern giving dates (Paragraph 5: 'On April 18th' – 'Am 18. April 1994'), and percentages (i.e. using commas in German, e.g. '2.6%' – '2,6%').

Another example are *culture-specific idioms*, specifically the idiom 'fingers crossed' in the sub-heading of the ST. This idiom reflects the culture-specific way of crossing one's fingers to express hope and support. Corresponding actions in Germany are pressing one's thumb into one's fist to give support to somebody (and the corresponding idiomatic expression is 'Daumen drücken') and knocking on some wooden object to wish for luck (with the idiomatic expression 'auf Holz klopfen', see 'touch wood'). Since we argued that German texts of that kind are usually formal in style, we have opted not to use an idiom here, but a sentence adverb:

It may, fingers crossed, be right this time. – diesmal hoffentlich zu Recht

Interlingual translation problems

(i) Infinitive structures

The examples will illustrate that examining the text from a global perspective will result in structures which are not necessarily listed in grammar books or translation guidelines (e.g. Friederich, 1969). In other words, the choice of the specific structure for the TT, i.e. the decision as to which transpositions and/or modulations would be appropriate is guided mainly by the immediate context, and by text-typological and stylistic considerations.

(a) Infinitive after passive structure

Paragraph 2:
The rich industrial economies are expected to expand . . . – . . . im Vergleich zu . . . in den hochentwickelten Industrieländern.

By combining two sentences in the ST into a complex sentence in the TT (i.e. an example of Chesterman's (1997a) syntactic strategy *sentence structure change*), a verb phrase ('are expected to expand') has become redundant (see also previous comments on theme–rheme structure):

Paragraph 4:
Japan, . . . is now expected to grow . . . Western Germany is tipped to see growth of only 0.5% . . . growth is expected to speed up . . . – So wird . . . für Japan nur noch ein Wachstum . . . erwartet, . . . Für Deutschland (West) wird . . . ein Wachstum von 0,5% angesetzt. . . . gehen die Prognosen . . . von einem beschleunigten Wachstum . . . aus.

The agentless passive constructions with an infinite after verbs of permission, order, or – as in this case – expectation have here been rendered as passive sentences in the first two cases, with the agents of the growth (Japan, Western Germany) treated in the semantic role of beneficiary (indicated by the preposition 'für'). In the third case, we have opted for an active sentence structure, with an abstract subject, i.e. 'Prognosen', in the semantic role of agent. We have also introduced more lexical variation in the TT.

(b) Infinitive after adverb

Paragraph 7:
that America's spare capacity is likely to be fully absorbed – daß es in den USA . . . wahrscheinlich zu einer vollen Kapazitätsauslastung kommen wird.

Due to the different linguistic systems, we have used an indicative verb form (in a passive sense) after the adverb.

(c) Object with infinitive (AcI)

Paragraph 10 (preposition in the TT):
In 1995, the IMF expects unemployment to be almost 12% – Für 1995 erwartet der IWF eine Arbeitslosenrate von fast 12%

Paragraph 11:
making labour markets work better – ein besseres Funktionieren des Arbeitsmarktes

Since we have a list structure here, we have opted for nouns (to conform to the nominal style which we have described as a characteristic feature of the German text and genre), which also makes accounting for the verbal noun in the ST ('making') redundant. An alternative solution could have been 'einen effektiveren Arbeitsmarkt', in this case the aspect of 'working' would be implied.

(d) Infinitive after noun

Paragraph 11:
that hamper . . . the incentive to seek work. – . . . keine Anreize zur Jobsuche bieten

The decision to choose a noun has been made for stylistic reasons (the activity expressed by the verbal structure 'seek work' is implied by the noun 'Jobsuche', i.e. 'Suche' indicates an activity).

Paragraph 12:
firms will have little incentive to hire low-skilled workers, and workers will
have little incentive to acquire more skills. – . . . haben weder die
Unternehmen einen Anreiz, gering qualifizierte Arbeitskräfte einzustellen,
noch die Arbeitnehmer einen Anreiz, höhere Qualifikationen zu erwerben.

The infinitive structures in the TT have been preferred because the objects of
those infinitives ('gering qualifizierte Arbeitskräfte', 'höhere Qualifikationen')
are more complex.

Paragraph 13:
there are better ways to achieve distribution objectives. – gibt es bessere
Mittel, um die Verteilungsziele zu erreichen

The infinitive in the ST functions as an attribute to 'ways', and this function is
expressed by 'um . . . zu'. An alternative version could have been a nominal
structure: 'gibt es bessere Mittel zur Erreichung der Verteilungsziele'.

(ii) -ing structures

Gerund after preposition
In most cases we have used a nominal structure in the TT (Paragraphs 5, 11,
13). The choice of an expanded infinitive structure in Paragraph 12 has been
motivated by a complex object following the gerund (placed as a pre-modification in the TT).

Paragraph 5:
to prevent inflation from accelerating. – um eine Beschleunigung der Inflation zu verhindern.

Paragraph 11:
. . . by removing distortions – . . . durch Beseitigung von Faktoren

Paragraph 12:
This may dissuade European governments from swallowing the
labour-market medicine the IMF prescribes. – Das könnte europäische
Regierungen davon abhalten, die vom IWF verschriebene
Arbeitsmarktmedizin zu schlucken.

Paragraph 13:
instead of imposing minimum wages – anstelle solcher Methoden wie der
Vorgabe von Mindestlöhnen

(iii) Participles
The past participle in a passive sense is used in a with-construction. The
semantic relationship between the sub-clause and the following main clause is
one of cause and effect, which has been made explicit in the TT (indicated by the
conjunction 'da', see Königs, 1998):

Paragraph 5:
With America's recovery now established, . . . – Da die wirtschaftliche
Gesundung der USA nunmehr als gesichert gilt, . . .

Text-specific translation problems

(i) Lexical-semantic fields
   Due to its specific topic, the text is characterised by technical vocabulary from
the lexical-semantic fields (or frames) of (a) economy (e.g. 'economic recovery,
recession, growth, industrial production, labour force, economic theory, productivity'), with 'growth' being a key concept; (b) forecasting (e.g. 'forecast,
expect'); and (c) investment (e.g. 'interest rates, bond investors, long-term government bond yields'). Due to stylistic aspects of the German genre (see previous
comments in *(iii) Style*) some lexical choices have been determined by the existence of these three frames, in addition to choosing more technical terms in the
TT for the colloquial expressions in the ST (e.g. 'Konjunktur- und
Rezessionsphasen' for 'booms and busts', 'wirtschaftlicher Niedergang' for
'went into a dive' in Paragraph 3). The following choices relate to the lexical field
of economy, or the *economy frame:*

   Paragraph 3 (specification ['Wirtschaftsentwicklung' for 'fortunes'] and generalisation ['Länder' for 'economies']):
   big differences in the fortunes of individual economies – erhebliche
   Unterschiede in der Wirtschaftsentwicklung der einzelnen Länder.

   Paragraph 6 (specification):
   America's growth – Das Wirtschaftswachstum der USA

   Paragraph 6 (compression [in the context of economic growth, the effects of
   bad weather can be implied]):
   despite the depressing impact of bad weather. – und dies trotz des schlechten
   Wetters.

   Paragraph 7 (specification through de-metaphorisation (see also *(vi) Abstract
   agents):*
   even though inflation is at present dormant – obwohl es derzeit keine
   Hinweise auf eine Inflationsgefahr gibt

   Paragraph 12 (choice of more general terms as they are usually found in
   German texts on economic topics):
   firms will have little incentive . . . and workers will have little incentive . . . – . . .
   haben weder die Unternehmen einen Anreiz, . . . , noch die Arbeitnehmer
   einen Anreiz

   On the other hand, we have opted for more general expressions in order to
prevent an inappropriate interpretation, which would be based on the readers'
knowledge of the system in the target culture, e.g.

   Paragraph 13:
   centralised wage fixing – zentrale Lohnfestsetzungen

'Aushandlung von Tariflöhnen' would not be appropriate here since it applies too specifically to the target culture (i.e. Germany). Other lexical choices concerning the field of economy are:

Paragraph 6:
figures for total GDP – Zahlen für das gesamte BIP

Using abbreviations is typical of economic texts, the full names are 'Gross domestic product (GDP)' and 'Bruttoinlandsprodukt (BIP)', respectively.

Paragraph 11:
... notably making labour markets work better by removing distortions (e.g. rigid hiring and firing rules – ... vor allem ein besseres Funktionieren des Arbeitsmarktes durch Beseitigung von Faktoren, die ... Solche störenden Faktoren sind zum Beispiel die starren Regelungen für Einstellung und Entlassung von Arbeitnehmern, ...

In addition to opting for two sentences, the lexical choices are again frame-determined. Alternative versions could have been 'einen effektiveren Arbeitsmarkt' or 'eine Reform des Arbeitsmarktes' (which would imply the aspect of working better). For 'rigid hiring and firing rules', an alternative version could have been 'unflexible Beschäftigungspolitik'. In some contexts, e.g. in reports about the USA or the UK, 'Hire and Fire' are used as loanwords in German texts. But since this paragraph refers to Europe, and due to the fact that German texts of this genre are generally characterised by a more formal style (see *(iii) Style*), we have decided against the use of the loanwords.

The *lexical field of forecasting* is generally closely related to economy and growth. In the ST, the two words 'forecast(ing)' and 'expect' are predominantly used, whereas we have chosen somewhat more lexical variety in the TT (e.g. 'rechnen mit', 'erwarten', 'ausgehen von', 'ansetzen', 'veranschlagen'). 'Prognosen' has been preferred to (the equally appropriate) 'Vorhersagen' due to the context of economics (with 'Vorhersagen' more characteristic than 'Prognosen' in the context of fortune telling and weather), and to contribute to the fairly formal style of the TT.

Concerning the *lexical field of investment*, we have some expressions in the ST which reflect different systems in various countries. We have already commented about 'fed-funds rate' (see point (iii) under *Pragmatic translation problems*). The following lexical choices have been motivated by this lexical field:

Paragraph 7 (specification):
the rise in short-term rates should have reassured bond investors about inflation. – ... hätte die Anhebung der kurzfristigen Zinssätze den Besitzern von festverzinslichen Anleihen die Gewißheit geben sollen, daß keine Inflation bevorsteht.

Bonds pay a regular interest rate and are generally adversely affected by inflation (interest rates cause bond prices to change). We have opted for a specification because 'Anleger' would have been too vague in this context.

(ii) Metaphors
The metaphors in the ST come mainly from the domains movement and health. Both in English and German texts on political and economic issues, development is frequently conceptualised as movement (i.e. the conceptual met-

aphor can be formulated as 'Development is Movement along a Path'), thus also allowing for entailments concerning the method ('synchronised', 'out of step'), the direction ('moved into', 'move out', 'went into a dive'), and the speed ('pace', 'slow') of development. References to health are evidence that the economy is conceptualised as a person (i.e. the conceptual metaphor is Economy is a Person); more specifically, the aim is for the Economy to be healthy (as it is for a person), and in the case of problems, some medicine is required (e.g., 'recovery', 'prescribe remedies', 'swallow the labour-market medicine').

Because of their relevance, these two conceptual metaphors (movement, health) are also reflected at the global level of the TT, although at the micro-level, not every individual metaphorical expression in the ST corresponds to a metaphorical expression in the TT (on metaphors and translation from a cognitive point of view see Stienstra (1993), Schäffner (1997b, 1998b, in press). The relevance of these two conceptual metaphors has also made it possible to replace a metaphorical expression from one domain by a metaphorical expression from the other domain ('move out' – 'erholen' in Paragraph 3):

Paragraph 3:
... the synchronised booms and busts ..., the economies ... have been unusually out of step .... America, Britain and Canada moved into recession in 1990, and started to move out of it in 1992, just as the economies of Japan and continental Europe went into a dive. – ... in denen Konjunktur- und Rezessionsphasen . . . nahezu synchron verliefen, ist das . . . erstaunlicherweise nicht mehr der Fall. Die USA, Großbritannien und Kanada gerieten 1990 in eine Rezession, von der sie sich ab 1992 schrittweise wieder erholten, während sich zur selben Zeit in Japan und auf dem europäischen Festland ein wirtschaftlicher Niedergang abzeichnete.

Paragraph 4 (different word groups within identical metaphor):
growth is expected to speed up – gehen die Prognosen . . . von einem beschleunigten Wachstum . . . aus.

In the following two cases, the conceptual metaphor has been expanded in the TT, by explicitly introducing a means ('ankurbeln', 'Drosselung') which will lead to the intended effect ('boost', 'slow'):

Paragraph 2:
boost economic activity – die Wirtschaft . . . ankurbeln

Paragraph 7:
. . . to slow the pace of growth, . . . help to slow the economy. – . . . zur Drosselung des Wirtschaftstempos . . . zu einer Verlangsamung des Wirtschaftswachstums beitragen.

Since the conceptual metaphor of the economy as a (healthy) person is known in German as well, a more literal translation has been opted for in the following cases:

Paragraph 11:
The IMF prescribes the usual remedies – Der IWF verschreibt die üblichen Heilmittel

Paragraph 12:
... swallowing the labour-market medicine the IMF prescribes.- die vom IWF
verschriebene Arbeitsmarktmedizin zu schlucken.

It is due to the textual relevance of the conceptual metaphor of health that we
have opted for 'Gesundung' (in Paragraphs 5 and 9), and not for 'Erholung'
(which would also have been possible). The choice of an antonymic translation
in Paragraph 9 has been motivated by the fact that the focus is on the process
(expressed by 'Gesundung', in contrast to 'Gesundheit' which denotes a state,
see the collocations 'starke Gesundheit', 'robuste Gesundheit', but these adjectives do not collocate with 'Gesundung'):

Paragraph 9:
recovery will not be as robust – wird die wirtschaftliche Gesundung . . .
schwächer ausfallen

The use of 'Diagnose' (Paragraph 13) also contributes to the overall textual
function of the metaphorical domain of health:

Paragraph 13:
this part of its economic advice deserves the full attention of governments. –
so verdient doch dieser Teil seiner Diagnose der Wirtschaftslage die volle
Aufmerksamkeit der Regierungen.

Proof against heart attacks
A study touts the benefits of moderate drinking

[1]

Does a drink a day keep heart attacks away? Over the past 20 years, numerous studies have found that moderate alcohol consumption – say one or two beers, glasses of wine or cocktails daily – helps to prevent coronary heart disease. Last week a report in the *New England Journal of Medicine* added strong new evidence in support of that theory. More important, the work provided the first solid indication of how alcohol works to protect the heart.

[2]

In the study, researchers from Boston's Brigham and Women's Hospital and Harvard Medical School compared the drinking habits of 340 men and women who had suffered recent heart attacks with those of healthy people of the same age and sex. The scientists found that people who sip one to three drinks a day are about half as likely to suffer heart attacks as nondrinkers are. The apparent source of the protection: those who drank alcohol had higher blood levels of high-density lipoproteins, or HDLs, the so-called good cholesterol, which is known to ward off heart disease.

[3]

As evidence has mounted, some doctors have begun recommending a daily drink for cardiac patients. But most physicians are not ready to recommend a ritual happy hour for everyone. The risks of teetotaling are nothing compared with the dangers of too much alcohol, including high blood pressure, strokes and cirrhosis of the liver – not to mention violent behavior and traffic accidents. Moreover, some studies suggest that even moderate drinking may increase the incidence of breast and colon cancer. Until there is evidence that the benefits of a daily dose of alcohol outweigh the risks, most people won't be able to take a doctor's prescription to the neighborhood bar or liquor store.

Source: Time, 27 December 1993, p. 31

Translation Assignment

A German version of this text is to be published in the weekly magazine *Der Spiegel* in January 1994, in the regular section 'Prisma-Wissenschaft', i.e. the section reporting on new scientific findings and developments.

Medizin
Promille für das Herz

[1]
Trinkt Alkohol, und ihr bleibt gesund – stimmt das? In den letzten 20 Jahren wurde in zahlreichen Untersuchungen nachgewiesen, daß mäßiger Alkoholgenuß, zum Beispiel ein oder zwei Glas Bier, Wein oder Cocktail pro Tag, zur Verhinderung von Herzkrankheiten beitragen kann. Im *New England Journal of Medicine* wurden kürzlich neue überzeugende Beweise zur Stützung dieser These vorgelegt. Darüber hinaus liefert der Beitrag die ersten stichhaltigen Angaben darüber, auf welche Weise die schützende Wirkung des Alkohols für das Herz zustande kommt.

[2]
Bei ihren Untersuchungen verglichen Forscher des Bostoner Brigham and Women's Hospital der Harvard Universität die Trinkgewohnheiten von 340 Männern und Frauen, die kürzlich einen Herzinfarkt erlitten hatten, mit denen gesunder Menschen der gleichen Altersgruppe und des gleichen Geschlechts. Die Wissenschaftler fanden heraus, daß die Wahrscheinlichkeit eines Herzinfarkts bei Menschen, die sich ein bis drei Gläschen pro Tag genehmigen nur halb so hoch ist wie bei Nichttrinkern. Die wahrscheinliche Ursache für diesen Schutz ist die folgende: Diejenigen, die Alkohol tranken, wiesen im Blut eine höhere Konzentration von Lipoproteinen hoher Dichte (HDL) auf, dem sogenannten 'guten Cholesterin', von dem man weiß, daß es vor Herzerkrankungen schützt.

[3]
Aufgrund der zunehmenden Beweise raten jetzt schon einige Ärzte ihren Herzpatienten, täglich ein Gläschen Alkohol zu trinken. Aber die meisten Ärzte sind noch nicht bereit, den täglichen Alkoholgenuß prinzipiell für alle gutzuheißen. Die Gesundheitsrisiken bei Abstinenz sind unbedeutend im Vergleich zu den Gefahren, die übermäßiger Alkoholgenuß verursacht, wie zum Beispiel hoher Blutdruck, Schlaganfall und Leberzirrhose, von Gewalttätigkeit und Verkehrsunfällen ganz zu schweigen. Darüber hinaus lassen manche Untersuchungen den Schluß zu, daß sogar mäßiger Alkoholgenuß zu einem erhöhten Risiko von Brust- und Darmkrebs führen kann. Solange nicht eindeutig bewiesen ist, daß eine tägliche Dosis Alkohol eher nützt als schadet, werden wir wohl noch nicht mit einem Rezept ins Lokal oder den Laden an der Ecke gehen können.

Annotations

Translation Assignment

A German version of this text is to be published in the weekly magazine *Der Spiegel* in January 1994, in the regular section 'Prisma-Wissenschaft', i.e. the section reporting on new scientific findings and developments.

ST Characterisation

The text was published in the American weekly magazine *Time* on 27 December 1993. It is an exemplar of the genre popular-scientific text, i.e. it reports on a scientific topic, but the addressees are laypeople. This is reflected in the structure and argumentation of the text, especially in a more personal tone, a more informal style, indicated by colloquialisms (e.g. 'sip a drink'), idioms (e.g. in the first sentence), puns (e.g. in the title).

As is typical of titles in *Time*, there are two headings: the main one at the top, printed in bold and in larger size, and below it a smaller one, with a coherent link between these two headings (to be discussed in detail in the following annotations). The original text is accompanied by a small photo, depicting some people having a drink in a bar, and with the caption 'Will people one day be indulging in ritual happy hours for health as well as pleasure?' (this photo has not been reproduced here, since it is not part of the translation assignment, i.e. the clients, the editors of *Der Spiegel*, intend to use a different photo).

This is a text about a specific medical finding. Although these findings originate in the USA (reflected in names of institutions), the topic is not source culture specific but of equal interest to humankind all over the world, and particularly for Western Europe, due to the lifestyle in industrially highly developed countries. The ST poses, above all, pragmatic and text-specific translation problems.

TT Specification

In general, popular-scientific texts in German are often characterised by a more neutral and impersonal style, with puns and colloquialisms not frequently found there. Although the German magazine *Der Spiegel* is known for its particular style, which has been characterised as 'brisk and punchy' by Sandford (1976: 216, see also Yang 1990), the texts in the section 'Prisma – Wissenschaft' are usually stylistically neutral. The client, i.e. the German newspaper, has asked for a ready-to-print TT. Therefore, the stylistic characteristics of popular-scientific texts in *Der Spiegel* have to be taken into account for the production of an appropriate TT. Texts on new developments in the field of medicine, which have been published in *Der Spiegel* can serve as parallel texts.

Annotations

Pragmatic translation problems

(i) Situation of TT

According to the assignment, the TT is to be published in January 1994, and therefore the temporal references have been adapted accordingly:

Paragraph 1:
last week – kürzlich

We have opted for 'kürzlich' due to the short time lapse since the ST publication. Alternative appropriate solutions could be 'im Dezember 1993' or 'im Dezember letzten Jahres', or 'im Dezember des vergangenen Jahres', or, if the exact date of the TT publication is known, 'vor vier Wochen' or 'vor drei Wochen'.

(ii) Terminology in relation to the genre and to the addressees

There are a number of medical terms in the ST. In the German language, there are frequently two words for diseases and other medical concepts, one technical medical term (which is often derived from Greek or Latin, and shows some formal similarity to the English term); and a non-technical word. The difference is a pragmatic one; more specifically, the use of the medical or the more general word is determined by the communicative situation and the communicative partners. The use of the technical term is the convention in scientific discourse (e.g. a text in a medical journal, where the addressees are medical experts). In other situations, e.g. doctor–patient communication, laypeople talking among themselves, the non-medical term would be preferred. In popular-scientific texts, either the more general term is used, or a combination of the medical term and a more general word. In this case, the analysis of parallel texts has revealed that – with respect to popular-scientific texts on medical topics – *Der Spiegel* frequently uses a combination of the technical term and the corresponding general word, and/or an explanation (see examples from the section 'Prisma – Wissenschaft': 'Schmerzen des Gesichtsnervs ('Trigeminusneuralgie')' in issue 25/1997, p. 195, 'erster Fall von Gedächtnisverlust (Amnesie)', 'Schädigungen des Globus pallidus ('Pallidum'), einer Struktur des Zwischenhirns' – all in issue 16/1997, on p. 225).

These conventions have determined our solutions for the TT. In most cases we have opted for the more general word as appropriate to the purpose of the TT, see:

Paragraph 1: coronary heart disease – Herzkrankheiten
Paragraph 3: breast and colon cancer – Brust- und Darmkrebs.

In the following case we have opted for a combination of the specific medical term and a more general word because the findings of the scientists are described in more detail:

Paragraph 2:
high-density lipoproteins, or HDLs, the so-called good cholesterol – höhere Anteile von Lipoproteinen hoher Dichte (HDL), dem sogenannten 'guten Cholesterin'

For the genre popular-scientific text, 'Anteile des guten (HDL) Cholesterins' or 'hoher Anteil des schützenden ('guten') HDL-Cholesterins' would be equally appropriate (the second version was actually used in a text in *Der Spiegel* 39/1994, p. 237). Sometimes a more simple '(überhöhte) Blutfettwerte' oder '(erhöhter) Cholesterinspiegel (im Blut)' would be sufficient for the purpose of the TT. In a more scientific text, the actual medical term would be required (for example, in a text in the German consumer magazine *Test*, issue 7/1995, p. 771, which discussed the medical conditions and symptoms, the original English terms were given with an explanation in German, as: 'HDL: high density lipoprotein, Fett-Eiweißkomplexe hoher Dichte, and LDL: low density lipoprotein, Fett-Eiweißkomplexe niedriger Dichte').

The medical terms are used in the following two cases because they have also become established in non-medical discourse:

Heart attacks – Herzinfarkt
Paragraph 3: cirrhosis of the liver – Leberzirrhose

'Herzinfarkt' is the proper German medical term, although due to interference from English (or 'translationese'), 'Herzanfall' is sometimes found in German texts (which is an example of a false friend – 'attacks' can correspond to 'Anfall' in other contexts, e.g. 'ein Asthmaanfall'). The typical collocation is 'einen Herzinfarkt erleiden'. The singular form is the typical usage (see also in Paragraph 3: 'strokes' – 'Schlaganfall').

(iii) Proper names

The proper names concern journals and institutions:

Paragraph 1:
in the *New England Journal of Medicine* – im *New England Journal of Medicine*

The degree of specification depends on various factors, especially the knowledge of the TT addressees. In conformity with the conventions in *Der Spiegel*, the proper name has been kept in the TT. In the case of a formal similarity of words (as here 'journal' and 'Journal', and 'medicine' and 'Medizin'), the addition of a generic cover term (e.g. 'Zeitschrift') is not absolutely necessary since it can be considered as redundant. In less obvious cases, a more specific explanation would be more appropriate, i.e. explaining the type of the publication to the TT readers (e.g. 'medizinische Fachzeitschrift', 'amerikanische medizinische Fachzeitschrift'). A systematic analysis of parallel texts in *Der Spiegel* confirms this procedure: the less transparent the title of the journal, the more specific the explanation (see examples from the section 'Prisma – Wissenschaft': 'im *New England Journal of Medicine*' – issue 25/1997, p. 195, 'im *Journal of Neurology, Neurosurgery and Psychiatry*', 'das britische Wissenschaftsblatt *New Scientist*', 'in dem Fachblatt *Oikos*' – all in 16/1997, p. 225).

Paragraph 2:
researchers from Boston's Brigham and Women's Hospital and Harvard Medical School – Forscher des Bostoner Brigham and Women's Hospital der Harvard Universität

The phrase we have used was found twice in texts in *Der Spiegel* in 1994 and 1995, respectively (which proves once more the effectiveness of using background texts and parallel texts for solving translation problems). In other contexts, a more general 'der Medizinischen Fakultät der Harvard Universität', or simply 'der Harvard Universität', could be sufficient, i.e. in contexts where details are not absolutely necessary for the purpose of the TT and its addressees. Since it can safely be assumed that the readers of *Der Spiegel* know that Harvard University is in the USA, we have not found it necessary to add 'amerikanisch'.

(iv) Culture-specific references

There are two cases in which we have a reference to culture-specific customs and traditions, which are encapsulated in lexical structures: 'happy hour' and 'liquor store':

Paragraph 3:
But most physicians are not ready to recommend a ritual happy hour for everyone. – Aber die meisten Ärzte sind noch nicht bereit, den täglichen Alkoholgenuß prinzipiell für alle gutzuheißen.

'Ritual happy hour' in the English text is meant to put emphasis on the daily routine. 'Happy hour' has recently been introduced in German, but only in the context of pubs, and it is therefore restricted in its use and context. In a pub context, both in English and in German, 'happy hour' evokes a specific scene: a specific time of the day, cheaper prices, a specific atmosphere. These features, however, are not dominant in the ST. The relevant idea is rather the daily routine, the regularity, the normality, which we have decided to convey in the TT by 'täglich' and 'prinzipiell'. It could be argued that our solution is stylistically not very elegant (i.e. there is lexical repetition: 'täglich ein Gläschen Alkohol zu trinken' in the sentence before and 'täglichen Alkoholgenuß' here). But we hesitated to use ' . . . ein solches Ritual prinzipiell für alle gutzuheißen', where we would have had an alternative structure (with co-reference). A typical scene evoked by 'Ritual' would include a certain number of actions, usually following each other in a fixed order, a number of people, usually linked by some common purpose, e.g. a religious group), a sense of festivity and / or strictness, even rigidity (see collocations such as 'feierliches Ritual', 'strenges Ritual', 'das Ritual der alljährlichen Abschlußfeier', 'rituelle Vorschrift', 'rituelle Tänze und Gesänge'). Having a drink daily to prevent heart attacks might ironically be called a 'Ritual', but doing so here would change the style of the TT.

Paragraph 3:
. . . most people won't be able to take a doctor's prescription to the neighborhood bar or liquor store. – werden wir wohl noch nicht mit einem Rezept ins Lokal oder den Laden an der Ecke gehen können.

'Liquor store' involves a cultural reference, it is related to the practice of issuing a licence to sell alcohol to restaurants, pubs, etc., and also to specific shops. In other words, in the USA (and also in the UK), alcohol cannot be bought in practically any shop. In Germany, however, there are hardly any restrictions concerning shops where alcohol can be bought. Therefore a more general 'Laden' will be sufficient. Similarly, the more general 'Lokal' has been chosen for 'neighborhood bar' instead of 'Restaurant' (normally a place where one would eat, and a stylistically neutral umbrella term for a whole range of restaurants), or 'Bar' (mainly used in the context of night clubs, a place often with music, for dancing), or 'Kneipe' (a colloquial term for 'pub', which would be stylistically inappropriate for this specific text and assignment). 'Stammlokal' could be used as well, although such a high degree of precision is not necessary in this context. Or alternatively, since the main idea simply is that you cannot have alcohol prescribed, it would be totally appropriate to say 'können wir Alkohol noch nicht auf Rezept bekommen.'

The introduction of 'wir' (despite the fact that a personal style is not typical of popular-scientific texts in German) and of the particle 'wohl' has been motivated

by the slightly ironical touch of this very last sentence (see the comments on *(ii)*
Style below).

Intercultural translation problems

(i) Title and sub-heading
   The ST has a main title in bold, and a sub-title. We have decided to use only
one main title and indicate the subject (the field) by a sur-title, since this is the
in-house convention for the special section of *Der Spiegel,* where the TT is to be
published (as to the specific semantic content and the stylistic features, see (i)
under *Text-specific translation problems*).

(ii) Style
   In general, the genre of popular-scientific texts in German news magazines is
characterised by a neutral, impersonal style, and also – related to this – by a
nominal style. Therefore, we have opted for a slight elevation of style in the TT.
An analysis of parallel texts has revealed that in this particular section in *Der
Spiegel*, the style is predominantly neutral, but there is also the odd colloquialism
when the topic can be related to human vice or virtue (e.g. in a text on the link
between the choice of food and sexuality in mice we read 'Dieses Ergebnis
erzielten Wissenschaftler . . . die in einem Laborversuch männliche Wühlmäuse
mit einer Nahrung unterschiedlichen Einweißgehalts päppelten . . . :' – issue
16/1997, p. 225 – hence our choice of 'wir' in the last sentence, see above).

   Paragraph 2 (modulation: displacement):
   people who sip one to three drinks a day – . . . bei Menschen, die sich ein bis
   drei Gläschen pro Tag genehmigen

   'Sip' emphasises the small quantity of the alcohol that is consumed, in addition to the delight in drinking. It does not refer to a specific way of drinking. This
interpretation is based on the context. The German equivalents for 'sip', found in
bilingual dictionaries ('nippen, schlürfen, schlückchenweise trinken') indicate a
specific mode of drinking, i.e. different semantic features would be stressed
(foregrounded) by these German verbs. We have opted for a more neutral verb
('sich genehmigen'), and have attached the feature of small quantity to the noun
('Gläschen'). Since drinking alcohol is the topic of the text, 'Gläschen' can be said
to imply alcohol in this context. This is an example of the translation strategy
'displacement', or 'dislocation' (here of a connotation). But see Paragraph 3,
where we opted for a modulation, i.e. a specification ('a daily drink' – 'täglich ein
Gläschen Alkohol'), mainly for stylistic reasons, and to reintroduce the aspect of
regular drinking, after the explanation of medical details in Paragraph 2.
   In the following examples, we opt for a nominal style to comply with this characteristic feature of German popular-scientific texts:

   Paragraph 1:
   . . . moderate alcohol consumption . . . helps to prevent coronary heart
   disease. – daß mäßiger Alkoholgenuß, . . . zur Verhinderung von
   Herzkrankheiten beitragen kann

   (*NB*: Alternative collocations to 'mäßiger Alkoholgenuß' could be 'maßvoller
Alkoholkonsum' or 'mäßiger Alkoholkonsum'.)

Paragraph 1:
... indication of how alcohol works to protect the heart. – ... Angaben darüber, auf welche Weise die schützende Wirkung des Alkohols für das Herz zustande kommt.

Paragraph 3:
... are nothing compared with the dangers ... – ... sind unbedeutend im Vergleich zu den Gefahren ...

(iii) Abstract agents

Abstract agents are characteristic of English texts of the genre in question. Transpositions have been used as translation strategies (mostly using passive structures in the TT), resulting in modulations at the same time, see:

Paragraph 1:
Over the past 20 years, numerous studies have found that ... – In den letzten 20 Jahren wurde in zahlreichen Untersuchungen nachgewiesen, daß ...

'Studies' in the ST functions syntactically as the subject of the sentence, and semantically as agent of the action 'finding'. Logically speaking, the agents are scientists, and the studies are the results. According to German conventions, results do not usually take the semantic function of agent, and therefore only rarely occupy the subject position. In the TT, a passive structure has been used, allowing for the logical agent (implicit in the ST too) to be implied, and the result is rephrased as a prepositional phrase 'in zahlreichen Untersuchungen'. For referring to the process, as in the ST, 'Untersuchungen' is the appropriate word, whereas 'Studie' is normally used to refer to the product of some scientific study, i.e. a publication.

A change of agent and subject has also been used as a translation procedure in the following example:

Paragraph 1:
Last week a report ... added stong new evidence ... – Im *New England Journal of Medicine* wurden kürzlich neue überzeugende Beweise ... vorgelegt.

Paragraph 3: impersonal structure in TT
Moreover, some studies suggest that ... – Darüber hinaus lassen manche Untersuchungen den Schluß zu, daß ...

This last example is again evidence of the resulting nominal style in the TT. A slightly alternative solution could be: ' ... legen manche Untersuchungen den Schluß nahe, daß ... '.

(iv) Combining sentences by colons

Another feature characteristic of the style of popular-scientific texts (and of journalistic texts in general) is a verbless clause with a colon at the end. Such structures allow the information to be presented in a condensed way. The semantic relation between the propositions, indicated by the colon, may be different in each case. Although such a structure is also typical in German texts of the genre concerned, it has been changed here into a complete sentence for syntactic reasons, i.e. a verb has been added, which calls for a subject complement, and thus the semantic relation of explication has been made lexically explicit in the TT:

> Paragraph 2:
> The apparent source of the protection: – Die wahrscheinliche Ursache für diesen Schutz ist die folgende:

Another possibility would be to use a complex sentence, i.e. a main phrase plus a subordinate clause, thus doing away with the colon, i.e. 'Die wahrscheinliche Ursache ist, daß . . . '.

Interlingual translation problems
Some changes in the syntactic structure (transpositions) have been made because of different linguistic conventions, as in the following examples.

(i) Number

> Paragraph 1:
> say one or two beers, glasses of wine or cocktails daily – zum Beispiel ein oder zwei Glas Bier, Wein oder Cocktail pro Tag

The ST uses plural for 'beers' and 'cocktails', but adds 'two glasses' in the case of wine. 'Bier, Wein, Cocktail' in German are treated as quantity/mass nouns which are used in the singular only, they are uncountable nouns. Used in the plural, i.e. 'Biere', 'Weine' would mean that different brands are being referred to. In the combination with 'Bier', 'Glas' is mostly used in the singular form, it can even be considered redundant (e.g. when ordering in a pub, one can ask for 'zwei Glas Bier' or 'zwei Bier'). In the context of wine, too, 'Glas' can be used in the singular, but it is normally not redundant (or only in some regions in Germany). Alternatively, we could have said 'ein oder zwei Gläser Bier, Wein oder Cocktails', but we have opted against this formulation because it is less conventional in the context with which we are concerned here.

We have also opted for plural forms in the case of some abstract nouns in the ST. Although these nouns are in the singular, they indicate a quantity. In such cases, plurals are more common in German texts.

> Paragraph 1:
> a report . . . added stong new evidence in support of that theory. – wurden kürzlich neue überzeugende Beweise zur Stützung dieser These vorgelegt.

The plural 'Beweise' is more typical in such cases in German, particularly if the following propositions provide more information (the following paragraphs give a more detailed description of the complexity of the study). The choice of 'überzeugend' (literally 'convincing') for 'strong' is determined by taking typical collocations into account (e.g. 'schwerwiegender Beweis' is preferred in the context of judicial evidence).

> Paragraph 3:
> As evidence has mounted, some doctors have begun recommending a daily drink for cardiac patients. – Aufgrund der zunehmenden Beweise raten jetzt schon einige Ärzte ihren Herzpatienten, täglich ein Gläschen Alkohol zu trinken.

The quantitative aspect is also obvious in the verb 'mounted' in the ST, expressed by a participle as pre-modification in the TT. In addition, 'as' denotes a causal relationship (cause–effect), which has determined the choice of the German prepositional phrase ('aufgrund').

Paragraph 1:
More important, the work provided the first solid indication . . . – Darüber hinaus liefert der Beitrag die ersten stichhaltigen Angaben darüber, . . .

The choice of the adjective ('stichhaltig') has been determined by consideration of typical collocations. 'More important' in the ST functions as a sentence adverb, i.e. modifies the whole following proposition. It is a reduced clause ('what is more important is'). Semantically, it is linked to the previous sentence by indicating the increasing novelty of the findings. We have conveyed this semantic aspect (coherence) by the sentence adverb 'darüber hinaus' in the front position. An alternative version could have been 'Mehr noch, der Beitrag liefert . . .'.

(ii) Infinitives

(a) Infinitive after verb

Paragraph 1 (ST, infinitive expresses a consequence; TT, indicative verb form, consequence expressed more explicitly by 'zustande kommt'):
. . . indication of how alcohol works to protect the heart – . . . Angaben darüber, auf welche Weise die schützende Wirkung des Alkohols für das Herz zustande kommt.

In addition, we have an adnominal relative clause in the ST ('indication of how'), where the 'how' is merged with its antecedent (cf. 'of the way in which'). In the TT we have opted for a pronominal adverb ('darüber') plus a modal clause (the mode indicated by 'auf welche Weise').

(b) Infinitive after passive structure

Paragraph 2 (ST, passive structure; TT, sub-clause, impersonal structure):
the so-called good cholesterol, which is known to ward off heart disease – . . . dem sogenannten 'guten Cholesterin', von dem man weiß, daß es vor Herzerkrankungen schützt.

(c) Infinitive after adjective

Paragraph 2:
people who sip one to three drinks a day are about half as likely to suffer heart attacks as non drinkers are – daß die Wahrscheinlichkeit eines Herzinfarkts bei Menschen, die sich ein bis drei Gläschen pro Tag genehmigen, nur halb so hoch ist wie bei Nichttrinkern.

The choice of a noun ('Wahrscheinlichkeit') also contributes to the nominal style as a characteristic feature of the genre. The genitive structure ('Wahrscheinlichkeit eines Herzinfarkts') makes a verb ('suffer' – 'erleiden') redundant.

Alternative solution:
Die Wissenschaftler fanden folgendes heraus / Die Wissenschaftler kamen zu

der folgenden Erkenntnis: wer sich jeden Tag ein bis zwei Gläschen Alkohol genehmigt, hat gegenüber Abstinenzlern nur ein halb so großes Risiko, einen Herzinfarkt zu erleiden.

We have not opted for this alternative version because of similar structures in the sentences before (i.e. 'Herzinfarkt erleiden') and after (i.e. the use of a colon).

Paragraph 3:
most physicians are not ready to recommend a ritual happy hour – Aber die meisten Ärzte sind noch nicht bereit, den täglichen Alkoholgenuß prinzipiell für alle gutzuheißen.

Since infinitives can be used as attributes after adjectives in German as well, we have opted for this solution here as the appropriate structure.

(iii) -ing structures

Paragraph 3 (gerund in ST – indicative verb form in TT):
some doctors have begun recommending a daily drink for cardiac patients – . . . raten jetzt schon einige Ärzte ihren Herzpatienten, täglich ein Gläschen Alkohol zu trinken.

The gerund after the verb 'begin' indicates some intentional activity ('recommend') on the part of the agent. This activity is expressed by a full verb ('raten') in the main clause, with the temporal aspect (i.e. a beginning activity) expressed by the adverb 'jetzt', intensified by 'schon'.

Paragraph 3 (gerund ofter noun plus preposition in ST; noun in TT):
The risks of teetotaling – Die Gesundheitsrisiken bei Abstinenz . . .

(iv) Antonymic translations

Paragraph 3:
. . . – not to mention violent behaviour and traffic accidents. – . . . von Gewalttätigkeit und Verkehrsunfällen ganz zu schweigen.

'Ganz zu schweigen von' is a typical German idiomatic expression.

Paragraph 3:
Until there is evidence that the benefits of a daily dose of alcohol outweigh the risks . . . – Solange nicht eindeutig bewiesen ist, daß eine tägliche Dosis Alkohol eher nützt als schadet, . . .

In addition to the antonymic translation ('until there is' – 'solange . . . nicht'), there is a lexical problem: 'Outweigh' sometimes corresponds to 'überwiegen' or to 'schwerer wiegen als'. The main idea expressed in the text is that one thing ('benefits') is more important than the other ('risks'), or, that one thing is beneficial whereas the other is harmful. We have opted to express this contrast by a verbal structure with a comparative 'eher . . . als'. An alternative solution could have been ' . . . daß der tägliche Alkoholgenuß mehr Vorteile als Nachteile bringt' (for the choice of 'Dosis' see below, (ii) Lexical-semantic fields).

Text-specific translation problems

(i) Allusions, proverbs, puns

A specific translation problem is posed by the heading, in combination with the sub-heading. Headings typically function to attract the reader's attention. In the ST, this has been achieved by the semantic ambiguity in the title based on the word 'proof' (followed by the preposition 'against'), used for stylistic effects. Read together with the sub-headline, the ambiguity becomes clear, and the pun can be appreciated.

For the production of the TT, several factors have to be taken into account, for example, title conventions for the respective genre in the target culture, the relevance of the pun for the overall effect of the text, and the linguistic possibilities which the TL offers. Since in the target culture, too, the main function of the heading is to attract readers, finding some attractive heading could be advisable. On the other hand, as stated earlier, German popular-scientific texts, including those in *Der Spiegel*, are typically characterised by a neutral style. Due to this aspect, we have opted for a more neutral, but still attractive heading 'Promille für das Herz', and added the subject area as a sur-title (see previous comments under *(i) Title and sub-heading*).

An alternative and equally neutral solution could be 'Alkohol fürs Herz' (which was actually the title of an article in *Der Spiegel*, issue 51/1997, p. 20. In a later, lengthy article on the same subject in *Der Spiegel*, issue 38/1999, pp. 144 ff, the subject area is introduced as 'Herzinfarkt' above the main heading 'Schmackhafte Arznei', with the quotation marks indicating that this is taken from a quote, which is then used in full later in the text, and which is a quote by the Greek poet Plutarch).

Also, in German publications it is relatively frequent for popular-scientific texts to have a main title and a sub-heading (depending on in-house styles for respective publications). In this case, the main title is often a short and attractive one, and the sub-title is a kind of summary information of the content of the text. In such cases, i.e. for a different translation assignment, an appropriate solution could have been a combination of 'Promille für das Herz' as main title, followed by 'Positive Wirkung von mäßigem Alkoholgenuß nachgewiesen' as sub-heading.

If the translation assignment had asked for a more 'catchy' title, we could have tried to find some ambiguous heading, either one with some semantic ambiguity in German as well, or by formal means, e.g. 'Auf Ihr Wohl!?', i.e. the combination of exclamation mark and question mark.

In the first sentence of the ST, there is an allusion to a proverb or a saying ('An apple a day keeps the doctor/dentist away') which has been changed semantically and syntactically (i.e. turned into a question) and, in addition, there is rhythm and rhyme:

Paragraph 1:
Does a drink a day keep heart attacks away? – Trinkt Alkohol, und Ihr bleibt gesund – stimmt das?

A decision as to (a sound balance of) gain and loss has to be taken for the translation, based on the relevance of the information content, the structure of the proverb, and rhythm and rhyme. In this case, we have opted for a generalised formulation of the message, i.e. the link between alcohol and health, especially the health of the heart as a body organ (which has become clear from the

heading). We have also kept the question format, since the question indicates
that there is still uncertainty as to the truth of the proposition. Everything else,
however, i.e. allusion to a proverb, rhythm and rhyme, has been sacrificed or, in
other words, it has not been found relevant in view of the purpose of the TT.

For another text purpose, i.e. with a different translation assignment, it might
well be appropriate to have a more informal style and use proverbs, allusions,
puns, rhyme, etc. In such cases, the (re)search process could start by looking for
German proverbs and sayings that refer to alcohol and health. A useful starting
point would be looking up keywords (e.g. 'Gesundheit', 'gesund', krank',
'Krankheit', 'Herz', 'Doktor') in special dictionaries (such as Idiomatic Dictionaries, Dictionaries of Proverbs and Sayings) or reference books (useful ones are,
for example, Büchmann *Geflügelte Worte* for German, or *The Oxford Dictionary of
Political Quotations* for English). Possible solutions could then be, for example,
'Ein Gläschen in Ehren – auch für's Herz?' (i.e. a variation of the proverb 'Ein
Gläschen in Ehren kann niemand verwehren' – which we were thinking of using
for the TT here, but then rejected due to stylistic considerations), or 'Der Wein
erfreut des Menschen Herz' (a quotation from the Bible, and not chosen here
because the text reports on the effects of alcohol in general, not only of wine).

(ii) Lexical-semantic fields

The dominant lexical-semantic fields, which reflect underlying conceptual
frames, are related to medicine and health, and to research. These frames have
influenced the lexical choices for the TT, including specifications and generalisations (see also previous comments as to the specification of 'Gläschen (Alkohol)'
for 'drink'), e.g.:

Paragraph 3:
. . . some doctors have begun recommending . . . But most physicians . . . – . . .
raten jetzt schon einige Ärzte . . . Aber die meisten Ärzte . . .

A more specific word than 'Ärzte' is not necessary for the purpose of the TT. In
addition, the important message here is the contrast (some doctors recommend
but most physicians do not recommend), but it is not a question of different types
of doctors.

Paragraph 3:
The risks of teetotaling are nothing compared with the dangers . . . – Die
Gesundheitsrisiken bei Abstinenz sind unbedeutend im Vergleich zu den
Gefahren

The specification ('Gesundheitsrisiken') has also been determined by the
frame health, as has the choice of 'Dosis' (for 'dose') and the generalisation
'Rezept' (for 'a doctor's prescription'):

Paragraph 3:
. . . the benefits of a daily dose of alcohol . . . a doctor's prescription . . . – . . . eine
tägliche Dosis Alkohol . . . einem Rezept . . .

Political Texts: Introductory Comments

Political texts are also frequently translated, often by in-house translators employed by national governments, political parties and other institutions (and also by supranational institutions, e.g. the European Commission's Translation Service). 'Political text' is an umbrella term covering a variety of genres. The characterisation of a text as political can best be based on functional and thematic criteria. Political texts are a part and/or the result of politics, they are historically and culturally determined, and their topics are primarily related to politics, i.e. political activities, political ideas, political relations, etc. They fulfil different functions due to different political activities. Political discourse includes both inner-state and inter-state discourse, and it may take various forms. Examples are bilateral or multilateral treaties, speeches made by politicians at various occasions, contributions by members of parliament to a parliamentary debate, editorials or commentaries in newspapers, press conferences or interviews with politicians, or a politician's memoirs.

Political discourse is often of relevance not only for the specific culture of the text producer(s) but may be of interest for a wider audience. Since politics is more and more internationalised, translation, too, is becoming more and more important. Depending on the wider (political) context in which the texts are embedded, the addressees of a TT may be politicians, special interest groups, or the public at large. In some cases, the notions of source culture and target culture may even become blurred, as, for example, in the case of translations within the institutions of the European Union, where texts are translated both for internal use in committees and for use by national governments (see, for example, Dollerup, 1996; Koskinen, 2000). Very frequently, however, political topics are, by their very nature, of supra-national relevance, and texts are therefore also addressed to an audience outside the boundaries of the home state and the national language, even if only implicitly or potentially. In other situations, political texts are primarily addressed to an audience in a target culture, for example, speeches delivered by politicians during state visits abroad. In all these cases, translations are relevant. Translation-specific issues posed by political texts are varied and depend, above all, on the purpose of the text for political action. Only a few points will be discussed here (see also Schäffner, 1992a, b, 1995b, 1997a, c, d, 1998a).

Culture-specific Aspects

Due to their purpose, STs display different degrees of culture-boundedness. If the text was produced primarily for the source culture audience (e.g. an interview with a politician on home TV, a politician's speech during an electioneering campaign), addressees and text producer(s) share a large amount of background knowledge because they are members of the same community (see the notion of 'community co-membership' as basis of mutual knowledge in Clark & Marshall, 1981). The texts may then be highly culture-specific, and the translator is often faced with the question of how much implicit information of the ST will need to be made explicit for the TT addressees (see in particular the pragmatic translation strategies information change and explicitness change in Chesterman's (1997a) classification). Similarly, abbreviations and other short forms may be used to refer to institutions, people, historical events, etc. which are known to members of the source culture. The translator's decision will require an analysis of the translation brief, reflecting, in particular, on the knowledge and experience that can be expected of the TT readers.

With reference to political institutions of the source culture (e.g. names of political parties, government bodies, governmental institutions), there are usually standardised expressions in the target culture. Therefore, background texts that were published in the target culture can be consulted. However, these background texts are often written for the home audience and may use more explanatory discriptions in combination with a proper name (e.g. 'Spaniens Sozialistische Arbeiterpartei PSOE', 'die britische TV-Gruppe BSkyB', see also references to German institutions in the English media, e.g. 'the Bundestag, the second chamber of parliament'). If the TT addressees are politicians, such a more extensive label may not be required, and indeed not be appropriate.

Ideological Aspects

Political texts may also be characterised by a certain degree of sensitivity and/or a certain discretion for diplomatic reasons. This may be reflected in the choice of (ideologically relevant or problematic) topics, words and formulations. For example, some more general and, thus, vague expressions are often used in diplomatic discourse in the case of highly sensitive political issues. The translated texts often fulfil a different function in their target communities, and it cannot always be assumed that TT readers have all the background knowledge which the ST readers had. Thus, communication may be impaired if the surface structures are not interpreted in the light of their purpose. Consulting background texts that were published in the target culture may only be of limited use to translators here. Background texts are often written from a specific political and/or ideological position, which is reflected, for example, in the evaluative adjectives that are chosen to characterise those political institutions of the foreign culture in question. Therefore, a translator has to be extremely careful not to copy those evaluations, since they may be totally opposite to the evaluation expressed by the ST author. For example, in German newspaper texts we often come across evaluations such as 'die Terroristenorganisation IRA, militante Unionisten, radikale Republikaner'. Adding such evaluative phrases would be totally inappropriate in a translation of a text by a politician, as in our Sample Text 5. Newmark (1981: 149ff.) provides more examples of translation problems posed by abstract political concepts.

Genre Conventions and Personal Style

Political texts can belong to a variety of genres, and genre conventions apply as well. Such conventions are, for example in the case of a speech, ritual forms of addressing the audience or commissive speech acts. Some political texts belong to the argumentative text type and, in such cases, text-typological conventions apply (e.g. problem–solution structure, contrastive evaluations). Newmark (1981) says that speeches by politicians normally belong to what he calls 'authoritative texts'. He argues that such texts should not be changed when translated. However, such a prescriptive view does not cover all specific cases. A functionalist approach leaves the translator more leeway in his or her choices or, in other words, requires the expertise of the translator. The (re)search process undertaken by the translator may have to include a comparison to other speeches of a politician in order to find out whether there is a characteristic personal speech style, preferences in the use of terms and/or soundbites, or preferences in the use of specific rhetorical features (e.g. analogies, contrastive pairs, see also Beard (2000) on the characteristic features of the language of politics). If politicians quote other politicians or political documents, it may be necessary – depending on the purpose of the TT – to check authoritative translations in order to ensure consistency.

Sample Texts

The two sample texts in this volume reflect different communicative settings and, thus, different purposes. The authors of both texts are politicians, dealing with topics of different degrees of relevance for the

target culture. One text (Sample Text 5, a text by Gerry Adams, published in a national UK newspaper) is highly culture specific. It is
predominantly addressed to source culture addressees, who, due to
community co-membership, share vast knowledge of a social kind, i.e.
knowledge about the political situation and about the historical background of a sensitive issue. Therefore, there are a lot of culture-specific
references in the text. The translator is faced with the question of how
much of the culture-specific information that is implicit in the ST needs
to be made explicit for the TT addressees. In the second case, Sample
Text 6, we have a speech (more precisely, a commemorative address) by
a politician (John Major) that was originally addressed to an audience
outside his own home culture and also outside the culture of the TT (on
commemorative addresses, see also Sauer, 1996). Shared background
knowledge cannot immediately be taken for granted, which is already
reflected in the structure of the ST itself. Speeches of this kind have
usually a wider audience, including the immediate audience, but also
politicians at home and in other countries.

For the ST characterisation, reference can also be made to House's
(1997) model of translation quality assessment which consists of two
dimensions: (i) dimensions of the language user (with sub-categories
geographical origin, social class, and time); and (ii) dimensions of language use (with sub-categories medium, participation, social role
relationship, social attitude, and province; (see House 1997: 39)).
Applied to Sample Text 6, we have an asymmetrical role relationship
(i.e. John Major has authority over his addressees), he speaks in his position role as Prime Minister, in his situational role he is representing his
country at a commemorative ceremony abroad, and his relationship to
the addressees is characterised by diplomatic indirectness and evasive-
ness.

Due to the different constellations concerning the purpose of the TTs
in both cases and their addressees (general public in one case, politicians
in the other), different translation strategies were opted for, as will be
illustrated in the annotations (e.g. explications, additions, translator's
notes).

Bad Faith and Dishonesty

[1]

'If the focus remains on the past, the past will become the future and that is some-thing that no one can desire'.

[2]

In that one small sentence, Senator George Mitchell and his colleagues in their international report last month captured the heartfelt aspirations of the people of Ireland for a lasting peace. A peace process, any peace process, if it is to be meaningful and enduring, must tackle the issues at the heart of a conflict. Success, a permanent peace, depends upon a nego-tiated settlement firmly rooted in democracy and self-determination.

[3]

For nearly a year-and-a-half, the guns of war in Ireland were silenced. For several years in advance of that, myself, the SDLP leader John Hume, the former Irish Taoiseach Albert Reynolds and Irish-America painstak-ingly put together a package which persuaded the IRA to call a complete cessation of military operations on the basis that it would lead to an inclusive process of negotiations. Regrettably, both British government and unionist intransigence, and their refusal to engage imaginatively or flexibly with the peace process, prevented the urgent and necessary con-solidation of that process.

[4]

On Friday night last, the IRA ended its 18-month-long cessation. The announcement was greeted universally with disappointment and regret. At this time my thoughts are with the families of those killed and injured in the London explosion. I understand the pain they are going through. I speak from the personal experience of losing many relatives, friends and colleagues in 25 years of conflict. It may be difficult for some people to absorb this after what happened on Friday night, but the reality is that the IRA was undefeated when 18 months ago it took a very courageous decision to create what was universally recognised to be the greatest opportunity since partition to resolve the conflict and secure a lasting peace settlement. But the British government and the unionists erected one obstacle after another to frustrate every attempt to sit down around the negotiating table.

[5]

Inclusive negotiations, without preconditions or vetoes, is the key to advancing the peace process to a peace settlement. This was the commit-ment given by the two governments, publicly and repeatedly in the

run-up to the IRA cessation. This was the context in which the IRA in
August 1994 made their historic announcement. Since that time there
has not been one word of real negotiations. Nor is there even the prospect of negotiations beginning.

[6]

For 18 months Sinn Fein and others have been standing at the negotiating table waiting for the British government and the unionists to sit
down with the rest of us to agree a new and peaceful future. The cumula-
tive evidence points damningly to a British-government strategy locked
into a psychology of war; a mindset which demands victory over republicans rather than agreement and compromise. We have witnessed bad
faith and dishonesty, new preconditions, stalling, negativity and provocation. British bad faith and dishonesty which confounded those who
believed that the British would approach the peace process positively;
bad faith and dishonesty which was so barefaced that it surprised even
those of us with a healthy cynicism about British intentions.

[7]

We watched as Private Lee Clegg was released and then promoted, as
David Trimble marched through the nationalist community in
Garvaghy Road, as Irish prisoners were mis-treated in English jails, as
plastic bullets were fired at peaceful demonstrators, as RUC raids
wrecked nationalist homes. We pointed out, with growing desperation,
that there could be no negotiated peace without peace negotiations. That
without peace talks there was no peace process.

[8]

Yet Sinn Fein maintained its positive approach to the peace process. Last
November, the two governments established the twin-track approach.
The Irish Taoiseach, John Bruton, described it as the means to remove
preconditions to all-party talks. But when Senator George Mitchell's
international body issued its report, the British government dumped it,
reneging again on its commitment to begin all-party talks.

[9]

When the IRA announced its complete cessation of military operations,
it presented everyone, but particularly the two governments, with a
unique and unprecedented opportunity. The hope and expectation was
most effectively summed up by Seamus Heaney, when he described the
new situation as a 'space in which hope can grow'.

[10]

Our goal was to deepen that hope, to nourish it and to build a new beginning for all of the Irish people, and to open a new chapter in the
relationship between the Irish and British people. Regrettably that hope

was dashed on the rock of John Major's self-interest and the need for unionist votes at Westminster. While the IRA must bear the responsibility for its actions in London, the British government must bear its total responsibility for the collapse of the peace process. It has been guilty of criminal neglect.

[11]

One thing is clear: it is not possible to have peace in Ireland unless the British government is committed to that objective.

[12]

Clearly, the question now must be what happens next? In any conflict, there are two ways of bringing it to an end. Either one side defeats the other, seeks a surrender of the other, or we somehow find a way to rebuild the peace process and work for and secure a negotiated peace settlement.

[13]

Sinn Fein has repeatedly pointed out, with others, that the peace process could not stand still. If it was not moving forward it was always in grave danger of moving back. That has now happened.

[14]

But despite the tragic breakdown of the IRA cessation, Sinn Fein's peace strategy remains as the main function of our party. Our efforts to build an effective peace process must be redoubled.

[15]

What is clearly needed is a negotiated peace settlement. We needed that before Friday night's events; we need it more than ever now. How do we achieve that goal? In his submission to the Forum for Peace and Reconciliation in Dublin just before Christmas, F W De Klerk recommended that a peace process should be played like a one-day, and not a three-day, game of cricket. In other words, it is crucial that people sit down around the table and treat each other as human beings.

[16]

Peace in Ireland can only be achieved through honest dialogue and democratic negotiations based on equality. This is not a military problem. It is a political problem, which was militarised by the British. It needs a political solution; that can only be achieved by dialogue.

[17]

This is not a time for knee-jerk reactions or for slamming the door on dialogue. That will only aggravate the situation. People in Ireland and Britain want above all to see their governments and political representatives more positively and decisively to engage in dialogue to resolve our difficulties.

[18]

For Sinn Fein's part, we are firmly committed to democratic and peaceful means of resolving political issues and to the objective of an equitable and lasting agreement that can commend the consent and allegiance of all the people on the island of Ireland.

[19]

Sinn Fein also remains committed to the total disarmament of all armed groups and to the removal, forever, of all guns, republican, loyalist and British, from the political equation in Ireland. Sinn Fein's commitment to our peace strategy and to a lasting peace based on democratic negotiations remains absolute.

Gerry Adams is President of Sinn Fein.

Source: The Guardian, 12 February 1996, p. 14

Translation Assignment

The German weekly *Die Zeit* wants to report on the current (i.e. February 1996) political situation in the UK after the IRA had declared an end to the cease-fire. In order to have a politically well balanced account, they decide to include statements from various politicians. The text by Gerry Adams was chosen among others to be translated for subsequent publication in *Die Zeit*. The publication is intended for the end of February 1996. *Die Zeit*'s motivation for dealing with this topic was that with the UK being a member of the European Union, every development concerning Northern Ireland is of relevance and news-worthiness for Germany as well. The German text is to be submitted to the editors of *Die Zeit*.

Mißtrauen und Unehrlichkeit

Von Gerry Adams

[1]
'Wenn man immer nur auf die Vergangenheit blickt, dann wird die Vergangenheit zur Zukunft, und das kann niemand wünschen.'

[2]
In diesem einen Satz aus dem letzten Monat verabschiedeten Bericht der internationalen Kommission unter Leitung von US-Senator George Mitchell wird der tiefverwurzelte Wunsch des irischen Volkes nach dauerhaftem Frieden kurz und prägnant ausgedrückt. Ein Friedensprozeß, das heißt ein jeder Friedensprozeß, der zu einem ehrlichen und dauerhaften Ergebnis führen soll, muß sich mit den Problemen befassen, die dem Konflikt zugrundeliegen. Der Erfolg, ein dauerhafter Frieden, ist abhängig von einer Vereinbarung, die fest auf dem Boden der Demokratie und Selbstbestimmung steht.

[3]
Fast anderthalb Jahre lang haben die Waffen in Irland geschwiegen. Bereits zuvor haben ich selbst, der Parteichef der SDLP John Hume, der ehemalige irische Premier Albert Reynolds und Vertreter der Iren in den USA in jahrelanger anstrengender Arbeit ein Verhandlungspaket zusammengestellt, das die IRA zu einer vollständigen Einstellung der Kampfhandlungen veranlaßte, als Voraussetzung für einen Verhandlungsprozeß unter Beteiligung aller Seiten. Bedauerlicherweise hat die Unnachgiebigkeit sowohl der britischen Regierung als auch der pro-britischen Unionisten in Nordirland und ihre Weigerung, sich konstruktiv und flexibel am Friedensprozeß zu beteiligen, die dringend notwendige Konsolidierung dieses Prozesses verhindert.

[4]
Letzten Freitag (d.h. 9. Februar 1996 – Anm. d. Üb.) beendete die IRA ihren achtzehn Monate währenden Waffenstillstand. Diese Entscheidung wurde überall mit Enttäuschung und Bedauern aufgenommen. Meine Gedanken sind bei den Familien, deren Angehörige bei der Explosion in London getötet und verwundet wurden. Ich kann ihren Schmerz nachempfinden, da ich selbst viele Verwandte, Freunde und Mitstreiter in den 25 konfliktreichen Jahren verloren habe. Es mag manchen Menschen schwer fallen, das zu begreifen angesichts der Geschehnisse von Freitag nacht. Aber in der Tat war die IRA unbesiegt, als sie vor 18 Monaten die mutige Entscheidung traf, einen Waffenstillstand zu verkünden. Diese

Entscheidung wurde allgemein als die beste Chance seit der Teilung des Landes bewertet, den Konflikt beizulegen und eine Regelung für einen dauerhaften Frieden zu schaffen. Die britische Regierung und die Unionisten errichteten jedoch eine Hürde nach der anderen und machten damit jeglichen Versuch zunichte, die Plätze am Verhandlungstisch wieder einzunehmen.

[5]
Verhandlungen, an denen alle Seiten beteiligt sind, ohne jegliche Vorbedingungen und ohne Vetorechte, sind der Schlüssel zur erfolgreichen Weiterführung des Friedensprozesses bis hin zum Abschluß eines Friedensvertrages. Dazu hatten sich die britische und die irische Regierung vor dem IRA-Waffenstillstand wiederholt und öffentlich verpflichtet. Und in diesem politischen Klima traf die IRA im August 1994 ihre historische Entscheidung. Seitdem ist es jedoch zu keinem einzigen echten Verhandlungsgespräch gekommen. Es gibt nicht einmal das geringste Anzeichen eines Verhandlungsbeginns.

[6]
Achtzehn Monate lang haben Sinn Fein und andere Parteien am Verhandlungstisch gestanden und darauf gewartet, daß die britische Regierung und die Unionisten ihre Sitze einnehmen, um gemeinsam mit uns eine Zukunft in Frieden zu vereinbaren. Es gibt immer mehr erdrückende Beweise, die die Schlußfolgerung nahelegen, daß die britische Regierung in ihrer Verhandlungsstrategie der psychologischen Kriegsführung gefangen ist. Diese Strategie zielt auf einen Sieg über die republikanischen Iren, und nicht auf Vereinbarungen und Kompromisse. Wir haben Mißtrauen und Unehrlichkeit erfahren, immer neue Vorbedingungen, Verzögerungen, Ablehnung und Provokationen. Mißtrauen und Unehrlichkeit seitens der britischen Regierung, das sogar diejenigen irritierte, die der Meinung waren, daß die britische Regierung dem Friedensprozeß positiv gegenüberstehe. Mißtrauen und Unehrlichkeit in einer solchen Schamlosigkeit, daß sogar diejenigen von uns enttäuscht waren, die den Absichten der britischen Regierung immer mit gesundem Zynismus gegenübergestanden haben.

[7]
Wir haben stillschweigend zugesehen, als der Soldat Lee Clegg aus dem Gefängnis entlassen und danach befördert wurde (Lee Glegg war 1993 wegen Mord an einer jungen Irin zu lebenslänglicher Haft verurteilt worden, wurde jedoch 1995 entlassen. – Anm. d. Üb.). Wir haben zugesehen, als der UUP-Parteichef David Trimble an der Spitze einer protestantischen Prozession über die fast ausschließlich von Katholiken

bewohnte Garvaghy Road von Portadown marschierte, als irische Gefangene in englischen Gefängnissen mißhandelt wurden, als Plastikgeschosse auf friedliche Demonstranten abgefeuert wurden, und als die protestantischen Milizen Häuser der katholischen Nationalisten zerstörten. Wir haben mit wachsender Verzweiflung darauf hingewiesen, daß es ohne Friedensverhandlungen keine Friedensvereinbarung geben kann, und ohne Friedensgespräche keinen Friedensprozeß.

[8]
Trotz allem hat Sinn Fein seine positive Haltung gegenüber dem Friedensprozeß beibehalten. Im November 1995 haben die britische und die irische Regierung eine Doppelstrategie vereinbart, die der irische Premier John Bruton als ein Mittel zur Beseitigung aller Vorbedingungen für Allparteiengespräche bezeichnete. Aber als die internationale Kommission unter Leitung von Senator George Mitchell ihren Bericht veröffentlichte, hat die britische Regierung ihn abgelehnt und ist damit erneut ihrer Verpflichtung zum Beginn der Allparteiengespräche nicht nachgekommen.

[9]
Als die IRA die vollständige Einstellung ihrer Kampfhandlungen verkündete, hat sie allen, aber vor allem den beiden Regierungen, eine einzigartige und noch nie dagewesene Chance geboten. Die Hoffnungen und Erwartungen hat Seamus Heaney (irischer Poet, 1995 Nobelpreisträger für Literatur – Anm. d. Üb.) auf eindrucksvolle Weise zusammengefaßt, als er die neue Situation als 'Raum, in dem Hoffnung wachsen kann' beschrieb.

[10]
Unser Ziel war es, diese Hoffnung zu verstärken, sie gedeihen zu lassen und einen neuen Anfang für das ganze irische Volk zu ermöglichen. Wir wollten ein neues Kapitel in den irisch-britischen Beziehungen aufschlagen. Leider zerschellte diese Hoffnung an den eigennützigen Interessen John Majors, dem die Stimmen der irischen Unionisten für die Wahlen wichtig waren. So wie die IRA die Verantwortung für die Ereignisse in London zu tragen hat, muß auch die britische Regierung die volle Verantwortung für das Scheitern des Friedensprozesses tragen, den sie sträflich vernachlässigt hat.

[11]
Eines ist klar: Frieden in Irland ist nicht erreichbar, wenn die britische Regierung sich diesem Ziel nicht verpflichtet fühlt.

[12]
Jetzt stehen wir vor der Frage, wie es weitergehen soll. Es gibt zwei

Möglichkeiten, einen Konflikt zu beenden. Entweder besiegt die eine Seite die andere bzw. zwingt sie zur Kapitulation, oder wir finden einen Weg, um den Friedensprozeß wieder in Gang zu setzen und um auf den Abschluß einer dauerhaften Friedensvereinbarung hinzuarbeiten.

[13]

Sinn Fein hat, gemeinsam mit anderen, immer wieder betont, daß der Friedensprozeß nicht zum Stillstand kommen darf. Wenn er nicht vorangetrieben wird, dann besteht immer die große Gefahr des Rückschritts. Genau das ist jetzt eingetreten.

[14]

Dennoch bleibt auch trotz des bedauerlichen Zusammenbruchs des Waffenstillstands der IRA die Friedensstrategie weiterhin die Hauptaufgabe von Sinn Fein. Unsere Anstrengungen zur Gewährleistung eines effektiven Friedensprozesses müssen verdoppelt werden.

[15]

Was wir brauchen ist eine Friedensvereinbarung. Wir hätten sie eigentlich schon vor den Ereignissen vom Freitag voriger Woche gebraucht, und wir brauchen sie jetzt mehr als je zuvor. Wie können wir dieses Ziel erreichen? In seinem Bericht kurz vor Weihnachten an das Forum für Frieden und Versöhnung in Dublin, plädierte der Vize-Präsident Südafrikas, F.W. de Klerk, für zügige Verhandlungen bei Friedensprozessen. Es ist wichtig, daß sich alle beteiligten Seiten an den Verhandlungstisch setzen und einander als menschliche Wesen respektieren.

[16]

Frieden in Irland kann nur durch ehrlichen Dialog und durch demokratische Verhandlungen auf der Grundlage von Gleichberechtigung erreicht werden. Es handelt sich nicht um ein militärisches Problem, sondern um ein politisches Problem, das durch die britische Seite eine militärische Dimension erhielt. Es bedarf einer politischen Lösung, die nur durch Dialog erreicht werden kann.

[17]

Dies ist nicht die Zeit für eingefahrene Trotzreaktionen, und auch nicht die Zeit, Dialoge rundweg abzulehnen. Dadurch würde die Lage nur erschwert. Die Menschen in Irland und Großbritannien erwarten von ihren Regierungen und den politischen Repräsentanten vor allem, daß sie sich überzeugter und entschiedener für einen Dialog engagieren, um unsere schwierigen Probleme zu lösen.

[18]

Was Sinn Fein betrifft, so fühlen wir uns zutiefst demokratischen und friedlichen Mitteln zur Lösung der politischen Probleme verpflichtet.

Unser Ziel ist weiterhin eine gerechte und dauerhafte Vereinbarung, die die Zustimmung und Unterstützung aller Iren erhält.

[19]

Ebenso bleibt Sinn Fein der vollständigen Entwaffnung aller Gruppen verpflichtet, damit die Waffen für immer aus den politischen Kalku-lationen in Irland entfernt werden, ganz gleich ob es sich dabei um die Waffen der Republikaner, der Loyalisten oder der Briten handelt. Sinn Fein bleibt uneingeschränkt seiner Friedensstrategie und dem Ziel eines dauerhaften Friedens auf der Grundlage demokratischer Verhandlungen verpflichtet.

Gerry Adams ist Präsident von Sinn Fein, dem politischen Arm der Irisch-Republikanischen Armee.

Annotations

Translation Assignment

The German weekly *Die Zeit* wants to report on the current (i.e. February 1996) political situation in the UK after the IRA had declared an end to the cease-fire. In order to have a politically well balanced account, they decide to include statements from various politicians. The text by Gerry Adams was chosen among others to be translated for subsequent publication in *Die Zeit*. The publication is intended for the end of February 1996. *Die Zeit*'s motivation for dealing with this topic was that with the UK being a member of the European Union, every development concerning Northern Ireland is of relevance and news-worthiness for Germany as well. The German text is to be submitted to the editors of *Die Zeit*.

ST Characterisation

The ST was published in the daily *The Guardian* on 12 February 1996 as part of two pages of comment entitled 'The end of the cease-fire', next to an editorial, a cartoon, and other statements by politicians, e.g. MPs. *The Guardian*'s heading for these statements reads as follows: 'Following the IRA bomb, Gerry Adams accuses the British government of criminally neglecting the peace process. Below and right key players and commentators assess where politicians can go now.'

The fact that Gerry Adams was asked by *The Guardian* to write an article is remarkable in itself. Until the beginning of the cease-fire (autumn 1994), Gerry Adams was not allowed to make public statements in the UK media (in fact, whenever he was shown on TV-news, there was a voice-over by an actor).

The text is, first of all, a political text, written by a politician who is arguing not from his personal position but as the leader of his party, i.e. Sinn Fein, which is the political wing of the IRA. This is indicated by the use of 'we' or 'Sinn Fein'. The only personal comments are in Paragraph 4 (see the use of 'I' there). In a sense, Gerry Adams is also replying to the demands by the British and Irish governments that Sinn Fein disassociates itself from the deliberate bomb attack by its allies in the IRA as a precondition for resuming the negotiations.

The text was written in the knowledge that it is meant for publication in a leading daily newspaper with a liberal political orientation and a wide circulation, both at home and abroad. The text refers to the topical event, i.e. the bomb explosion, but this event is put in the wider political and historical context. The text is argumentative; on the one hand, it criticises the position of the British government and, on the other hand, it praises and defends the position of Sinn Fein and the IRA. This is clearly reflected in the choice of the nouns, verbs and adjectives for those positions, which are associated with specific connotations and evaluations (e.g. 'intransigence, refusal, prevent' *versus* 'courageous, historic announcement, firmly committed'). The text also contains a lot of references to the socio-cultural background, e.g. names of parties, organisations or institutions, and people. This is proof of the fact that the text was written with the home audience in mind who could be assumed to share a lot of common knowledge with the author, both about the specific event of the bombing and about the situation of Northern Ireland in general.

Political and Historical Background of the ST

The political situation in Northern Ireland is a very important but also a highly sensitive topic for the UK. After 18 months of cease-fire, which had been announced in September 1994, the IRA was responsible for a bomb explosion in London's Docklands (South Quay, on the evening of Friday, 9 February 1996). The period of the cease-fire had been characterised by debates about which parties would be allowed to take part in the negotiations to reach a peace settlement and under which conditions. The British government had repeatedly turned down Sinn Fein's wish to be part of the all-party talks or had set conditions, respectively, such as committing the IRA to decommission their arms. With the bomb in London, which took practically everybody by surprise, the IRA wanted to demonstrate its power in the hope that the British government would make concessions and let Sinn Fein be part of the talks.

TT Specification

The TT is intended for publication in *Die Zeit*, about two weeks after the ST was published. *Die Zeit* is a liberal paper. Its readers are mainly intellectuals. It is a weekly and the reports on political issues normally provide background information and/or additional comments.

The most important translation problems are due to the culture-specificity of the ST. The political situation of Northern Ireland is, although predominantly an internal problem of the UK, also of relevance at a multi- and international level, and therefore a topic which has regularly been covered in the international media. The German audience, i.e. the readers of *Die Zeit*, can therefore be assumed to have some general knowledge about the conflict in Northern Ireland (due to previous articles and news reporting), but they will probably not have sufficient knowledge to fully comprehend the references to more recent events in Northern Ireland. The decision of what to do in these cases, i.e. whether additional information would need to be given to account for differences in the background knowledge of the readers, or whether information can be deleted etc., needs to be based on the purpose of the TT and on the relevance of the micro-level information for the text as such. The identification of the text as a position paper by a representative of a political party makes it possible for the TT readers to clearly identify the referents of the personal pronouns. Genre conventions are not of high relevance here since the ST was written by an individual politician. In other words, the TT cannot be adapted to characteristic features of the style of German politicians.

(*Die Zeit* actually did publish a statement by Gerry Adams in its issue of 23 February 1996, however without any detailed information as to its origin. That text contained largely the same arguments as the current ST from *The Guardian*, but also additional ideas. It may well be that *Die Zeit* had asked Gerry Adams for an article and had it translated. As happens very often with translations commissioned by newspapers, the editors/journalists will do some kind of editorial work in preparing the final version of the text that will be published.)

Annotations

Pragmatic translation problems

These result mainly from the culture specificity of the topic of the ST. In the case of highly source-culture-specific texts, where the average reader of the TT will probably have less background knowledge than the reader of the ST, the translator has a number of options available to deal with these problems. For example, adding information, either (in brackets) in the text itself or as footnotes, deleting information, and using generalisations are all potential strategies. The translation assignment for the present text is the submission of a German text to the editors of *Die Zeit* who, as is common practice with news reports, will do some more editorial work in preparing the final version of the text that will be published. However, the client, or commissioner, of the TT (i.e. journalists and editors of *Die Zeit*) is not identical to the ultimate audience (i.e. the readers of the article in the newspaper). Because of the purpose of the TT, and also in awareness of the ultimate use of the text, it has been decided to provide explanations to culture-specific references, and, in the case of longer explanations, indicate them by adding *Anm. d. Üb.* (= Anmerkung des Übersetzers, i.e. translator's note – an example of the pragmatic translation strategy *visibility change* in Chesterman's (1997a) classification). Which of these will be adopted for the published version will be decided by the editors. In a published version, explanations are usually indicated by *Anm. d. Red.* (= Anmerkung der Redaktion, i.e. editors' note).

(i) Culture-bound terms and proper names

(a) Names and abbreviations of parties, organisations, and institutions

Sinn Fein: This proper name has become established in German texts reporting about Northern Ireland (sometimes with the spelling variation as Sinn Féin). Normally, an explanation is added, the most frequent one being: 'Sinn Fein, der politische Arm der Irisch-Republikanischen Armee'. In the TT itself, only 'Sinn Fein' is used, because we decided to provide a more specific characterisation of the author, Gerry Adams, at the very end of the text as 'Gerry Adams ist Präsident von Sinn Fein, dem politischen Arm der Irisch-Republikanischen Armee'.

A related problem is that of the gender to choose. In articles in the German press (for example in the German news magazine *Der Spiegel,* 2 December 1996, p. 158), Sinn Fein was treated as a masculine noun ('Sinn Fein und seine Wähler'). This gender has been adopted in Paragraphs 8 and 19:

Yet Sinn Fein maintained its positive approach – Trotz allem hat Sinn Fein seine positive Haltung . . . beibehalten.
Sinn Fein's commitment to our peace strategy – Sinn Fein bleibt uneingeschränkt seiner Friedensstrategie . . . verpflichtet. (The change from 'our' to 'sein' is motivated by the change in the syntactic structure.)

IRA: the ST uses only the abbreviation. As is the case with 'Sinn Fein', the abbreviation 'IRA' too has become established in German texts that report on Northern Ireland, so that it can be used in the TT. The gender is feminine because 'Armee' in the full name is a feminine noun:

Paragraph 3:
a package which persuaded the IRA . . . – ein Verhandlungspaket . . . , das die IRA . . . veranlaßte

Alternatively, the German version of the full name (i.e. 'Irisch-Republikanische Armee') could be added to the first textual occurrence of

'IRA', with the abbreviation added (in brackets or as an apposition). In the present text, however, this option has not been chosen because of the explication of Gerry Adams' position at the very end of the text.
SDLP:

Paragraph 3:
the SDLP leader John Hume – der Parteichef der SDLP John Hume

This stands for the Social Democratic Labour Party. In the TT, only the abbreviation is used because a number of politicians are listed, and the reference to the political party is obvious in the specification 'Parteichef'. In other contexts, particularly those that focus on the religious affiliation of the political parties, it might be appropriate to provide a further specification as, for example, 'katholische SDLP', or 'Katholikenpolitiker John Hume' (as was the case in an issue of *Der Spiegel*, 2 December 1996 p. 157); in other contexts the full name of the party might be required (with German newspapers often using the original English name in such cases).

RUC (the Royal Ulster Constabulary): this is the police force in Northern Ireland. In other contexts, a more specific version, such a 'Polizisten der Royal Ulster Constabulary' may be required, but such a higher degree of specificity is not necessary here. Therefore, a specification as 'protestantische Milizen' has been opted for due to the context (see also *(b) Names and labels for political and religious groupings* below):

Paragraph 7:
as RUC raids wrecked nationalist homes – als die protestantischen Milizen Häuser der katholischen Nationalisten zerstörten

Paragraph 15:
Forum for Peace and Reconciliation – Forum für Frieden und Versöhnung

The Forum was established in October 1994 with the specific purpose to pursue lasting peace and reconciliation among all the people of Ireland. It had a consultative role, and comprised representatives from most of the political parties. The label we used in the TT was found as the standard name in German journalistic texts for this body.

(b) Names and labels for political and religious groupings

Based on their political and / or religious orientation, parties and groupings are referred to by the general labels 'unionists' (mainly protestants, and those who want Northern Ireland to remain part of the UK, e.g. David Trimble's UUP), 'nationalists' (Catholics in Northern Ireland who want a closer cooperation with the Republic of Ireland and ultimately a united Ireland by means of negotiations, e.g. John Hume's SDLP), 'republicans' (those who want Northern Ireland to join the independent Republic of Ireland, also by military operations, e.g. the IRA). For a ST reader, these labels identify the referents. In the TT, specifications and / or additions have been opted for whenever the context did not provide sufficient information which would allow the reader to identify the political or religious orientation of the referents (as in Paragraph 3). In subsequent occurrences within the text, the shorter version is sufficient (as in Paragraphs 4 and 6):

Paragraph 3 (specification by addition of 'pro-britisch'):
both British government and unionist intransigence – Unnachgiebigkeit

sowohl der britischen Regierung als auch der pro-britischen Unionisten in Nordirland

Alternatively, 'Anhänger der Union mit Großbritannien' could be used as a specification of 'unionist'. Since a resulting syntactic structure in Paragraph 3 would have been 'Unnachgiebigkeit sowohl auf Seiten der britischen Regierung als auch auf Seiten der Anhänger der Union mit Großbritannien in Nordirland', it has been avoided for reasons of economy and style. The introduction of 'Unionisten' also allows its use without an explanation in the subsequent paragraphs, see:

Paragraphs 4 and 6:
the British government and the unionists – die britische Regierung und die Unionisten

Subsequent references to 'the British' in Paragraph 6 have been rendered as 'britische Regierung':

. . . that the British would approach the peace process positively; . . . British intentions – . . . daß die britische Regierung dem Friedensprozeß positiv gegenüberstehe. . . . Absichten der britischen Regierung . . .

In the ST, the reference to the government can be implied. In the TT, an explicitation has been opted for in order to avoid any misinterpretation in a political text on a sensitive issue (using 'die Briten' could be interpreted as referring to all the people, an inappropriate generalisation).

Paragraph 6 (specification):
a mindset which demands victory over republicans – Diese Strategie zielt auf einen Sieg über die republikanischen Iren

'Republikanische Iren' had been used in German texts before (e.g. in *Der Spiegel*, 2 December 1996, p. 158). 'Republikaner' would be an alternative expression in contexts where associations with the German extreme right-wing party of the same name can be excluded.

In contexts, where the dominant aspect is the religious affiliation of the political groupings, we have opted for specification. Referring to the religious affiliation is a common strategy in German newspaper texts (e.g. 'protestantische Unionisten', 'katholische Nationalisten' – see *Die Welt*, 14 February 1996).

In Paragraph 7, we opted for a specification of 'nationalist' as 'katholisch' to emphasize the contrast between Protestants and Catholics in this context (see also the comments in: *(ii) Political and historical background*).

Paragraph 7:
as David Trimble marched through the nationalist community in Garvaghy Road . . . . . . as RUC raids wrecked nationalist homes – als der UUP-Parteichef David Trimble an der Spitze einer protestantischen Prozession über die fast ausschließlich von Katholiken bewohnte Garvaghy Road von Portadown marschierte . . . als die protestantischen Milizen Häuser der katholischen Nationalisten zerstörten

Paragraph 18:
. . . removal, forever, of all guns, republican, loyalist and British – Waffen der Republikaner, der Loyalisten oder der Briten

An alternative solution could have been a specification as 'der protestantischen Milizen' instead of 'Loyalisten' to account for a lack in the background knowledge of the TT readers. Our choice to use three nouns was made for stylistic reasons and was based on the assumption that the TT readers will be able to interpret the referent of 'Loyalisten' due to the previous context.

Paragraph 3:
Irish-America – Vertreter der Iren in den USA

The formulation in the ST is a reference to the large group of Americans who claim some Irish heritage and who are politically active within the USA and outside. We opted for a specification here.

(c) Names and titles of individual people
Paragraphs 2 and 8: Senator George Mitchell, the former US Senator, chaired the political talks between the various political parties in Northern Ireland, and drafted the settlement agreement. Politicians from other countries were also involved in these negotiations, but they are unspecified and only expressed by 'Senator George Mitchell and his colleagues' (Paragraph 2), and 'Senator George Mitchell's international body' (Paragraph 8). In the first occurrence, a specification has been used, both to account for differences in readers' background knowledge and to comply with conventions of the target culture and the genre:

Paragraph 2:
Senator George Mitchell and his colleagues – internationale[n] Kommission unter Leitung von US-Senator George Mitchell

The second occurrence (Paragraph 8) refers back to the commission and its report, therefore the addition of 'US' is not needed once more:

when Senator George Mitchell's international body issued its report – als die internationale Kommission unter Leitung von Senator George Mitchell ihren Bericht veröffentlichte

In other journalistic texts, the name alone would be sufficient in repeated occurrences (e.g. 'internationale Kommission unter Leitung von George Mitchell', or 'die Mitchell-Kommission'), but with the author here being a politician himself, reporting about a sensitive political issue, the use of the full title and name is part of political etiquette and style.

Paragraphs 3 and 8:
the former Irish Taoiseach Albert Reynolds – der ehemalige irische Premier Albert Reynolds
The Irish Taoiseach, John Bruton – der irische Premier John Bruton

'Taoiseach' is the Irish equivalent to the British 'Prime Minister', usually referred to in German as 'Premier' or 'Premierminister'.

Paragraph 9 (specification/addition in translator's note to account for potential lack in background knowledge):
Seamus Heaney – Seamus Heaney (irischer Poet, 1995 Nobelpreisträger für Literatur – Anm. d. Üb.)

Paragraph 15 (specification):
F W De Klerk – der Vize-Präsident Südafrikas F W De Klerk

The former President of South Africa (until 1994) was instrumental in dismantling the Apartheid system. After freeing the ANC leader Nelson Mandela from prison he opened negotiations with the ANC. The first democratic elections resulted in the ANC's victory and a coalition government. In 1993, Mandela and de Klerk shared the Nobel Peace Prize. When De Klerk addressed the Forum for Peace and Reconciliation, he did so in his (then) function as Executive Deputy President of the Republic of South Africa. We have opted for a specification because of the implicit reference to the peace process in South Africa in the ST. This specification is also in line with the conventions in German newspaper texts, where names of politicians are usually combined with their titles and/or positions.

(ii) Political and historical background and source culture-specific events and traditions

The whole of Paragraph 7 lists some events which had happened shortly before and whose political significance is obvious to the ST readers. The first reference (to Lee Clegg) concerns a specific event which had caused considerable debate all over the UK. The second reference concerns one of the annual marches by members of the Protestant Orange Order. David Trimble, the leader of the Protestant Ulster Unionist Party (UUP), marched at the head of the parade that forced its way through Garvaghy Road in a besieged Catholic neighbourhood from Portadown to Drumcree. In 1996, when the ST was produced, Trimble had a reputation as a hard-liner, ill-disposed to compromise, who for a long time had refused to join in any negotiations with Sinn Fein.

In order for the TT readers to understand this paragraph fully with all its implications, extensive explanations would be necessary, which, however, would be detrimental to the genre. Moreover, such extensive explanations would not be necessary for the specific purpose of the TT. In other words, the necessary degree of differentiation (Hönig & Kussmaul, 1982) does not require further details. Therefore, a compromise has been opted for, keeping the additions to a minimum. In the case of David Trimble and Garvaghy Road, the references to the leader of a protestant party and a catholic residential area are important for the TT audience to understand that sensitive issue. Although we have added the abbreviation for the party (UUP), the full name 'Ulster Unionist Party' (original English names are frequently used in German newspapers) has not been deemed necessary here, since the focus is on the contrast between protestant and catholic. In the reference to Lee Clegg, a translator's note has been added, providing the background information:

> We watched as Private Lee Clegg was released and then promoted, as David Trimble marched through the nationalist community in Garvaghy Road, ... – Wir haben stillschweigend zugesehen, als der Soldat Lee Clegg aus dem Gefängnis entlassen und danach befördert wurde (Lee Glegg war 1993 wegen Mord an einer jungen Irin zu lebenslänglicher Haft verurteilt worden, wurde jedoch 1995 entlassen. – Anm. d. Üb.). Wir haben zugesehen, als der UUP-Parteichef David Trimble an der Spitze einer protestantischen Prozession über die fast ausschließlich von Katholiken bewohnte Garvaghy Road von Portadown marschierte, ...

Alternative solutions:
. . . an der Spitze einer protestantischen Prozession durch die katholische Siedlung an der Garvaghy Road von Portadown marschierte, . . .
or:
an der Spitze einer protestantischen Prozession über die Garvaghy Road in der katholischen Enklave / in dem katholischen Stadtviertel von Portadown marschierte, . . .

There are some more references in the ST that require activation of culture-specific background knowledge and/or of knowledge about the historical development of Ireland. In these cases, specifications, additions, or translator's notes have been considered most appropriate strategies:

Paragraph 3 (specification / addition):
an inclusive process of negotiations – Verhandlungsprozeß unter Beteiligung aller Seiten

Various political parties have been listed before in this paragraph, so that our decision has been motivated by inferencing processes from the context, in addition to the reliance on our background knowledge. We have then opted for lexical consistency in the subsequent occurrence in Paragraph 5, and in Paragraph 8 for a contextual synonym ('all-party talks' – 'Allparteiengespräche').

Paragraph 4 (specification in the TT by addition to account for different background knowledge of the TT readers):
the greatest opportunity since partition – die beste Chance seit der Teilung des Landes

Paragraph 5 (specification):
the two governments – die britische und die irische Regierung

The definite article signals to the ST reader that the referents are known, either because they have been introduced in the text before, or because they are common knowledge for author and addressees and can thus be activated. In this case in Paragraph 5, we have a combination of these two possibilities. In the ST, there has been an explicit reference to the government of the UK shortly beforehand, and there has also been a reference to the Irish Taoiseach, which allows for the interpretation that the governments of the UK and of the Republic of Ireland are meant. Both governments sponsored the peace talks. Since this knowledge cannot be assumed for the TT readers, a specification has been used. In the second occurrence of this phrase in Paragraph 8, the specification has been repeated in the TT because of the context (the two paragraphs before comment only on activities of the British government). But when 'the two governments' occurs again immediately in the following Paragraph 9, no specification is necessary in the TT since the referents can easily be established, therefore 'den beiden Regierungen' has been used.

Paragraph 8 (specification):
the two governments established the twin-track approach. – haben die britische und die irische Regierung eine Doppelstrategie vereinbart

Paragraph 9:

the two governments – den beiden Regierungen

Paragraph 10 (specification and generalisation):

. . . John Major's self-interest and the need for unionist votes at Westminster. – . . . eigennützigen Interessen John Majors, dem die Stimmen der
irischen Unionisten für die Wahlen wichtig waren.

ST readers have the relevant background knowledge about Westminster
(which denotes the Parliament, i.e. the House of Commons, in a metonymic relationship) and the voting procedure there (i.e. Northern Ireland being a part of
the UK, the parties send their representatives to the Parliament. The unionist
parties supported Major's Conservative Party). For the TT readers, a specification ('irische Unionisten') has been used to account for their different
background knowledge. Due to the intended purpose of the TT, we have opted
for a generalisation ('für die Wahlen'), although a specification ('britisches
Unterhaus') could have been an alternative solution. There is also no need to
specify John Major any further.

(iii) Other culture specific references

Paragraph 15 (generalisation):

. . . FW De Klerk recommended that a peace process should be played like a
one-day, and not a three-day, game of cricket. – plädierte . . . F W de Klerk für
zügige Verhandlungen.

Cricket is not a highly popular game in Germany, and the rules as well as the
length of a game are not widely known. Since cricket functions only as a metaphorical comparison to the negotiations (see the immediately following
sentence: 'In other words, it is crucial that people sit down around the table and
treat each other as human beings.'), any reference to cricket can safely be
avoided in favour of a more general formulation in the TT (an alternative, and
equally metaphorical, version could be 'daß der Friedensprozeß nicht auf die
lange Bank geschoben werden darf'). Indeed, keeping the reference to cricket
(e.g. by a more literal translation such as 'verglich er den Friedensprozeß mit
einem Cricketspiel und argumentierte, daß ein solches Spiel nur einen Tag lang
gespielt werden soll statt drei Tage') would introduce comprehension problems for the TT readers and would require additional information about the
rules of the game. We have also opted against keeping the cricket comparison
and adding a translator's note, and then leave the final decision to the editors,
because the editors, too, are in all probability not familiar with the rules of the
game.

Since the following sentence repeats the same proposition in a different way,
and due to the generalisation in the TT, there is no need to account for 'in other
words'.

(iv) Situation of TT

The TT is intended for publication in *Die Zeit*, about two weeks after the ST
was published. Therefore, the translator has to take a decision as to how to deal
with references to time and place. Due to the translation assignment, it can be
assumed that the editorial process will include specifications as to the topical
event, i.e. the bomb explosion on 9 February 1996 in the London docklands.

Therefore, references to time and place have not been specified or adapted, but translator's notes were added when deemed appropriate:

Paragraph 4:
On Friday night last, . . . in the London explosion. – Letzten Freitag (d.h. 9. Februar 1996 – Anm. d. Üb.) . . . bei der Explosion in London . . . (alternatively, in den Londonder Docklands)

It may be difficult for some people to absorb this after what happened on Friday night – angesichts der Geschehnisse von Freitag Nacht

In Paragraphs 10 and 15, there are repeated references to the bomb attack, albeit in a rather general way. The identification of the specific event that is referred to is no problem for a reader, neither for a reader of the ST nor of the TT. Therefore a more general formulation has been used in the TT too. Moreover, the author of the text, having to account for that negative event, probably uses those more general and vague expressions deliberately.

Paragraph 10:
the actions in London – die Ereignisse in London

Paragraph 15:
before Friday night's events – vor den Ereignissen vom Freitag voriger Woche

Paragraph 8 (specification):
Last November, the two governments established the twin-track approach. – Im November 1995 haben die britische und die irische Regierung eine Doppelstrategie vereinbart

A temporal specification has been opted for because of the reference to a political decision with which the ST readers are familiar (see the definite article: 'the twin-track approach'; it has been changed into the indefinite article 'eine' because the TT readers are not familiar with its content).

Paragraph 15:
. . . just before Christmas – kurz vor Weihnachten

There is no need for a further specification (e.g. as 'Weihnachten 1995' or 'Weihnachten letzten Jahres') due to the topic and the purpose of the TT.

Intercultural translation problems

(i) Genre conventions

(a) Positioning of the name of the author
In the ST, the name of the author is given in the additional information to the text that has been provided by the editors and which has been placed immediately before the text, and it also includes information about the other articles that are devoted to the bomb explosion and published on that page. At the end of the ST, there is a specification as to Gerry Adams' position ('Gerry Adams is President of Sinn Fein'). In the TT, amendments have been made to comply with the genre convention in Die Zeit, i.e. to conventions of the genre comment article:

'Von Gerry Adams' has been put at the beginning of the text, immediately after the title. Additional information about the author has been put at the end: 'Gerry Adams ist Präsident von Sinn Fein, dem politischen Arm der Irisch-Republikanischen Armee.'

(b) Changes in syntactic structures to comply with genre conventions of the target culture

Paragraph 2:
In that one small sentence, Senator George Mitchell and his colleagues in their international report last month captured the heartfelt aspirations ... – In diesem einen Satz aus dem letzten Monat verabschiedeten Bericht der internationalen Kommission unter Leitung von US- Senator George Mitchell wird der tiefverwurzelte Wunsch . . . kurz und prägnant ausgedrückt.

A complex pre-modification structure, as is common in German exemplars of that genre (particularly concerning references to time, place, instruments) has been introduced in the TT. One change in the syntactic structure normally calls for additional changes. Here the change from an active structure 'captured' to a passive structure 'wird ausgedrückt', which, in turn, goes hand in hand with a modulation, i.e. the ST subject 'Senator George Mitchell and his colleagues' (semantic relation: agentive) has become a genitive object (semantic relation: originator, source).

(ii) Number

Political parties and other groupings can be treated either as a collective whole or as a collection of individuals. In the second case, verbs in plural form are used, or plural pronouns as co-referents. Due to the German conventions, a singular form has been chosen:

Paragraph 5:
This was the context in which the IRA in August 1994 made their historic announcement. – Und in diesem politischen Klima traf die IRA im August 1994 ihre historische Entscheidung.

This is the only occurrence in the ST where a pronoun in plural form was used for IRA (see: 'the IRA ended its 18-month-long cessation' in Paragraph 4).

(iii) Conceptual metaphors

Source culture and target culture sometimes employ identical, but sometimes different conceptual metaphors to refer to certain phenomena. This has consequences for the translator's strategies.

Paragraph 2 (change of metaphorical expression):
issues at the heart of a conflict – Probleme[n] . . . die dem Konflikt zugrundeliegen

The metaphor of the heart is frequently used in English texts to express the idea of centrality. In German texts, this idea is sometimes expressed metaphorically by 'Kern', but hardly by 'Herz' (see 'das Herzstück einer Sammlung' as the most precious thing, i.e. in a positive sense). In the context of problems and conflicts, there is, by implication, a logical link between the centrality of an issue and its origin and subsequent growth. Growth is conceptualised in (at least) two ways, the one is outwards, growing from a centre in all directions, resulting in outer layers, the other one is upwards, growing from the bottom into a vertical direction. If we want to find the origin of a problem, we go back to the starting point, either by going to the centre, or to the bottom. Both in the English and in the German language there is evidence of these conceptual metaphors, e.g. 'a core issue, a fundamental problem, zum Kern der Sache vorstoßen, einer Sache auf den Grund gehen'.

These reasoning processes become evident in the TT solution. The result of the translation strategy is a different perspective in the TT, i.e. where the ST focuses on the centre, the TT focuses on the bottom, but we are still within the same conceptual macro-domain, i.e. origin of a conflict. Alternative solutions, all operating in the same conceptual domain, could have been:

Probleme, die den Kern des Konflikts bilden
Probleme, die die Wurzel des Übels sind

Our decision has also been motivated by the fact that 'conflict' is a key concept (see *(iii) Textual lexical-semantic fields and key concepts*).

Paragraph 12 (change of conceptual metaphor):
to rebuild the peace process – um den Friedensprozeß wieder in Gang zu setzen

Construction metaphors are very common in political texts. In German texts, they are more typically used with objects that denote something concrete or static (e.g. 'ein vereintes Europa bauen'). Since a process is something dynamic, a movement metaphor has been used. The conceptual metaphor *Politics is Movement Along a Path* (see Lakoff & Johnson, 1980) is also highly typical of conceptualising politics, as illustrated in Paragraph 13:

Paragraph 13:
Sinn Fein has repeatedly pointed out, . . . that the peace process could not stand still. If it was not moving forward it was always in grave danger of moving back. – Sinn Fein hat, . . . immer wieder betont, daß der Friedensprozeß nicht zum Stillstand kommen darf. Wenn er nicht vorangetrieben wird, dann besteht immer die große Gefahr des Rückschritts.

Since the movement metaphor is a fairly common metaphor in both English and German political discourse (see Chilton & Lakoff, 1995; Schäffner, 1996), it has been preserved in the TT, thus also ensuring coherence to Paragraph 12. Nouns have been chosen predominantly for the TT ('Stillstand, Rückschritt') instead of verbs as in the ST ('stand still, moving forward, moving back') for stylistic reasons. A passive structure has been opted for in the TT ('wenn er nicht vorangetrieben wird') instead of the syntactically possible active structure 'wenn er nicht vorankommt', since a logical agent (a driving force) is implied. An alternative version, which also elaborates the movement metaphor, could be ' . . . dann läuft er ständig Gefahr, zurückgerollt zu werden'.

The past tense in the second sentence of the ST ('was') is an indication of the ongoing reported speech, signalled by the verb 'pointed out'. In German, reported speech is often indicated by subjunctive verb forms. Subjunctives could have been used here as well ('dürfe . . . Wenn er nicht vorangetrieben werde, dann bestehe . . . '). However, since indicative verb forms for reported speech are also very common in German, especially when there is a verb of speaking/ reporting (as is the case here: 'betont') and since the speaker is still the same (i.e. IRA), we have opted for the indicative forms.

Interlingual translation problems

(i) Infinitive structures in the ST

(a) Infinitive after passive structure
In Paragraph 4 in the ST, the infinitive indicates a semantic relation of specification. In the TT, the specification is expressed by 'als':

> Paragraph 4:
> ... what was universally recognised to be the greatest opportunity ... – Diese Entscheidung wurde allgemein als die beste Chance ... bewertet, ..

(b) Infinitive after noun
Infinitive as expressing a semantic relation of intention or of consequence, as in the following paragraphs:

> Paragraph 4:
> But the British government and the unionists erected one obstacle after another to frustrate every attempt ... – Die britische Regierung und die Unionisten errichteten jedoch eine Hürde nach der anderen und machten damit jeglichen Versuch zunichte, ...

In the ST, the interpretation as consequence is determined by the context and the background knowledge. The TT uses an indicative verb form, the two propositions are linked, and the consequence is expressed by 'und damit'.

> Paragraph 17 (intention expressed by 'um ... zu ... ' in TT):
> ... engage in dialogue to resolve our difficulties. – ... für einen Dialog engagieren, um unsere schwierigen Probleme zu lösen.

(c) Object plus infinitive in ST
We have opted for a subordinate clause in the TT, as in the following examples:

> Paragraph 4 (ST) for + object + infinitive, with the object as agent of the infinitive construction; TT: subordinate clause introduced by 'daß', agent as grammatical subject, indicative verb form):
> ... waiting for the British government and the unionists to sit down ... – ... darauf gewartet, daß die britische Regierung und die Unionisten ihre Sitze einnehmen

Paragraph 17 (ST, object plus infinitive as complex sentence object, with the object as agent of activity expressed by an infinitive; TT: subordinate clause introduced by 'daß', addition of the pronoun 'sie' to express the agent [subject of the subordinate clause], which is co-referent to 'Regierungen und politische Repräsentanten', which has been moved to the main clause in the TT to allow for a closer coherent link to 'erwarten'):

People in Ireland and Britain want above all to see their governments and political representatives more positively and decisively to engage in dialogue to resolve our difficulties. – Die Menschen in Irland und Großbritannien erwarten von ihren Regierungen und den politischen Repräsentanten vor allem, daß sie sich überzeugter und entschiedener für einen Dialog engagieren, um unsere schwierigen Probleme zu lösen.

Alternative solution:
Die Menschen in Irland und Großbritannien erwarten vor allem, daß sich ihre Regierungen und die politischen Repräsentanten überzeugter und entschiedener für einen Dialog engagieren, um unsere schwierigen Probleme zu lösen.

(d) Infinitive as attributive after noun in the ST
Although the German language does allow for infinitive structures in such cases, nouns have been opted for in the TT for stylistic reasons, as in the following paragraphs:

Paragraph 8:
. . . reneging again on its commitment to begin all-party talks. – . . . ist damit erneut ihrer Verpflichtung zum Beginn der Allparteiengespräche nicht nachgekommen..

The grammatically equally correct version 'ist damit erneut ihrer Verpflichtung, Allparteiengespräche zu beginnen, nicht nachgekommen' has been avoided because its complexity results in two verbs following each other and, thus, in a stylistically less elegant structure.

Paragraph 14:
Our efforts to build an effective peace process must be redoubled. – Unsere Anstrengungen zur Gewährleistung eines effektiven Friedensprozesses müssen verdoppelt werden.

(e) Infinitives as subject complements
In the TT, we have opted for the addition of 'es' as place holder (dummy subject):

Paragraph 10:
Our goal was to deepen that hope, to nourish it and to build . . . – Unser Ziel war es, diese Hoffnung zu verstärken, sie gedeihen zu lassen und . . . zu ermöglichen,

(f) Infinitive as attribute after adjective
Paragraph 11 (ST) infinitive as attribute after adjective in an impersonal structure and with the proposition relating to some future state, which is linked to a condition ('unless'); TT: object in ST as subject in TT, adjective as subject complement, the reference to the conditional future state expressed by 'erreichbar' (the suffix '-bar' indicating the semantic feature of possibility):

it is not possible to have peace in Ireland unless . . . – Frieden in Irland ist nicht
erreichbar, wenn . . . nicht . . .
Alternative solutions to express the conditional future state of affairs:
Frieden in Irland ist nicht möglich, wenn . . . nicht . . . (i.e. adjective alone)
or: Es kann keinen Frieden in Irland geben, wenn . . . nicht . . . (i.e. modal
verb)

(ii) -ing structures

(a) verbal nouns ending in -ing
For verbal nouns ending in -ing, we have used nouns in the TT, as in the following paragraphs:

Paragraph 6:
We have witnessed . . . stalling, . . . – Wir haben . . . erfahren, . . . Verzögerungen, . . .

Paragraph 10:
Our goal was . . . to build a new beginning for all of the Irish people, . . . – Unser
Ziel war es, . . . einen neuen Anfang für das ganze irische Volk zu ermög-
lichen, . . .

(b) Gerund after abstract nouns + preposition as object or as attribute
In the TT we have normally opted for a nominal structure (frequently a verbal
noun) or verbal structure (often an infinitive structure):

Paragraph 4 (indicative verb form in TT):
I speak from the personal experience of losing many relatives – . . . da ich
selbst viele Verwandte, . . . verloren habe.

Paragraph 5 (verbal noun in TT):
Inclusive negotiations, . . . is the key to advancing the peace process to a peace
settlement. – Verhandlungen, an denen alle Seiten beteiligt sind, . . . sind der
Schlüssel zur erfolgreichen Weiterführung des Friedensprozesses bis hin
zum Abschluß eines Friedensvertrages.

Paragraph 12 (verb in infinitive structure in TT):
In any conflict, there are two ways of bringing it to an end. – Es gibt zwei
Möglichkeiten, einen Konflikt zu beenden.

Paragraph 13 (noun in TT):
If it was not moving forward it was always in grave danger of moving back. –
Wenn er nicht vorangetrieben wird, dann besteht immer die große Gefahr
des Rückschritts.

Paragraph 17 (verb in infinitive structure in TT):
This is not a time . . . for slamming the door on dialogue. – Dies ist nicht die
Zeit . . . Dialoge rundweg abzulehnen.

Paragraph 18 (verbal noun in TT):
. . . we are firmly committed to democratic and peaceful means of resolving
political issues – . . . so fühlen wir uns zutiefst demokratischen und friedlichen Mitteln zur Lösung der politischen Probleme verpflichtet.

(c) Present participle

Paragraph 5 (ST, participle as attribute after the noun; TT, compound noun):
Nor is there even the prospect of negotiations beginning. – Es gibt nicht
einmal das geringste Anzeichen eines Verhandlungsbeginns.

Present participles as attributes are frequently put before the noun (see 'a
lasting peace', 'with growing desperation'), placing them after the noun may be
done for stylistic reasons.

In the following two cases, the present participle indicates attendant circumstances, i.e. expressing one action which accompanies another one. In the TT,
the two verbs (in indicative form and identical tense) have been linked by
'und':

Paragraph 4:
For 18 months Sinn Fein and others have been standing at the negotiating
table waiting . . . – Achtzehn Monate lang haben Sinn Fein und andere
Parteien am Verhandlungstisch gestanden und darauf gewartet, daß . . .

Paragraph 8
the British government dumped it, reneging again on its commitment to
begin all-party talks. – hat die britische Regierung ihn abgelehnt und ist
damit erneut ihrer Verpflichtung zum Beginn der Allparteiengespräche nicht
nachgekommen.

(iii) Idiomatic expressions
Idiomatic expressions may reflect quite different origins and motivation in
source and TL. Based on their function in the text, i.e. both at the micro- and
macro-level, we have opted for using idiomatic expressions or for generalisations in the TT, e.g.

Paragraph 17:
This is not a time for knee-jerk reactions or for slamming the door on dialogue. – Dies ist nicht die Zeit für eingefahrene Trotzreaktionen, und auch
nicht die Zeit, Dialoge rundweg abzulehnen.

(iv) Other translation solutions that are related to the linguistic structures
Some of the transpositions and modulations have not been caused by differences in the linguistic systems of source and TL but rather by contextual and / or
stylistic considerations. We will only mention a few examples:

Changes in relationship between implicit and explicit information
Paragraph 4 (omission and explication of implicit semantic relations in the
ST):
I understand the pain they are going through. I speak from the personal expe-

rience of losing many relatives, friends and colleagues in 25 years of conflict. – Ich kann ihren Schmerz nachempfinden, da ich selbst viele Verwandte, Freunde und Mitstreiter in den 25 konfliktreichen Jahren verloren habe.

The immediacy of the pain and the author's empathy has been rendered by combining the two sentences into one for the TT, thus making the implicit semantic relation of cause and effect explicit by 'da' and by the choice of the verb ('nachempfinden').

Paragraph 12 (implication in TT):
. . . or we somehow find a way to rebuild the peace process and work for and secure a negotiated peace settlement. – . . . oder wir finden einen Weg, um den Friedensprozeß wieder in Gang zu setzen und um auf den Abschluß einer dauerhaften Friedensvereinbarung hinzuarbeiten.

The change in the syntactic structure has been motivated by the following considerations: the ST links two propositions (expressed by the verbs 'work for' and 'secure'), with 'and' indicating a semantic relation of temporal sequence (i.e. in 'work for a negotiated peace settlement', 'peace settlement' is the aim of the action, to be achieved by means of negotiations, whereas in 'secure a negotiated peace settlement', 'peace settlement' is a fact, a result of negotiations, which needs to be made permanent). These different semantic relations have been expressed in the TT by different syntactic structures, i.e. 'Abschluß' for the aspect of aim, and 'dauerhafte Friedensvereinbarung' for the aspect of permanence. The semantic relation of temporal sequence is implied by 'dauerhaft'.

Text-specific translation problems

(i) Heading/title
The heading, 'Bad faith and dishonesty', is taken from the text itself (and it was probably chosen as a heading by the editors, and not by the author himself). This procedure is common for news texts. 'Bad faith' and 'dishonesty' are key concepts in the text. They are introduced in a sentence in Paragraph 6 and taken up again twice in the two following sentences. Lexical consistency is therefore required in the TT too:

> We have witnessed bad faith and dishonesty, . . . British bad faith and dishon-
> esty . . . bad faith and dishonesty . . . – Wir haben Mißtrauen und Unehrlich-
> keit erfahren, ... Mißtrauen und Unehrlichkeit seitens der britischen
> Regierung . . . Mißtrauen und Unehrlichkeit . . .

(ii) Contrastive evaluations
The text is argumentative in that, on the one hand, it criticises the position of the British government and, on the other hand, it praises and defends the position of Sinn Fein and the IRA. This is clearly reflected in the choice of the nouns, verbs and adjectives for those opposing positions, attitudes, and actions. There are, on the one hand, words with negative connotations for the position of the British government and the unionists: 'psychology of war, bad faith and dishonesty, stalling, negativity and provocation, criminal neglect, intransigence,

refusal, erect obstacles, renege on commitment, self-interest'. On the other hand, there are words with positive connotations for the position of the IRA and Sinn Fein: 'courageous decision, greatest opportunity, historic announcement, positive approach to the peace process, unique and unprecedented opportunity, hope, commitment'.

For the TT too, we made every effort to make sure that these opposing connotations are obvious in the lexical choices (e.g. on the one hand, 'psychologische Kriegsführung, sträflich vernachlässigt, Unnachgiebigkeit', and, on the other hand, 'mutige Entscheidung, positive Haltung gegenüber dem Friedensprozeß, verpflichtet'). These oppositions and contrasts as a characteristic feature of the text were also the motivation for the addition of 'stillschweigend' in paragraph 7:

Paragraph 7:
We watched as . . . – Wir haben stillschweigend zugesehen, als . . .

The adverb has been added to emphasise the textual contrast between (partly violent) actions by one party but restraint by another party. An alternative solution could be 'wir haben tatenlos zugesehen'.

(iii) Textual lexical-semantic fields and key concepts
There are two dominant and interrelated frames (lexical-semantic fields) in the text, a negotiation frame and a peace frame. Both frames are reflected in the lexical-semantic fields that structure the text:

negotiated settlement, process of negotiations, negotiating table, real negotiations, honest dialogue, democratic negotiations, agreement, compromise, all-party talks – vereinbarte Regelung, Verhandlungsprozeß, Verhandlungstisch, echtes Verhandlungsgespräch, ehrlicher Dialog, demokratische Verhandlungen, Vereinbarung, Kompromisse, Allparteiengespräche

lasting peace, permanent peace, peace process, peace settlement, negotiated peace, peace negotiations, peace talks, peace strategy – dauerhafter Frieden, Friedensprozeß, Friedensvertrag, Friedensvereinbarung, Friedensverhandlungen, Friedensgespräche, Friedensstrategie

The presence of these frames accounts for specifications, e.g. the addition of 'Verhandlung-' in the TT:

Paragraph 3:
put together a package – haben . . . ein Verhandlungspaket zusammengestellt

Paragraph 6:
a British-government strategy locked into a psychology of war – in ihrer Verhandlungsstrategie der psychologischen Kriegsführung gefangen

The political reason for the need to achieve peace by means of negotiations, i.e. the military conflict in Northern Ireland, is not equally dominant. It is rarely explicitly referred to (e.g. 'conflict, guns were silenced, cessation of military operations, disarmament, removal of guns'), although it implicitly contributes to the structure of the text. The key concept is 'conflict', a more general and thus vague description, as is characteristic of diplomatic discourse, especially in the case of highly sensitive political issues. For the TT, an equally general 'Konflikt' has therefore been opted for:

Paragraph 1:
the issues at the heart of a conflict – Probleme . . ., die dem Konflikt zugrundeliegen

Paragraph 4:
25 years of conflict – 25 konfliktreiche[n] Jahren

Paragraph 4:
. . . to resolve the conflict – . . . den Konflikt beizulegen

Paragraph 12:
In any conflict, there are two ways of bringing it to an end. – Es gibt zwei Möglichkeiten, einen Konflikt zu beenden.

The presence of a conflict-frame, or a fighting-frame, in the ST allows for a translation strategy of implicitation in the TT, and it also determines lexical choices:

Paragraph 3 (implicitation by compression, i.e. due to the context, 'Waffen' implies that they are meant for fighting):
the guns of war in Ireland were silenced – haben die Waffen in Irland geschwiegen

Paragraph 19 (frame-determined lexical choice / implicitation):
Sinn Fein also remains committed to the total disarmament of all armed groups . . . – Ebenso bleibt Sinn Fein der vollständigen Entwaffnung aller Gruppen verpflichtet, . . .

'Entwaffnung aller Gruppen' implies that they are armed, with 'guns' ('Waffen') following immediately in the sentence (a repetition of the identical word stem – 'Entwaffnung aller bewaffneten Gruppen' – would sound clumsy). 'Abrüstung' is more typically used in the context of the weapon arsenals of states (i.e. a slightly different frame).

Paragraph 4 (frame-determined lexical choice):
I speak from the personal experience of losing many relatives, friends and colleagues . . . – . . . da ich selbst viele Verwandte, Freunde und Mitstreiter . . . verloren habe.

'Mitstreiter' has been opted for as most appropriate for a frame of 'fighting'. The formally similar 'Kollegen' is typically used in the context of work, i.e. people with whom one is working together in employment. For a group of people working together on a specific project but only temporarily, it is more common in German texts to focus on the collective rather than the individuals. This accounts for the strategy adopted in the other occurrence of 'colleagues' in the ST, where, moreover, 'colleague' is not part of the fighting-frame:

Paragraph 2:
George Mitchell and his colleagues – internationale Kommission unter Leitung von US-Senator George Mitchell

In addition to 'negotiation' and 'peace', 'commitment' is another key concept. It is used in particular to structure the final part of the ST. The repetition of the key concept in the last two paragraphs (with variation between verb and noun) functions as a stylistic means to emphasise the message. The same cohesive device of lexical repetition (only verbs for stylistic reasons), has been used in the TT to achieve the same effect, i.e. emphasis:

Paragraphs 18 and 19:
For Sinn Fein's part, we are firmly committed . . . Sinn Fein also remains committed . . . Sinn Fein's commitment . . . – Was Sinn Fein betrifft, so fühlen wir uns . . . verpflichtet. . . . Ebenso bleibt Sinn Fein . . . verpflichtet, . . . Sinn Fein bleibt uneingeschränkt . . . verpflichtet.

(iv) Quotations from other texts

Paragraph 1:
'If the focus remains on the past, the past will become the future and that is something that no one can desire'. – 'Wenn man immer nur auf die Vergangenheit blickt, dann wird die Vergangenheit zur Zukunft, und das kann niemand wünschen.'

This sentence has been taken from the report by Senator George Mitchell's committee, as said in the next sentence. Should an authorised German translation of this document exist, the version given there would need to be used in official German documents. Since the existence of an authorised German translation is rather unlikely (due to the nature of the issue) and in view of the purpose of the TT (i.e. for the press), the sentence has been translated by us.

Paragraph 9:
. . . Seamus Heaney, when he described the new situation as a 'space in which hope can grow'. – . . . Seamus Heaney . . . , als er die neue Situation als 'Raum, in dem Hoffnung wachsen kann' beschrieb.

It is fairly common in argumentative texts that politicians, intellectuals or other public figures are quoted when they have commented on political developments. Such quotes function as rhetorical devices in that they add weight to an argument. In this particular case, we need not bother to check whether that quote had been translated before. It would be different should one of Heaney's poems have been quoted, for which an authorised German translation might exist.

Address by John Major, Prime Minister of the United Kingdom of Great Britain and Northern Ireland, on the occasion of the Warsaw Uprising 50th Anniversary Commemoration, at Warsaw, Krasinski Square, 1 August 1994

[1]

Mr President,

Ladies and Gentlemen,

[2]

This year and next, in many of the countries of Europe, we commemorate the inspiring but tragic events of 50 years ago.

We honour the bravery and sacrifices of those who fought in a just cause.

And we celebrate half a century of peace and reconciliation.

Your guests from abroad today, Mr President, embody that spirit of reconciliation.

[3]

I am proud to represent my country here. Britain stood with Poland in 1939. Your Government then found refuge in London. Through the War, Poles and Britons served side by side in the air, on land and at sea.

[4]

It was in a broadcast from London that the world first heard of the 1944 Uprising. Winston Churchill declared that Britain felt itself responsible for the restoration to the Poles of their own country.

[5]

He was deeply moved by what he called 'the martyrdom of Warsaw.' In his History of the War, he later gave a moving account of the struggle by Warsaw's people to save their city, of their hardships, and of how they saw it almost totally destroyed.

[6]

Britain tried to help, though no country could do enough.

During the fighting 186 sorties were flown from British bases on the other side of Europe, in the south of Italy. Of those that reached Warsaw, one in three of those aircraft did not return.

[7]

Earlier today I laid a wreath at the spot where one of them crashed, in the Skaryszewski Park, just across the river. I met there veterans from Britain and other Commonwealth countries and allies who risked their lives so that Poland might be free. They are a living witness to the values which bind our free nations. So are thousands of Polish veterans who live in Britain today.

[8]

The Uprising was Poland's decision to assert her sovereignty and independence. But Poland's tragedy was that the outcome of the war and of the Uprising left her under another occupation. It took 45 years fully to reassert your country's independence and sovereignty.

[9]

After the destruction of Warsaw in 1944, the people of Warsaw and of Poland rebuilt this capital city. The world can see your success and your pride: in the Old Town, the Royal Castle, the streets and stones of Warsaw.

[10]

Now you grapple with another challenge: to rebuild your economy and society after the devastation of Communism. With your other friends, we are taking part in the rebuilding of Poland: through trade, through investment, through transfer of know-how.

[11]

And now a democratic and independent Poland has made the sovereign decision to apply for membership in the European Union. I welcome that. Europe will not be complete without Poland as a full member of our Union. The values of the Union are the values for which your citizens and ours fought and died 50 years ago.

[12]

This evening we remember and honour those dead. We honour also all those who lived through that time of pity and terror. Soldiers and civilians. Men and women; and children, symbolized by the statue of the little boy soldier with the helmet. The brave people of Warsaw.

[13]

Let the past be an inspiration for the future, for the new challenges of peace and freedom.

[14]

Perhaps those who were not there cannot fully understand. But we can stand beside you now, as we stood then; and offer thanks and honour.

[15]

In the words of one of the last broadcasts from Warsaw in October 1944:
'Immortal is the nation that can muster such universal heroism. For those who have died have conquered, and those who live on will fight on, will conquer and again bear witness that Poland lives when the Poles live.'

Source: Texts according to *Materials and Documents* 7–8/1994 from the Polish Ministry of Foreign Affairs, published by Polska Agencja Informacyjna, Warsaw (pp. 9–10)

Translation Assignment

The German government would like to have translations of all addresses spoken at the Commemoration ceremony on the occasion of the 50th Anniversary of the Warsaw Uprising, Warsaw, on 1 August 1994. These addresses are meant to be studied and analysed by government advisors.

John Major

Premierminister des Vereinigten Königreichs von Großbritannien und Nordirland

[1]
Herr Präsident, meine Damen und Herren,
[2]
In diesem und dem kommenden Jahr gedenken wir in vielen Ländern Europas der Ereignisse vor 50 Jahren, die inspirierend, aber dennoch tragisch waren.
Wir ehren den Mut und die Opferbereitschaft derjenigen, die für eine gerechte Sache kämpften.
Und wir feiern 50 Jahre des Friedens und der Versöhnung.
Herr Präsident, Ihre Gäste aus aller Welt, die heute hier anwesend sind, verkörpern diesen Geist der Versöhnung.
[3]
Ich bin stolz darauf, mein Land hier zu repräsentieren. Großbritannien stand 1939 an der Seite Polens. Ihre Regierung fand damals Zuflucht im Exil in London. Während des Krieges kämpften Polen und Briten Seite an Seite, in der Luft, zu Land und zur See.
[4]
Durch eine Rundfunksendung aus London hörte die Welt zum ersten Mal vom Warschauer Aufstand 1944. Winston Churchill erklärte, daß sich Großbritannien dafür verantwortlich fühle, daß die Polen ihr Heimatland zurück bekämen.
[5]
Er war zutiefst berührt von dem 'Martyrium Warschaus', wie er es nannte.
In seinem Werk über den Zweiten Weltkrieg berichtete er in bewegenden Worten über den Kampf der Warschauer Bevölkerung um die Rettung ihrer Stadt, über ihre Not, und darüber, wie sie die fast vollständige Vernichtung ihrer Stadt miterleben mußten.
[6]
Großbritannien versuchte zu helfen, aber kein Land konnte genug tun.
Während der Kämpfe wurden von britischen Stützpunkten in Süditalien aus 186 Einsätze geflogen. Von den Flugzeugen, die Warschau erreichten, kehrte jedes dritte nicht zurück.

169

[7]
Heute morgen habe ich im Skaryszewski Park auf der anderen Seite des
Flusses einen Kranz niedergelegt, genau an der Stelle, wo eines dieser
Flugzeuge abgestürzt war. Dort habe ich Kriegsveteranen aus Großbritannien, anderen Commonwealth-Staaten und von den Alliierten
getroffen. Sie alle setzten ihr Leben aufs Spiel, für ein freies Polen. Sie
verkörpern auf anschauliche Weise die Werte, die unsere freien Völker
verbinden, genauso wie die Tausende von polnischen Veteranen, die
jetzt in Großbritannien leben.
[8]
Mit der Entscheidung für den Warschauer Aufstand machte Polen
seinen Anspruch auf Souveränität und Unabhängigkeit geltend. Aber es
war Polens tragisches Schicksal, daß es nach dem Krieg und dem
Aufstand erneut unter Fremdherrschaft geriet. Nach 45 Jahren konnte
nunmehr die Unabhängigkeit und Soveränität Ihres Landes endgültig
wieder hergestellt werden.
[9]
Nach der Zerstörung Warschaus im Jahre 1944 hat die Bevölkerung
Warschaus und ganz Polens ihre Hauptstadt wieder aufgebaut. Die
ganze Welt kann sehen, was Sie erreicht haben und worauf Sie stolz sein
können: die Altstadt, das Königsschloß, die Straßen und Gassen, ein
jeder Stein in Warschau.
[10]
Jetzt stehen Sie vor einer erneuten schweren Herausforderung: dem
Wiederaufbau Ihrer Wirtschaft und Ihrer Gesellschaft nach den
Verheerungen durch das kommunistische System. Gemeinsam mit
anderen Freunden Ihrens Landes beteiligen wir uns am Wiederaufbau
Polens, durch Handel, Investitionen und Transfer von Know-how.
[11]
Und jetzt hat Polen als ein demokratischer und unabhängiger Staat die
souveräne Entscheidung getroffen, sich um Mitgliedschaft in der
Europäischen Union zu bewerben. Ich begrüße diesen Entschluß.
Europa wäre unvollständig ohne Polen als vollwertiges Mitglied
unserer Union. Die Werte der Europäischen Union sind dieselben
Werte, für die die Menschen unserer beiden Länder vor 50 Jahren
gekämpft haben und gestorben sind.
[12]
Heute abend gedenken wir der Toten und ehren sie. Wir ehren auch all
jene, die die Zeit der Not und des Terrors überlebt haben, Soldaten und
Zivilisten, Männer und Frauen, und auch die Kinder, die in dem
Denkmal durch den kleinen Soldaten mit dem Helm verewigt sind, die
gesamte mutige Bevölkerung von Warschau.

[13]

Möge die Vergangenheit eine Inspiration für die Zukunft sein, für die neuen Herausforderungen von Frieden und Freiheit.

[14]

Wer das Geschehen der Vergangenheit nicht selbst miterlebt hat, kann das alles vielleicht nicht ganz verstehen. Aber wir können auch jetzt wieder an Ihrer Seite stehen, genauso wie damals, und unseren Dank und unsere Ehrerbietung aussprechen.

[15]

Um es mit den Worten einer der letzten Rundfunksendungen aus Warschau vom Oktober 1944 zu sagen:

'Unsterblich ist die Nation, die solch einen großen Heldenmut hervorgebracht hat. Diejenigen, die gestorben sind, haben gesiegt, und diejenigen, die leben, kämpfen weiter, siegen und beweisen erneut, daß Polen noch nicht verloren ist.'

Annotations

Translation Assignment

The German government would like to have translations of all addresses spoken at the Commemoration ceremony on the occasion of the 50th Anniversary of the Warsaw Uprising, Warsaw, on 1 August 1994. These addresses are meant to be studied and analysed by government advisors.

ST Characterisation

The ST is a political speech by John Major, the Prime Minister of the UK, that was delivered on the occasion of a ceremony held on 1 August 1994 in Warsaw to commemorate the 1944 Warsaw Uprising. Altogether, there were 11 addresses by representatives of their respective states or governments. All the addresses were embedded in a larger event, which also included parades, the laying of wreaths, and musical performances. The addresses were subsequently translated into Polish and into English by the Polish Ministry of Foreign Affairs and published.

John Major represented the United Kingdom at the ceremony in Warsaw. His speech reflects the characteristic features of a commemorative address (see Sauer, 1996), both in content and in form, i.e. references to the immediate public ceremony, to the event that is commemorated (usually some event which happened in the past and which is of importance to the country), and formal aspects of the genre such as ritual opening, declarative and commissive speech acts (especially promises). Due to the functional and situational constraints of the address (e.g. limited time, consideration of political alliances in the past and at present, political diplomacy), some of the sensitive political issues are not explicitly spelled out.

The original addressees of the speech were the Polish people, notably those present at the ceremony. However, as is generally the case with political texts, there is always a wider audience in the sense that some statements are (also) meant for the home audience or other countries. This aspect of multiple audiences is further complicated by the changed political constellations after the end of the Cold War. Therefore, Major's task was to find a balance between references to the allies and partners of the past and those of the present and the future, and he did this by frequently avoiding any explicit references to former political enemies and by using abstract nouns.

Political and Historical Background of the ST

The 1944 Warsaw Uprising

On 1 August 1944, the citizens of Warsaw started a revolt against the German oppressor. The main reason for the choice of this day was the fact that the Russian Red Army had by then reached the city. The Warsaw citizens had thought that, together with the support of the Red Army, they had a realistic chance of overthrowing the German command. However, the Red Army refused to support the Uprising, and within a few weeks, the Germans succeeded in suppressing the revolt, killing and wounding thousands of Warsaw's citizens. Immediately after regaining full command of the city, the Germans

172

deported the citizens from Warsaw and started to destroy the city systematically.

The 1994 Commemoration

On the evening of 1 August 1994, a ceremony took place in Warsaw to commemorate the 50th anniversary of the Uprising. The Polish President Lech Walesa intended it to be an occasion for reconciliation and for establishing new political relationships. For that reason, he had invited the former allies and liberators (UK, USA, France), the former enemy (Germany), as well as Russia which became the official liberator of Poland, but (at least according to the Poles) had betrayed the Poles during the Warsaw Uprising, and, moreover, had become the new oppressor of Poland from 1945 onwards.

Why is the topic a sensitive issue for the UK?

The UK was one of the allied powers during the Second World War and, as such, one of the winners of the war. The UK had supported Poland during the Second World War (e.g. the Polish government worked in exile in London). In speaking about the bilateral relations between the UK and Poland, Major focuses on the UK's support during the War and at the present and in future. He does not speak about the relations during the Cold War. Major does also not explicitly mention the other key players in the Uprising, i.e. Germany and Russia (more exactly, the Soviet Union), neither does he mention their roles for Poland during the Cold War. He rather implicitly refers to them, which is motivated by the changed political alliances: the Soviet Union no longer exists, and Russia today (more precisely, in 1994, at the time of speaking) is a democratic state (or at least on the path to democracy). Britain and Germany have for decades been partners, e.g. in NATO and in the EU. In other words, former enemies are today's friends and partners. The past is a delicate and sensitive topic, also for Britain, although more so for Germany and Russia. At a ceremonial commemoration, criticism is not opportune, offence is not appropriate to the occasion. Therefore Major uses more general references and abstract nouns, i.e. structures which are linked to presuppositions and implicatures.

TT Specification

The TT is intended for internal use by the German government, specifically for detailed content analysis by government advisors. The change in the addressees (i.e. the German government is the immediate audience of the TT compared to having been part of the indirect multiple audience of the ST) is related to a change in the textual function: from a commemorative address functioning for external communication (ST) to a document functioning for internal communication (TT). In other words, ST and TT are in a heterofunctional relationship (see Nord, 1997). The TT addressees are familiar with the events, i.e. the Warsaw Uprising, the commemoration ceremony, and with the underlying political relations between the states and governments involved. They are interested in finding out how Major dealt with the sensitive and delicate political issues. The TT therefore has to be what Nord (1993, 1997) calls documentary translation. This means, for example, that ST statements that require activation of background knowledge, e.g. knowledge about the Polish history in general and about the Warsaw uprising in particular, or statements in which the referents are implied or presupposed, would not be made more specific or explicit in the TT. Due to the genre and the purpose of the TT, footnotes would also not be considered appropriate.

The most important translation problems are text-specific ones.

Annotations

Pragmatic translation problems

(i) Proper names

Since ST and TT addressees share the relevant political background knowledge, there are no serious pragmatic translation problems. The proper names in the ST are the names of the countries (Britain, Poland), of groupings of countries (Commonwealth countries, European Union), of towns (London, Warsaw), and references to places in Warsaw (Skaryszewski Park, the Old Town, the Royal Castle). In the ST, the standard English proper names are used (and not the Polish ones, a strategy sometimes applied by politicians when speaking at public occasions in their host country). Naturally, in the TT, the standardised German proper names are used: 'Großbritannien, Polen, die Commonwealth-Staaten, London, Warschau, Skaryszewski Park, die Altstadt, das Königsschloß'.

The only person mentioned by name is Winston Churchill, British Prime Minister during the Second World War. Again, there is no need for a specification in the TT due to its purpose and addressees. There is a reference to one of his books, i.e. to the six volumes of *'The Second World War'*. Since in this particular context, there is no need for an exact bibliographical reference, the TT too gives a more general reference; however, adding the specification 'Zweiter Weltkrieg', and indicating by 'Werk' that a book is referred to, but not providing the exact title of the German version (the exact title for the volumes as published in German being *Der Zweite Weltkrieg*):

> Paragraph 5:
> In his History of the War, ... – In seinem Werk über den Zweiten Weltkrieg ...

The commemorated event is referred to by 'the (Warsaw) Uprising', which can also be considered as a proper name (note the capital letter), i.e. a proper name for a culture-specific event (the culture being Poland, the Polish name for this event is 'powstanie Warszawskie'). In German, this event is referred to as 'Warschauer Aufstand'. Since also the German President Roman Herzog gave an address at the 1994 commemoration ceremony, the terminological consistency is an important feature to be kept in mind by the translator. Throughout the TT, the full proper name 'Warschauer Aufstand' has therefore been used.

The other historical event referred to is the Second World War, which in the ST is only referred to by 'war' or 'War' (there is no consistency as to capitalisation). Due to the purpose of the text and its situational context, 'war' can readily be identified as referring to the Second World War. The same holds true for the TT, so that, again, no specification is required (but see previous comments on Churchill's volume).

(ii) Situation of ST and TT

The ST being an address that was delivered at a specific ceremony, there are references to the immediate place and time of the ceremony, which cannot be changed bearing the purpose of the TT in mind: 'this year' – 'in diesem Jahr' (Paragraph 2), 'today' – 'heute' (Paragraphs 2 and 7), 'here' – 'hier' (Paragraph 3), 'this evening' – 'heute abend' (Paragraph 12).

In Paragraph 7, 'earlier today' is not further specified (the ceremony took place in late afternoon/evening, see 'this evening' in Paragraph 12). In the TT, we have opted for a specification ('heute morgen'), which has been motivated by general encyclopaedic knowledge (e.g. diplomatic protocol of state visits). The second 'today' refers more generally to the present time. Therefore, the less specific 'jetzt' has been preferred for the TT, although 'heute' or 'heutzutage' would have been equally appropriate:

Paragraph 7:
... thousands of Polish veterans who live in Britain today. – ... Tausende von polnischen Veteranen, die jetzt in Großbritannien leben.

There are also temporal references to the commemorated event, i.e. the Uprising, although the formulations are usually a bit more general and may, thus, also refer to the whole time of the Second World War. Again, since the TT addressees are interested in seeing how the ST reflected the event, any temporal adjustments would be inappropriate to the TT purpose, see:

Paragraphs 2 and 11:
50 years ago – vor 50 Jahren

Paragraphs 3 and 14:
then – damals

In the ST, there is a reference to a detail in the monument in the square where the ceremony was held. Since the immediate referent is no longer visible to the TT addressees, an explanatory specification has been added in the TT:

Paragraph 12:
... and children, symbolised by the statue of the little boy soldier with the helmet – ... und auch die Kinder, die in dem Denkmal durch den kleinen Soldaten mit dem Helm verewigt sind,

Intercultural translation problems
There are certain conventions of the genre commemorative address. Those referring to content and style (e.g. references to the commemorated event, diplomatic style) are discussed in respect to pragmatic and text-specific translation problems. More formal conventions concern the ritual opening and addressing the host.

(i) Ritual opening
Ritual openings of speeches are forms with which to address the audience, in this case:

Mr President, Ladies and Gentlemen, – Herr Präsident, meine Damen und Herren,

Alternative structures that are equally ritual openings, are 'Sehr geehrter Herr Präsident, meine Damen und Herren', 'Herr Präsident, meine sehr verehrten Damen und Herren'. A comma at the end has become the conventional form, and has replaced the older form of putting an exclamation mark after forms of address (e.g. 'Sehr geehrter Herr Präsident, meine Damen und Herren!').

(ii) Addressing the host
Repeatedly addressing the host (and/or the audience) during a commemorating address is a characteristic feature of the genre. Apart from being a sign of politeness, it normally signals the beginning of a new idea (a new macrostructure) and thus also functions as a cohesive device. In German texts (as in English ones), such forms are usually found at the beginning of a sentence. They can also be moved to other positions, mainly for stylistic reasons (e.g. for emphasis), as is the case in the ST. We have opted for front position in the TT in conformity with genre conventions and for syntactic reasons (i.e. the need for a relative clause):

Paragraph 3:
Your guests from abroad today, Mr President, . . . – Herr Präsident, Ihre Gäste aus aller Welt, die heute hier anwesend sind, . . .

(iii) Commemorative address as spoken discourse
The ST shows some characteristic features of spoken language, although it is usual diplomatic practice that such addresses are produced in writing, since after delivery at the respective event they will be kept for the records, will be distributed to the media, etc. However, since the primary purpose of the speech is its oral delivery, this aspect has an influence on the structure and the style of the text, for example, the use of short, and/or grammatically incomplete sentences. Due to the changed function of the TT (i.e. it is intended as a document for internal use by the German government), this textual feature has not always been kept for the TT; in other words, the TT has been produced with its purpose as a written document in mind, see:

Paragraph 11 (specification in TT as more characteristic of written political discourse):
And now a democratic and independent Poland has made the sovereign decision to apply for membership in the European Union. I welcome that. – Und jetzt hat Polen als ein demokratischer und unabhängiger Staat die souveräne Entscheidung getroffen, sich um Mitgliedschaft in der Europäischen Union zu bewerben. Ich begrüße diesen Entschluß.

Paragraph 12 (one complex sentence in TT for list of groups):
We honour also all those who lived through that time of pity and terror. Soldiers and civilians. Men and women; and children, symbolised by the statue of the little boy soldier with the helmet. The brave people of Warsaw. – Wir ehren auch all jene, die die Zeit der Not und des Terrors überlebt haben, Soldaten und Zivilisten, Männer und Frauen, und auch die Kinder, die in dem Denkmal durch den kleinen Soldaten mit dem Helm verewigt sind, die gesamte mutige Bevölkerung von Warschau.

(iv) Empathy
Another characteristic feature of a commemorative address is that the speaker expresses empathy and solidarity with the audience, recounting the hardship

they had to go through during the event in the past and which is being commemorated. Such a feature of empathy is the reason for the following translation
strategies:

Paragraph 5 (transpositions and modulations):
... he later gave a moving account of ... and of how they saw it almost totally
destroyed – ... berichtete er in bewegenden Worten über ... und darüber, wie
sie die fast vollständige Vernichtung ihrer Stadt miterleben mußten

We have opted for a verbal structure ('berichtete') since verbs express
empathy more forcefully. This transposition goes hand in hand with a modulation in that the evaluation ('moving') has been transferred from the result
('account') to the manner ('in bewegenden Worten' or, alternatively, 'berichtete
er auf bewegende Weise'). The more specific 'miterleben' has been opted for in
order to focus on the process aspect of 'destroy', thus also contributing to the
element of empathy.

Narrative structures too can function to express empathy, for example in
Major's recounting of his meetings with veterans. We have opted for the use of
the present perfect as grammatical tense to focus on the immediacy of the events:

Paragraph 7:
Earlier today I laid a wreath ... I met there veterans ... – Heute morgen habe
ich ... einen Kranz niedergelegt, ... Dort habe ich Kriegsveteranen ... getroffen.

Empathy can also be highlighted by expansions and additions, see:

Paragraph 9 (addition):
The world can see your success and your pride: in the Old Town, the Royal
Castle, the streets and stones of Warsaw. – Die ganze Welt kann sehen, was
Sie erreicht haben und worauf Sie stolz sein können: die Altstadt, das
Königsschloß, die Straßen und Gassen, ein jeder Stein in Warschau.

Adding 'ganze', 'und Gassen' and 'ein jeder Stein' contributes to the narrative
structure and also complies with the emphatic element of the commemorative
address.

(v) Speech acts

Speech acts (see Searle, 1969), preferably declarative and commissive speech
acts (e.g. promises), can frequently be found in commemorative addresses. Most
of the speech acts in the ST are representatives, simple statements, and are largely
descriptive, i.e. descriptions of facts, events, and emotions, with one exception:

Paragraph 13:
Let the past be an inspiration for the future, for the new challenges of peace
and freedom. – Möge die Vergangenheit eine Inspiration für die Zukunft
sein, für die neuen Herausforderungen von Frieden und Freiheit.

The ST sentence has the form of an indirect request, or an order. But the
addressees are left vague and ambiguous. Since it is not appropriate for the communicative situation to give orders to one's hosts, the interpretation as a request
is more fitting. The addressees may deliberately have been left vague so that
everybody can feel called upon, thus once more contributing to empathy. This
interpretation has been the basis for the choice of a modal verb in subjunctive
form in the TT.

Interlingual translation problems

(i) Gender
Countries have different genders in German, in the case of 'Polen', the gender is neuter:

Paragraph 8:
. . . Poland's decision to assert her sovereignty . . . left her under another occupation. – . . . machte Polen seinen Anspruch . . . geltend. . . . daß es . . . erneut unter Fremdherrschaft geriet.

(ii) Number
Paragraph 7 (plural in ST, but singular in TT due to linguistic conventions):
. . . who risked their lives . . . – Sie alle setzten ihr Leben aufs Spiel . . .

(iii) Grammatical cases
German verbs require specific grammatical cases. Whenever two verbs are combined which require different cases, the grammatical structure needs to be adapted accordingly:

Paragraph 12 (transposition ('gedenken' requires genitive, 'ehren' requires accusative)):
This evening we remember and honour those dead. – Heute abend gedenken wir der Toten und ehren sie.

(iv) Reported speech
Paragraph 4 (subjunctive verb form in TT to comply with linguistic conventions):
Winston Churchill declared that Britain felt itself responsible for the restoration to the Poles of their own country. – Winston Churchill erklärte, daß sich Großbritannien dafür verantwortlich fühle, daß die Polen ihr Heimatland zurück bekämen.

Due to the accompanying transposition from a nominal structure ('restoration') to a verbal structure, a subjunctive verb form has also been used as an indication of the ongoing reported speech ('zurück bekämen').

(v) Theme–rheme structure
Paragraph 4:
It was in a broadcast from London that the world first heard of the 1944 Uprising. – Durch eine Rundfunksendung aus London hörte die Welt zum ersten Mal vom Warschauer Aufstand 1944.

The syntactic structure in the ST indicates emphasis (it was + emphasised element + conjunctional clause), thus making 'in a broadcast from London' the rheme of the sentence. This structure of the cleft sentence ensures the coherent link to Paragraph 3, i.e. the supportive role of Britain as the dominant idea (macro-proposition) in Paragraphs 3 and 4. Since this emphasis is significant for the text, it has been rendered by the front position of the rheme in the TT ('durch eine Rundfunksendung aus London').

Paragraph 7:
They are a living witness . . . So are thousands of Polish veterans who live in Britain today. – Sie verkörpern . . ., genauso wie die Tausende von polnischen Veteranen, die jetzt in Großbritannien leben.

In the sentence starting with 'so', the verb is placed before the subject of the sentence, which is the rheme and carries the stress. It is also an economic way of repeating the information in the previous sentence, i.e. 'so are' is synonymous with 'they too are a living witness'. In the TT, we have opted for an equally economic form by linking the sentence to the previous one, using a verbless structure and making the repetitive aspect explicit ('genauso wie'), thus keeping 'Tausende von polnischen Veteranen, die . . . ' as sentence rheme.

(vi) Wh-clauses
In the two following cases we have interrogative clauses which take over the function of their antecedents, with the *wh*-element being merged with its antecedent.

In Paragraph 5 the ST has an interrogative clause taking over the function of its antecedent (i.e. object complement), and 'what' merged with its antecedent (cf. 'by that which', also an adnominal relative clause). In the TT we have subject complement plus modal clause:

Paragraph 5:
He was deeply moved by what he called 'the martyrdom of Warsaw.' . . . – Er war zutiefst berührt von dem 'Martyrium Warschaus', wie er es nannte.

In the same paragraph, the ST has an interrogative clause taking over the function of its antecedent (i.e. prepositional object), and 'how' merged with its antecedent (see: 'of the way in which they saw', also an adnominal relative clause). The TT has a pronominal adverb ('darüber') plus modal clause:

Paragraph 5:
he later gave a moving account of . . . and of how they saw it almost totally destroyed. – . . . berichtete er in bewegenden Worten über . . . und darüber, wie sie die fast vollständige Vernichtung ihrer Stadt miterleben mußten.

In addition, the past participle ('destroyed') in the ST, functions as predicate complement to the object ('it' = 'town') after a verb of perception ('saw'). In the TT, we have used a subordinate clause with an indicative verb form. (For the accompanying change of a verb of perception ('saw') into a verb of emotion ('miterleben'), see previous comments on empathy.)

Text-specific translation problems

(i) Repetition of initial idea at later stage
An idea, which John Major uses at the beginning of his speech, is taken up again in a later paragraph:

Paragraph 2:
we commemorate the inspiring but tragic events of 50 years ago. – gedenken wir . . . der Ereignisse vor 50 Jahren, die inspirierend, aber dennoch tragisch waren.

Paragraph 13:
Let the past be an inspiration for the future, . . . – Möge die Vergangenheit eine Inspiration für die Zukunft sein, . . .

This stylistic feature provides both a structural frame to the text and ensures intratextual coherence. Since this is a characteristic feature of the ST, we have kept it in the TT by opting for the repetition of the key concept, 'inspirierend', 'Inspiration'.

(ii) Dominant lexical-semantic fields (frames) in the text
The dominant lexical-semantic fields (frames) in the address are commemoration, fighting, and support. These frames are linked continuously in the text, thus also bringing in the temporal aspect of linking past, present, and future. The fact that these frames are relevant to the purpose of the TT as well (i.e. the TT is intended for a detailed content analysis by advisors to the German government) has guided our choice of lexical expressions and some other translation strategies, such as specifications.

Paragraph 7 (specification):
I met there veterans . . . – Dort habe ich Kriegsveteranen . . . getroffen.

The specification 'Kriegsveteranen' is determined by the (war-)fighting frame.

Paragraph 3 (specification and lexical repetition):
Britain stood with Poland . . . Poles and Britons served side by side . . . – Großbritannien stand . . . an der Seite Polens. . . . kämpften Polen und Briten Seite an Seite

Paragraph 14 (specification):
But we can stand beside you now, as we stood then – Aber wir können jetzt wieder an Ihrer Seite stehen, genauso wie damals

The specification ('stand an der Seite') has been motivated by the support frame, and since the cohesive device of lexical repetition ensures intratextual coherence, we have opted for identical structures in Paragraphs 3 and 14.

Paragraph 3 (specification / addition):
Your Government then found refuge in London. – Ihre Regierung fand damals Zuflucht im Exil in London.

This specification, too, has been motivated by the support frame.
In Paragraphs 9 and 10, the support frame (i.e. Britain supporting Poland) is linked to a rebuilding frame, with moving from rebuilding in a concrete sense in Paragraph 9 to an abstract sense (i.e. a metaphor) in Paragraph 10. To be precise, it is in the metaphorical sense that the rebuilding frame and the support frame are linked. Since a rebuilding frame is present in both a concrete and a metaphorical sense in German too, we have opted for reproducing it in the TT (with variation between verbal and nominal structures):

Paragraphs 9 and 10:
. . . the people of Warsaw and of Poland rebuilt this capital city. . . . rebuild your economy and society . . . we are taking part in the rebuilding of Poland – . . . hat die Bevölkerung Warschaus und ganz Polens ihre Hauptstadt

wieder aufgebaut. . . . Wiederaufbau Ihrer Wirtschaft und Ihrer Gesellschaft . . . beteiligen wir uns am Wiederaufbau Polens

(iii) Vagueness, presuppositions, and implicatures as characteristic features of diplomatic discourse

There are some implicit references, which require the activation of background knowledge and a recognition of presuppositions and implicatures.
Major uses more abstract and / or vague formulations, e.g. abstract nouns for
actions, events, with the agent (agentive role) being left implicit. This is a strategy frequently found in political and diplomatic discourse, especially when
sensitive issues are at stake, as is the case here. With regard to the purpose of the
TT, this stylistic feature has been kept:

Paragraph 8:
But Poland's tragedy was that the outcome of the war and of the Uprising left
her under another occupation. – Aber es war Polens tragisches Schicksal, daß
es nach dem Krieg und dem Aufstand erneut unter Fremdherrschaft geriet.

The identification of the implicit agent in this sentence requires the activation
of background knowledge, which is based on the presupposition of 'another': at
first Germany had occupied Poland, then the Soviet Union. However, Poland
was not under direct Soviet occupation, but the implication is that in Poland a
Communist system had been installed by the Soviet Union, and that the Soviet
Union actively influenced Poland's political affairs. Based on this interpretation,
we opted for 'Fremdherrschaft' ('Okkupation' denotes a direct occupation, with
decisions being taken by another state).

Paragraph 11:
. . . after the devastation of Communism – nach den Verheerungen durch das
kommunistische System

'Kommunismus' in German usually denotes the social system in a more
abstract sense, or the ideology. Since in the text it is combined with a result ('devastation') of some action (which implies an agent of this action), the more
concrete 'kommunistisches System' has been opted for in the TT, with the causal
relationship having been made explicit in the TT.

Paragraph 14 (explication):
Perhaps those who were not there cannot fully understand. – Wer das
Geschehen der Vergangenheit nicht selbst miterlebt hat, kann das alles
vielleicht nicht ganz verstehen.

The referent of 'those who' is most probably the people in Britain, and 'there'
refers to Poland during the Uprising and the Second World War. This interpretation is based on the context (see the following sentence) and on background
knowledge. For the TT, a specification has been opted for, since we considered a
more general expression ('dabei', for example) to be too vague for the purpose of
the TT (i.e. the TT is a written document, thus the interpretation of vague expressions of time and place is no longer supported by the immediacy of the original
content, i.e. the commemoration ceremony). The choice of the verb ('miterleben')
has been motivated by the textual feature of empathy (see comments above).

(iv) Use of personal pronouns in the address

Pronouns are related to positioning, i.e. the use of pronouns reflects, and even constitutes, social and political relationships. This works at two levels; the communicative setting and the level of the political relationships (see Chilton & Schäffner, 1997). John Major, speaking as the official representative of his country, uses the personal pronoun 'I' to denote his political role as Prime Minister. 'I' has consistently been rendered as 'ich' in the TT. The pronoun 'you' always refers to Poland (e.g. 'Your Government . . . – Ihre Regierung . . .), with sentence (4) as the only exception, where the host, President Walesa, is addressed: 'your guests from abroad, Mr President, . . . '. In the TT, the context allows for the specification in this case, despite the identical form of the German pronoun ('Herr Präsident, Ihre Gäste . . . ').

The personal pronoun 'we' (or 'our') can have different referents, which sometimes overlap. The referent of 'we' is first, all those present at the commemoration ceremony ('we remember, we honour'), second, Britain ('we are taking part in the rebuilding of Poland', 'we can stand beside you now as we stood then', 'your citizens and ours', and third, the member states of the European Union ('our Union'). In 'our free nations' (Paragraph 7) the referent could be either the two countries Poland and Britain, or a group of nations. Since vagueness of the referents of 'we', or blending of potential referents, is a typical feature of political discourse, the 'we' has consistently been rendered as 'wir' in the TT.

(v) Perspective of the speech

Paragraph 6 (omission):
During the fighting 186 sorties were flown from British bases on the other side of Europe, in the south of Italy. – Während der Kämpfe wurden von britischen Stützpunkten in Süditalien aus 186 Einsätze geflogen.

Although the address was delivered in Poland, this sentence in the ST reports from a local British perspective, which is signalled by 'on the other side of Europe'. For the TT we have opted for omission.

(vi) Quotations from other texts

Paragraph 5:
He was deeply moved by what he called 'the martyrdom of Warsaw.' – Er war zutiefst berührt von dem 'Martyrium Warschaus', wie er es nannte.

In this reference to Churchill, the inverted commas indicate that it is a quote from his book. The fact that it is a quote is, in addition, signalled by 'what he called', which is a meta-communicative signal to the audience of the speech (i.e. as oral delivery). For the written version, and due to the changed function of the TT, it could also be omitted (i.e. alternative version: 'Er war zutiefst von dem 'Martyrium Warschaus' berührt.'). Since this quote is not of major significance for the speech, there is no need to check for an authorised German translation.

At the very end of the address, John Major quotes, in an English translation, from a broadcast from Warsaw, which itself includes a reference to the Polish national anthem.

Paragraph 15:
'Immortal is the nation that can muster such universal heroism. For those

who have died have conquered, and those who live on will fight on, will conquer and again bear witness that Poland lives when the Poles live.' – 'Unsterblich ist die Nation, die solch einen großen Heldenmut hervor-gebracht hat. Diejenigen, die gestorben sind, haben gesiegt, und diejenigen, die leben, kämpfen weiter, siegen und beweisen erneut, daß Polen noch nicht verloren ist.'

Since no exact source of the broadcast is given, searching for an authorised translation in German (which may not exist at all) would be highly time-con-suming, and is also not necessary for the purpose of the TT. However, there is a reference to the text of the Polish National Anthem, albeit not explicitly men-tioned, but identifiable by the primary audience of the address. This reference is evident in the words 'that Poland lives when the Poles live', more precisely, it is a reference to the first words of the national anthem (the original Polish is 'Jeszcze Polska nie zginela, kiedy my zyjemy', literally: 'Poland hasn't died when we live'). The function of this reference is to use the recognition effect to establish common ground between speaker and hearers (empathy again). Since this is a characteristic feature of this particular ST, it would also be of relevance to the TT addressees (due to the purpose of the TT). German politicians can be assumed to know that the national anthem has played a significant role as a symbolic reflec-tion of Poland's national identity in the long history of division and defeat of the country. They can also be expected to know the anthem's words 'Noch ist Polen nicht verloren' (in fact, this phrase is relatively widely known in Germany). The first two lines in an authorised translation are 'Noch ist Polen nicht verloren, solang wir noch leben'.

In this last sentence, we have also opted for a more 'poetical' style. An alterna-tive solution could be:

'Die Toten haben gesiegt, und die Lebenden kämpfen weiter, siegen und beweisen erneut, daß Polen noch nicht verloren ist.'

Reviews: Introductory Comments

Reviews are critical assessments of some work of art, e.g. a book, film, theatre or concert performance, TV or radio programme. Since reviews are usually published in newspapers and news magazines (i.e. they can be characterised as belonging to journalistic texts in the widest sense), many of the translation-relevant aspects presented for popular-scientific texts will apply here as well.

The main function of reviews is to describe the piece of work (or art) and to express an opinion about it. That is, reviews belong to the informative text type (see Reiss, 1971), but they may also have expressive elements (and maybe also appellative elements, although reviews do not usually attempt to make readers agree with the opinion expressed, i.e. they are not usually persuasive texts). Reviews are not highly conventionalised genres, although there are a few characteristic features which are also of relevance for translation. Reviews, however, are not too frequently translated for publication in the target culture, but rather for internal use by the clients themselves (e.g. a publishing company, an artist, or an agent). It does happen fairly regularly, though, that extracts of reviews (also from different countries) are used for promotional purposes (e.g. on book covers and in catalogues).

Titles and Proper Names

Pieces of art (e.g. films, novels, dramas, songs) have their specific titles. When they are translated, the title might change (due to copyright regulations, to avoid duplication, etc., see Nord, 1993). Whenever titles are referred to in a review (e.g. titles of other publications of the same author), or if quotations are used, it will become necessary for the translator (unless the skopos does not demand this) to check for the exact title (and if necessary the quote) in an authorised translation (should one exist). In the case of reviews of books which have not (yet) been translated, the reviewer may introduce his or her own keywords (as in our sample text with reference to the concept 'mogul'). If the addressees of the TT are the original publishers of the book, the translator's (re)search process may have to include checking the original book for titles, keywords, etc.

In referring to the author (or to other characters of a book, for example), English reviews often use 'Mr/Mrs' followed by the surname.

In German reviews, first name and surname, or surname alone, are typically used ('Herr' or 'Frau' are forms of direct address and are, thus, inappropriate in the genre review). These conventions in referring to people are characteristic of a variety of journalistic texts, e.g. Hicks (1999: 42) argues that the 'convention in journalism is full name ('John/Joan Smith') for the first use, then either courtesy title ('Mr/Mrs/Miss/Ms Smith') or surname or first name for the rest of the story'. He adds that in-house styles may request a slight variation of this pattern. In German journalistic texts, on the other hand, a combination of title and name (depending on the length of the title, placed either before or after the name) or the name alone are conventionally used (but without 'Herr' or 'Frau').

Position of Bibliographical Data

Depending on the newspaper, journal, or magazine where the review (i.e. the ST) is published, there is usually some in-house style as to the format. This concerns, in particular, the arrangement of the bibliographical information. The sample text in this volume is a book review that was published in the weekly magazine *The Economist*. The magazine's conventions are: two kinds of headings (one at the top, indicating what the book is about; then the major heading, providing a kind of subjective evaluation of the content). These headings are followed by presentation of the bibliographical data, usually in the following order: title, author, publisher, number of pages, price (this conventional arrangement has largely been confirmed by looking at a number of exemplars of the genre). The placement and arrangement of these data in the TT and the choice of a heading will depend on the purpose of the TT (for example, book reviews published in German newspapers give these data either at the beginning or at the end of the text, depending on the preferred in-house style of the media).

Style

Reviews are often written by literary critics and similar experts in the respective field (sometimes also by professional journalists). Thus, their personal writing style will have to be taken into account for the translation-oriented ST analysis. Review writers will also take the status of the journal where the review is published into account, and subsequently they know (more or less) what they can expect on the part of their readers (in terms of background knowledge). For example, when writing a review for a quality newspaper or a feminist magazine, reviewers may make use of a variety of stylistic means (such as modifying well-known quotes, allusions to other works of arts or artists) because they can be fairly confident that their readers will have the required knowledge to understand (and appreciate) the reference.

Reviews are combinations of providing a summary of the content and providing an evaluation, a critical assessment. There are no fixed rules as to the quantitative distribution of these two elements, nor to the positioning of the evaluation. The summing-up of the reviewer's judgement may be right at the beginning of the text, but it may equally well be the very last sentence (see Gilbert, 1999: 99ff).

Sample Text

In the sample text we have chosen, these aspects become relevant too, albeit less so with respect to an in-house style concerning the positioning of the bibliographical data. The decision as to how much information to use for the TT and where to place it is predominantly influenced by the purpose of the text (the TT is intended for internal use, i.e. we have a case of documentary translation). In this particular case, *culture-specific aspects* are of a certain relevance. The ST is a review of a book that reports about Germany. Therefore, there are a number of references to culture-specific items known in Germany (e.g. people, newspapers, films), which have been explained to the ST readers. Again here, the skopos helps the translator to decide on the appropriate amount of information for the TT addressees. In the annotations, translation strategies of omission, compression, implication will be discussed in their relevance to the specific translation assignment.

German Media Moguls
SOUL-SEARCHING
Götterdämmerung. **By Herbert Riehl-Heyse.**
Siedler Verlag; 224 pages, DM 39.80

[1]
Like many journalists, Herbert Riehl-Heyse of *Süddeutsche Zeitung* bemoans the emergence of a soulless, business school approach to press management. It is an approach so at odds with the exuberance of the remarkable people who created the German press as well as its television and film industries after the second world war. Their characters are entertainingly diverse, from Gerd Bucerius, the patrician (and recently deceased) Hamburg lawyer who published *Die Zeit,* the left-liberal weekly, to Aenne Burda, a former secretary who now runs one of Europe's big women's magazine groups.

[2]
There are also similarities. Rudolf Augstein and Reinhard Mohn both came home from lost battles and prisoner-of-war camps to create new media empires in rubble littered cities. Mr Augstein made *Der Spiegel,* a less conservative and more muck-raking version of America's *Time,* into Germany's most read weekly magazine. Mr Mohn turned Bertelsmann, his family's bible-printing firm in the provincial town of Gütersloh, into a world media giant.

[3]
By the author's own admission his collection is fragmentary as it deals just with people who are still alive, leaving out such moguls as Axel Springer, the conservative newspaper publisher without whom any story of the post-war German media is incomplete. Still, it is a fascinating book stuffed with remarkable tales which offer an insight not only into the German media but also into the post-war history of the German film industry.

[4]
The most interesting story is not about a media mogul but a movie mogul. Artur Brauner, a young Jew, flees to the woods when the Nazis invade Poland. After six terrifying years, during which 49 members of his family are murdered, he moves to Berlin and launches a career as a film producer with *Heimatfilme* – the cosy pictures, bereft of controversy, loved by German audiences in the 1950s. This schmaltz he justified as a means to making better films – his 1991 *Hitlerjunge Salomon* for example (called *Europa, Europa* in English), which is about a Jewish boy who joins

the Hitler Youth to survive. It was neither put forward for an Oscar nor included in the Berlin Film Festival. Audiences loved it.

Source: *The Economist*, 3 February 1996

Translation Assignment
The Berlin publishing company *Siedler Verlag* is interested in finding out how its publications are reviewed in other countries. In spring 1996, the *Siedler Verlag* asks you to prepare a German version of the review of the book *Götterdämmerung* that appeared in *The Economist* (3 February 1996), for internal use of the publishing company.

Auf der Suche nach Herz – Deutschlands Medienmagnaten

Herbert Riehl-Heyse, *Götterdämmerung*

[1]
Wie viele andere Journalisten beklagt auch Herbert Riehl-Heyse von der *Süddeutschen Zeitung* das Entstehen einer herzlosen, rein geschäftsmäßigen Art und Weise des Pressemanagements. Diese Art und Weise steht völlig im Widerspruch zu dem Enthusiasmus jener bemerkenswerten Persönlichkeiten, die nach dem Zweiten Weltkrieg den Boden für Presse, Fernsehen und Film in Deutschland bereitet haben. Sie unterscheiden sich in ihrem Wesen und ihrem Lebensweg auf äußerst erfrischende Weise. Ihr Spektrum reicht von Gerd Bucerius, dem aus wohlhabender Familie stammenden (und kürzlich verstorbenen) Hamburger Rechtsanwalt und Herausgeber der links-liberalen *Zeit*, bis zu Aenne Burda, einer ehemaligen Sekretärin und heute Besitzerin einer der bedeutendsten europäischen Verlage von Frauenzeitschriften.

[2]
Es gibt jedoch auch Ähnlichkeiten, z.B. zwischen Rudolf Augstein und Reinhard Mohn. Beide kehrten nach dem verlorenen Krieg aus der Gefangenschaft in die Heimat zurück und gründeten neue Medienimperien in den zerbombten Städten. Augstein machte den *Spiegel*, eine weniger konservative, aber stärker zum Enthüllungsjournalismus neigende Version des amerikanischen *Time* Magazins, zu Deutschlands meistgelesener Wochenzeitschrift. Mohn verwandelte Bertelsmann, seinen auf den Druck von Bibeln spezialisierten Familienbetrieb im verschlafenen Gütersloh, zu einem weltweit operierenden Mediengiganten.

[3]
Der Autor gesteht selbst ein, daß seine Auswahl fragmentarisch ist, da sie nur lebende Personen erfaßt. Es fehlen solche Pressezaren wie der konservative Axel Springer, ohne den eine jede Geschichte der Medienlandschaft im Nachkriegsdeutschland unvollständig ist. Es ist dennoch ein faszinierendes Buch, voller bemerkenswerter Berichte, die nicht nur einen Einblick in die deutschen Medien gestatten, sondern auch in die Nachkriegsgeschichte der deutschen Filmindustrie.

[4]
Der interessanteste Bericht handelt nicht von einem Pressezaren, sondern von einem Filmbaron. Artur Brauner, ein junger Jude, flieht beim Einfall der Nazis in Polen in die Wälder. Nachs sechs unheilvollen

Jahren, in denen 49 Mitglieder seiner Familie ermordet werden, siedelt er nach Berlin über und beginnt eine Karriere als Filmproduzent mit den beim deutschen Publikum in den 50er Jahren so beliebten Heimatfilmen. Er rechtfertigte diese sentimentalen Kitschfilme, da sie ihm die finanziellen Mittel beschafften, um bessere Filme zu drehen. Ein Beispiel ist sein *Hitlerjunge Salomon* vom Jahre 1991, ein Film über einen jüdischen Jungen, der der Hitlerjugend beitritt, um zu überleben. Dieser Film wurde weder für einen Oscar nominiert noch bei den Berliner Filmfestspielen aufgeführt. Aber er wurde ein großer Publikumserfolg.

Annotations

Translation Assignment

The Berlin publishing company *Siedler Verlag* is interested in finding out how its publications are reviewed in other countries. In spring 1996, the *Siedler Verlag* asks you to prepare a German version of the review of the book *Götterdämmerung* that appeared in *The Economist* (3 February 1996), for internal use of the publishing company.

ST Characterisation

The text was published in the book review section of *The Economist* on 3 February 1996. Following the in-house style for reviews, there are three kinds of headings: a small one at the top indicating what the book is about; the major one, printed in larger size ('Soul-searching'), and providing a kind of subjective evaluation of the content on the part of the reviewer (who is anonymous); and then the bibliographical data, i.e. title, author, publisher, number of pages, price. Since the title is given in German and the price in the German currency, it can be assumed that this is a review of the German version of the book, i.e. it has not (yet) been translated and is not (yet) for sale in Great Britain.

This is a text about a book that reports about Germany, specifically the role of the media in Germany. The dominant lexical-semantic field of the text is the media. There are a number of references to people in Germany and to names of newspapers, journals, publishing companies, and films. Since the author in all probability assumed insufficient background knowledge about the media in Germany on the side of the British readership, he or she frequently explained the character of papers, journals and films. Therefore, the ST poses, above all, pragmatic and intercultural translation problems.

TT Specification

The client, i.e. the German publishing company, is above all, interested in the evaluation its book received in a British journal. This information is required for internal use, i.e. the TT will not subsequently be published in full. However, the *Siedler Verlag* normally publishes quotations from international reviews, both on book covers and in their catalogues, which they may eventually do in this case as well. Due to the characteristics of the client, ST information that is common knowledge to the client, or that was specifically provided to account for insufficient background knowledge on the part of the ST addressees, can be left out in the TT. However, it is sometimes difficult to clearly draw a line between redundant information for the TT addressees and useful information. When in doubt, we have decided to include the information in the TT (these cases are discussed in the annotations).

Annotations

Pragmatic translation problems

(i) Addressees

Due to the specified translation assignment, the bibliographical details in the heading can be left out, because they are known to the client. It is more typical of reviews in German to have the name of the author in front of the title of the book.

Götterdämmerung. By Herbert Riehl-Heyse. Siedler Verlag; 224 pages, DM 39.80
Herbert Riehl-Heyse, *Götterdämmerung*

(ii) Culture-bound terms and proper names

The ST author has used the German names for the listed publications, together with a characterisation of the political stance of the journal and how often it is published. In addition to giving their names, publishing companies and people are also characterised. If it can safely be assumed that the function of this characterising information is to add background knowledge about Germany on the behalf of the ST readers, it can be deleted in the TT. If, however, the characterisation reflects a more or less subjective evaluation, i.e. if the characterisation is different or controversial in the target culture Germany, then it is advisable to include it in the TT.

Paragraph 2:
Die Zeit, the left-liberal weekly – links-liberalen *Zeit*

The information 'weekly' can be left out because it is common knowledge for the client, i.e. there is no need to include 'Wochenzeitschrift' in the TT.

Der Spiegel, a less conservative and more muck-raking version of America's *Time*, . . . Germany's most read weekly magazine – *Spiegel*, eine weniger konservative aber stärker zum Enthüllungsjournalismus neigende Version des amerikanischen *Time* Magazins, . . . Deutschlands meistgelesener Wochenzeitschrift

The characterising information is included in the TT because it reflects a subjective evaluation. 'Enthüllungsjournalismus' has been chosen as an appropriate label for this kind of journalism of a serious and influential quality journal ('Sensationsjournalismus' is more common for gossip in the yellow press; the other possible characterisation 'eine Zeitschrift, die Korruption aufdeckt' would have required a more complex syntactical structure). The historical connotation of 'muck-raking' (in 1906, the American President Roosevelt called critics of the social system 'muckrakers') is not relevant here and might not even be obvious to ST readers. Moreover, 'muck-raking' was intended in a negative sense by Roosevelt, but in the ST it is a positive evaluation. German words such as 'Netzbeschmutzer' or 'Schmutzfinken' are sometimes used (also by politicians) to reject media criticism, but since they have negative connotations, they would be inappropriate in the TT.

Paragraph 2:
turned Bertelsmann, his family's bible-printing firm in the provincial town of Gütersloh, into a world media giant – Bertelsmann, seinen auf den Druck von Bibeln spezialisierten Familienbetrieb im verschlafenen Gütersloh, zu einem weltweit operierenden Mediengiganten

The information is included in the TT because it reflects a subjective evaluation. 'Verschlafen' has been preferred to 'Provinzstadt' because of the connotations: 'Provinzstadt' denotes a small town, but it has also a very strong connotation of backwardness, of being out of touch with new developments, a place where nothing is going on (these connotations are even stronger with reference to people, see 'jemand kommt aus der Provinz', 'ein Provinzler'). In the context of the ST, the focus is on the size and the implication of unexpectedness, i.e. it is surprising that a small town (Gütersloh has about 80,000 inhabitants) is the seat of a huge company (lexically expressed by the contrast between 'provincial town' and 'world media giant'). 'Verschlafen' captures this implication of unexpectedness.

Paragraph 3:
such moguls as Axel Springer, the conservative newspaper publisher – solche Pressezaren wie der konservative Axel Springer

'Konservativ' could also have been left out because it is common knowledge for the client, and also not a controversial issue in Germany. 'Moguls' and 'newspaper publisher' are compressed to 'Pressezar' (see below (ii) *Textual keywords* under *Text specific translation problems*).

There is one case in the ST where no characterisation of a newspaper is given, but the occurrence of 'journalist' in the immediate context allows the ST readers to imply that it is a newspaper, which again is common knowledge for the client of the TT (and, in addition, the generic term 'Zeitung' is part of the proper name):

Paragraph 1:
journalists, Herbert Riehl-Heyse of *Süddeutsche Zeitung* – Journalisten . . . Herbert Riehl-Heyse von der *Süddeutschen Zeitung*

Paragraph 4:
Hitlerjunge Salomon for example (called *Europa, Europa* in English) – *Hitlerjunge Salomon*

This is a clear case of information being provided in the ST as information for its audience, therefore there is no need to account for '(called *Europa, Europa* in English)' in the TT.

Paragraph 4:
It was neither put forward for an Oscar nor included in the Berlin Film Festival. – Dieser Film wurde weder für einen Oscar nominiert, noch bei den Berliner Filmfestspielen aufgeführt.

An alternative solution could be the use of the proper name 'Berlinale', but since the ST is not about film festivals, the more general noun is appropriate for the TT purpose. 'Oscar' is the standard term in German for the American film prize.

Paragraph 4:
Heimatfilme – the cosy pictures, bereft of controversy, loved by German audiences in the 1950s. This schmaltz he justified . . . – beim deutschen Publikum in den 50er Jahren so beliebten Heimatfilmen. Er rechtfertigte diese sentimentalen Kitschfilme, . . .

'Heimatfilme' is a case of a culture-specific term, denoting a special type of German film. The ST author used the German word in italics, which is indicative of its culture-specificity, and added an explanation ('the cosy pictures, bereft of controversy'). It can be argued that this explanation is not necessary in the TT. It could even be considered redundant if accounted for in the TT (this is the decision taken here), and 'diese sentimentalen Kitschfilme' in the following sentence adds explicitly to the explanation. However, it could also be argued that we have again a subjective evaluation in the ST, which would indeed be useful to render in the TT. An alternative version could then be: 'beim deutschen Publikum in den 50er Jahren so beliebten Heimatfilmen, voller Sentimentalität und bar großer Probleme', or 'beim deutschen Publikum in den 50er Jahren so beliebten Heimatfilme, die eine heile Welt vorführten'.

Although 'schmaltz' is a loanword in German (via Yiddish), we have opted for the specification 'sentimentale Kitschfilme'. The words 'Schmalz' and 'schmalzig' can also be found in German in connection with over-sentimental films, however in more colloquial contexts and in an absolutely negative sense.

We can use this example to illustrate briefly the creative processes in arriving at our solution: due to the stylistic and genre constraints of 'Schmalz', and also due to the fact that it would introduce a somewhat excessive negative evaluation into the TT, we decided against its use. The respective propositions in Paragraph 4 deal with a specific film genre (i.e. Heimatfilme); in other words, we are thinking in terms of a 'film frame'. What we need is an evaluative expression for this genre (evaluation being a characteristic feature of the ST, see also the later comments about lexical-semantic fields, and the TT addressees are particularly interested in all evaluative aspects). The evaluative elements (semantic features) of 'schmaltz', which are relevant in this context, can be said to be 'over-sentimental', 'tear-jerker', 'low quality', 'not intellectually challenging and appealing'. 'Sentimentale Filme' alone would not have covered the negative evaluation of 'low quality' (the film *Casablanca*, too, can be characterised as 'sentimentaler Film'), and although 'Kitschfilm' does convey a negative evaluation, the features 'over-sentimental' and 'tear-jerker' are not prominent ('Kitschfilm' can also be used to characterise a comedy). To account for all the features that are relevant in the context of the ST we then opted for 'sentimentale Kitschfilme'.

Incidentally, there is much more culture-specificity in the title of the German book *Götterdämmerung* – for example, allusions to Greek mythology and to the music of Richard Wagner. But since the ST does not have any reference to them, they are not relevant for the specific translation assignment and need not be considered further.

(iii) Situation
There is only time reference of relevance for the TT:

Paragraph 1:
Gerd Bucerius, the patrician (and recently deceased) Hamburg lawyer – Gerd Bucerius, dem aus wohlhabender Familie stammenden (und kürzlich verstorbenen) Hamburger Rechtsanwalt

Due to the time specification of the translation assignment (the TT is requested in spring 1996, Gerd Bucerius died in autumn 1995) 'kürzlich verstorben' is sufficienctly specific for the purpose of the TT and its addressees.

Intercultural translation problems

(i) Genre conventions

(a) Headings
Reviews are not a highly conventionalised genre, although there are a few

characteristic features (see introductory comments). There is usually some in-house style as far as their format is concerned. The arrangement of the headings is an example of the in-house style of *The Economist*. Since the TT is meant for internal use by *Siedler Verlag*, there is no need to take any in-house style into account. Therefore, one heading has been chosen which combines the two headings of the ST:

German media moguls
Soul-searching
Auf der Suche nach Herz – Deutschlands Medienmagnaten

(b) Lexical repetition in heading
Another conventional aspect of English journalistic texts refers to headings where very often the heading is a shortened structure taken from the first sentence of the text (see also the introductory comments):

Soul-searching
Like many journalists, Herbert Riehl-Heyse of *Süddeutsche Zeitung* bemoans the emergence of a soulless, business school approach to press management.

Auf der Suche nach Herz – Deutschlands Medienmagnaten
Wie viele andere Journalisten beklagt auch Herbert Riehl-Heyse von der *Süddeutschen Zeitung* das Entstehen einer herzlosen, rein geschäftsmäßigen Art und Weise des Pressemanagements.

'Soul' is not taken up again explicitly in the text, but there is a semantic contrast to 'exuberance' in the next sentence. In the TT, lexical repetition as a feature of intratextual coherence has also been applied (and also the semantic contrast to 'Enthusiasmus' in the next sentence has been kept). 'Soul' is used as a metonym for deep feelings, emotions, and 'soulless' then expressing an attitude to business, which is lacking in personal involvement and emotional commitment. To express this attitude, 'herzlos' has been used in the TT, because in German the heart ('Herz') is the organ which is typically linked to emotions (it is seen as the centre of human life, as the seat of the human soul, as evidenced in ancient myths and religious texts). For example, if a person is pursuing a task with enthusiasm and personal involvement, one can say that he or she is 'mit dem Herzen bei der Sache'. ('Seele', too, is related to inner feelings, but it is commonly associated with religion and psychoanalysis and would bring in associations, which are not part of the textual message).

For another purpose, e.g. publication of the TT in a German journal, one could find a totally different heading (maybe one linked to the allusions evoked by the book title, such as 'Sturz vom Olymp'), and then instead of 'herzlos' other expressions could be used, e.g. 'nüchtern', 'finanziell denkend'.

(ii) References to people
In English reviews referring to aspects of Germany, it is typical to refer to people by first name plus second name, or by adding Mr, Mrs in front of the family name (at least this is the convention in *The Economist*; a cursory analysis of some texts in various English newspapers has confirmed the frequent use of Mr or Mrs followed by surname). According to the stylistic and genre conventions

of German reviews, the surname alone is used, in other words, adding 'Herr' would not conform to the conventions in the target culture.

Paragraph 2:
Mr Augstein – Augstein
Mr Mohn – Mohn

(iii) Tense
In the report about the life of Artur Brauner in Paragraph 4, the present tense is used in two sentences ('flees, moves, launches'). The function of the present tense in such historical reporting is to make the experience more vivid to the reader. Since in German narrative texts, the present tense fulfils the same purpose (*historisches Präsens*) it has been used in the TT, too ('flieht, siedelt über, beginnt').

Interlingual translation problems
Some changes in the syntactic structure (transpositions) become necessary due to differences in the linguistic systems, especially infinitive and gerund structures. Such transpositions go usually hand in hand with modulations, e.g.

(i) Infinitives

Paragraph 2:
both came home from lost battles and prisoner-of-war camps to create new media empires in rubble littered cities – Beide kehrten nach dem verlorenen Krieg aus der Gefangenschaft in die Heimat zurück und gründeten neue Medienimperien in den zerbombten Städten

The infinitive structure in the ST ('to create new media empires') has been rendered as an indicative verb form in the TT ('und gründeten neue Medienimperien'), logically implying a temporal sequence of the actions expressed in the propositions (i.e. coming home and then creating media empires). An infinitive structure in the TT ('Beide kehrten . . . in die Heimat zurück, um neue Medienimperien . . . zu gründen') would be wrong because it expresses an intention on the part of the agents.

The modulations concern the lexical references to the war and the post-war time: we used the specification 'Krieg' for 'battles' due to the fact that 'battles' is part of a 'war frame' which is elaborated in the same sentence by 'prisoner-of-war camps' and by 'rubble littered cities'. In the TT, the introduction of 'Krieg' allows for the generalisation 'Gefangenschaft' (i.e. the more specific meaning 'Kriegsgefangenschaft' is implicit). The modulation 'zerbombte Städte' for 'rubble littered cities', i.e. the reason ('zerbombt') for the result ('rubble littered') has been made explicit in the TT, can also be justified by the reference to the identified 'war frame'.

(ii) -ing structures

Paragraph 3
his collection is fragmentary as it deals just with people who are still alive,

leaving out such moguls as . . . – seine Auswahl fragmentarisch ist, da sie nur
lebende Personen erfaßt. Es fehlen . . .

One ST sentence has been rendered as two sentences in the TT (see Chesterman's (1997a) syntactic translation strategy *Sentence structure change*) mainly for
reasons of clarity and style, thus changing the gerund structure ('leaving out')
into an indicative verb form. The relative clause ('people who are still alive') has
been changed into a structure of adjective plus noun ('lebende Personen') for
reasons of economy.

Paragraph 4
This schmaltz he justified as a means to making better films – Er rechtfertigte
diese sentimentalen Kitschfilme, da sie ihm die finanziellen Mittel beschafft-
en, um bessere Filme zu drehen

The phrase 'as a means' expresses a causal relationship, the gerund ('making')
expresses an intention. The intention is captured by the infinitive ('um . . . zu . . .
'), the causal relationship has been made explicit by using a sub-clause in the TT
(conjunction 'da', or alternatively 'weil'; and there is also a specification 'finanz-
ielle Mittel' because 'Mittel' alone would be too vague). The syntactic structure
in the TT has resulted in a change of the theme–rheme structure. The rheme position of 'this schmaltz' contributes to the evaluative explanation of 'Heimatfilme'
to the ST readers. Since the TT readers are familiar with this specific film genre
(as commented earlier), the evaluation need not be highlighted in a particular
way. Putting 'sentimentale Kitschfilme' in rheme position in the TT would
require to make the causal relationship even more explicit by adding 'Begründung', e.g.

Diese sentimentalen Kitschfilme rechtfertigte er mit der Begründung, daß sie
ihm die finanziellen Mittel beschafften, . . .
or:
Diese sentimentalen Kitschfilme rechtfertigte er mit der Begründung, sie
beschafften ihm die finanziellen Mittel, . . .

(iii) Style
Most of the other changes in the syntactic structures have been made for stylistic reasons mainly (and could also be listed as text-specific translation problems),
e.g.

Paragraph 1:
Their characters are entertainingly diverse, from Gerd Bucerius . . . to Aenne
Burda . . . – Sie unterscheiden sich in ihrem Wesen und ihrem Lebensweg auf
äußerst erfrischende Weise

The personal pronoun 'sie' has been used in the TT to establish a cohesive link
to 'Persönlichkeiten' in the sentence before. Subsequently, the adjective 'diverse'
has been changed into the verb 'sich unterscheiden', and the subject of the ST
('their characters') corresponds to the propositional object in the TT ('in ihrem
Wesen und ihrem Lebensweg'; note that in German the singular is common). We
have rendered 'characters' by a combination of two nouns ('Wesen und Lebensweg') because the following information in the ST concerns differences in the
social background of people who have turned into media moguls. This range in

the social background, indicated by 'from . . . to' in the ST, has been made more explicit in the TT by the addition of 'ihr Spektrum reicht':

Paragraph 1:
. . . from Gerd Bucerius, the patrician (and recently deceased) Hamburg lawyer who published *Die Zeit*, the left-liberal weekly, to Aenne Burda, a former secretary who now runs one of Europe's big women's magazine groups. – Ihr Spektrum reicht von Gerd Bucerius, dem aus wohlhabender Familie stammenden (und kürzlich verstorbenen) Hamburger Rechtsanwalt und Herausgeber der links-liberalen *Zeit*, bis zu Aenne Burda, einer ehemaligen Sekretärin und heute Besitzerin einer der bedeutendsten europäischen Verlage von Frauenzeitschriften.

The ST uses a parallel structure for the characterisation of the two people, i.e. a noun to indicate the previous profession and then a verb to express the activity in the media industry. German (mainly journalistic) texts have been looked at and it has been found that they typically use a combination of nouns. Therefore the verbs in the ST have been changed into nouns in the TT, and subsequently the relative clauses have been replaced by a combination of the two nouns, linked by the conjunction 'und'. Although pre-modifications are more common in German journalistic texts (e.g. 'die frühere Sekretärin Aenne Burda'), this structure has not been chosen here because the contrast between the social origin and the media position can be more forcefully represented in a parallel structure as previously explained.

Text-specific translation problems

(i) Lexical-semantic fields
The lexical-semantic field of 'media' structures the ST and assures intratextual coherence (e.g. 'press management, weekly magazine, newspaper publisher, film producer'). It is linked to 'mogul', which, together with other lexical units (e.g. 'empire', 'giant') expresses the connotation of largeness and importance. It is important to have this lexical-semantic field of 'media' reflected in the TT as well, regardless of changes in the word class (e.g. 'publish' – 'Herausgeber') or specifications (e.g. 'women's magazine groups' – 'Verlage von Frauenzeitschriften'; 'post-war German media' – 'Medienlandschaft im Nachkriegsdeutschland'; 'making better films' – 'um bessere Filme zu drehen') which have been motivated by contextual and stylistic considerations.

Another significant lexical-semantic field is related to the purpose of the text: there are a large number of words (mainly adjectives and nouns) that are used for evaluation. Due to the translation assignment, i.e. the German publisher wants to know what the British reviewer thinks about the book, it is important to keep the – overall positive – tone of the evaluation.

(ii) Textual keywords
The ST uses only 'mogul' throughout the text. In the TT, we have opted for more variation. A first decision has to be taken as to the rendering of 'mogul'. In German texts we find both 'Mogul' and 'Magnat' which are typically used with the more general, superordinate term 'Medien', whereas for the more specific labels (i.e. subordinate terms) other compounds are more common. The choice

here has been made for labels of nobility ('Zar', 'Baron', see the English 'media czar' or 'media baron'), which also ensures intratextual coherence to 'Medienimperium' in Paragraph 2. Both 'Mogul' and 'Magnat' are also originally titles of nobility, but this connotation has largely been lost, and nowadays both terms are used to denote rich and powerful people.

German media moguls – Medienmagnaten

moguls (Paragraph 3) – Pressezaren

media mogul . . . movie mogul (Paragraph 4) – Pressezar . . . Filmbaron

If possible, the translator should try to check which words are actually used in the German book (e.g. by getting hold of a copy of the book, or by contacting the publishing company or the author). In real life, however, this is not always possible (particularly due to time pressures). In this particular case, we did indeed check the original German book and found that there is no consistency in the use of terms, and that 'Medienmagnat', 'Mediengigant' and 'Tycoon' are used as synonyms. 'Mogul' is used in the German book in the context of films. For this reason, we opted for lexical variation in the TT.

Promotional Texts: Introductory Comments

The label 'promotional texts' is used here to cover a variety of genres which belong to the operative text type (Reiss, 1976, 2000) and which have predominantly an appellative and/or persuasive function. That is, text addressees (or customers) are expected to do something; in particular, to buy a product or to accept the service offered. Advertising texts, tourist information, and similar texts of a commercial nature belong to what we have called promotional texts. Such texts, which are published in mass media, such as flyers, leaflets, or brochures, on posters, etc., account for a considerable amount of the professional translation market (see Schmitt, 1998a: 10). Some of the translation problems already discussed in the previous introductory comments apply to promotional texts as well and will not be repeated here (e.g. use of direct quotes to give support to a claim, forms of referring to names, titles, functions of people). Additionally relevant aspects are culture-specific advertising conventions and the interplay of text and other visual material (on translation and advertising see also, for example, Séguinot, 1994; Smith, 1998; Smith & Klein-Braley, 1997).

Culture-specific Aspects of Advertising Conventions

It has frequently been argued that in advertising, texts are produced that make no linguistic sense, do not respect the advertising conventions and have no respect for the cultural identity of the people addressed (see Snell-Hornby, 1999). One of the reasons for this is a certain neglect of the fact that linguistic and cultural issues are inextricably intertwined. In product advertisements, multinational companies frequently use an identical strategic marketing concept (including visual material) for a variety of cultures. Adaptations to the respective culture (localisation) may be required for the campaign to be successful (for non-successful campaigns due to neglect of the culture-specific relevance of colours, traditions, etc. see Séguinot, 1994). Adaptations to the respective target culture may involve changes in the propositional content (see *cultural filtering* as a pragmatic translation strategy in Chesterman's (1997a) classification). For example, in an advertising text for a watch, the propositional content of the English ST and of the German TT reflect slight differences which are evidence of the fact that the culture-specific background knowledge of the respective addressees had been taken into account (e.g. 'winning his third British Open championship' compared to 'British Open '88 [. . .] der 1988 ein zweites Mal auch die German Open gewann'). It is an integral part of the work of the translator as an expert in intercultural communication to apply such pragmatic strategies in the process of translation, or at least to negotiate their application (and potential consequences) with the client. The dominant criterion for deciding on translation strategies in each case is the intended function of the text in its target culture for the target addressees.

In the case of tourist information, as another genre of promotional texts, TL texts will often actually function within the source culture. That is, the TT addressees are usually visitors who have come to the ST culture and who wish to obtain more information about the place they are visiting (of course, tourist information may also be read inside the target culture itself, e.g. before a visit is made as part of the preparation, or out of general interest for the place, or for various other purposes). It may therefore be argued that the tourist who is reading the TT while visiting the ST culture can be described as the prototypical TT addressee. Since visitors may come from a variety of cultures, tourist information often comes in the form of an illustrated leaflet with texts in two or more languages side by side, i.e. addressed to an international readership, with the aim of presenting a specific self-image to the outside world. The content of tourist information is often highly specific to the source culture, which is reflected in references to culture-specific institutions, historical events, traditions, lifestyles.

Another kind of promotional material are more extensive texts published in company brochures, or newsletters, and which include reports from satisfied customers who lend support to a specific product. In such texts the appellative function is less straightforward, and an additional aim is to contribute to the reputation and respectability of the company.

Textual and Extra-textual Information

In advertising texts and tourist information, the textual information is often supported by extra-textual information. In some kinds of advertising texts (e.g. on billboards) the textual information is considerably reduced compared to the extra-textual information. The appeals to the emotions of the potential customers are predominantly made via pictures, i.e. through visual stimulation. Here again, the appropriateness of a certain visual motive for the respective culture needs to be considered (see, for example, Séguinot (1994) on the culture-specific significance of flowers). The text itself may have an explicit reference to an accompanying photograph (e.g. in tourist brochures). It is advisable for the translator to consult the client to find out which visual material is intended to be included in the TT and, if necessary, to provide advice about the appropriateness of pictures etc.

Stylistic Means

The function of advertising texts is to appeal to the readers (i.e. the consumers). The linguistic and stylistic means chosen for the text thus contribute to fulfilling this function. Promotional texts, and advertising texts in particular, frequently make use of a variety of stylistic elements. Stolze (1998) differentiates between stylistic elements that appeal to the emotions of the customers (e.g. appeals to stereotypes in a culture via keywords, suggestive linguistic elements that highly evaluate the product, puns) and stylistic elements that are meant to stimulate the customers by means of factual statements, claims, direct address, questions, etc. Based on empirical analyses of sample texts (i.e. advertising texts from Germany and Brazil), Stolze concludes that emphasising the high quality of the product is more typical of German advertising texts (i.e. stressing the quality of the product, referring to technical aspects and to technological innovation is meant to achieve trust in the company and in the reliability of its products). In Brazil, on the other hand, advertising texts make more frequently use of rhetorical means for emotional influence.

Based on a comparative analysis of some English and German advertising texts, we have also noticed that German texts (especially advertising texts for technological products) are more neutral than English ones, stressing mainly the quality and technical aspects. For example, in an advertising text about a model car, the evaluative adjectives in the English ST were replaced in the German TT by adjectives expressing an element of quantity or precision or they were deleted altogether:

- The ultimate in elegance and design, captured forever in the last XX ever created by YY. – Im Maßstab von 1:24 aus über 100 Einzelteilen präzisionsgefertigt. Die authentische Replik eines legendären Automobils.
- exciting detail – exakte Details
- reveal every fascinating detail of the six-cylinder engine – kann man den aufwendig gearbeiteten Sechszylindermotor bewundern
- the handsome toolboxes – Werkzeugkoffer

As a result, the German TT has fewer adjectives and nouns that express sensual impressions and appeal to the emotions. In the TT, the focus is on precision, workmanship, whereas in the ST, the focus is on the feelings and emotions of the readers (see also Steiner [1998] who arrived at similar results, and who concludes that reliability has a higher social value in Germany than in the UK).

Direct forms of address (e.g. speech acts of request, recommendation) are another typical feature of promotional texts, also of tourist information brochures. For this genre, the use of parallel texts can be very helpful for translators. For example, English tourist brochures published by local tourist offices, often have as a closing formula 'We will do everything possible to make your stay here a very pleasant one'. A corresponding German phrase could be 'Wir bemühen uns, Ihnen Ihren Aufenthalt so angenehm wir möglich zu machen'.

Other stylistic features characteristic of promotional texts are the use of proverbs, puns, slogans, slang, alliteration, rhyme, etc. Such stylistic means can be introduced in the TT where appropriate. For example, in an advertising text for a cosmetics product, the German TT introduced an allusion to a well-known slogan ('Milch macht müde Männer munter'), thus also allowing for an alliteration as an additional stylistic feature:

> This time honoured synergy of delicate hand picked field flowers [...] cools and uplifts tired eyes. – Diese altbewährte Kombination aus zarten handgepflückten Feldblumen [...] kühlt die Augenpartie und macht müde Augen wieder munter.

In tourist information it is also common practice to use SL expressions in the TT, both to help the readers to find their way and to add to the local flair of the text. In addition, a slogan or a campaign motto is frequently used, often to structure the text. The promotion purpose can also be supported by reference to historic or technical achievements, to awards and prizes received, or by quoting authoritative voices (e.g. politicians, scientists, famous artists).

Sample Text

The sample text in this volume is a tourist information text (since the authentic German TT shows some defects, we have added our own alternative version). The text is addressed to the general public; and culture-specific and stylistic aspects are of relevance, for example alliteration, idiomatic expressions, and allusions. Extra-textual information, however, is not highly relevant in our sample text.

Birmingham
Europe's meeting place

Illustrated Brochure published by Birmingham Marketing Partnership

[1]
Europe's meeting place meets your needs. Where communication networks converge, where cultures co-exist, where industry and commerce combine, the City of Birmingham forms the focal point of a unique concentration of resources and facilities It is, in every sense, Europe's meeting place.

[2]
A sense of place. Birmingham is not just the centre of the United Kingdom, it is central to the European experience, a gateway for transatlantic trade, a focus for business and business people. By road, by rail, by air, the city is a pivot for all points of the compass and for travel to and from Europe and the United States. Birmingham is, geographically and culturally, central to European life.

[3]
A flying start. Handling over four million passengers a year, Birmingham International Airport – with its dedicated 'Eurohub' terminal – is truly international. It operates direct scheduled flights to and from 39 destinations throughout Europe, Scandinavia and the United States. In other words, all the major business centres are connected to Birmingham.

[4]
Show business is BIG business. The National Exhibition Centre, largest in the UK, is perfectly positioned for its international role. In its sixteen halls, it hosts 110 exhibitions a year and welcomes some 4 million visitors. On site is an 800 bed luxury hotel and the famous 12,600 seat NEC Arena, which provides a complementary venue for international rock concerts, world championships and conventions. It lies at the heart of Britain's motorway network, has its own InterCity railway station and is linked directly to the airport.

[5]
Money matters. The city which boasts the world's oldest Mint, which saw the establishment of two of the leading clearing banks and which has been home to the Bank of England since 1827, is a financial and business centre of international standing. One of the largest business

communities in Europe draws on an established infrastructure of multi-disciplinary expertise to underpin more than £1 billion of business a year, including Europe's second largest insurance market.

[6]

This is Convention City. The most prestigious conference centre in the UK and Europe stands prominently in the centre of the city. In its short life, the International Convention Centre has already played host to the European Summit and other high profile political, cultural and corporate conferences. The eleven meeting halls, which include the magnificent Symphony Hall, can accommodate from 30 to 3000 delegates in comfort, in style, in safety and security.

[7]

Eclectic, eccentric, exciting. Birmingham's music scene cannot be simply categorized. If it revolves around the high-profile City of Birmingham Symphony Orchestra under Simon Rattle in their new home – the acoustic perfection of Symphony Hall – it can also include UB40 at the NEC Arena, the D'Oyly Carte Opera and an extraordinary cosmopolitan diversity of Asian and Afro-Caribbean sounds. Jazz is at Ronnie Scott's all year round and during the International Jazz Festival, gets out into the streets and malls and clubs and bars of the UK's 'City of Music'.

[8]

The big occasion. Centrally located adjacent to the International Convention Centre is the UK's leading indoor sporting arena, tailor-made for the big events in international athletics and tennis, boxing and ice-skating. But the National Indoor Arena does not restrict itself to sport. Up to 12,000 people have watched everything from TV extravaganzas like The Gladiators to Aida to spectacular product launches in this world class stadium.

[9]

The world's workshop. The home and heart of the industrial revolution continues to be a major manufacturing centre, with more than a third of Britain's manufacturing exports emanating from the region. Now, however, as finance and commerce support and supplement manufacturing, as new companies join established international names like Cadbury's, Rover, Lucas and IMI, new industries are being created. Today, it is Birmingham's advanced manufacturing technology which is ensuring the future prosperity of the region.

[10]

For art's sake. Birmingham is a major cultural destination. The world's leading Pre-Raphaelite collection hangs in the City Museum and Art Gallery contrasting sharply with the innovative work of contemporary artists at the Ikon Gallery. Its literary scene is diverse: the city has been home to writers as different as JRR Tolkien and Conan Doyle. Meanwhile, The Birmingham Royal Ballet dance at the Hippodrome, the Repertory Theatre remains centre stage, and a wealth of independent organisations and festivals ensure that the arts continue to enhance the city's quality of life.

[11]

The skill factor. Traditional skills in leather, glass and jewellery still flourish. But in the new science, computer and business parks, new skills, new technologies and new commitment to training are continuing the tradition of scientific endeavour that produced Joseph Priestley, James Watt, Matthew Boulton and William Murdoch. From the city's three Universities, new generations of science, engineering and arts specialists are applying their innovative skills to the advanced requirements of today's industry and commerce.

[12]

Bed room. For visitors to the meeting place of Europe more than 35,000 beds may be found within twenty miles of the city centre. The Birmingham Convention & Visitor Bureau will find everyone a place to eat well and sleep soundly: from a modest but comfortable Bed & Breakfast to the elegance and quality of the Swallow Hotel, the Hotel of the Year in 1994. But whichever choice is appropriate, Birmingham meets everyone with high standards and an unfailingly friendly welcome.

[13]

The name of the game. Birmingham loves its sport and hosts more World and European championship events than any other UK city. The Belfry, one of thirty golf courses in the area, is the UK PGA headquarters and hosted the Ryder Cup on three occasions. Villa Park, the home of Aston Villa, will be one of the venues for the 1996 European Football Championship. The city has two world-class indoor venues and close to the site of the world's first ever game of lawn tennis in Edgbaston, is one of the world's finest test cricket stadiums. Whatever your sport, Birmingham is the place to enjoy it.

[14]

Ancient and modern. Birmingham's buildings are milestones in its development from market town to major city and meeting place for Europe. Its Jacobean roots and Regency elegance are still evident among the proud Victorian and Edwardian civic buildings, built as symbols of prosperity and progress. Joseph Chamberlain, the Lord Mayor of Birmingham in its Victorian heyday and the man who personified Birmingham's confident approach to the world, would appreciate the city's commitment to re-shaping its centre and share its pride in today's powerful and contemporary architecture, public art and open squares. **[15]**

The quality of life. The busy bustle of Birmingham belies the fact that it has more public parks than any other European city. Chief among these are Sutton Park, bequeathed by Henry VIII, and the beautiful Botanical Gardens. Away from the pressures of business, Birmingham people and their guests can wander along pleasant walkways and canal sides to discover designer shops and fine stores. And they can always find peace and tranquillity in a city which boasts no less than six million trees and puts its wide open spaces to good use with a continuing programme of carnivals and festivals. **[16]**

The business of pleasure. At night Birmingham comes alive to entertain itself and its visitors, offering everything you would expect from a major European meeting place – and a few that are unique to Birmingham itself. Everyone will enjoy the wine bars and bistros, pubs and clubs. Lovers of good food will find some of the best Balti and Chinese restaurants in Europe as well as opportunities to sample every kind of international cuisine. When business is completed, Birmingham takes its pleasure seriously. **[17]**

Rural Birmingham. The true diversity of metropolitan Birmingham is matched by the diversity of the surrounding countryside. London is merely an hour and a half by train, but within a short drive are the historic towns of Stratford-upon-Avon and Ironbridge. To the south is Warwick Castle, the finest medieval castle in England. To the north is Stoke-on-Trent, where Spode and Wedgwood founded their great potteries, which may be seen in operation today. With the Cotswold and Malvern hills close by, Birmingham is surrounded by country walks and country pubs.

Translation Assignment
Birmingham Marketing Partnership wants to produce a trilingual illustrated brochure (English, French, and German) to promote Birmingham. For this purpose, the English text has to be translated. In the brochure, the three language versions will be printed side by side, interspersed by photos and other illustrations. The brochure is meant to be freely available for distribution in travel agencies, information offices, at the airport, etc., within Birmingham, i.e. it is not primarily intended to send the brochure abroad.

Birmingham

[1]

Europas Treffpunkt, der keine Wünsche offenläßt. Wo Kommunikationsnetze zusammenlaufen, wo unterschiedliche Kulturen in friedlichem Nebeneinander existieren und Industrie und Handel mit vereinter Kraft zusammenwirken – dort liegt Birmingham, Mittelpunkt der einmaligen Konzentration von Ressourcen und Möglichkeiten. Birmingham ist, in jeder Hinsicht, der Treffpunkt Europas.

[2]

Standortbestimmung. Birmingham bildet nicht nur das Herz des Vereinigten Königreichs: Es steht auch fest im Mittelpunkt des europäischen Geschehens, ist ein Tor im transatlantischen Handel und ein wichtiger Brennpunkt der Geschäftswelt. Im Schienen-, Straßen- und Luftverkehr ist die Stadt ein zentraler Knotenpunkt für Reisende aus Ost und West, Nord und Süd, von und nach Europa und den USA. Birmingham steht geographisch und kulturell fest im europäischen Leben.

[3]

Hier heben Sie ab! Mit jährlich über vier Millionen Fluggästen ist der Birmingham International Airport mit seinem Spezialterminal 'Eurohub' ein im wahrsten Sinne internationaler Flughafen. Direkte Linienflüge nach 39 Reisezielen in Europa, Skandinavien sowie nach den USA werden hier abgewickelt. Alle wichtigen Geschäftszentren sind mit Birmingham verbunden.

[4]

Showbusineß ist 'Big Business'. Der Standort des National Exhibition Centre, das größte in England, ist perfekt für die internationale Rolle des Messezentrums. In den sechzehn Hallen finden jährlich 110 Ausstellungen mit rund vier Millionen Besuchern statt. Weitere 'Platzvorteile' sind ein 800-Betten-Luxushotel und die berühmte, 12600 Zuschauer fassende NEC Arena, ein Treffpunkt für internationale Rockkonzerte, Weltmeisterschaften und Tagungen. Das NEC liegt im Zentrum des britischen Autobahnnetzes, besitzt einen eigenen Inter-City-Bahnhof und direkten Anschluß zum Flughafen.

[5]

Geldangelegenheiten. Die Stadt, die die älteste Münzstätte der Welt ihr eigen nennt, in der zwei der führenden Clearingbanken gegründet wurden und wo seit 1827 die Bank of England zu Hause ist, ist ein Finanz- und Geschäftszentrum von internationalem Rang. Einer der größten Wirtschaftskreise Europas (u.a. der zweitgrößte europäische

Versicherungsmarkt) profitiert von der etablierten Infrastruktur zahlreicher Fachdisziplinen, die das Fundament des jährlich mehr als 1 Milliarde Pfund starken Wirtschaftsaufkommens der Stadt bilden.
[6]
Es wird getagt. Das renommierteste Kongreßzentrum Großbritanniens und Europas nimmt einen stolzen Platz im Herzen der Stadt ein. In der kurzen Zeit seines Bestehens hat das International Convention Centre bereits einen europäischen Gipfel und andere wichtige politische, kulturelle und Firmenereignisse erlebt. Elf Veranstaltungssäle, darunter die großartige Konzerthalle Symphony Hall, bieten 30 bis 3000 Gästen bequem in elegantem, sicherem Ambiente Platz.
[7]
Eklektisch, exzentrisch und erregend. Birminghams Musikszene läßt sich in keine Schublade pressen. Das renommierte City of Birmingham Symphony Orchestra unter Leitung von Dirigent Simon Rattle, das in der Symphony Hall mit ihrer perfekten Akustik eine neue Heimstatt gefunden hat, spielt hier ebenso eine Rolle wie UB40 in der NEC Arena, die D'Oyly Carte Opera und das bunte kosmopolitische Spektrum asiatischer und afro-karibischer Klänge. Und während des Internationalen Jazzfestivals dringt der Jazz, der ganzjährig im Ronnie Scott's zu Hause ist, hinaus auf die Straßen und in die Einkaufszentren, Clubs und Bars der britischen 'City of Music'.
[8]
Großes Ereignis. In zentraler Lage, direkt neben dem International Convention Centre, befindet sich die führende britische Hallen-Sportarena mit maßgeschneiderten Spezialanlagen für große internationale Leichtathletik-, Tennis-, Box- und Eislaufveranstaltungen. Doch in der National Indoor Arena dreht sich nicht nur alles um den Sport. Bis zu 12.000 Zuschauer erleben in dem Weltklassestadium eine Vielfalt von Ereignissen, die von der Aufzeichnung des TV-Spektakels The Gladiators über die Oper Aida bis hin zu eindrucksvollen Produkteinführungen reicht.
[9]
Die Werkstatt der Welt. Die Region, die einst Ausgangspunkt der industriellen Revolution war, ist auch heute ein wichtiges Fertigungszentrum. Mehr als ein Drittel der britischen Industrieexporte kommen noch immer von hier. Heute erhält das verarbeitende Gewerbe durch Finanz- und Handelsbetriebe Unterstützung, und mit der Ansiedlung neuer Unternehmen entstehen neue Industriezweige neben renommierten internationalen Namen wie Cadbury's, Rover, Lucas und IMI. Birminghams fortschrittliche Fertigungstechnik sichert auch den zukünftigen Wohlstand der Region.

[10]

Kunst als Selbstzweck. Birmingham ist ein kulturelles Terrain par excellence. Ein größerer Kontrast als zwischen der führenden Prä-Raffaeliten-Sammlung im City Museum and Art Gallery und den innovativen Werken zeitgenössischer Künstler in der Ikon Gallery beispielsweise ist kaum vorstellbar. Nicht weniger vielseitig ist die literarische Szene der Stadt: Zu den berühmten Söhnen der Stadt zählen so unterschiedliche Autoren wie JRR Tolkien und Conan Doyle. Das Birmingham Royal Ballet tanzt im Hippodrome, das Repertory Theatre steht weiterhin im Mittelpunkt des Bühnengeschehens, und ein breites Spektrum von unabhängigen Organisationen und Festivals sorgen dafür, daß die Kunst auch weiterhin die Lebensqualität der Stadt positiv prägt.

[11]

Hier wird Können großgeschrieben. Überlieferte Fertigkeiten spielen auch heute noch in der Leder-, Glas- und Schmuckwarenindustrie eine wichtige Rolle, während die neuen Wissenschafts-, Computer- und Geschäftsparks durch neue Fachkenntnisse, Technologien und Ausbildungsschwerpunkte die Tradition wissenschaftlichen Unternehmertums fortsetzen, die einst so klingende Namen wie Joseph Priestley, James Watt, Matthew Boulton und William Murdoch [sic!]. Aus den drei Universitäten der Stadt geht eine neue Generation von Wissenschaftlern, Technikern und Künstlern hervor, die in den modernen Anforderungen von Industrie und Handel ein breites Betätigungsfeld für ihre innovativen Fertigkeiten finden.

[12]

Betten-Kapazität. Im Umkreis von rund 30 Kilometern um das Stadtzentrum warten über 35.000 Betten aud [sic!] die Besucher, die sich im Treffpunkt Europas einfinden. Das Birmingham Convention & Visitor Bureau arrangiert Unterbringungen für jeden Geschmack und Geldbeutel: Das Angebot reicht von bescheidenen, aber einladenden Bed-&-Breakfast-Pensionen bis hin zum erstklassigen, eleganten Swallow Hotel, das 1994 als 'Hotel des Jahres' ausgezeichnet wurde. Egal, für welche Preisklasse Sie sich entscheiden, Birmingham bietet hohen Standard und ein jederzeit freundliches Willkommen.

[13]

Aus Freude am Spiel. Birmingham ist eine sportbegeisterte Stadt und jährlich Austragungsort von mehr weltweiten und europäischen Meisterschaftsereignissen als jeder andere britische Ort. The Belfry, einer von dreißig Golfplätzen in der Region, ist die Zentrale des britischen Profigolfverbandes PGA; dreimal wurde hier bereits der

Ryder Cup ausgetragen. Villa Park, das Stadion des Fußballclubs Aston Villa, ist 1996 einer der Austragungsorte der Fußball-Europameisterschaft. Die Stadt besitzt zwei Sporthallen von Weltrang, und in der Nähe des international renommierten Cricket-Platzes in Edgbaston wurde einst das erste Rasentennis-Match der Welt ausgetragen. In Birmingham kommt jeder Sportliebhaber auf seine Kosten.

[14]

Alt und neu. An Birminghams Gebäuden läßt sich die Entwicklung vom Marktstädtchen zum europäischen Treffpunkt nachvollziehen. Überreste der architektonischen Wurzeln aus der Zeit Jakobs I. und die Eleganz des Regency sind heute noch zwischen den stolzen öffentlichen Gebäuden aus der Zeit Königin Victorias und König Eduards, einst errichtet als Symbol des Wohlstands und Fortschritts, zu finden. Joseph Chamberlain, der als Birminghams Oberbürgermeister in der viktorianischen Blütezeit die selbstsichere Haltung der Stadt gegenüber dem Rest der Welt verkörperte, wäre sicherlich stolz auf die heutigen engagierten Bemühungen um eine Erneuerung des Stadtzentrums und die eindrucksvolle, zeitgenössische Architektur, das öffentliche Kunstangebot und die offenen Plätze der Stadt.

[15]

Lebensqualität. Doch wenden wir uns vom geschäftigen Treiben der Stadt einmal ab: Birmingham besitzt mehr öffentliche Parkanlagen als jede andere Stadt in Europa. Erwähnung verdienen hier besonders der von Heinrich VIII. gestiftete Sutton Park und die eindrucksvollen Botanische [sic!] Gärten. Losgelöst von der Hektik des städtischen Lebens laden hier freundliche Spazierwege durch Parkanlagen und an Kanälen Einheimische und Besucher zum Bummeln und zum Entdecken von Designerläden und anderen feinen Geschäften ein. Ruhe und Stille sind überall zu finden in dieser Stadt, die nicht weniger als 6 Millionen Bäume ihr eigen nennt und auf seinen zahlreichen offenen Plätzen ein ständiges Karneval- und Festivalprogramm bietet.

[16]

Spaß am Vergnügen. Birmingham bei Nacht bietet Einheimischen und Besuchern all das, was man von einem wichtigen europäischen Treffpunkt erwarten würde – und zudem einige ganz spezielle Birminghamer Spezialitäten. Neben einladenden Weinstuben, Bistros, Pubs und Clubs finden Gourmets hier einige der besten chinesischen und Balti-Restaurants Europas und zahlreiche Gelegenheiten, internationale Speisen aus aller Welt zu probieren. Denn nach getaner Arbeit weiß Birmingham nach allen Regeln der Kunst zu feiern.

[17]

Birmingham – die ländliche Seite. Die umgebende Landschaft steht der
städtischen Metropole Birmingham in Sachen Vielfältigkeit in nichts
nach. London ist per Bahn in ganzen 1 1/2 Stunden zu erreichen, die
historischen Städte Stratford-upon-Avon und Ironbridge sind nur eine
kurze Autofahrt entfernt. Im Süden liegt Warwick Castle, das
prächtigste   mittelalterliche   Schloß   Englands,   im   Norden
Stoke-on-Trent, wo die berühmten Porzellanmanufakturen von Spode
und Wedgwood heute noch in Betrieb sind. Und in den umgebenden
Cotswolds und Malvern Hills laden Wanderwege und ländliche Pubs
zum Verweilen ein.

Annotations

Translation Assignment

Birmingham Marketing Partnership wants to produce a trilingual illustrated brochure (English, French, and German) to promote Birmingham. For this purpose, the English text has to be translated. In the brochure, the three language versions will be printed side by side, interspersed by photos and other illustrations. The brochure is meant to be freely available for distribution in travel agencies, information offices, at the airport, etc., within Birmingham, i.e. it is not primarily intended to send the brochure abroad.

ST Characterisation

The ST is a visitor information leaflet, and in a sense thus also a kind of advertising text. As such, it is a persuasive text, i.e. the main aim is to present Birmingham and its facilities to the international world in order to attract them to come to the city, maybe primarily for business (this characterisation is motivated by the knowledge that the Birmingham Marketing Partnership commissioned the production of the brochure), but also for pleasure. The ST addressees are English speaking people (not necessary English as mother tongue) who (plan to) visit Birmingham. The brochure is meant to give the readers some brief information about the town they are visiting (short-term, immediate purpose), and also persuade them to come back and to promote Birmingham in their own hometown (long-term purpose).

The style of the ST contributes to its main function: short sentences (sometimes elliptical sentences), the audience is directly addressed (personal pronouns 'you, your'; request, recommendation as frequent speech acts), positive evaluative expressions (especially adjectives with positive connotations, such as 'unique, prestigious, magnificent'). With respect to its content, the ST is highly source culture specific. This is reflected in the large number of source-culture-specific references (place names, names for traditional events, meals, etc.). The central motto of the promotion campaign is 'Birmingham, Europe's meeting place'. The idea of meeting is a central one for the structure of the text. Other characteristic formal features are short phrases to introduce each new piece of information (pseudo-headings).

TT Specification

The TT is intended for inclusion into the trilingual brochure. As the ST, it will be an advertising text, with persuasion as its main function. The TT addressees are, first of all, German-speaking business people, but also tourists, who arrive in Birmingham. That is, the brochure will be used by them.

The TT presented here is actually the German translation that was published in the trilingual brochure (which was produced by the Birmingham Marketing Partnership in 1995). In this brochure, the English, French and German texts were printed in different sizes and fonts, with the English text printed much larger, and the short phrases which introduce each new piece of information were printed in bold. In the French and the German versions, these pseudo-headings have not been set off by a special print style.

What is to be expected is a TT whose structure and content are appropriate for the intended function (advertising, promotion) in a specific communicative context (distribution within Birmingham). Since the ST is highly source culture specific in its content, we also expect that the TT will account for a lack in background knowledge of the TT addressees.

We have identified pragmatic and text-specific translation problems as the most important ones in this text. For the following annotations, the translation strategies that were applied for the authentic TT are discussed and, where deemed necessary, evaluated. In this sense, the annotations for this text are partly a translation criticism. In some cases, alternative versions are suggested as improvements of the existing TT. There are also a few typing errors and grammatical mistakes in the published TT, which we have indicated by [sic!].

Annotations

Pragmatic translation problems

The purpose of the text is to provide information about Birmingham to people who do not (yet) know the town, thus promoting the town and attract visitors. Since ST and TT addressees do not share the culture-specific background knowledge, the translator has to decide on the amount of explanation that will be necessary in order to produce a TT, which is appropriate for its purpose (i.e. Chesterman's (1997a) pragmatic translation strategies, *information change* and *visibility change*, will be relevant). The ST contains only the most essential facts, without going into detail (e.g. no specification of industries associated with company names, the three universities are not named, historical personalities are just mentioned by name). Some explanation will be necessary, and the translator will have to balance the amount of required additions and/or specifications to the characteristic features of the genre tourist information (with space restrictions and layout considerations also playing a role). In other words, to decide on the required quantity of information in the TT, one needs to bear in mind that the TT will have to be an advertising text, as is the ST (i.e. equifunctional translation, 'Funktionskonstanz'). It can equally be argued that there will also be readers of the ST who do not have the relevant background knowledge to fully comprehend all the proper names (i.e. English-speaking readers who are not familiar either with Birmingham or with the UK as a whole).

In the published TT, explanations and additions have mainly been provided for place names, institutions, and other culture specific phenomena (*realia*).

(i) Place names

Paragraph 1: the City of Birmingham – Birmingham

Birmingham is officially designated a 'City' (it has a cathedral). Since there is no comparable procedure in Germany (see 'Stadtrecht verleihen', which means that a village becomes a town), and since this aspect is not of relevance in Paragraph 1, the proper name on its own in the TT is sufficient.

In subsequent paragraphs, 'city' has consistently been rendered as 'Stadt' (with the exception of 'Ort' in Paragraph 13 for stylistic reasons, i.e. to avoid repetition of 'Stadt'), or it has been deleted (Paragraph 14), unless 'City' is part of a more complex proper name (e.g. City of Birmingham Symphony Orchestra in

Paragraph 7, City Museum and Art Gallery in Paragraph 10 – see *(ii) Proper names for buildings, institutions, and other bodies* below).

In Paragraph 14, there is an explicit contrast between 'city' and 'town':

Paragraph 14:
Birmingham's buildings are milestones in its development from market town to major city and meeting place for Europe. – An Birminghams Gebäuden läßt sich die Entwicklung vom Marktstädtchen zum europäischen Treffpunkt nachvollziehen.

In the TT, the diminutive form 'Marktstädtchen' reflects the aspect of unimportance, and 'europäischer Treffpunkt' implies 'major city' (translation strategy: compression), with this aspect having been presented in the text before (see also *(ii) Textual key concepts* under *Text-specific translation problems*).

Paragraph 17:
London . . . the historic towns of Stratford-upon-Avon and Ironbridge . . . Stoke-on-Trent . . . With the Cotswold and Malvern hills close by, Birmingham is surrounded by country walks . . . – die historischen Städte Stratford-upon-Avon und Ironbridge . . . Stoke-on-Trent, . . . Und in den umgebenden Cotswolds und Malvern Hills laden Wanderwege . . .

The context clarifies that these are names for towns. The heading of this paragraph ('Rural Birmingham' – 'Birmingham – die ländliche Seite') and the reference to 'Wanderwege' will, in all probability, allow for an interpretation of Cotswolds and Malvern Hills as regions of a rural character. Alternatively, a generic noun could have been added (e.g. 'Die Landschaft der Cotswolds und der Malvern Hills in unmittelbarer Nähe'; see also below *(iii) References to source-culture-specific traditions, historical events, and people*).

(ii) Proper names for buildings, institutions, and other bodies
The translator has opted generally for the strategy of keeping the original name and adding a superordinate term for the category. This strategy is highly appropriate for the purpose of the TT:

Paragraph 3:
Birmingham International Airport – with its dedicated 'Eurohub' terminal – is truly international. – . . . ist der Birmingham International Airport mit seinem Spezialterminal 'Eurohub' ein im wahrsten Sinne internationaler Flughafen.

The proper names are kept in the TT, and the generic noun 'Flughafen' has been added (but mainly for stylistic reasons, 'Airport' is widely used in German-speaking countries). 'Terminal', too, is increasingly used on German airports. 'Spezialterminal' conveys a sense of use for specific purposes. A more appropriate TT version would be 'mit seinem zweiten Terminal 'Eurohub'.

Paragraph 4:
The National Exhibition Centre, . . . is perfectly positioned for its international role. . . . NEC Arena, . . . It lies . . . – . . . National Exhibition Centre, . . . ist perfekt für die internationale Rolle des Messezentrums. . . . NEC Arena . . . Das NEC liegt . . .

The proper name has been kept and a superordinate category name ('Messe-zentrum') has been added. The ST uses the abbreviation NEC for the next textual occurrence, and so does the TT. In texts of this kind (i.e. tourist information), it is advisable to add the abbreviation (preferably in brackets) immediately after the first occurrence of the full name. In this particular case, we would also suggest an alternative version to make clear that 'Messezentrum' refers to NEC:

Alternative version:
Der Standort des National Exhibition Centre (NEC), des größten in England, ist perfekt für seine internationale Rolle als Messezentrum.

Paragraph 6:
This is Convention City. The most prestigious conference centre . . . the Inter-national Convention Centre . . . Symphony Hall – Es wird getagt. Das renommierteste Kongreßzentrum . . . das International Convention Centre . . . Konzerthalle Symphony Hall . . .

Here again, the translator has opted for a combination of a superordinate term ('Kongreßzentrum', 'Konzerthalle') and the English proper name. For reasons of consistency, it is advisable to add the abbreviation 'ICC' after 'International Con-vention Centre'. The allusion to the proper name in the heading, however, has disappeared in the TT.

Paragraph 7:
Birmingham's music scene . . . City of Birmingham Symphony Orchestra under Simon Rattle . . . UB40 at the NEC Arena, the D'Oyly Carte Opera . . . at Ronnie Scott's . . . – Birminghams Musikszene . . . City of Birmingham Sym-phony Orchestra unter Leitung von Dirigent Simon Rattle . . . UB40 in der NEC Arena, die D'Oyly Carte Opera . . . im Ronnie Scott's

The topic of this paragraph is introduced by 'music scene/Musikszene', which makes further specifications unnecessary. The formal similarities between 'orchestra' and 'Orchester' and between 'opera' and 'Oper', in addition to the activated frame 'music', facilitate comprehension. Previously introduced proper names can easily be taken up again. The contrast between classical music at Symphony Hall and pop music at the NEC Arena might not be immediately obvious to those visitors who do not know the rock band UB40. However, in Paragraph 4, information was provided about rock concerts being held at the NEC. Alternatively, a specification could have been used: 'die Rockband UB40'. The music frame would also make the specification/addition of 'unter Leitung von Dirigent Simon Rattle' unnecessary. A shorter version is sufficient (either 'unter Leitung von Simon Rattle' – which is the more conventional formulation – or 'mit dem Dirigenten Simon Rattle'). 'Ronnie Scott's' is the name of a jazz club, named after its founder (the first club was opened in London in 1959). It would go too far to provide all these details to the TT readers, but 'im Ronnie Scott's' is in our view rather unspecified. We would therefore suggest adding a generic noun (i.e. 'im Ronnie Scott's Club').

Paragraph 8:
. . . indoor sporting arena . . . the National Indoor Arena . . . – . . . Hallen-Sportarena . . . National Indoor Arena . . .

Both in the ST and in the TT, the category term is used before the proper name. For textual consistency we would suggest adding the abbreviation ('NIA') to the TT.

Paragraph 9:
... major manufacturing centre ... established international names like Cadbury's, Rover, Lucas and IMI. – ... Fertigungszentrum ... renommierten internationalen Namen wie Cadbury's, Rover, Lucas und IMI.

Both in the ST and in the TT, the explicit reference to 'manufacturing centre/ Fertigungszentrum' (although 'Industriezentrum' would be more appropriate) facilitates the interpretation of the names ('Cadbury's, Rover, Lucas, IMI') as company names. The purpose of this particular text does not require further specification as to the respective branches of industry. Moreover, the characterisation as 'established international names' indicates an assumption that the readers too, are familiar with these companies (with 'international renommierte Namen' being a more appropriate collocation).

In Paragraphs 5 and 10, superordinate terms are not required due to the formal identity or similarity of the English and German words. The gender specifications are based on the gender of the corresponding German words:

Paragraph 5:
the Bank of England – die Bank of England

Paragraph 10:
... Pre-Raphaelite collection ... the City Museum and Art Gallery ... contemporary artists at the Ikon Gallery. ... The Birmingham Royal Ballet dance at the Hippodrome, the Repertory Theatre ... – ... Prä-Raffaeliten-Sammlung im City Museum and Art Gallery ... Werken zeitgenössischer Künstler in der Ikon Gallery ... Das Birmingham Royal Ballet tanzt im Hippodrome, das Repertory Theatre ...

The purpose of the TT does not require a further explanation of 'Pre-Raphaelite' (but see also below *(ii) Theme–rheme structure* under *Interlingual translation problems*). Due to the specification 'contemporary artists', it can safely be assumed that 'Ikon' will not be misinterpreted as icon (i.e. a painting of a sacred person, associated with the Eastern Church), due to the formal similarity to 'Ikone'.

Paragraph 12:
The Birmingham Convention & Visitor Bureau ... the Swallow Hotel ... – Birmingham Convention & Visitor Bureau ... Swallow Hotel ...

'Birmingham Convention & Visitor Bureau' needs to be kept in the original since visitors would need to know where to go when in need of accommodation. The context should be sufficient for identification; alternatively, a category name (e.g. 'Touristeninformation', 'Informationszentrum') could be added.

Paragraph 15:
... it has more public parks ... among these are Sutton Park, ... and the beautiful Botanical Gardens. – ... öffentliche Parkanlagen ... Sutton Park und die eindrucksvollen Botanische [sic!] Gärten.

The generic noun 'Parkanlagen' facilitates the identification of Sutton Park as a proper name (supported also by the formal similarity between the English 'park' and the German 'Park'. 'Botanischer Garten' is normally used in the singular form. Moreover, the TT sentence is grammatically incorrect since with the plural form it would need to read 'die eindrucksvollen Botanischen Gärten'.

Corrected version:
Birmingham besitzt mehr öffentliche Parkanlagen als jede andere Stadt in Europa. Erwähnung verdienen hier besonders der von Heinrich VIII. gestiftete Sutton Park und der eindrucksvolle Botanische Garten.

Paragraph 17:
To the south is Warwick Castle, the finest medieval castle in England. . . . where Spode and Wedgwood founded their great potteries . . . – Im Süden liegt Warwick Castle, das prächtigste mittelalterliche Schloß Englands, . . . wo die berühmten Porzellanmanufakturen von Spode und Wedgwood . . .

The context itself provides generic nouns ('castle', 'potteries') and sufficient explanation. In view of the purpose of the text (i.e. visitors read the brochure in Birmingham, they will [have to] look out for signs, inscriptions, etc. in English), the proper name 'Warwick Castle' is the preferred choice, instead of the alternative version 'Schloß Warwick'. A specification ('Porzellanmanufakturen') accounts for (assumed) lacking background knowledge of the TT readers.

(iii) References to source culture specific traditions, historical events, and people

Paragraph 1: specification/expansion in TT
. . . where cultures co-exist, . . . – wo unterschiedliche Kulturen in friedlichem Nebeneinander existieren

Birmingham is a city where people from different ethnic groups live together. The translator opted for a more explicit rendering of this fact, which is implicit in the ST.

Paragraph 8:
But the National Indoor Arena does not restrict itself to sport. . . . from TV extravaganzas like The Gladiators to Aida . . . – Doch in der National Indoor Arena dreht sich nicht nur alles um den Sport. . . . von der Aufzeichnung des TV-Spektakels The Gladiators über die Oper Aida . . .

'The Gladiators' is actually a kind of sports game, albeit more for amusement. For readers who do not know what it is about, the previous sentence ('does not restrict itself to sport') might not be very helpful, and also 'TV Spektakel' is rather non-descriptive. The purpose of the TT does not require a detailed explication as to what kind of TV programme it is, but we would nevertheless suggest something more descriptive, e.g. 'Sport-Spiel-Show' (also to set it apart from 'Oper').

Paragraph 11:
. . . continuing the tradition of scientific endeavour that produced Joseph Priestley, James Watt, Matthew Boulton and William Murdoch. – . . . die Tra-

dition wissenschaftlichen Unternehmertums fortsetzen, die einst so klingende Namen wie Joseph Priestley, James Watt, Matthew Boulton und
William Murdoch.

The context allows for an interpretation as names of famous scientists and
inventors of the past. A more detailed explanation of their inventions and/or
their specific fields of expertise is not required in this particular text. However,
the TT sentence is grammatically incomplete, since a verb phrase is missing. The
translator might have been thinking of 'hervorbrachte', but in that case
'klingende Namen' would not be an appropriate collocation.

Alternative versions:
. . . die Tradition wissenschaftlichen Unternehmertums fortsetzen, die einst
von so berühmten Erfindern wie Joseph Priestley, James Watt, Matthew
Boulton und William Murdoch begründet wurde.

or:
. . . die einst so berühmte Erfinder wie Joseph Priestley, James Watt, Matthew
Boulton und William Murdoch hervorbrachte.

or:
. . . die mit so klingenden Namen wie Joseph Priestley, James Watt, Matthew
Boulton und William Murdoch verbunden ist.

Paragraph 12:
. . . the Swallow Hotel, the Hotel of the Year in 1994 – . . . Swallow Hotel, das
1994 als 'Hotel des Jahres' ausgezeichnet wurde.

The translator opted for the addition of 'ausgezeichnet' to indicate that 'Hotel
of the Year' is a title of honour.

Paragraph 13:
The Belfry, one of thirty golf courses in the area, is the UK PGA headquarters
and hosted the Ryder Cup on three occasions. Villa Park, the home of Aston
Villa, . . . close to the site of the world's first ever game of lawn tennis in
Edgbaston, is one of the world's finest test cricket stadiums. – The Belfry,
einer von dreißig Golfplätzen in der Region, ist die Zentrale des britischen
Profigolfverbandes PGA; dreimal wurde hier bereits der Ryder Cup ausgetragen. Villa Park, das Stadion des Fußballclubs Aston Villa, . . . in der Nähe
des international renommierten Cricket-Platzes in Edgbaston wurde einst
das erste Rasentennis-Match der Welt ausgetragen.

The translator has again opted for some specifications (i.e. an explanation of
the abbreviation 'PGA', the addition of 'Fußballclub' or more exactly, a specification as 'Stadion des Fußballclubs' – or, alternatively, 'das Heimstadion'). In
the last sentence, the propositions have been exchanged, resulting in a change
of the theme–rheme structure (i.e. giving more prominence to the tennis game
instead of the cricket stadium – see *emphasis change* as a semantic translation
strategy in Chesterman's (1997a) classification). In other words, whereas the
rheme in the ST is cricket (which is more in line with culture-specific interests),
the rheme in the TT is tennis, in a historical perspective. Since the purpose of

this paragraph is to provide brief information about the variety of sports offered in Birmingham, this change does not have any major impact (and both the tennis and the cricket stadium are located in Edgbaston). One could even argue that since cricket is of hardly any relevance to German speakers (see also the comments in the annotations to Sample Text 5), this change may be even more in line with readers' expectations and experience with this kind of tourist information in German. An alternative version, keeping the theme–rheme structure of the ST, could be:

... und in der Nähe des Platzes, wo einst das erste Rasentennis-Match der Welt ausgetragen wurde, befindet sich das international renommierte Cricket-Stadion in Edgbaston.

A more literal version (. . . befindet sich in Edgbaston eines der besten Cricket-Stadien der Welt) would mean a repeated use of 'Welt' and would therefore sound stylistically clumsy.

Paragraph 14:
Its Jacobean roots and Regency elegance . . . Victorian and Edwardian civic buildings, . . . Joseph Chamberlain, the Lord Mayor of Birmingham in its Victorian heyday . . . – Überreste der architektonischen Wurzeln aus der Zeit Jakobs I. und die Eleganz des Regency . . . öffentlichen Gebäuden aus der Zeit Königin Victorias und König Eduards, . . . Joseph Chamberlain, der als Birminghams Oberbürgermeister in der viktorianischen Blütezeit . . .

In this paragraph there are references to architectural styles, which are named after the reign of kings and queens, and explained to the TT reader by additions ('aus der Zeit Königin Victorias und König Eduards'). In German texts of this kind, it is more common to refer to English kings and queens of the past by German names (Jakob, Eduard). For visitors to Birmingham who are not too familiar with the English history and who cannot easily link kings to historical periods, it will, however, be rather difficult to 'place' the architectural styles in their time. We would therefore suggest including a further specification as to the historical time in the TT. Facts, figures, and data too, can contribute to the purpose of the text, i.e. promoting Birmingham. Moreover, 'Wurzeln' (i.e. using the same metaphor as in the ST) is not normally used in the context of architectural style, 'Beispiele', 'Zeugnisse' or 'Zeugen' would be more appropriate.

Alternative version:
Beispiele für die Architektur zur Zeit Jakobs I. vom frühen 17. Jahrhundert und für die Eleganz des Regency-Stils vom frühen 19. Jahrhundert findet man noch heute zwischen den stolzen öffentlichen Gebäuden, die als Symbol des Wohlstands und Fortschritts während der Regentschaft von Königin Victoria (1837–1901) und König Eduard VII. (1901–1910) errichtet wurden.

Paragraph 15:
... Henry VIII, . . . a continuing programme of carnivals and festivals. – Heinrich VIII. . . . ein ständiges Karneval- und Festivalprogramm . . .

In this paragraph, there is no need to add 'König' in the TT since Heinrich VIII. is 'famous' in German-speaking target cultures as well. 'Karneval' is a specific event in Germany, with a long tradition especially in southern regions of the country, and celebrated at the end of February. What happens there is not the same as what happens in Birmingham, but at least parades and dressing up are part of the event. For the purpose of the TT, it is not necessary to elaborate or to give more detailed information.

Paragraph 16:
. . . wine bars and bistros, pubs and clubs. . . . Balti and Chinese restaurants . . . – . . . Weinstuben, Bistros, Pubs und Clubs . . . chinesischen und Balti-Restaurants

'Pub' has become an established concept in Germany, due to, for example, the growing number of 'Irish Pubs' in Germany. The use of the English word 'Pub' in the TT also adds to the 'local flair' which the text is meant to convey (although the rhyming effect of the ST – 'pubs and clubs' – has got lost). 'Balti' is part of the proper name and acts as a 'guide' to visitors looking for restaurants. In this context, however, it would have been helpful to add the regional origin, since 'Balti' is not (yet) known in the target culture.

Alternative version:
Neben einladenden Weinstuben, Bistros, Pubs und Clubs finden Gourmets hier einige der besten chinesischen sowie der indischen 'Balti' Restaurants . . .

Paragraph 17:
With the Cotswold and Malvern hills close by, Birmingham is surrounded by country walks and country pubs. – Und in den umgebenden Cotswolds und Malvern Hills laden Wanderwege und ländliche Pubs zum Verweilen ein.

Again here, 'Pub' contributes to the local flair (see *cultural filtering* as a pragmatic translation strategy in Chesterman's (1997a) classification), but the sentence is clumsy. The translator may have aimed at a phrase which is appropriate for advertising texts, but has ended up with inappropriate and slightly illogical collocations: Both 'Wanderwege' and 'Pubs' are used in agentive roles and as grammatical subjects of the TT sentence, but whereas pubs can invite ramblers to have a rest ('zum Verweilen einladen'), this is surely not the purpose of a 'Wanderweg'. The modulation here is accompanied by a deletion of 'Birmingham' (i.e. it is implied in this sentence, since it is explicitly mentioned before in the paragraph). The shift from 'Birmingham is surrounded by country walks and country pubs' (locative) to 'umgebende Cotswolds und Malvern Hills', moreover, has resulted in geographically not quite accurate information (i.e. the Cotswolds and the Malvern Hills do not surround Birmingham, but are close by).

More appropriate version:
Die Landschaft der Cotswolds und der Malvern Hills in unmittelbarer Nähe hat viele Wanderwege, und ländliche Pubs laden zum Verweilen ein.

or:
Und in den naheliegenden Cotswolds und Malvern Hills gibt es viele Wanderwege, und ländliche Pubs laden zum Verweilen ein.

or:
Die reizvolle Landschaft der Cotswolds und der Malvern Hills lädt zum Wandern ein, und ländliche Pubs laden zum Verweilen ein.

(iv) Situationality

The brochure was produced at the end of 1995, but such promotion material is usually intended to be used for a few years, with any updated version requiring only minor changes. There is only one explicit and one implicit reference to the actual time of publication in the ST:

Paragraph 13:
Villa Park, . . . will be one of the venues for the 1996 European Football Championship. – Villa Park, . . . ist 1996 einer der Austragungsorte der Fußball-Europameisterschaft.

Paragraph 6:
In its short life, the International Convention Centre has already played host to the European Summit – In der kurzen Zeit seines Bestehens hat das International Convention Centre bereits einen europäischen Gipfel . . . erlebt.

The ST refers to the summit meeting of heads of government of EU member states, which took place in Birmingham in the autumn of 1992 (note the definite article). The TT formulation, however, is rather vague, and we would suggest the more conventional term 'EU-Gipfeltreffen' (which in a sense is also a proper name). For future publications, it may be advisable to add the year. On the other hand, the text itself does not specify when the International Convention Centre was built (in 1991 actually, but there is only a reference to 'its short life'). These are cases where we would recommend that the translator contact the authors to negotiate what information to include.

Alternative solution:
In der kurzen Zeit seit seiner Eröffnung 1991 hat das International Convention Centre bereits ein EU-Gipfeltreffen (1992) . . . erlebt.

Intercultural translation problems

(i) Culture specific measures and currency

Paragraph 5:
. . . more than £1 billion of business a year . . . – . . . des jährlich mehr als 1 Milliarde Pfund starken Wirtschaftsaufkommens der Stadt . . .

There is no need to convert money due to the TT purpose. In other genres, especially journalistic texts, it is more common to add the approximate sum as converted into the target culture currency. Syntactically, however, a more appropriate collocation would be:

. . . des Wirtschaftsaufkommens der Stadt von jährlich mehr als 1 Milliarde Pfund . . .

Paragraph 12:
. . . more than 35,000 beds may be found within twenty miles of the city centre. – Im Umkreis von rund 30 Kilometern um das Stadtzentrum warten über 35.000 Betten aud [sic!] die Besucher, . . .

The conversion of 'miles' into the target culture conventional 'kilometres' is an appropriate strategy for this kind of genre. Figures in German do not

usually put a full stop, i.e. '35 000' would be appropriate (*NB*: there is no consistency in the published version of the TT with giving figures). There is also a
typing error in the TT, it should be 'auf'. (Our alternative version makes use of a
different structure: 'Im Umkreis von rund 30 Kilometern um das Stadtzentrum
stehen den Besuchern des Treffpunkt Europas über 35 000 Betten zur Verfügung.')

(ii) Text-typological and genre conventions

(a) Use of personal pronouns

The function of tourist information is both to provide information and to
promote the town. A characteristic feature is therefore talking to the addressees
in a direct way, as a kind of dialogue with the readers. This is reflected in the use
of personal pronouns, especially second person singular and/or plural
('you/your'), and also first person plural ('we/our/us'). In this particular text,
however, there are only three occurrences of personal pronouns, which have
been rendered in an impersonal way in the TT:

Paragraph 1:
Europe's meeting place meets your needs. – Europas Treffpunkt, der keine
Wünsche offenläßt.

Paragraph 13:
Whatever your sport, Birmingham is the place to enjoy it. – In Birmingham
kommt jeder Sportliebhaber auf seine Kosten.

Paragraph 16:
At night Birmingham comes alive to entertain itself and its visitors, offering
everything you would expect from a major European meeting place – Birmingham bei Nacht bietet Einheimischen und Besuchern all das, was man
von einem wichtigen europäischen Treffpunkt erwarten würde

However, a personal style has been introduced in the TT occasionally for
impersonal formulations in the ST (see Chesterman's (1997a) pragmatic translation strategy of *interpersonal change*), thus overall accounting for that characteristic feature of the genre, see:

Paragraph 2:
A flying start. – Hier heben Sie ab!

Paragraph 12:
But whichever choice is appropriate, . . . – Egal, für welche Preisklasse Sie sich
entscheiden, . . .

In Paragraph 15, the TT lets the authors speak (also in a colloquial style),
which reflects a speech act recommendation/invitation:

Paragraph 15:
The busy bustle of Birmingham belies the fact that it has more public parks
than any other European city. – Doch wenden wir uns vom geschäftigen
Treiben der Stadt einmal ab: Birmingham besitzt mehr öffentliche Parkanlagen als jede andere Stadt in Europa.

However, since this is the only case where the authors speak directly to the readers, this structure is a bit 'out of place'. Moreover, splitting the sentence into two in the TT has resulted in a change of the theme–rheme relation and also in a slight loss of coherence: there is a semantic relation of opposition in the ST, whereas in the TT the semantic relation is not immediately obvious (a colon can indicate a variety of links). We would therefore prefer an alternative version, which makes the relation of opposition more explicit:

> Bei all diesem geschäftigen Treiben in der Stadt kann man kaum glauben, daß Birmingham mehr öffentliche Parkanlagen besitzt . . .

> or:
> Bei all dem geschäftigen Treiben in der Stadt mag man überrascht sein zu erfahren, daß Birmingham mehr öffentliche Parkanlagen besitzt . . .

(b) Implicit speech acts and evaluative adjectives

Another characteristic feature of advertising texts and promotional literature is the frequent use of the speech acts request and recommendation, which often go hand in hand with personal pronouns. But in this particular text, these two speech acts are not used, at least not explicitly. One could argue that recommendations/invitations are implied, e.g. in Paragraph 17:

> . . . where Spode and Wedgwood founded their great potteries which may be seen in operation today. – . . . wo die berühmten Porzellanmanufakturen von Spode und Wedgwood heute noch in Betrieb sind.

The phrase 'may be seen' in the ST can be interpreted as an indirect invitation, which is not obvious in the TT formulation. In other cases, an implicit speech act 'promise' may be identified:

> Paragraph 12:
> But whichever choice is appropriate, Birmingham meets everyone with high standards and an unfailingly friendly welcome. – Egal, für welche Preisklasse Sie sich entscheiden, Birmingham bietet hohen Standard und ein jederzeit freundliches Willkommen.

> Paragraph 13:
> Whatever your sport, Birmingham is the place to enjoy it. – In Birmingham kommt jeder Sportliebhaber auf seine Kosten.

> Paragraph 16:
> Lovers of good food will find some of the best Balti and Chinese restaurants in Europe . . . – . . . finden Gourmets hier einige der besten chinesischen und Balti-Restaurants Europas

Apart from Paragraph 12, where the personal style in the TT (see previous comments on *Use of personal pronouns*) allows for an interpretation as a promise, the other cases read rather like factual statements (speech act 'representatives'). This textual feature (i.e. no explicit speech acts of recommendation, related to the relatively few occurrences of personal pronouns) is motivated by the respectability of the company that commissioned the brochure (i.e. the Birmingham

Marketing Partnership) and its main addressees (business people). The authors seem to rely more on promoting the town by references to its importance in terms of central location, high-quality facilities, and historical innovation. This is reflected in the adjectives, often in the superlative form (e.g. 'unique, central, largest, perfectly positioned, leading, magnificent, high-profile, extraordinary, world class, one of the world's finest, the world's oldest, the world's first ever'), and also in comparisons (e.g. 'the most prestigious conference centre in the UK and Europe, it has more public parks than any other European city').

In a few cases, the translator added an adjective in the TT, thus increasing emphasis:

Paragraph 14:
Joseph Chamberlain, . . . would appreciate the city's commitment to re-shaping its centre . . . . – Joseph Chamberlain, . . . wäre sicherlich stolz auf die heutigen engagierten Bemühungen um eine Erneuerung des Stadt-zentrums . . .

(c) Other stylistic features typical of the genre: foreign words, alliteration, parallel structure, pairs, lists of three items

We have already mentioned the use of English proper names (see previous comments on *(ii) Proper names*). There are two more cases where English words contribute to the local flair of the TT:

Paragraph 12:
from a modest but comfortable Bed & Breakfast – Bed-&-Breakfast-Pensionen

Paragraph 15:
discover designer shops and fine stores – Entdecken von Designerläden und anderen feinen Geschäften

'Bed & Breakfast' has become established in the German language, the generic noun ('Pensionen') has been added for syntactic reasons (but since it is actually a synonym, a structure such as 'Bed & Breakfast Unterkunft' would be more appropriate). 'Designerläden' too, has become established in German in the context of fashion. In two cases, French (idiomatic) expressions have been chosen for the TT:

Paragraph 3:
Birmingham is a major cultural destination. – Birmingham ist ein kulturelles Terrain par excellence.

Paragraph 16:
Lovers of good food will find . . . – . . . finden Gourmets hier . . .

The use of French expressions is fairly common in German advertising texts, especially in the context of food and fashion, and in order to emphasise high quality. In tourist information, we also often find examples of rhyme, alliteration, idiomatic expressions, and allusions, which contribute to the function of promot-ing a place. These features are especially obvious in the short phrases, which introduce each paragraph. They will be discussed later (see *(i) Short sentences* under *Text-specific translation problems*). The ST makes use of alliterations, parallel structures, pairs (e.g. 'the streets and malls and clubs and bars', 'athletics and tennis, boxing and ice-skating', 'a place to eat well and sleep soundly', 'public art and open squares', 'wine bars and bistros, pubs and clubs', 'country walks and country pubs'), lists of three (e.g. 'by road, by rail, by air', 'skills in leather, glass and jewellery', 'the new science, computer and business parks', 'new skills, new technologies and new commitment', 'new generations of science, engineering and arts specialists'). These features, which contribute to the rhythm of the text, have somewhat 'got lost' in the TT. Admittedly, not every alliteration can be recreated in the same position in the TT, and this need not be attempted either. But it is highly advisable to introduce some of these stylistic features where possible and appropriate in the TT, in order to achieve the desired effects of promotion material. In this specific text, the translator has made some effort to create effects, but more could have been done.

For example, in Paragraph 1, the alliteration ('converge, co-exist, combine') can probably not be recreated (although the translator made an effort to do so – 'Kommunikationsnetze, Kulturen, Kraft' – and using two verbs that start with 'zusammen-'). Alternatively, the parallel sentence structure could have been even more emphasised by adding another 'wo' before 'Industrie', see:

Paragraph 1:
Where communication networks converge, where cultures co-exist, where industry and commerce combine, the City of Birmingham . . . – Wo Kommunikationsnetze zusammenlaufen, wo unterschiedliche Kulturen in friedlichem Nebeneinander existieren und [wo] Industrie und Handel mit vereinter Kraft zusammenwirken – dort liegt Birmingham . . .

In Paragraph 2, one stylistic feature (i.e. ambiguity) has been replaced by two other ones (i.e. ambiguity, personal style):

Paragraph 2:
A flying start. – Hier heben Sie ab!

'A flying start' is slightly ambiguous. It is definitely not used here in its specific meaning in sports, but rather in the transferred meaning of an 'excellent start'. However, since the paragraph deals with Birmingham's airport, the literal meaning of flying can also be activated, thus allowing for two readings: flying into or out of Birmingham corresponds to an excellent start of any activity, be it for business or pleasure. In the TT, we have a similar effect due to two potential interpretations of 'abheben': a literal one (a plane taking off) and one based on the transferred meaning (become supercilious, high-spirited, effusive, wild – with a slightly negative connotation, though). Although in this transferred meaning, ST and TT are no longer absolutely identical, this is of no major relevance, since the formal feature (ambiguity) as a characteristic feature of the genre contributes to the desired effect (appreciate the stylistic feature by recognising the allusion to a familiar phrase). The phrase chosen for the TT is thus a highly appropriate one for the purpose of the text.

In Paragraph 6, one stylistic feature characteristic of advertising texts (i.e. alliteration: 'style, safety, security') has been replaced by another one (i.e. a foreign word: 'Ambiente', with connotations of style and elegance):

Paragraph 6:
The eleven meeting halls, . . . can accommodate . . . delegates in comfort, in style, in safety and security. – Elf Veranstaltungssäle, . . . bieten . . . Gästen bequem in elegantem, sicherem Ambiente Platz.

In Paragraph 7, the translator has opted for an idiomatic expression in the TT for a neutral formulation in the ST:

Paragraph 7:
Birmingham's music scene cannot be simply categorised. – Birminghams Musikszene läßt sich in keine Schublade pressen.

In Paragraph 12, an informal collocation has been chosen to re-create a formal feature (the alliteration), which also results in a minor change in the propositional content (i.e. 'eat well' disappears in the TT):

Paragraph 12:
The Birmingham Convention & Visitor Bureau will find everyone a place to eat well and sleep soundly: from a modest but comfortable Bed & Breakfast to the elegance and quality of the Swallow Hotel, – Das Birmingham Convention & Visitor Bureau arrangiert Unterbringungen für jeden Geschmack und Geldbeutel: Das Angebot reicht von bescheidenen, aber einladenden Bed-&-Breakfast-Pensionen bis hin zum erstklassigen, eleganten Swallow Hotel

The translator has opted for lexical expressions which contribute to the overall textual feature of alliteration ('Geschmack und Geldbeutel', 'erstklassigen, eleganten'). This could even have been enhanced by substituting 'bequem' for 'einladend'. Another characteristic feature (pairs) is evident in both ST and TT.

In this way, it is possible to compensate for other cases where a phrase / structure with a specific stylistic feature in the ST had been rendered in a neutral way in the TT. This strategy is known as re-location ('Disloziierung') of features, and it contributes to ensuring the overall effect of the text (in Chesterman's (1997a) classification this would be an example of the pragmatic translation strategy of *coherence change*). We find a similar case of re-location in Paragraph 15, where a more personal style in a speech act has been chosen to compensate for the alliteration in the ST (but see also previous comments):

Paragraph 15:
The busy bustle of Birmingham belies the fact that it has more public parks . . . – Doch wenden wir uns vom geschäftigen Treiben der Stadt einmal ab: Birmingham besitzt mehr öffentliche Parkanlagen . . .

In Paragraph 11, the repetition of 'new' in the ST (lists of three) contributes to the persuasive function of an advertising text. The TT does not opt for the same textual feature:

Paragraph 11:
. . . new skills, new technologies and new commitment to training are continuing the tradition of scientific endeavour . . . – neue Fachkenntnisse, Technologien und Ausbildungsschwerpunkte die Tradition wissenschaftlichen Unternehmertums fortsetzen,

However, the repetition of 'neu' in the TT would result in increased emphasis and would be more appropriate for the genre (for the ultimate lexical choices see also *(ii) Textual key concepts* under *Text-specific translation problems*).

Alternative version:
. . . neue Fachkenntnisse, neue Technologien und neue Ausbildungsschwerpunkte . . .

A re-location of the text-typical structure of pairs has been used in the following case:

Paragraph 2:
the city is a pivot for all points of the compass ... – ... ist die Stadt ein zentraler Knotenpunkt für Reisende aus Ost und West, Nord und Süd, ...

In this way, a lexical translation problem ('compass') has been solved. The German word 'Kompaß' denotes the object, and in tourist brochures it is normally not used in the sense intended here, i.e. directions (it could be used in this sense in poetic texts). An alternative solution could have been 'aus allen Himmelsrichtungen' (see also *(iv) Change of perspective* under *Interlingual translation problems*).

In Paragraph 17, the stylistic feature of repetition of the same word ('diversity') has not been copied in the TT, but the effect (focusing on the diversity of the countryside) has been achieved by a change of the theme–rheme structure (the rheme in the ST is 'countryside', the rheme in the TT is 'Vielfältigkeit'):

Paragraph 17:
The true diversity of metropolitan Birmingham is matched by the diversity of the surrounding countryside. – Die umgebende Landschaft steht der städtischen Metropole Birmingham in Sachen Vielfältigkeit in nichts nach.

The translator has opted for an antonymic translation to achieve the effect: the ST focuses on equality ('is matched by'), whereas the TT focuses on competitiveness ('steht in nichts nach'). 'Städtische Metropole', however, is redundant, with 'Metropole' being another label for a big and important town.

(iii) Naming conventions

Paragraph 3:
It operates direct scheduled flights to and from 39 destinations throughout Europe, Scandinavia and the United States. – Direkte Linienflüge nach 39 Reisezielen in Europa, Skandinavien sowie nach den USA werden hier abgewickelt.

In English, 'Europe' can denote different referents, e.g. the European continent, or the European Union. In the ST, the referent is vague. But since Scandinavia is geographically part of Europe, it sounds strange to the TT reader to see it separated from 'Europa'. 'Europa' in German is dominantly used to denote the geographical area (including the United Kingdom). Moreover, 'abgewickelt' has a slightly negative connotation ('routine, but without much enthusiasm'). A more appropriate alternative solution would therefore be:

Es gibt direkte Linienflüge von und zu 39 Zielorten in Europa und den USA.

or:
Es gibt Direktflugverbindungen mit 39 Städten in Europa und den USA.

Paragraph 10:
... the city has been home to writers as different as JRR Tolkien and Conan Doyle. – Zu den berühmten Söhnen der Stadt zählen so unterschiedliche Autoren wie JRR Tolkien und Conan Doyle.

'Berühmte Söhne' (translation strategy: modulation) is a common way of expression in German which is also characteristic of tourist texts. However, adding the first name is more common in German texts, and formal conventions require a full stop after initials (i.e. : J. R. R. Tolkien und Arthur Conan Doyle).

Interlingual translation problems

In this section of the annotations we will not give a detailed comment of all modulations and transpositions which are due to differences in the linguistic systems of source and TL. We will focus mainly on those cases where corrections are required or where we would suggest an alternative version, linked to a more general discussion of potential translation strategies for identified phenomena.

(i) Gender

Paragraph 2:
Birmingham is not just the centre of the United Kingdom, it is central to the European experience, – Birmingham bildet nicht nur das Herz des Vereinigten Königreichs: Es steht auch fest im Mittelpunkt des europäischen Geschehens,

Although towns are usually treated as neuter in German, it is not common practice to use the pronoun 'es' in co-referential function. It is rather more common in German texts to use either 'die Stadt' or the proper name. The corrected version could therefore be:

Birmingham bildet nicht nur das Herz des Vereinigten Königreichs, die Stadt steht auch fest im Mittelpunkt des europäischen Geschehens.

A replacement of a co-referential pronoun by the proper name has been done in Paragraphs 1 and 15:

Paragraph 1:
the City of Birmingham forms the focal point ... It is, in every sense, Europe's meeting place. – dort liegt Birmingham, Mittelpunkt ... Birmingham ist, in jeder Hinsicht, der Treffpunkt Europas.

Paragraph 15:
... it has more public parks ... in a city which ... puts its wide open spaces to good use ... – Birmingham besitzt mehr öffentliche Parkanlagen ... in dieser Stadt, die ... auf seinen zahlreichen offenen Plätzen ...

However, in the second part of Paragraph 15, the gender has become mixed up: 'Stadt' being feminine, the pronoun should be 'ihre' (in contrast to the proper name, i.e. 'Birmingham ... seine Plätze', with 'freie Plätze' being a more appropriate collocation).

When pronouns are used, then mainly possessive pronouns. In some cases, modulations and transpositions have been used, thus allowing to avoid a replacement of a possessive pronoun. In Paragraph 14, possessive pronouns have been replaced by definite articles, in Paragraph 16 they have been deleted; see:

Paragraph 13:
Birmingham loves its sport . . . – Birmingham ist eine sportbegeisterte Stadt

Paragraph 14:
Birmingham's buildings are milestones in its development . . . Its Jacobean roots . . . in its Victorian heyday . . . the city's commitment to re-shaping its centre . . . – An Birminghams Gebäuden läßt sich die Entwicklung . . . Überreste der architektonischen Wurzeln aus der Zeit Jakobs I. . . . in der viktorianischen Blütezeit . . . Bemühungen um eine Erneuerung des Stadtzentrums . . .

Paragraph 16:
. . . Birmingham comes alive to entertain itself and its visitors, . . . Birmingham takes its pleasure seriously. – Birmingham bei Nacht bietet Einheimischen und Besuchern all das, . . . weiß Birmingham nach allen Regeln der Kunst zu feiern.

An alternative version could be: 'Birmingham . . . bietet Einheimischen und seinen Besuchern . . . '

(ii) Theme–rheme structure

Paragraph 1:
Where communication networks converge, where cultures co-exist, where industry and commerce combine, the City of Birmingham forms the focal point . . . – Wo Kommunikationsnetze zusammenlaufen, wo unterschiedliche Kulturen in friedlichem Nebeneinander existieren und Industrie und Handel mit vereinter Kraft zusammenwirken – dort liegt Birmingham, Mittelpunkt . . .

The addition of 'dort liegt' and the change in the syntactic structure emphasise the topic (i.e. the rheme) 'Birmingham'.

Paragraph 9:
Now, however, as finance and commerce support and supplement manufacturing, as new companies join established international names like Cadbury's, Rover, Lucas and IMI, new industries are being created. Today, it is Birmingham's advanced manufacturing technology, which is ensuring the future prosperity of the region. – Heute erhält das verarbeitende Gewerbe durch Finanz- und Handelsbetriebe Unterstützung, und mit der Ansiedlung neuer Unternehmen entstehen neue Industriezweige neben renommierten internationalen Namen wie Cadbury's, Rover, Lucas und IMI. Birminghams fortschrittliche Fertigungstechnik sichert auch den zukünftigen Wohlstand der Region.

In the ST, there is a semantic relation of contrast, i.e. established industries are contrasted with new branches (indicated by 'however, as'). The following cleft sentence contributes to this contrast by emphasising the importance of the new industries. In the TT, the semantic links between the propositions are dominantly additive. A more appropriate alternative solution would be:

Heute jedoch kooperieren die neuen Finanz- und Handelsbetriebe immer enger mit der verarbeitenden Industrie, treten neue Unternehmen an die Seite solch international renommierter Namen wie Cadbury's, Rover, Lucas und IMI, so daß ganze neue Industriezweige entstehen. Heute ist es die fortschrittliche Fertigungstechnik Birminghams, die den zukünftigen Wohlstand der Region sichert.

Paragraph 10:
For art's sake. Birmingham is a major cultural destination. The world's leading Pre-Raphaelite collection hangs in the City Museum and Art Gallery contrasting sharply with the innovative work of contemporary artists at the Ikon Gallery. – Birmingham ist ein kulturelles Terrain par excellence. Ein größerer Kontrast als zwischen der führenden Prä-Raffaeliten-Sammlung im City Museum and Art Gallery und den innovativen Werken zeitgenössischer Künstler in der Ikon Gallery beispielsweise ist kaum vorstellbar.

The reordering of the propositions in the TT has somewhat destroyed the logic of the argumentation. In the ST, the topic art/culture is introduced at the beginning of the paragraph (as rheme), followed by examples, which are arranged in parallel structures (type of art, place), and linked by an explicit reference explaining their difference ('contrasting sharply', which is supported by the lexical choices 'innovative, contemporary', but only a ST reader would be able to understand the implicit link to 'more traditional, past, 19th century'). Due to the fronting position of 'Kontrast', this aspect gets much more prominence in the TT. An alternative solution, which keeps to the theme–rheme structure and also accounts for lacking knowledge of TT readers could be:

Da ist die bedeutendste Prä-Raffaeliten-Sammlung der Welt im City Museum and Art Gallery, die sich in ihrem Stil augenfällig von den innovativen Werken zeitgenössischer Künstler in der Ikon Gallery unterscheidet.

(iii) Non-human and/or abstract agents
There are cases where non-human or abstract nouns function in the semantic role of agentive and take the subject position in a sentence. Since these structures seem to be more frequent in English texts, independent of the genre, they could also be listed under the heading *Intercultural translation problems*. In the TT, prepositional phrases are frequently used.

Paragraph 4:
The National Exhibition Centre, ... In its sixteen halls, it hosts 110 exhibitions a year and welcomes some 4 million visitors. – Der Standort des National Exhibition Centre, . . . In den sechzehn Hallen finden jährlich 110 Aus-stellungen mit rund vier Millionen Besuchern statt.

The verbs associated with the subject in its semantic role of agentive ('hosts', 'welcomes') are typically used with human beings. In the TT, the syntactic structure of a prepositional phrase functions in the semantic role of locative in the first part, and instrument in the second part ('mit . . . Besuchern'). However, this instrument relation does not make much sense, so that we would suggest as a different TT solution:

In den sechzehn Hallen finden jährlich 110 Ausstellungen statt, die rund vier Millionen Besucher anziehen.

(NB: In this example too, we see that the possessive pronoun ('its') has been replaced by a definite article ('den').)

A change from an agentive role (subject) in the ST to a locative role (prepositional phrase) in the TT (see clause structure change as a syntactic translation strategy in Chesterman's (1997a) classification) is also obvious in the following case:

Paragraph 8:
But the National Indoor Arena does not restrict itself to sport. – Doch in der National Indoor Arena dreht sich nicht nur alles um den Sport.

Alternatively, as in Paragraph 13, subject complements ('X ist Y') can be used, and/or nouns or verbs, which semantically denote the role of 'locative' (e.g. 'Austragungsort', 'austragen', here in a passive structure), see:

Paragraph 13:
Birmingham loves its sport and hosts ... The Belfry, ... is ... and hosted ... – Birmingham ist eine sportbegeisterte Stadt und jährlich Austragungsort ... The Belfry, ... ist ... wurde hier ... ausgetragen.

In the following examples, however, we have non-human agentives also in the TT:

Paragraph 5:
The city which boasts the world's oldest Mint, which saw the establishment of two of the leading clearing banks ... – Die Stadt, die die älteste Münzstätte der Welt ihr eigen nennt, in der zwei der führenden Clearingbanken gegründet wurden ...

Here we find a prepositional phrase for the locative role in the second part of the sentence. In the first part, 'Stadt' as a non-human agentive takes the subject position. In German, such a structure seems appropriate whenever the agent can logically be interpreted as referring to human beings (e.g. the people of Birmingham), or when some space is involved (see later, 'bieten Platz', which, in addition, is not a verb denoting an activity performed by an agent):

Paragraph 6:
the International Convention Centre has already played host to ... The eleven meeting halls, ... can accommodate from 30 to 3000 delegates ... – hat das International Convention Centre bereits einen europäischen Gipfel ... erlebt. Elf Veranstaltungssäle, ... bieten 30 bis 3000 Gästen ... Platz.

In the first proposition, the passive structure is an indication that 'International Convention Centre' functions in the semantic role of 'experiencer'. In such structures, and also in the case of the semantic role 'beneficiary', non-human and/or abstract nouns are also in German frequently used in subject position (cf. 'Das Haus erhält einen neuen Farbanstrich'). Moreover, 'from 30 to 3000 delegates' in the ST is a reference to the different sizes of the halls, which is implicit in the TT. (Alternative solution: 'Elf Veranstaltungssäle unterschiedlicher Größe ... bieten 30 bis 3000 Gästen ... Platz', or a changed perspective – see later – as: '30 bis 3000 Gäste finden in elegantem, sicherem Ambiente bequem Platz in den elf Veranstaltungssälen unterschiedlicher Größe . . . ').

'City' is again used as agentive in both ST and TT in the following example:

Paragraph 15:
. . . in a city which boasts no less than six million trees – in dieser Stadt, die nicht weniger als 6 Millionen Bäume ihr eigen nennt

However, 'etwas sein eigen nennen' is normally used in contexts of material possessions, i.e. when the aspect of ownership is highlighted. Since in this paragraph the focus is on quantity, and not on ownership, a more appropriate solution could be suggested. In addition, in advertising genres, when it comes to quantities, normally the positive form ('mehr als') is preferred.

More appropriate version:
. . . in dieser Stadt mit mehr als 6 Millionen Bäumen / in dieser Stadt, in der es mehr als 6 Millionen Bäume gibt

(iv) Change of perspective
In some other cases we see a change in the perspective when comparing ST and TT.

Paragraph 14:
Birmingham's buildings are milestones in its development . . . – An Birminghams Gebäuden läßt sich die Entwicklung . . . nachvollziehen.

There is an attributive relation between 'buildings' and 'milestones' in the ST, a metaphorical comparison, whereas in the TT 'Gebäude' functions in a locative sense (directing the visitors' gaze towards the buildings).

In addition, the demetaphorisation in the TT is quite an appropriate translation strategy here. The formally similar 'Meilenstein' in German is mainly related to developments in science, industry, and politics. It is more common to describe a specific discovery (e.g. the steam engine) as a milestone for the development of a scientific field. In the context of architectural styles of buildings, 'Meilenstein' does not fit. If a metaphorical expression were considered as most appropriate in view of the purpose of the text (which, however, is not the case here), 'Zeuge' could have been used (i.e. 'Die Gebäude Birminghams sind Zeugen für die Entwicklung . . . ', or 'Die Gebäude Birminghams bezeugen auf anschauliche Weise . . . ').

Paragraph 15:
. . . Birmingham people and their guests can wander along pleasant walkways and canal sides – laden hier freundliche Spazierwege durch Parkanlagen und an Kanälen Einheimische und Besucher zum Bummeln . . . ein

The semantic relations are exchanged: in the ST, 'people and their guests' functions as agentive and 'walkways and canal sides' as locative. In the TT, 'Spazierwege' is used as an agentive, and the people are put in a semantic relation of objective. In addition, in the TT the translator added that the people are invited to wander along, making the possibility thus more explicit. This is a structure which can frequently be found in advertising texts. However, treating 'Spazierwege' as agentive has resulted in a somewhat inappropriate collocation: 'freundlich' is a characteristic feature of people, in relation to walkways one could speak of 'angenehme Spazierwege' or 'schöne Spazierwege'.

Paragraph 16:

Everyone will enjoy the wine bars and bistros, pubs and clubs. – Neben einladenden Weinstuben, Bistros, Pubs und Clubs . . .

Here too, the localities function as agentive in the TT: there is a change of the perspective, from being inside a place in the ST to being invited to get inside a place in the TT, and from guests as agents of the enjoyment to the places as inviting. 'Einladend' implies that the guests will enjoy the place once they are inside.

At the end of this section, we will shortly present some examples of inappropriate lexical and/or syntactic choices and provide corrected versions (without giving longer explanations).

Inappropriate lexical choices and/or collocations

Paragraph 6:

. . . high profile political, cultural and corporate conferences. – . . . wichtige politische, kulturelle und Firmenereignisse

'Firmenereignis' is rather general and vague (it could also be a ball, which would not necessarily be 'high profile' though). Alternative solution: 'Kongresse zu politischen, kulturellen und wirtschaftlichen Themen'.

Paragraph 10:

. . . the Repertory Theatre remains centre stage – . . . das Repertory Theatre steht weiterhin im Mittelpunkt des Bühnengeschehens

The collocation 'im Mittelpunkt des Bühnengeschehens' would be used in the context of some character who is at the centre of a play. More appropriate solution: 'das Repertory Theatre bietet ein Bühnenereignis nach dem anderen'.

Paragraph 13:

Birmingham . . . hosts more World and European championship events than any other UK city. – Birmingham ist . . . jährlich Austragungsort von mehr weltweiten und europäischen Meisterschaftsereignissen als jeder andere britische Ort.

The conventional way of referring to such events is 'Welt- und Europameisterschaften'. There is also no real motivation for the addition of 'jährlich'.

More appropriate version:

Birmingham ist . . . weitaus häufiger Austragungsort von Welt- und Europameisterschaften als jede andere britische Stadt.

Paragraph 15:

And they can always find peace and tranquillity . . . – Ruhe und Stille sind überall zu finden . . .

'Ruhe' and 'Stille' are synonyms so that their combination sounds a bit strange and odd. In this context, one word would suffice. However, since combinations of related words are a characteristic feature of advertising texts, a more appropriate version could be: 'Ruhe und Entspannung kann man überall finden . . .'.

Paragraph 16:
Lovers of good food will find . . . opportunities to sample every kind of international cuisine. – . . . finden Gourmets . . . zahlreiche Gelegenheiten,
internationale Speisen aus aller Welt zu probieren.

'Internationale Speisen aus aller Welt' says the same thing twice, with 'aus
aller Welt' and 'international' being synonyms. The adjective 'international' is
commonly used in contexts of politics, commerce, sports, and evokes aspects of
many people being present and active together. More appropriate version: ' . . .
Speisen aus aller Welt zu probieren.'

Inappropriate syntactic structures

Paragraph 2:
By road, by rail, by air, the city is a pivot for all points of the compass and for
travel to and from Europe and the United States. – Im Schienen-, Straßen- und
Luftverkehr ist die Stadt ein zentraler Knotenpunkt für Reisende aus Ost und
West, Nord und Süd, von und nach Europa und den USA.

'By road, by rail, by air' function semantically as means of transport, which the
translator tried to account for by the addition of 'für Reisende'. But the resulting
TT is syntactically odd because 'im Schienen-, Straßen- und Luftverkehr' is syntactically linked to 'die Stadt', but semantically to 'Reisende'.

More appropriate version:
Ob Sie per Bahn, Auto oder Flugzeug kommen, die Stadt ist ein zentraler
Verkehrsknotenpunkt für Reisen in alle Himmelsrichtungen, von und nach
Europa und den USA.

or:
. . . für Reisen aus Ost und West, Nord und Süd, . . .

The introduction of a more personal style is in conformity with the genre conventions (see previous comments in *(ii) Genre conventions*).

Paragraph 10:
. . . a wealth of independent organisations and festivals ensure that . . . – ein
breites Spektrum von unabhängigen Organisationen und Festivals sorgen
dafür, daß . . .

There is a number problem here: 'Spektrum' is in the singular and thus
requires a singular form of the verb ('sorgt'). However, due to the plural forms
('Organisationen und Festivals'), a plural verb is more logical (German native
speakers too often mix singular and plural in such cases). This grammatical
problem could be avoided by opting for alternative solutions (e.g.: ' . . . vielfältige
unabhängige Organisationen und Festivals sorgen dafür').

Text-specific translation problems

(i) Short sentences
   Short and sometimes elliptical sentences can be found especially at the beginning of each paragraph, where these phrases function as a kind of heading. A
similar stylistic feature has been adopted for the TT. These short headings

display specific stylistic features (alliteration, ambiguity, etc). We have already commented (under *Intercultural translation problems*) that the translator tried to compensate for certain stylistic features (e.g. alliteration) by other features (e.g. personal style) which are equally characteristic of tourist information in particular and advertising texts/promotional texts in general. Another relevant point is that there is coherence within each paragraph, i.e. very frequently we have in the paragraph heading a word which stands for the key idea of the paragraph, thus contributing to the lexical-semantic field (or the frame) of the paragraph. Decisions as to other appropriate lexical choices within the paragraph can thus often have been made on the basis of the relevant frame. We will comment on these aspects by going through each of the paragraphs (but only adding cross-references when certain aspects have already been discussed in other sections of the annotations).

Paragraph 1:
Europe's meeting place meets your needs. – Europas Treffpunkt, der keine Wünsche offenläßt.
(see later comments in *(ii) Textual key concepts*)

Paragraph 2:
A sense of place. – Standortbestimmung.
(see later comments in *(ii) Textual key concepts*)

Paragraph 3:
A flying start. – Hier heben Sie ab!
(see previous comments on genre conventions under *Intercultural translation problems* for ambiguity and personal style)

Paragraph 4:
Show business is BIG business. – Showbusineß ist 'Big Business'.
'Showbusineß' has become an established term in German too (however, in the spelling 'Business'). It needs no explanation for the intended primary addressees of the TT. It can also be assumed that most readers will see the allusion to the song 'There's no business like show business'. It could be argued that this paragraph in the ST deals predominantly with the suitability of the NEC for large events (therefore the capital letters 'BIG') and that the TT readers might expect more information about cultural events. Although this argument is true in a sense, it could also be said that due to the formal features (allusion, retaining foreign words) the heading contributes to the function of an advertising text (attract attention, keep 'exotic flair'), which is more important here.

Some lexical choices in this Paragraph 4 are related to the frame business, more specifically, the location for business, e.g.:

(a) On site is an 800 bed luxury hotel . . . – Weitere 'Platzvorteile' sind ein 800-Betten-Luxushotel . . .

The specification ('Platzvorteil') is also in conformity with the genre convention (advertising style).

(b) . . . the famous 12,600 seat NEC Arena . . . a complementary venue for international rock concerts, world championships and conventions. – die berühmte, 12600 Zuschauer fassende NEC Arena . . . ein Treffpunkt für internationale Rockkonzerte, Weltmeisterschaften und Tagungen.

The specification in the TT ('Zuschauer fassende Arena') complies with German conventions. However, since events are referred to, 'Austragungsort' would be more appropriate than 'Treffpunkt' (which is normally used with reference to people, e.g. 'ein Treffpunkt für Geschäftsleute').

Paragraph 5:
Money matters. – Geldangelegenheiten.

There is a word play in the ST due to syntactic ambiguity (i.e. 'matters' may be either a noun or a verb). Word plays too, are characteristic of the genre and of advertising discourse in general. The TT heading is rather neutral and informative. For the purpose of advertising, a similarly catchy phrase could have been used, e.g. 'Money makes the world go around . . . ' – another allusion to a song which should be known to the majority of the addressees. Moreover, the English text would contribute to keeping the culture-specific flair and it would also be coherent to the heading 'Showbusiness . . . ' in Paragraph 4. Alternatively, 'Wenn's um Geld geht' could be used as a heading, which is an allusion to an advertising slogan for a bank, which is known to German addressees. There is a frame clash in this paragraph, though:

. . . draws on an established infrastructure of multi-disciplinary expertise . . . – profitiert von der etablierten Infrastruktur zahlreicher Fachdisziplinen, . . .

'Fachdisziplinen' evokes a frame of education which, however, is not intended here. The focus is rather on the fact that expertise in various domains has been available for a long time. A more appropriate solution could therefore be: ' . . . etablierten Infrastruktur von Fachwissen auf vielen Gebieten, . . . '.

Paragraph 6:
This is Convention City. – Es wird getagt.

'Tagen' is derived from the noun 'Tagung' which is a synonym to 'Kongress' or 'Konferenz'. Since repetition of key concepts within and between the paragraphs is a characteristic feature of this text (and of promotional texts in general), 'Stadt der Kongresse' may be a more appropriate solution.

Paragraph 7:
Eclectic, eccentric, exciting. – Eklektisch, exzentrisch und erregend.

The alliteration in the ST has been recreated in the TT, thus contributing to the style of advertising texts (see also previous comments under *Intercutural translation problems*).

Paragraph 8:
The big occasion. – Großes Ereignis.

The plural 'Großereignisse' is more typical in these kinds of texts.

Paragraph 9:
The world's workshop. – Die Werkstatt der Welt.

'Workshop' is used metaphorically here, a characteristic feature of advertising texts. The same applies to 'Werkstatt', which is normally used in contexts referring to smaller places where some kind or repair work is carried out. In its metaphorical sense here it contributes to the style of the text, also supported by the alliteration which has been recreated.

Paragraph 10:
For art's sake. – Kunst als Selbstzweck.

'Selbstzweck' has slightly negative connotations in German. Alternative solutions could be 'Alles für die Kunst' or 'Aus Liebe zur Kunst', which would convey the required sense of positive attitudes. One might also think of a version such as 'L'art pour l'art', i.e. using a French phrase, thus providing a coherent link to 'Terrain par excellence' in the following sentence in the TT (see also previous comments on the use of foreign phrases as a characteristic feature of advertising genres).

Paragraph 11:
The skill factor. – Hier wird Können großgeschrieben.

'Skill' is the keyword in this paragraph, frequently repeated, and contributing to the semantic contrast of old and new, of tradition and innovation. 'Skill' refers both to manual skills and to intellectual capacities, knowledge. The translator opted for lexical variation to account for these different aspects:

The skill factor. Traditional skills . . . new skills, . . . innovative skills . . . – Können . . . Überlieferte Fertigkeiten . . . neue Fachkenntnisse, . . . innovativen Fertigkeiten . . .

Our alternative version too, accounts for these aspects, introducing a few more changes (e.g. the choice of 'Technologiepark' as the more conventional term in German requires a substitution of 'Technologie' by 'Fähigkeiten und Fertigkeiten' – these two concepts often going hand in hand). The other main point of this paragraph, i.e. the focus on new developments has been accounted for by repeatingly using 'neu'. In addition, the explication 'Leder-, Glas- und Schmuckwarenindustrie' is determined by the dominant frames of the paragraph.

Alternative version:
Hier wird Können großgeschrieben. Überlieferte Fertigkeiten spielen auch heute noch in der Leder-, Glas- und Schmuckwarenindustrie eine wichtige Rolle, während die neuen Technologie-, Computer- und Geschäftsparks mit neuem Wissen, neuen Fähigkeiten und Fertigkeiten sowie neuen Ausbildungsschwerpunkten die Tradition wissenschaftlichen Unternehmertums fortsetzen, . . . ein breites Betätigungsfeld für ihre innovativen Fertigkeiten finden.

Paragraph 12:
Bed room. – Betten-Kapazität.

This is the conventional expression in German tourist brochures.

Paragraph 13:
The name of the game. – Aus Freude am Spiel.

The whole paragraph is about sports, and similar to the polysemous 'game', 'Spiel' is used in the context of sports (especially team sports, and often in compounds, e.g. 'Fußballspiel, Handballspiel'), but also in the context of spare time activities. The ST uses a vogue cliché (see Kirkpatrick,

1996: 129), mainly for exploiting the rhyme potential of 'game'. To help the readers understand immediately that the paragraph deals with sports, we would suggest 'Sport und Spiel' as alternative version (a heading which makes use of the stylistic feature alliteration, which we identified as characteristic of advertising texts).

Paragraph 14:
Ancient and modern. – Alt und neu.

This is the conventional and commonly used collocation in German.

Paragraph 15:
The quality of life. – Lebensqualität.

'Lebensqualität' is typically used in contexts of a more sociological character, e.g. speaking about standards of living, mainly in a material sense. This paragraph deals with what Birmingham can offer for relaxation (e.g. parks, walkways) during the day (in contrast to the night-time events in the following paragraphs). More appropriate solutions for the heading could thus be 'Entspannungsmomente', or 'Zur Entspannung', or 'Abschalten und entspannen'.

Paragraph 16:
The business of pleasure. – Spaß am Vergnügen.

The beginning and end of this paragraph work on the same idea and structure: business and pleasure are contrasted:

The business of pleasure. . . . When business is completed, Birmingham takes its pleasure seriously. – Spaß am Vergnügen. . . . Denn nach getaner Arbeit weiß Birmingham nach allen Regeln der Kunst zu feiern.

The concept of 'pleasure' is specified in the paragraph predominantly with reference to cuisine. The TT has the same focus on cuisine, but the framing structure at the beginning and the end of this paragraph ('Vergnügen, feiern') would activate expectations as to parties and dancing. The structure 'Spaß am Vergnügen' may remind readers of the idiom 'Spaß an der Freude'. This exists as a standard expression, but would not quite fit here because it is normally used in the context of everyday life. The ST works on the contrast between 'business during the day' and 'pleasure of enjoying a good meal afterwards'. The TT, however, sets up an argument of 'business during the day' and 'eating and dancing and partying afterwards'. It could be argued that this minor change in the TT can be justified with regard to the purpose of the text and the genre. Alternatively, we could substitute 'genießen', which is wider in its meaning than 'feiern', and covers both eating/drinking (see 'einen guten Wein genießen') and other cultural events (see 'ein Konzert genießen').

Paragraph 17:
Rural Birmingham. – Birmingham – die ländliche Seite.

The heading in the TT could be interpreted as Birmingham itself showing aspects of rural life, whereas the paragraph reports about the surroundings of the city (indicated by the repeated use of 'country'). A more appropriate alternative heading could be 'Birmingham und seine Umgebung', or 'Sehenswertes außerhalb Birminghams'. Note that London is mentioned in the paragraph, which would not be part of the 'surrounding countryside', but it is used in a syntactic structure which implies a contrast ('merely . . . but . . . '):

> London is merely an hour and a half by train, but within a short drive are the historic towns . . . – London ist per Bahn in ganzen 1½ Stunden zu erreichen, die historischen Städte . . . sind nur eine kurze Autofahrt entfernt.

For visitors who come from larger countries, 'an hour and a half' might not seem to be anything else but a 'short' trip, and the duration of 'a short drive' too is relative. To account for such differences, we have introduced adverbs in the TT to make the contrast more explicit.

> Alternative version:
> Sogar London ist schon in 1½ Stunden Bahnfahrt zu erreichen, aber bereits nach 30 Minuten Autofahrt ist man in den historischen Städten Stratford-upon-Avon und Ironbridge.

The addition of a verb ('erreichen') is required by the syntactic structure in the TT ('Bahnfahrt' denotes a process, which is normally explicitly combined with a verb). The specification 'Autofahrt' for 'drive' is motivated by a 'travelling' frame, with the car as prototypical means of transport implicit in the ST. (For dealing with place names see also previous comments *(ii) Place names* under *Pragmatic translation problems*).

(ii) Textual key concepts

(a) Europe's meeting place

The central motto of the promotion campaign, 'Birmingham, Europe's meeting place', is used to structure the ST. It is used in the main title of the text, and again in Paragraphs 1, 12, 14, and 16 (in slight variations: 'Europe's meeting place, the meeting place of Europe, meeting place for Europe, a major European meeting place'). Due to the relevance of this key concept, lexical consistency is required in the TT too ('Treffpunkt Europas' and 'europäischer Treffpunkt' are the synonymous phrases). In Paragraph 1, a formal element of this key concept is exploited for stylistic reasons:

> Paragraph 1:
> Europe's meeting place meets your needs. – Europas Treffpunkt, der keine Wünsche offenläßt.

This formal feature cannot be imitated in German. But this is no loss, since this is the heading to the paragraph, and the version chosen for the TT fulfils its purpose equally well.

(b) Centre and heart

Another key idea of the text, which is repeatedly used, is the central location. This aspect of a centre is linked to the idea of a heart. The first explicit reference to 'centre' is in Paragraph 2:

> Paragraph 2:
> Birmingham is not just the centre of the United Kingdom, it is central to the European experience, . . . the city is a pivot . . . Birmingham is, geographically and culturally, central to European life. – Birmingham bildet nicht nur

das Herz des Vereinigten Königreichs: Es steht auch fest im Mittelpunkt des europäischen Geschehens, . . . ist die Stadt ein zentraler Knotenpunkt . . . Birmingham steht geographisch und kulturell fest im europäischen Leben.

In advertising leaflets, Birmingham has often been characterised as the 'heart of England' (but during the last few years, this slogan has been replaced by the slogan 'Europe's meeting place'). The choice of 'Herz' (translation strategy: metaphorisation) may thus have been motivated by the translator's knowledge of the use of 'heart' in other texts with an advertising and promotional function. The metaphor of the heart expresses both a central location and an emotional feeling of being at home and comfortable. However, the dominant idea of this second paragraph is only the central location of the town for travel (see the lexical choices 'centre, central, pivot, central'). Moreover, the addition of 'fest' (twice) changes the perspective from locality (space) to firmness (attitude). As a consequence, the idea of geographical centrality is weakened in the TT. In addition, a colon (which is used in the TT) can have different functions in a text, it often indicates that the following proposition is a specification of the previous one. In this case, however, the semantic relation between the propositions is one of addition (indicated by 'nicht nur . . . auch'), for which a comma is more appropriate.

Alternative solution:
Standortbestimmung. Birmingham ist nicht nur der geographische Mittelpunkt des Vereinigten Königreichs, sondern auch der Mittelpunkt des europäischen Geschehens, ein Tor für den transatlantischen Handel und ein Zentrum für die Geschäftswelt. . . . Birmingham ist das geographische und kulturelle Zentrum Europas.

However, the metaphorical expression 'heart' is also used in other paragraphs of the ST (intratextual cohesion and coherence), but not in the sense of the advertising slogan 'Birmingham, the heart of England'. It is used when in addition to a central location a sense of vitality and / or emotional attachment is conveyed. In the TT, there is variation between 'Herz' and 'Zentrum' or synonymous expressions:

Paragraph 4:
at the heart of Britain's motorway network – im Zentrum des britischen Autobahnnetzes

Paragraph 6:
The most prestigious conference centre in the UK and Europe stands prominently in the centre of the city. – Das renommierteste Kongreßzentrum Großbritanniens und Europas nimmt einen stolzen Platz im Herzen der Stadt ein.

In addition to the central location, this proposition also expresses a sense of importance and pride ('stands prominently'). The collocation in the TT, however ('einen stolzen Platz einnehmen'), is somewhat inappropriate ('stolz' is usually combined with human beings). We would suggest 'nimmt einen exponierten Platz im Herzen der Stadt ein', with the choice of 'Herz' here contributing to the sense of importance, pride, and emotional attachment.

Paragraph 9:

The home and heart of the industrial revolution continues to be a major man-ufacturing centre. – Die Region, die einst Ausgangspunkt der industriellen Revolution war, ist auch heute ein wichtiges Fertigungszentrum.

The pride and emotional attachment associated with 'home and heart' in the ST had become lost in the TT (with 'Ausgangspunkt' being a rather neutral expression). A certain emotional attachment and a sense of feeling at home could be conveyed by 'Geburtsort'.

Alternative Solution for Target Text

Birmingham

[1]

Europas Treffpunkt, der keine Wünsche offenläßt. Wo Kommunikationsnetze zusammenlaufen, wo unterschiedliche Kulturen in
friedlichem Nebeneinander existieren und wo Industrie und Handel
mit vereinter Kraft zusammenwirken – dort liegt Birmingham,
Mittelpunkt der einmaligen Konzentration von Ressourcen und
Möglichkeiten. Birmingham ist, in jeder Hinsicht, der Treffpunkt
Europas.

[2]

Standortbestimmung. Birmingham ist nicht nur der geographische
Mittelpunkt des Vereinigten Königreichs, sondern auch der Mittel-
punkt des europäischen Geschehens, ein Tor für den transatlantischen
Handel und ein Zentrum für die Geschäftswelt. Ob Sie per Bahn, Auto
oder Flugzeug kommen, die Stadt ist ein zentraler Verkehrs-
knotenpunkt für Reisen aus Ost und West, Nord und Süd, von und nach
Europa und den USA. Birmingham ist das geographische und kulturelle
Zentrum Europas.

[3]

Hier heben Sie ab! Mit jährlich über vier Millionen Fluggästen ist der Birmingham International Airport mit seinem zweiten Terminal 'Eurohub'
ein im wahrsten Sinne des Wortes internationaler Flughafen. Es gibt
direkte Linienflüge von und zu 39 Zielorten in Europa und den USA.
Somit sind alle wichtigen Geschäftszentren mit Birmingham verbunden.

[4]

Show Business ist 'Big Business'. Der Standort des National Exhibition
Centre (NEC), des größten in England, ist perfekt für seine internationale Rolle als Messezentrum. In den sechzehn Hallen finden
jährlich 110 Ausstellungen statt, die rund vier Millionen Besucher
anziehen. Weitere 'Platzvorteile' sind ein 800-Betten-Luxushotel und
die berühmte, 12600 Zuschauer fassende NEC Arena, ein Treffpunkt für
internationale Rockkonzerte, Weltmeisterschaften und Tagungen. Das
NEC liegt im Zentrum des britischen Autobahnnetzes, besitzt einen
eigenen InterCity-Bahnhof und direkten Anschluß zum Flughafen.

[5]

Wenn's um Geld geht. Die Stadt, die die älteste Münzstätte der Welt ihr

eigen nennt, in der zwei der führenden Clearingbanken gegründet
wurden und wo seit 1827 die Bank of England zu Hause ist, ist ein
Finanz- und Geschäftszentrum von internationalem Rang. Einer der
größten Wirtschaftskreise Europas (u.a. der zweitgrößte europäische
Versicherungsmarkt) profitiert von der etablierten Infrastruktur von
Fachwissen auf vielen Gebieten, die das Fundament des Wirtschaftsaufkommens der Stadt von jährlich mehr als 1 Milliarde Pfund bildet.

[6]

Stadt der Kongresse. Das renommierteste Kongreßzentrum Großbritanniens und Europas nimmt einen exponierten Platz im Herzen der
Stadt ein. In der kurzen Zeit seit seiner Eröffnung 1991 hat das International Convention Centre bereits ein EU-Gipfeltreffen (1992) und andere
wichtige Kongresse zu politischen, kulturellen und wirtschaftlichen
Themen erlebt. 30 bis 3000 Gäste finden in elegantem, sicherem
Ambiente bequem Platz in den elf Veranstaltungssälen unterschiedlicher Größe, darunter die großartige Konzerthalle Symphony
Hall.

[7]

Eklektisch, exzentrisch und erregend. Birminghams Musikszene läßt
sich in keine Schublade pressen. Das renommierte City of Birmingham
Symphony Orchestra unter Leitung von Simon Rattle, das in der Symphony Hall mit ihrer perfekten Akustik eine neue Heimstatt gefunden
hat, gehört ebenso dazu wie die Rockband UB40 in der NEC Arena, die
D'Oyly Carte Opera und das bunte kosmopolitische Spektrum
asiatischer und afro-karibischer Klänge. Und während des Internationalen Jazzfestivals dringt der Jazz, der ganzjährig im Ronnie
Scott's Club zu Hause ist, hinaus auf die Straßen und in die
Einkaufszentren, in die Clubs und Bars der britischen 'City of Music'.

[8]

Großereignisse. In zentraler Lage, direkt neben dem International Con-
vention Centre, befindet sich die führende britische Hallen-Sportarena
mit maßgeschneiderten Spezialanlagen für große internationale
Leichtathletik-, Tennis-, Box- und Eislaufveranstaltungen. Doch in der
National Indoor Arena (NIA) dreht sich nicht nur alles um den Sport. Bis
zu 12 000 Zuschauer erleben in dem Weltklassestadium eine Vielfalt von
Ereignissen, von der Fernsehaufzeichnung der Sport-Spiel-Show 'The
Gladiators' über die Oper Aida bis hin zu eindrucksvollen
Produkteinführungen.

[9]

Die Werkstatt der Welt. Die Region, die einst der Geburtsort der
industriellen Revolution war, ist auch heute ein wichtiges Industrie-

zentrum. Mehr als ein Drittel der britischen Industrieexporte kommen noch immer von hier. Heute jedoch kooperieren die neuen Finanz- und Handelsbetriebe immer enger mit der verarbeitenden Industrie, treten neue Unternehmen an die Seite solch international renommierter Namen wie Cadbury's, Rover, Lucas und IMI, so daß ganze neue Industriezweige entstehen. Heute ist es die fortschrittliche Fertigungstechnik Birminghams, die den zukünftigen Wohlstand der Region sichert.

[10]

Aus Liebe zur Kunst. Birmingham ist ein kulturelles Terrain par excellence. Da ist die bedeutendste Prä-Raffaeliten-Sammlung der Welt im City Museum and Art Gallery, die sich in ihrem Stil augenfällig von den innovativen Werken zeitgenössischer Künstler in der Ikon Gallery unterscheidet. Nicht weniger vielseitig ist die literarische Szene: Zu den berühmten Söhnen der Stadt zählen so unterschiedliche Autoren wie J. R. R. Tolkien und Arthur Conan Doyle. Das Birmingham Royal Ballet tanzt im Hippodrome, das Repertory Theatre bietet ein Bühnenereignis nach dem anderen, und vielfältige unabhängige Organisationen und Festivals sorgen dafür, daß die Kunst auch weiterhin die Lebensqualität der Stadt positiv prägt.

[11]

Hier wird Können großgeschrieben. Überlieferte Fertigkeiten spielen auch heute noch in der Leder-, Glas- und Schmuckwarenindustrie eine wichtige Rolle, während die neuen Technologie-, Computer- und Geschäftsparks mit neuem Wissen, neuen Fähigkeiten und Fertigkeiten sowie neuen Ausbildungsschwerpunkten die Tradition wissenschaftlichen Unternehmertums fortsetzen, die einst von so berühmten Erfindern wie Joseph Priestley, James Watt, Matthew Boulton und William Murdoch begründet wurde. Aus den drei Universitäten der Stadt geht eine neue Generation von Wissenschaftlern, Technikern und Künstlern hervor, die in den modernen Anforderungen von Industrie und Handel ein breites Betätigungsfeld für ihre innovativen Fertigkeiten finden.

[12]

Betten-Kapazität. Im Umkreis von rund 30 Kilometern um das Stadtzentrum stehen den Besuchern des Treffpunkt Europas über 35 000 Betten zur Verfügung. Das Birmingham Convention & Visitor Bureau arrangiert Unterbringungen für jeden Geschmack und Geldbeutel: Das Angebot reicht von bescheidenen, aber bequemen Bed-&-Breakfast-Unterkünften bis hin zum erstklassigen, eleganten Swallow Hotel, das 1994 als 'Hotel des Jahres' ausgezeichnet wurde. Egal, für welche

Preisklasse Sie sich entscheiden, Birmingham bietet hohen Standard und ein jederzeit freundliches Willkommen.

[13]

Sport und Spiel. Birmingham ist eine sportbegeisterte Stadt und weitaus häufiger der Austragungsort von Welt- und Europameisterschaften als jede andere britische Stadt. The Belfry, einer von dreißig Golfplätzen in der Region, ist die Zentrale des britischen Profigolfverbandes PGA; dreimal wurde hier bereits der Ryder Cup ausgetragen. Villa Park, das Stadion des Fußballclubs Aston Villa, ist 1996 einer der Austragungsorte der Fußball-Europameisterschaft. Die Stadt besitzt zwei Sporthallen von Weltrang, und in der Nähe des Platzes, wo einst das erste Rasen-tennis-Match der Welt ausgetragen wurde, befindet sich das inter-national renommierte Cricket-Stadion in Edgbaston. In Birmingham kommt jeder Sportliebhaber auf seine Kosten.

[14]

Alt und neu. An Birminghams Gebäuden läßt sich die Entwicklung vom Marktstädtchen zum europäischen Treffpunkt nachvollziehen. Beispiele für die Architektur zur Zeit Jakobs I. vom frühen 17. Jahrhundert und für die Eleganz des Regency-Stils vom frühen 19. Jahrhundert findet man noch heute zwischen den stolzen öffentlichen Gebäuden, die als Symbol des Wohlstands und Fortschritts während der Regentschaft von Königin Victoria (1837–1901) und König Eduard VII. (1901–1910) errichtet wurden. Joseph Chamberlain, der als Birminghams Oberbürgermeister in der viktorianischen Blütezeit die selbstsichere Haltung der Stadt gegenüber dem Rest der Welt verkörperte, wäre sicherlich stolz auf die heutigen engagierten Bemühungen um eine Erneuerung des Stadtzentrums und die eindrucksvolle, zeitgenössische Architektur, das öffentliche Kunst-angebot und die freien Plätze der Stadt.

[15]

Abschalten und entspannen. Bei all diesem geschäftigen Treiben in der Stadt kann man kaum glauben, daß Birmingham mehr öffentliche Parkanlagen besitzt als jede andere Stadt in Europa. Erwähnung verdienen hier besonders der von Heinrich VIII. gestiftete Sutton Park und der eindrucksvolle Botanische Garten. Losgelöst von der Hektik des städtischen Lebens laden hier angenehme Spazierwege durch Parkanlagen und an Kanälen Einheimische und Besucher zum Bummeln und zum Entdecken von Designerläden und anderen feinen Geschäften ein. Ruhe und Entspannung kann man überall finden in dieser Stadt, in der es mehr als 6 Millionen Bäume gibt und auf deren zahlreichen freien Plätzen ständig Karneval- und Festivalprogramme angeboten werden.

[16]
Spaß am Vergnügen. Birmingham bei Nacht bietet Einheimischen und Besuchern all das, was man von einem wichtigen europäischen Treffpunkt erwarten würde – und zudem einige ganz spezielle Birminghamer Spezialitäten. Neben einladenden Weinstuben, Bistros, Pubs und Clubs finden Gourmets hier einige der besten chinesischen sowie indischen 'Balti' Restaurants Europas und zahlreiche Gelegenheiten, Speisen aus aller Welt zu probieren. Denn nach getaner Arbeit weiß Birmingham nach allen Regeln der Kunst zu genießen.

[17]
Birmingham und seine Umgebung. Die umgebende Landschaft steht der Metropole Birmingham in Sachen Vielfältigkeit in nichts nach. Sogar London ist schon in 1 1/2 Stunden Bahnfahrt zu erreichen, aber bereits nach 30 Minuten Autofahrt ist man in den historischen Städten Stratford-upon-Avon und Ironbridge. Im Süden von Birmingham liegt Warwick Castle, das prächtigste mittelalterliche Schloß Englands, im Norden Stoke-on-Trent, wo die berühmten Porzellanmanufakturen von Spode und Wedgwood noch heute in Betrieb sind. Und in den naheliegenden Cotswolds und Malvern Hills gibt es viele Wanderwege, und ländliche Pubs laden zum Verweilen ein.

Legal Texts: Introductory Comments

Legal texts belong to a variety of genres and cover a variety of topics, for example, national or international treaties and contracts, court proceedings, various kinds of legal documents, terms and conditions on a variety of services, service and guarantee conditions issued by companies, codes of practice. Legal texts typically belong to the informative text type (Reiss, 1971, 2000), although some genres may also show features of the operative text type. For example, Brinker (1985) in his text typology, lists statutory law with appellative texts ('Appelltexte'), treaties with obligation-centred texts ('Obligationstexte'), and certificates and wills with declarative texts ('Deklarationstexte'). In Rolf's (1993) text typology, summons to military service are listed as an example of assertive texts (sub-group 'transmittierende Textsorten'), statutory law and warrant of arrest as examples of binding directive texts, military treaties as examples of commissive texts (sub-group: bilaterally binding), and customs declaration and marriage certificate as examples of declarative texts (sub-groups: object-oriented ('sachdimensionierend') and person-oriented ['personendimensionierend'], respectively). All of these genres are more or less legally binding, at least for one of the communicative partners.

In a way similar to that which we used to characterise political texts, the specification of a text as a legal text too can best be based on functional and thematic criteria. That is, legal texts are a part and/or the result of some action that is legally relevant, an action that requires some form of codified regulation, and the resulting texts have (normally) a certain power within the legal system of the culture.

A number of genres which can be grouped under the label 'legal texts' are frequently translated (Schmitt (1998a: 10) explicitly lists treaties and contracts, various texts produced in the context of court proceedings, certificates and documents, norms and standards, patents). In the majority of cases, the TT will have an equally binding function for its addressees in the target culture as the ST had for its addressees in the source culture (i.e. equifunctional translation (Nord, 1997)). Depending on the specific text type and genre, text-typological and genre conventions will apply. I will only comment on a few translation issues that are relevant to our sample text as well (on wider expects on the translation of legal texts see Sarcevic (1997), Morris (1995), and the contributions and the extensive bibliography in Sandrini (1999)).

Superstructure Schemata

Some legal texts show conventional macrostructures and superstructures which are highly rigid, for example patents (see Lawson, 1983; Göpferich, 1998b), treaties (see Kupsch-Losereit, 1998: 229f.), court verdicts and sentences (see Arntz, 1992). Depending on the skopos, the superstructure of the ST may either be retained in the translation (documentary translation) or it may need to be adapted to the conventions of the target culture (instrumental translation).

Standard Formulations

In relation to highly conventionalised genre schemata, standard formulations are characteristic of specific genres. For example, in British patents, requests for the granting of a patent are typically formulated as

> We, . . . do hereby declare the invention, for which we pray that a patent may be granted to us, and the method by which it is to be performed, to be particularly described in and by the following statement: . . . . (Göpferich, 1998b: 223)

Legal terminology and conventionalised lexical expressions and syntactic structures also have to be taken into account for translation (see also Thiel & Thome, 1987; Rothkegel, 1984). International treaties have standardised phrases in the preamble which translators are expected to be aware of (a useful reference book is *Standardformulierungen für deutsche Vertragstexte mit Übersetzungen in englischer, französischer und spanischer Sprache*, edited by the Sprachendienst des Auswärtigen Amtes, Berlin: de Gruyter, 1992, 3rd edn) (see the following table).

English	French	Spanish	German
conscious	conscients	conscientes	in dem Bewußtsein; eingedenk
desiring; desirous	désirant; désireux	con el deseo, deseosos	in dem Wunsch; von dem Wunsch geleitet

Characteristic speech acts (e.g. declarative and commissive speech acts) are rendered by typical forms and structures. In treaties and contracts, obligations are typically expressed by 'shall' in English (and usually by present tenses or infinitive structures in the passive in German), promises to do some action are indicated by 'agree, undertake, acknowledge', but not by 'promise' (see Trosborg, 1994; Stolze, 1999: 165ff.). Other important aspects in translating legal texts are the need for consistency in terminology and clarity in the identification of the referents. Therefore, the specific terms and concepts are frequently repeated and not substituted by pro-forms (e.g. pronouns). The need for clarity also results in the use of characteristic syntactic structures, such as genitive structures with post-positions (and 'thereof' as a common preposition), and pre-modification structures in German texts. Some of these features are reflected in the following short example, taken from a contract, more specifically: from the superstructure category 'Time for Delivery' in General Conditions:

ST:
The Purchaser's remedies under-clauses (iii) and (iv) of this clause shall be in lieu of any other remedy in respect of the Vendor's failure to deliver goods in accordance with the Contract within the time fixed thereby or, if no time be fixed, within a reasonable time.

TT:
Nur die nach den Ziffern (iii) und (iv) eingeräumten Mittel des Rechtschutzes stehen dem Käufer zu in bezug auf das Versäumnis des Verkäufers, die Geräte vertragsgemäß innerhalb der festgesetzten Frist oder, in Ermangelung einer Frist, innerhalb eines angemessenen Zeitraums zu liefern.

Culture-specific Aspects

Translation problems may arise from the different legal systems in a country, e.g. Case Law in England and Statute Law in Germany. Related to this, legislative bodies, regulations and law-making procedures may be different (i.e. identical or similar terms may not at all denote the same body or procedure). Legal texts normally function within the legal system of their respective culture, and in the process of translation, the TT may be required to have the same position in the target system as the ST had in its own legal system. In other cases, a translator may be required to produce a documentary version, i.e. simply providing information on the original ST, with the resulting TT then having a different status than that of the ST had (see the Debate in *Current Issues in Language and Society* 6 (2, 1999): 130ff.; on the translation of certificates see Fleck (1998)). It is therefore highly important that translators are familiar (or familiarise themselves) with the legal systems in the respective cultures and with the textual conventions of legal texts, i.e. of the specific genres as belonging to legal texts.

Sample Text

The sample text in this volume, a mission statement and code of practice of an association, is not a prototypical exemplar of a legal text, but it does contain lexical and syntactic structures that are typically found in legal texts. In addition, a number of references to culture-specific phenomena present challenges for translation. In the annotations, the use of parallel texts (i.e. the *Satzung* of German associations) will be illustrated, in particular with respect to dealing with pragmatic translation problems (caused by different legal systems) and intercultural translation problems (especially genre conventions).

ASSOCIATION OF INDEPENDENT RAILWAYS
AND
PRESERVATION SOCIETIES LTD

MISSION STATEMENT AND CODE OF PRACTICE

MISSION STATEMENT

To help and encourage the promotion of high standards in the direction, management, restoration and operation of railway companies independent of the National Network and the preservation of historic railways and historic railway equipment.

1. To promote independent and 'heritage' railways, railway centres and railway museums to the public.
2. To maintain high standards by requiring members to conform with the AIRPS Code of Practice.
3. To encourage even higher standards by organising awards and competitions.
4. To keep members advised and informed of marketing trends and commercial affairs generally and to provide professional advice, a full information service and such other help and assistance as may be appropriate.
5. To provide a forum for the sharing of information and experience by organising open meetings and seminars.
6. To represent its members' interests to Government and other bodies.
7. To encourage members to provide regular training for both employees and volunteers in all aspects of railway operation, administration and maintenance and to further encourage them to provide advice and assistance in the obtaining of professional qualifications where appropriate.
8. To encourage members to promote and expand volunteer involvement in all activities whenever it is appropriate to their organisation and operation.
9. To encourage and advise members on the establishment and upkeep of an archive facility for documents, photographs and other artefacts relevant to their operations.

CODE OF PRACTICE

INTRODUCTION

[1]

In order to ensure safe, practicable operation and to enhance the reputation of independent and Heritage railways and to strengthen the

Association in its dealings with HM Railway Inspectorate and other Government Departments and Agencies as well as giving reassurance to members of the public, the Association has adopted the following Code of Practice as a condition of membership.

[2]

Applicants for membership of the Association of Independent Railways and Preservation Societies Ltd. must satisfy the Association that the objects for which it was formed are attainable and do not prejudice those of an already established scheme.

[3]

Applicants must also give an assurance that they conform to and will observe the Code of Practice.

[4]

Items of legislation mentioned in this Code of Practice relate to England, Wales and, in most cases Scotland. Organisations in Northern Ireland, Isle of Man and where appropriate, Scotland should relate this legislation to the appropriate regional equivalent.

[5]

Organisations in the Republic of Ireland should relate the equivalent Irish legislation as appropriate. References to HM Inspectorate should be related to the equivalent Government Department as appropriate.

[6]

GENERAL

1.1   The Chairman, Secretary and Treasurer / Accountant and all Directors / Council / Management Committee of the constituent member organisation, must be over eighteen years of age in order to accept legal responsibilities of office.

1.2   In the event of two or more Association Members seeking to preserve the same object, or having conflicting aims, they will agree to abide by the decision of three arbitrators appointed by the Association of Independent Railways and Preservation Societies Ltd.

[7]

CONSTITUTION

2.1   In the case of a member organisation whose own constituents are required as a condition of membership to make an annual subscription, there must be a written constitution, an up to date copy of which is lodged with the Association which contains the following principles.

(a)   The Objects for which the organisation is formed.

(b)   The Arrangements for the appointment of trustees or election of members to the Board/Council/Committee of Management and also their terms of service.

(c)   That all monies received shall be expended in the furtherance of its objectives, that proper books of accounts shall be kept and that at regular intervals there will be laid before members, a Statement of Income and Expenditure and a current Balance Sheet. The requirements of any legislation to which a member may be subject (eg the Companies Act of 1985 and, if applicable, the Charity Commissioners) requirements will be observed at all times.

(d)   That the books of accounts will be examined by a suitably qualified and properly appointed person (who will be independent of its members) in accordance with the requirements of the Registrar of Companies or if applicable, the Charity Commissioners.

(e)   That a General Meeting of members will be held at least once every calendar year for the election of officers and members of the Board/Council/Committee of Management for the appointment/reappointment of Trustees and for the acceptance of accounts which have been approved by the managing body and which have been audited in accordance with the appropriate statutory requirements.

(f)   That in the event of a dissolution or winding up of a body, provision has been made for the disposal of the assets of the body.

2.2   The Association of Independent Railways and Preservation Societies Ltd, reserves the right to suggest amendments to a constitution as submitted except in the case of:

(a)   Any body incorporated as either a Limited Company (whether by shares of Guarantee), or as an Industrial & Provident Society.

(b)   Any organisation properly registered as a charity or recognised as such by the Inland Revenue.

[8]
FINANCIAL & LEGAL

3.1   In the case of an Association member seeking donations from members of the public, it shall:

(a)   State the objects for which donations are required.

(b)   Make arrangements for any person who has made a donation to the appeal to receive a copy of the Statement of Account upon payment of a reasonable charge.

NB Regulars draws or lotteries which have to be licensed by a Local Authority are exempt from the provisions of the above clause.

3.2 In the case of an Association member operating a line or depot, that member will legally limit the financial liability of its members.

3.3 All Association members shall comply with all Statutory Requirements relating to the preparation and presentation of properly audited accounts.

[9]
INSURANCE REQUIREMENTS

4.1 When members of the public are to be admitted to an Association member's premises, whether on payment of an entrance fee or not, any Insurance Policy will be taken out with a reputable company to cover any claim for any loss, damage, injury or death whether caused by accident or negligence or otherwise of the Association member, its officers, staff (paid or unpaid) and its agents.

4.2 When any person (paid or unpaid) is working on behalf of the Association member, he/she will be covered by an Insurance Policy taken out with a reputable company against loss, damage, injury or death arising out of this work for which the member, its officers, staff (paid or unpaid) and its agents may be legally liable.

4.3 In the case of an Association member operating a steam locomotive(s) or having air receivers, the body will take out with a reputable company, adequate insurance against the risk of explosions.

[10]
STATUTORY REQUIREMENTS

5.1 All Association members shall comply with all appropriate Statutory Requirements and Codes of Practice.

[11]
RAILWAY OPERATING

6.1 Association members must maintain the highest standards of operation and must take adequate steps to ensure the safety of the public, staff and volunteers at all times.

6.2 Association members shall observe all Statutory Requirements and Codes of Practice relative to railway operation and safety.

6.3 Operating Rules must be prepared in a clear and easily understood format and must be adhered to by all staff and volunteers. A copy of the Operating Rules must be deposited with HM Railway Inspectorate.

6.4 All staff should have adequate training in operating duties and must be examined by a competent officer before being allowed to undertake such duties. Operating staff and volunteers should be re-examined in the Operating Rules and other relevant matters at regular intervals. Safety Critical Work Regulations must be observed where necessary, including appropriate medical standards.

6.5   The issuing of lineside photographic passes shall be carefully controlled. All pass holders should be required to wear suitably identified high visibility vests when or near [sic!] the operational railway. They shall be given clear instructions as to their conduct whilst on railway premises, any limitations on their movements and the importance of avoiding trespass.

Revised AIRPS 1/96

Translation Assignment
The Association of Independent Railways and Preservation Societies Ltd. (AIRPS) has contacts with a number of similar organisations world wide, among others in Germany. These organisations meet from time to time to discuss topics of common interest, to define common targets, and to harmonise their efforts to preserve the national heritage in the field of railways in their respective countries. In order to find out more about the work of AIRPS, the Bundesverband Deutscher Eisenbahn-Freunde e.V., the respective Association in Germany, ordered a translation of the Mission Statement and the Code of Practice.

SATZUNG der ASSOCIATION of INDEPENDENT RAILWAYS and PRESERVATION SOCIETIES Ltd (AIRPS), des britischen Dachverbands von privaten Eisenbahnunternehmen und Vereinen zur Erhaltung von Bahnanlagen

ZWECK UND AUFGABEN (Mission Statement)

Zweck des Verbandes ist die Gewährleistung eines hohen Niveaus bei der Verwaltung, Rekonstruktion und Betreibung von privaten Eisenbahnunternehmen sowie die Erhaltung und Pflege historischer Bahnanlagen, Fahrzeuge und Betriebsmittel. Der Verband sieht seine Aufgaben konkret im folgenden:

1. Förderung privater und Traditionsbahnunternehmen sowie Bewahrung historischer Bahnanlagen und Eisenbahnmuseen.
2. Einhaltung hoher Standards durch Gewährleistung eines satzungsgemäßen Verhaltens aller Mitglieder von AIRPS.
3. Qualitätserhöhung durch Verleihung von Preisen und Organisation von Wettbewerben.
4. Information und Beratung der Mitglieder über Markttrends und kommerzielle Entwicklungen, Gewährleistung von fachmännischer Beratung, umfassender Information und gegebenenfalls Hilfe und Unterstützung in speziellen Angelegenheiten.
5. Schaffung von Möglichkeiten des Informations- und Erfahrungsaustausches durch Organisation von öffentlichen Veranstaltungen und Seminaren.
6. Vertretung der Interessen der Mitglieder gegenüber der Regierung und anderen Institutionen.
7. Ermutigung der Mitgliedsvereine, Lehrgänge für Angestellte und Freiwillige zum Betrieb, zur Verwaltung und zur Instandhaltung der Bahnanlagen zu organisieren sowie gegebenenfalls Beratung und Unterstützung beim Erwerb von beruflichen Qualifikationen anzubieten.
8. Förderung der Mitgliedsvereine bei ihren Bemühungen um die Gewinnung immer mehr Freiwilliger für ihre Aktivitäten, wenn das mit der Organisation und der Arbeitsweise der Mitgliedsvereine in Einklang steht.
9. Förderung und Beratung der Mitgliedsvereine bei der Einrichtung und Aufrechterhaltung von Archiven mit Dokumenten, Photographien und anderen für ihre Tätigkeit relevanten Gegenständen.

LEITSÄTZE UND RICHTLINIEN (Code of Practice)
Einleitung
[1]
Die Association of Independent Railways and Preservation Societies Ltd. – nachfolgend Verband genannt – hat zum Zwecke der Gewährleistung eines sicheren Bahnbetriebs, der Festigung des Rufes der privaten und der Traditionseisenbahnen, der Unterstützung des Verbandes im Rahmen seiner Kontakte zur britischen Bahnaufsichtsbehörde (HM Railway Inspectorate), anderen Ministerien und Dienststellen sowie der Vertrauensbildung in der Öffentlichkeit folgende Satzung als Voraussetzung für die Mitgliedschaft angenommen.

[2]
Jeder Verein, der einen Antrag auf Mitgliedschaft in der Association of Independent Railways and Preservation Societies Ltd. stellt, hat gegenüber dem Verband zu gewährleisten, daß dieser seine im Mission Statement definierten Zwecke verfolgen kann und bereits bestehende Projekte nicht beeinträchtigt werden.

[3]
Jeder Verein, der einen Antrag auf Mitgliedschaft stellt, hat sich zur Anerkennung und Einhaltung der Satzung zu verpflichten.

[4]
Die gesetzlichen Bestimmungen, auf die in dieser Satzung Bezug genommen wird, gelten für England, Wales und in den meisten Fällen auch für Schottland. Für Vereine in Nordirland, auf der Isle of Man und gegebenenfalls in Schottland gelten die entsprechenden regionalen Gesetze.

[5]
Für Vereine in der Republik Irland gelten die entsprechenden irischen Gesetze. Bei Bezugnahme auf die britische Bahnaufsichtsbehörde (HM Railway Inspectorate) gilt dementsprechend die zuständige irische Regierungsbehörde.

[6]
Regelungen zur Mitgliedschaft

1.1   Der Vorsitzende, der Geschäftsführer und der Schatzmeister sowie alle Mitglieder des Verwaltungsrates / des Vorstands / der Geschäftsführung der einzelnen Mitgliedsvereine müssen das 18. Lebensjahr vollendet haben, um die mit einer offiziellen Funktion verbundenen rechtlichen Verpflichtungen übernehmen zu können.

1.2   Wenn sich zwei oder mehr Mitgliedsvereine um die Erhaltung und Pflege ein und desselben Objekts bemühen oder gegensätzliche Interessen vertreten, verpflichten sie sich zur Anerkennung der Entscheidung von drei Schlichtern, welche von der Association of Independent Railways und Preservation Societies Ltd. ernannt werden.

[7]
Statuten

2.1 Wenn die Angehörigen eines Mitgliedsvereins zur Zahlung eines Jahresbeitrages verpflichtet sind, muß der Verein über schriftliche Statuten verfügen. Die aktuelle Fassung dieses Dokuments ist dem Verband zu übergeben und muß folgende Grundsätze beeinhalten:

(a) Die Ziele des Vereins.

(b) Die Bestimmungen für die Ernennung von Treuhändern bzw. die Wahl von Mitgliedern des Verwaltungsrates/des Vorstands/der Geschäftsführung mit Angabe ihrer jeweiligen Amtszeit.

(c) Der Grundsatz, daß alle eingegangenen Gelder zur Durchsetzung der Ziele des Vereins verwendet werden, daß die Geschäftsbücher ordnungsgemäß geführt werden, und daß den Mitgliedern in regelmäßigen Abständen eine Aufstellung über Einnahmen und Ausgaben sowie eine aktuelle Bilanz vorgelegt wird. Die gesetzlichen Bestimmungen, denen ein Mitgliedsverein gegebenenfalls unterliegt (z.B. das britische Gesetz über Unternehmen und Gesellschaften von 1985, Company Act, oder die Bestimmungen für gemeinnützige britische Organisationen, Charity Commission) sind stets einzuhalten.

(d) Der Grundsatz, daß die Geschäftsbücher unter Beachtung der Anforderungen des Registers des Company Act bzw. der Charity Commission von einer entsprechend qualifizierten und ordnungsgemäß ernannten Person (die nicht Mitglied des Vereins ist) geprüft werden.

(e) Durchführung einer Hauptversammlung mindestens einmal pro Kalenderjahr, auf der die Funktionsträger und die Mitglieder des Verwaltungsrates/des Vorstands/der Geschäftsführung gewählt werden, Kuratoren ernannt bzw. bestätigt werden und der vom Vereinsvorstand genehmigte und satzungsgemäß geprüfte Jahresabschluß gebilligt wird.

(f) Vorkehrungen zur Veräußerung der Vermögenswerte des Vereins im Falle seiner Auflösung oder Abwicklung.

2.2 Die Association of Independent Railways und Preservation Societies Ltd. behält sich das Recht vor, im Hinblick auf die eingereichten Statuten Änderungen vorzuschlagen. Ausgenommen davon sind:

(a) alle Körperschaften in Form einer Gesellschaft mit beschränkter Haftung nach britischem Recht (Limited Company) (gegebenenfalls mit garantierten Aktien) oder einer Gegenseitigkeitsgesellschaft (Industrial & Provident Society).

(b) alle Körperschaften, die ordnungsgemäß als gemeinnützig eingetragen sind bzw. von der Finanzbehörde (Inland Revenue) als solche anerkannt sind.

[8]
Finanzrichtlinien

3.1 Wenn sich ein Mitgliedsverein mit einem Spendenaufruf an die Öffentlichkeit wendet, hat er:

(a) den Spendenzweck anzugeben;

(b) jeder Person, die dem Spendenaufruf folgt, gegen eine angemessene Gebühr eine Kopie des Kontoauszugs zuzustellen.

Hinweis: Regelmäßige Ziehungen oder Lotterien, die von einer örtlichen Behörde genehmigt werden müssen, sind von den Bestimmungen des vorgenannten Abschnitts ausgenommen.

3.2 Betreibt ein Mitgliedsverein eine Bahnstrecke oder ein Eisenbahndepot, hat er im Rahmen der gesetzlichen Bestimmungen dafür Sorge zu tragen, daß seine Einzelmitglieder finanziell nur beschränkt haftbar sind.

3.3 Alle Mitgliedsvereine haben die gesetzlichen Vorschriften zur Erstellung und Vorlage ordnungsgemäß geprüfter Jahresabschlüsse einzuhalten.

[9]
Versicherungsrechtliche Bestimmungen

4.1 Soll der Öffentlichkeit der Zutritt zum Betriebsgelände eines Mitgliedsvereins kostenlos oder gegen Zahlung eines Eintrittsgeldes gestattet werden, hat der betreffende Verein bei einer anerkannten Versicherungsgesellschaft eine Versicherung abzuschließen, um eventuellen Forderungen im Zusammenhang mit Verlust, Schaden, Verletzung oder Todesfall nachzukommen, die auf Unfälle, Fahrlässigkeit oder anderweitiges Verschulden des Mitgliedsvereins, seiner Funktionsträger, seiner (angestellten oder freiwilligen) Mitarbeiter und seiner Beauftragten zurückzuführen sind.

4.2   Wenn ein Mitgliedsverein (angestellte oder freiwillige) Mitarbeiter beschäftigt, ist für diese Personen bei einer anerkannten Versicherungsgesellschaft eine Versicherung abzuschließen, die Schutz bietet bei Verlust, Schaden, Verletzung oder Todesfall infolge der Ausübung der Tätigkeit, für welche der Mitgliedsverein, dessen Funktionsträger, (angestellte oder freiwillige) Mitarbeiter und Beauftragte laut Gesetz gegebenenfalls haftbar sind.

4.3   Wenn ein Mitgliedsverein eine oder mehrere Dampflokomotiven betreibt oder Dampfsammler besitzt, hat er bei einer angesehenen Versicherungsgesellschaft einen angemessenen Versicherungsschutz gegen Explosionsgefahr abzuschließen.

[10]
Einhaltung der Gesetze

5.1   Alle Mitgliedsvereine sind zur Einhaltung von Bestimmungen entsprechender Gesetze sowie von Richtlinien entsprechender Codes of Practice verpflichtet.

[11]
Eisenbahnbetrieb

6.1   Die Mitgliedsvereine haben stets für höchste Betriebsstandards zu sorgen und angemessene Sicherheitsmaßnahmen zum Schutz der Öffentlichkeit, ihrer Angestellten und freiwilligen Helfer zu ergreifen.

6.2   Die Mitgliedsvereine haben alle gesetzlichen Bestimmungen und Richtlinien in bezug auf den Eisenbahnbetrieb und dessen Sicherheit zu beachten.

6.3   Betriebsvorschriften sind klar und leicht verständlich zu formulieren und von allen Angestellten und freiwilligen Helfern zu befolgen. Eine Ausfertigung der Betriebsvorschriften ist bei der britischen Bahnaufsichtsbehörde zu hinterlegen.

6.4   Alle Angestellten sind hinreichend in die Betriebsabläufe einzuweisen und vor der Übernahme ihrer Aufgaben von einer qualifizierten Kraft zu prüfen. Das Bedienpersonal und die freiwilligen Helfer müssen in regelmäßigen Abständen ihre Kenntnis der Betriebsvorschriften sowie anderer wichtiger Fragen in Prüfungen nachweisen. Die Arbeitsschutzbestimmungen, einschließlich der entsprechenden Gesundheitsnormen, sind im erforderlichen Umfang zu beachten.

6.5   Die Ausgabe von Streckenausweisen mit Paßfoto ist sorgfältig zu kontrollieren. Alle Inhaber solcher Pässe haben deutlich gekennzeichnete Sicherheitswesten zu tragen, wenn sie sich an oder in der Nähe einer in Betrieb befindlichen Eisenbahnstrecke aufhalten. Ihnen sind für ihr Verhalten auf dem Bahngelände, die Einschränkung ihrer Bewegungsfreiheit und die Einhaltung der Zutrittsverbote eindeutige Instruktionen zu erteilen.

AIRPS, Stand 1/96.

Annotations

Translation Assignment

The Association of Independent Railways and Preservation Societies Ltd. (AIRPS) has contacts with a number of similar organisations world wide, among others in Germany. These organisations meet from time to time to discuss topics of common interest, to define common targets, and to harmonise their efforts to preserve the national heritage in the field of railways in their respective countries. In order to find out more about the work of AIRPS, the Bundesverband Deutscher Eisenbahn-Freunde e.V., the respective Association in Germany, ordered a translation of the Mission Statement and the Code of Practice.

ST Specification

The ST (combining a Mission Statement and a Code of Practice) is an official document of a specific limited company, which operates in the United Kingdom. The text serves both to present the association to the public (external function), and to give guidelines to its members (internal function). It contains a basic statement of the character of the respective entity, defining its aims and objectives, and laying down a set of rules for its operation. For the members of the association the text is binding in nature, and can therefore be considered a legal document. This is also reflected in the legal register of the text.

The ST has been made available in a small leaflet of four pages, with the Association's logo (a drawing of a locomotive inside a circle which represents rails) at the top left-hand corner of the front page. At the very end of the text there is a small reference to the validity of the text: 'revised AIRPS 1/96'.

TT Specification

As specified in the translation assignment, the TT is meant to be used by a German partner association for information purposes. They wish to learn more about the aims of AIRPS and also about the legal aspects involved in managing the association. In other words, the TT will have to fulfil a different function for its addressees than the ST does for its own addressees (hetero-functional translation). The TT needs to be recognisable as a legally binding text and, at the same time, the addressees want and need to be informed of the specific regulations and requirements in the source culture. The TT can therefore be characterised as an example of a documentary translation (see Nord, 1997: 47ff.).

The dominant translation problems are pragmatic and intercultural ones, and they often overlap. In the following annotations we will only discuss these two types. We will also illustrate the relevance of using parallel texts for solving intercultural translation problems.

Annotations

Pragmatic translation problems

The pragmatic translation problems of this text originate from its embeddedness in the economic and legal traditions and conventions of the source culture. This applies above all to the regulations for forming associations and their opera-

263

tion. These facts are subsequently reflected in the text (name of genre, information components and arrangement, lexical and syntactic structures). The corresponding economic and legal traditions of the target culture with their discourse conventions need to be taken into account in their relevance for the translation brief.

For solving some of these pragmatic translation problems, we searched the Internet to get information about culture-specific associations, organisations, and regulations.

(i) Proper names

(a) Name of the organisation

The full name, Association of Independent Railways and Preservation Societies Ltd., is given in the title. In the following Mission Statement, only the abbreviation AIRPS is used (point 2) which, however, has not been introduced before. In the Code of Practice, 'the Association' is used first (Introduction 1) before the full name is repeated in the following paragraph (Introduction 2). Throughout the following text, we mainly find 'the Association', with the full name being used again in 6.1.2 and 7.2.2. German texts of the genre *Satzung* (see later, under *Intercultural translation problems*) usually give the full name and an abbreviation (if there is one) in the first section of the text (i.e. in the section on name and legal status – on the typical macrostructure of this genre, *(ii) Genre conventions* under *Intercultural translation problems*), for example: 'Der Verein trägt den Namen XXX, abgekürzt YY', or 'Der Verein führt den Namen XXX mit der Abkürzung YY'.

In the second section of those German texts, on the purpose of the association, there is usually a statement as to the use of the general term 'Verband' throughout the text, for example: 'Zweck des YY – nachfolgend auch Verband genannt – ist es . . .'. In the TT, we have therefore given the proper English name in the title and have added the abbreviation, and in addition we have given a German explanation ('britischer Dachverband von privaten Eisenbahnunternehmen und Vereinen zur Erhaltung von Bahnanlagen') as an indication of the purpose of AIRPS (although the addressees of the German text can be expected to know that purpose, see the translation brief). Introducing the abbreviation in the title allows its use in the following Mission Statement. For the Code of Conduct, we have adopted the German principle of giving the full name again for the first occurrence (Introduction 1) and add a reference to using 'Verband' in the following text:

> Introduction 1:
> In order to . . . the Association has adopted the following Code of Practice as a condition of membership. – Die Association of Independent Railways and Preservation Societies Ltd. – nachfolgend Verband genannt – hat . . . folgende Satzung als Voraussetzung für die Mitgliedschaft angenommen.

The full name (i.e. the English proper name) has been used again in the second paragraph of the TT, as is the case in the ST. This paragraph specifies conditions for membership, and German parallel texts too, often – but not always – repeat the full name (or the abbreviation) instead of 'Verband' (for example: 'Mitglieder des XXX [FULL NAME] können werden: . . . ', but also: 'Als Mitglieder können . . . aufgenommen werden: . . . ').

> Introduction 2:
> Applicants for membership of the Association of Independent Railways and

Preservation Societies Ltd. must satisfy the Association . . . – Jeder Verein, der einen Antrag auf Mitgliedschaft in der Association of Independent Railways and Preservation Societies Ltd. stellt, muß gegenüber dem Verband gewähr-leisten, . . .

(b) Geographic names

For the geographic names in the text, the standard German equivalents have been used ('Isle of Man' is a proper name and as such used in German texts when a certain degree of officiality is required, in other texts, 'die Insel Man' could be equally appropriate):

Introduction 4:
. . . England, Wales . . . Scotland. . . . Northern Ireland, Isle of Man . . . – . . . England, Wales . . . Schottland. . . . Nordirland, auf der Isle of Man . . .

Introduction 5:
. . . Republic of Ireland . . . – . . . Republik Irland

(c) Reference to other institutions, which are specific of the source culture

The ST refers to a number of institutions and stipulations that are specific to the source culture (HM Railway Inspectorate, The Companies Act of 1985, Charity Commissioners, etc.). Pragmatic translation problems arise mainly because of the non-existence of certain bodies or regulations in the target community. In confor-mity with the translation brief, we have opted for more general descriptive terms in the TT, sometimes combined with the English proper name. The addition of the English proper names allows the TT addressees to follow up specific issues con-cerning the work of the British Association, if they so wish (e.g. in order to find out about legal and other requirements for starting bi-lateral cooperation):

Mission Statement:
. . . railway companies independent of the National Network . . . – . . . privaten Eisenbahnunternehmen . . .

'Independent' indicates that these railways are privately owned, they are not part of British Rail (which is meant by 'the National Network' in the ST). The German railway system is dominated by the Deutsche Bahn AG (since 1994 no longer state-owned but a shareholder company, with the state still owning a large part of the shares), but there are also a number of minor lines run by private companies. These are referred to as 'Privatbahnen' or 'Privatbahnunternehmen'. For this reason, we have opted for 'privat' in the TT. Due to the fact that the addressees of the TT are experts in the field of railway systems, an additional ref-erence to British Rail, i.e. as an explication of 'National Network' has been regarded redundant. For other translation purposes, such as a text on the work of AIRPS for a news magazine, a more explanatory TT version would be appro-priate (e.g. 'private Eisenbahnunternehmen, die unabhängig von dem Staats-unternehmen British Rail bestehen', or 'private Eisenbahnunternehmen, die neben dem Staatsunternehmen British Rail bestehen'). To ensure referential con-sistency, 'privat' has been used again in the next occurrences in the text:

Mission statement:
1. To promote independent and 'heritage' railways, railway centres and

railway museums to the public. – Förderung privater und Traditionsbahnunternehmen sowie Bewahrung historischer Bahnanlagen und
Eisenbahnmuseen.

Introduction 1:
. . . to enhance the reputation of independent and Heritage railways . . . – . . .
der Festigung des Rufes der privaten und der Traditionseisenbahnen, . . .

'Heritage' refers to historic railways that are regarded as part of the cultural
heritage (note that there is no consistency in the spelling in the ST, i.e. initial
capital letter, quotes). Their preservation, i.e. preserving the railway systems
and also ensuring their continuing operation, is one of the main goals of AIRPS.
In German texts, we find 'Traditions(eisen)bahnen' to indicate that the line is still
being operated, however mainly (or only) for touristic purposes and using 'historic' engines and carriages. When German texts refer to 'historische
Schienenfahrzeuge' and 'historische Bahnanlagen' it may also mean that they
are used in the sense of exhibits, for example in a museum, i.e. not actually being
in operation any more. For these reasons, we have opted for the more general
'historische   Bahnanlagen'   in   the   Mission   Statement   but   for
'Traditionseisenbahnen' in the Introduction.

Introduction 1:
. . . to strengthen the Association in its dealings with HM Railway Inspectorate and other Government Departments and Agencies . . . – . . . der Unterstützung des Verbandes im Rahmen seiner Kontakte zur britischen
Bahnaufsichtsbehörde (HM Railway Inspectorate), anderen Ministerien und
Dienststellen . . .

For 'HM Railway Inspectorate' we have opted for a descriptive term indicating the main status and function of the body. A more detailed explanation in the
TT (i.e. explaining that its main role is to secure the proper control of risks to the
health and safety of employees, passengers and others who might be affected by
the operation of Britain's railways) would go beyond the translation brief. The
relevant point in the ST is that AIRPS has contacts with government bodies. We
have also added 'britisch' in line with the translation purpose of informing the
TT addressees of regulations that are specific to the source culture, i.e. focus on
the 'local' aspect. It is important to ensure terminological consistency whenever
legal aspects are involved, as is the case here (see the repeated reference to 'HM
Railway Inspectorate' in Introduction 5 and Paragraph 11 / 6.3). The repetition of
the English name in addition to the German term is, however, not required in
each case (we have opted for repetition in Introduction 5 because of the reference
to legal aspects in another country). Since 'Government Departments and
Agencies' are not further specified in the ST, the more general 'Ministerien und
Dienststellen' can be considered appropriate for the specified translation
purpose.

Paragraph 7 / 2.1
(c) . . . The requirements of any legislation to which a member may be subject
(eg the Companies Act of 1985 and, if applicable, the Charity Commissioners)
requirements will be observed at all times – . . . Die gesetzlichen Bestimmungen, denen ein Mitgliedsverein gegebenenfalls unterliegt (z.B. das

britische Gesetz über Unternehmen und Gesellschaften von 1985, Company Act, oder die Bestimmungen für gemeinnützige britische Organisationen, Charity Commission) sind stets einzuhalten.

The 'Companies Act' and the 'Charity Commission' denote legal regulations and bodies in the source culture. The Companies Act of 1985, which regulates the manner in which companies are formed, carry out their business, and are wound up, applies exclusively to Britain (and AIRPS is a Limited Company), but may be compared to similar statutory regulations in the target culture. The Charity Commission is the government department, which maintains a database of all registered charities and controls how they are run (see the Internet, also *Longman's Dictionary of English Language and Culture*, 1992). The TT solution is to combine the original proper name with a generalisation, which contains the main information in a condensed form (in conformity with the translation brief). Thus, the readers of the TT will be able to compare the regulations which apply in the UK to their own ones, and the provision of the proper name will also facilitate their search for further information, if necessary.

The translation strategy therefore was to convey the basic information about the nature of this Act and the commission, respectively, supplemented by a reference to the country of origin.

There is also a minor syntactic error in the ST: there is no need to repeat 'requirements' after the information in brackets. Alternatively, the formulation could have been 'The requirements of . . . (e.g. the Companies Act of 1985 and, if applicable, the Charity Commissioners' requirements) will . . . '. Both in Paragraphs 7/2.1 (c) and (d) the ST actually refers to people in their social roles ('Charity Commissioner') instead of the body itself. The 'Registrar of Companies' functions under the Companies Act, and the primary duty is to register companies and ensure that they comply with the statutory requirements under the Act. In the TT, we opted for a focus on the documents containing the referenced requirements. This is in conformity with the conventions of the genre in German where references are usually made to statutory regulations or authoritative bodies, rather than to persons representing them (for example, 'laut Handelsregister', 'laut BGB', see 'Die Mitglieder des Geschäftsführenden Vorstands sind Vorstand im Sinne des §26 BGB' in der Satzung of the Bundesverband Deutscher Eisenbahn-Freunde e.V). See:

Paragraph 7/2.1
(d) That the books of accounts will be examined . . . in accordance with the requirements of the Registrar of Companies or if applicable, the Charity Commissioners. – . . . daß die Geschäftsbücher unter Beachtung der Anforderungen des Registers des Company Act bzw. der Charity Commission . . . geprüft werden.

Paragraph 7/2.2
(a) Any body incorporated as either a Limited Company . . . or as an Industrial & Provident Society. – alle Körperschaften in Form einer Gesellschaft mit beschränkter Haftung nach britischem Recht (Limited Company) . . . oder einer Gegenseitigkeitsgesellschaft (Industrial & Provident Society).

(b) the Inland Revenue. – Finanzbehörde (Inland Revenue)

Various legal forms of societies and companies are referred to in these paragraphs. 'Industrial & Provident Societies' are corporate bodies registered under the Industrial and Provident Societies Acts 1965–78, and dealing with issues of insurance. There are two differing formats available: the IPS cooperative format and the IPS society for the benefit of the community format (see the Internet). Although the company form of a Limited Company also exists under German law, the two are not completely identical in structure and liability. In order to point out the difference to the reader, it is common practice in target culture commercial and/or legal texts to give the corresponding German equivalent, expanded by the hint that the company was incorporated under a different legal system, and to add the English term (sometimes in italics in order to highlight it from the rest of the text). This gives the TT readers the chance of relating the term to their own background knowledge or to recognise it when they come across it in another context. The specification and compression 'alle Körperschaften' for 'any body incorporated' (see also the repetition of 'Körperschaften' in 2.2(b), there for 'any organisation') is motivated by the following enumeration of different forms of enterprises. In the case of the 'Inland Revenue', the standard term for the analogous body in the target culture has been substituted.

(d) Time reference

As is generally the case with legal documents, there is a reference to the date when they were approved and/or from when they will be valid. This is essential information, since such documents may be revised at regular intervals. In the ST, this reference is at the very end of the text (indicated by 'revised AIRPS, 1/96'). In the TT too, this information has been placed at the end of the text, and the actual format ('AIRPS, Stand 1/96') following the conventions of corresponding German documents.

Intercultural translation problems

As stated earlier, pragmatic and intercultural translation problems often overlap. Some of the issues we discuss under this heading could also have been listed in the previous section. We make the distinction mainly for methodological purposes. The points illustrated here are therefore those which primarily relate to lexical and syntactic choices that can be linked to genre conventions.

Parallel texts were extremely useful in solving intercultural translation problems (and also in solving some of the pragmatic translation problems, as previously indicated). The parallel texts we used were exemplars of the genre *Satzung* (see later) and, in particular, of associations active in the field of railways (e.g. Bundesverband Deutscher Eisenbahn-Freunde e.V., Sächsischer Museumseisenbahn Verein Windbergbahn e.V.). Most of these texts are available on the Internet. In addition, we used information on the home pages of the Deutscher Eisenbahn-Verein e.V., Interessengemeinschaft Harzer Schmalspur- und Brockenbahnen e.V., and leaflets of the Traditionsbahn Radebeul e.V.

(i) Name of the genre

Both in the source culture (UK) and in the target culture (Germany), registered companies and associations are required to follow certain legal rules and regulations. In this particular case, the UK association, i.e. AIRPS, is a Limited Company (subject to the Companies Act), and the German client, the

Bundesverband Deutscher Eisenbahn-Freunde e.V., is a 'eingetragener Verein' (that is what 'e.V.' stands for), an association, subject to the German 'Vereinsgesetz' and ultimately to the Civil Code (codified in the *Bürgerliches Gesetzbuch*, BGB). A German 'Verein' would formulate its aims and its operational principles in what is usually called a *Satzung*. Such a *Satzung* is a legal document, to be precise: a document with limited and specified jurisdiction and of a legal norm, which is derived from the German Civil Code. Therefore, a *Satzung* often includes references to the Civil Code (e.g. 'Der Vorstand ist Vereinsvorstand im Sinne des Bürgerlichen Gesetzbuches (BGB)' in the Satzung of the Sächsischer Museumseisenbahn Verein Windbergbahn e.V.).

A Mission Statement and a Code of Practice in the source culture function in an almost identical way as a *Satzung* in the target culture. They are legally binding in the sense that their members must act in conformity with the aims and purposes of the association. Minor differences in their status are due to the differences in English (case) law and German (codified) law. It is interesting to note, that more recently – maybe as a result of globalisation tendencies – a 'Mission Statement' has also been introduced in the target culture, i.e. using the English term to decribe the basic aims and objectives of a business company, an organisation, or an institution (gender: neuter, i.e. 'das Mission Statement'). *Eurodicautom* (the terminology data bank of the European Commission's Translation Service, accessible on the Internet) offers 'Unternehmensleitbild' for 'Mission Statement', and 'Grundregeln für . . . ' or 'Leitsätze für . . . ' for 'Code of Practice', which, however, are descriptive terms rather than labels for a genre.

In conformity with the translation brief, we have therefore taken the following decisions for the production of the TT. Since the client, the Bundesverband Deutscher Eisenbahn-Freunde e.V., has its own *Satzung*, we have decided to use 'Satzung' for the text as a whole in the title, i.e. as a cover term for Mission Statement and Code of Practice combined. For the individual headings we have then opted for a combination of a descriptive label (indicating the content of the respective paragraphs) and the English term (for ease of subsequent communication between the two associations), see the headings:

Mission Statement and Code of Practice – Satzung
Mission Statement – Zweck und Aufgaben (Mission Statement)
Code of Practice – Leitsätze und Richtlinien (Code of Practice)

These decisions have been motivated by reference to titles and section headings in German parallel texts (see also *(ii) Genre conventions*). For the subsequent occurrences of 'Code of Practice' in the ST, we have kept 'Satzung' throughout the TT whenever it refers to the specific one introduced in the text (in Introduction 1, 3, 4), and we have opted for more general expressions whenever additional codes or superordinate acts (e.g. Acts of Parliament) are implied (in Paragraphs 10/5.1, 11/6.2):

Mission Statement 2:
. . . requiring members to conform with the AIRPS Code of Practice. – . . .
Gewährleistung eines satzungsgemäßen Verhaltens aller Mitglieder von AIRPS.

Introduction 1:
. . . the Association has adopted the following Code of Practice . . . – Die Association . . . hat . . . folgende Satzung . . . angenommen.

Introduction 3:
. . . observe the Code of Practice. – . . . Einhaltung der Satzung . . .

Introduction 4:
Items of legislation mentioned in this Code of Practice, . . . – Die gesetzlichen
Bestimmungen, auf die in dieser Satzung Bezug genommen wird, . . .

Paragraph 10/5.1:
All Association members shall comply with all appropriate Statutory
Requirements and Codes of Practice. – Alle Mitgliedsvereine sind zur Einhaltung von Bestimmungen entsprechender Gesetze sowie von Richtlinien
entsprechender Codes of Practice verpflichtet.

Paragraph 11/6.2:
Association members shall observe all Statutory Requirements and Codes of
Practice . . . – Die Mitgliedsvereine haben alle gesetzlichen Bestimmungen
und Richtlinien . . . zu beachten.

Repeated co-references to a code of practice, or to a Satzung, are a characteristic feature of the legal register, both in the source and in the target culture. The
syntactically alternative formulation 'satzungsgemäß' (in Mission Statement 2)
conforms to genre conventions in German (see 'wenn ein Mitglied gegen die
satzungsgemäßen Pflichten verstößt' in the *Satzung* of the Bundesverband
Deutscher Eisenbahn-Freunde e.V.). Another conventional alternative formulation is 'im Sinne der Satzung' (see 'Dem Vorstand obliegt die Führung der
Vereinsgeschäfte im Sinne der Satzung' in the *Satzung* of the Sächsischer
Museumseisenbahn Verein Windbergbahn e.V.).

For 'constitution' in Paragraph 7, we have then opted for 'Statuten' in the TT in
order to have an explicit indication of the difference in application: 'Satzung'
when AIRPS as the umbrella association is concerned, and 'Statuten' for the regulations of it member organisations. (In the context of a country, 'constitution'
corresponds to 'Verfassung').

(ii) Genre conventions
Once the decision had been made to use 'Satzung' for the genre, other translation decisions could be made by reference to the genre conventions of a *Satzung*,
which in the German target culture is a fairly conventionalised genre (more conventionalised than a Mission Statement and a Code of Practice in the source
culture). These conventions concern the information arrangement (i.e. the components of the superstructure, or: the textual building blocks of the schema) and
also syntactic and lexical choices. In other words, we decided to produce a TT,
which largely follows the conventions established for the German genre
Satzung, as far as the labels for the textual building blocks and microstructural
aspects are concerned.

(a) Genre schema
A decision had to be made about the labels for the individual parts of the text.
The headings in the ST cannot be characterised as following any specific conven-

tions for superstructure components. In most cases, they provide more or less explicit information about the content of the following paragraph, for example:

- Introduction: general aims and conditions for membership, to whom it applies
- General: conditions for top functionaries (age, agreement)
- Constitution: conditions for member organisations (fees, book keeping, audit, rights of AIRPS in this respect)
- Financial and Legal: conditions concerning donations, lottery, account keeping
- Insurance requirements: liability
- Statutory requirements: only one general sentence
- Railway operating: detailed points concerning quality, safety, operating rules, training, passes

A systematic analysis of exemplars of the German *Satzung* reveals a highly conventional superstructure, i.e. the information arrangement and the labels used for the individual components are fairly consistent. A prototypical German *Satzung* is structured as follows (the components in brackets are optional):

- Name, Rechtsform und Sitz (sometimes with the addition of Geschäftsjahr)
- Zweck und Aufgaben
- (Gemeinnützigkeit – as a separate component)
- Erwerb der Mitgliedschaft
- Beendigung der Mitgliedschaft (alternatively Beginn und Ende der Mitgliedschaft)
- (Arten der Mitgliedschaft)
- Rechte der Mitglieder
- Pflichten der Mitglieder (alternatively Rechte und Pflichten der Mitglieder)
- Organe des Verbandes
- Die Delegiertenversammlung (alternatively Hauptversammlung, Jahreshauptversammlung, Mitgliederversammlung)
- Vorstand
- Rechnungsprüfer (alternatively Rechnungsprüfung)
- Auflösung des Verbandes

Usually, there is a reference to a 'Wahlordnung' (rules for election of board members) and/or a 'Beitragsordung' (rules for membership fees) which exist as separate documents.

In conformity with the translation brief (which asks for a documentary translation) we have not made any changes to the sequential arrangement of the information (the textual building blocks). In making decisions for the section headings, we cannot simply take those, which are conventionally used in the German genre either, since partial identical issues are not necessarily dealt with under different headings (there are only overlaps, e.g. with respect to membership and to financial arrangements). We have already discussed our motivation for the title and the main headings of the TT. We can add here that the information found in the Mission Statement corresponds to what would be listed in the genre component 'Zweck und Aufgaben' in a German *Satzung* (this is reflected in the headings we chose, and here are deliberately based on genre conventions). For the other headings, however, we opted for general descriptive terms, in order not to raise expectations on the part of the TT readers which will not be confirmed (e.g. choosing 'Rechnungsprüfung' instead of 'Finanzrichtlinien' might mean that the reader expects information about auditing accounts, which, however, does not show up here):

> Introduction – Einleitung
> General – Regelungen zur Mitgliedschaft
> Constitution – Statuten
> Financial and Legal – Finanzrichtlinien
> Insurance requirements – Versicherungsrechtliche Bestimmungen
> Statutory requirements – Einhaltung der Gesetze
> Railway operating – Eisenbahnbetrieb

The paragraphs about insurance requirements and railway operation are highy specific to this individual text. The German exemplars analysed did not have any reference to insurance requirements (so that we might conclude that such information is not part of the prototypical genre superstructure).

(b) Lexical choices

Some of the lexical choices concern rules for membership of the association. In the ST, there are repeated references to 'members' and to 'membership'. In most cases, 'members' (sometimes specified as 'Association members') denotes associations or organisations (i.e. legal entities) which are or want to become part of AIRPS, the umbrella organisation. For 'member' in this sense we have consistently used 'Mitgliedsverein' in the TT (translation strategy: modulation/specification; note that 'Vereinsmitglied' denotes the individual person). See also Introduction 2:

> Introduction 2:
> Applicants for membership of the Association of Independent Railways and Preservation Societies Ltd. . . . – Jeder Verein, der einen Antrag auf Mitgliedschaft in der Association of Independent Railways and Preservation Societies Ltd. stellt, . . .

In addition, the transposition (plural in ST – singular in TT, see the syntactic translation strategy of *phrase structure change* in Chesterman (1997a) classification) is also in conformity with German genre conventions, i.e. in German legal texts, the general viability of any condition is often expressed by the use of the indefinite pronouns 'alle' or 'jeder'.

In several other cases in the ST, reference is made to individual people as individual members of a member organisation (often both aspects combined in a single section). In the TT, we have used 'Mitglieder' in those cases or the more specific 'Einzelmitglieder', e.g.

> Paragraph 7/2.1:
> (c) . . . there will be laid before members, . . . The requirements of any legislation to which a member may be subject . . . – . . . daß den Mitgliedern . . . vorgelegt wird. . . . Die gesetzlichen Bestimmungen, denen ein Mitglieds-

verein gegebenenfalls unterliegt . . .

Paragraph 8/ 3.2:
In the case of an Association member operating a line or depot, that member will legally limit the financial liability of its members. – Betreibt ein Mitgliedsverein eine Bahnstrecke oder ein Eisenbahndepot, hat es im Rahmen der gesetzlichen Bestimmungen dafür Sorge zu tragen, daß seine Einzelmitglieder finanziell nur beschränkt haftbar sind.

In the Mission Statement, we have opted for 'Mitglied' to allow for the interpretation of both member organisations and individual members:

2. To maintain high standards by requiring members to conform with the AIRPS Code of Practice. – Einhaltung hoher Standards durch Gewährleistung eines satzungsgemäßen Verhaltens aller Mitglieder von AIRPS.

For denoting elected and / or appointed officers, etc. of the association, we used the terms that are typically found in the exemplars of the German *Satzung*, in particular:

Paragraph 6/1.1:
The Chairman, Secretary and Treasurer / Accountant and all Directors / Council / Management Committee . . . – Der Vorsitzende, der Geschäftsführer und der Schatzmeister sowie alle Mitglieder des Verwaltungsrates / des Vorstands / der Geschäftsführung . . .

'Schatzmeister' alone is sufficient here. Alternatively one could have used 'Schatzmeister / Kassierer', but normally these two functions are fulfilled by one and the same person (with 'Schatzmeister' being a more prestigious title as well). The elected officers ('Vorsitzender, Geschäftsführer, Schatzmeister') together are in the German texts typically referred to as 'Geschäftsführender Vorstand'. However, depending on the specific nature of the member organisation (i.e. whether a charity, a company, a professional body) there may be variation, indicated by the combination of 'Directors / Council / Management Committee'. For the TT, we have opted for a list of similarly possible arrangements ('des Verwaltungsrates / des Vorstands / der Geschäftsführung'). We have then opted for lexical consistency for the re-occurrence in Paragraph 7 / 2.1:

Paragraph 7/2.1:
(b) . . . election of members to the Board / Council / Committee of Management . . . – . . . Wahl von Mitgliedern des Verwaltungsrates / des Vorstands / der Geschäftsführung . . .

For the required meetings of associations, we found 'Delegiertenversammlung, Mitgliederversammlung, Hauptversammlung, Jahreshauptversammlung' in the German parallel texts. The variation is due to the size of the respective organisation. For the TT, we have therefore opted for the more general 'Hauptversammlung' which leaves implicit whether it is a meeting for all members or only for a certain number of delegated members:

Paragraph 7/2.1:
(e) That a General Meeting of members will be held at least once every calendar year . . . – Durchführung einer Hauptversammlung mindestens einmal pro Kalenderjahr, . . .

There are a number of terms in the ST that relate to the statutory requirements, to legal requirements and other aspects which are relevant for the operation of the association. For deciding on the most appropriate German expressions, we have again used parallel texts, i.e. exemplars of the German *Satzung*. The following lexical choices were subsequently made:

Paragraphs 4 and 5:
Items of legislation . . . legislation . . . the equivalent Irish legislation . . . – Die gesetzlichen Bestimmungen, . . . Gesetze. . . . die entsprechenden irischen Gesetze . . .

Paragraph 6 / 1.1:
. . . must be over eighteen years of age in order to accept legal responsibilities of office. – . . . müssen das 18. Lebensjahr vollendet haben, um die mit einer offiziellen Funktion verbundenen rechtlichen Verpflichtungen übernehmen zu können.

In addition, writing eighteen as a figure (das 18. Lebensjahr) in the TT is also in conformity with genre conventions. As a rule of thumb, in German texts, the figures from one to twelve are spelt out in full words; from thirteen onwards, only the figure itself is used. In certain genres (e.g. contracts), both forms are usually given (e.g. 'eighteen (18) days'). In those cases, the figure is put first in the German text, followed by the full word in brackets (e.g. '18 (achtzehn) Tage').

Paragraph 6 / 1.2:
. . . abide by the decision of three arbitrators . . . – Anerkennung der Entscheidung von drei Schlichtern . . .

Paragraph 7 / 2.1:
. . . make an annual subscription, . . . - . . . Zahlung eines Jahresbeitrages . . .

Paragraph 7 / 2.1:
(b) . . . terms of service – Amtszeit

Paragraph 7 / 2.1:
(c) . . . that proper books of accounts shall be kept . . . a Statement of Income and Expenditure and a current Balance Sheet. – daß die Geschäftsbücher ordnungsgemäß geführt werden . . . Aufstellung über Einnahmen und Ausgaben sowie eine aktuelle Bilanz . . .

Paragraph 7 / 2.1:
(d) That the books of accounts will be examined by a suitably qualified and properly appointed person – . . . daß die Geschäftsbücher . . . von einer entsprechend qualifizierten und ordnungsgemäß ernannten Person . . . geprüft werden.

Paragraph 7 / 2.1:
(f) . . . a dissolution or winding up of a body, . . . disposal of the assets of the body. – Vorkehrungen zur Veräußerung der Vermögenswerte des Vereins

im Falle seiner Auflösung oder Abwicklung

Paragraph 8/3.1:
... seeking donations ... Statement of Account ... a reasonable charge. – ...
Spendenaufruf ... Kopie des Kontoauszugs ... angemessene Gebühr

Paragraph 8/3.2:
... legally limit the financial liability ... – ... im Rahmen der gesetzlichen
Bestimmungen ... finanziell nur beschränkt haftbar sind.
We opted for a modulation/explicitation here ('im Rahmen der gesetzlichen
Bestimmungen'), i.e. explicitly mentioning the means which serve as a basis to
limit the liability in conformity with German genre conventions.

Paragraph 8/3.3:
... preparation and presentation of properly audited accounts. – ... Erstellung und Vorlage ordnungsgemäß geprüfter Jahresabschlüsse ...

Paragraph 9/4.1:
... any claim for any loss, damage, injury or death whether caused by accident
or negligence or otherwise ... – ... Forderungen im Zusammenhang mit
Verlust, Schaden, Verletzung oder Todesfall ... die auf Unfälle, Fahrlässigkeit oder anderweitiges Verschulden ... zurückzuführen sind.

We opted for the specification 'anderweitiges Verschulden' for 'otherwise' for
stylistic reasons, i.e. in order to keep the same word class (nouns) in the enumeration. Since 'negligence' carries the connotation of carelessness or even wilful
acts, we have decided to introduce the general notion of 'Verschulden' in the TT.

Paragraph 9/4.2:
... be covered by an Insurance Policy ... against loss, damage, injury or
death ... may be legally liable. – ... Versicherung abzuschließen, die Schutz
bietet bei Verlust, Schaden, Verletzung oder Todesfall ...... laut Gesetz
gegebenenfalls haftbar sind.

Paragraph 9/4.3:
... take out ... adequate insurance against the risk of explosions. – ... einen
angemessenen Versicherungsschutz gegen Explosionsgefahr abzuschließen.

(c) Syntactic structures
In this section we will only discuss those syntactic structures that are characteristic of legal texts and the subsequent decisions for producing the TT.

(c1) Verbal structures versus nominal structures
The aims and objectives of an association are usually listed at the beginning of
the text. In the ST (in the Mission Statement) infinitive structures are used ('to
help and encourage, to promote, to maintain, ...'). The German parallel texts we
analysed also typically formulate their aims (in the schema component 'Zweck
und Aufgaben') in the form of lists, however, usually in a nominal style, that is,
characteristic formulations in a German *Satzung* would be: 'Der Verein bezweckt

die Förderung . . . , Stärkung . . . , Erweiterung . . . , Anregung . . . ', or : 'Der Zweck des Vereins ist die Förderung . . . '. Verbal structures are also used, but less frequently (e.g. 'Der Verein sieht seine Aufgaben darin, . . . zu unterstützen, . . . zu fördern, . . . zu pflegen'). The most frequent verbs and / or nouns used to express aims and objectives are 'encourage, promote' in English texts, and 'Förderung, Stärkung, Unterstützung, fördern, unterstützen' in German texts.

Based on the fact that nominal structures are characteristic of the target culture genre, we have consistently used nouns in the Mission Statement (translation strategy: transposition), see, for example,

To help and encourage – Gewährleistung
To promote – Förderung
To maintain – Einhaltung
To encourage – Qualitätserhöhung
To keep members advised and informed . . . and to provide – Information und Beratung . . . Gewährleistung

We have applied the same strategy for the Introduction, see:

Introduction 1:
In order to ensure . . . and to enhance the reputation . . . and to strengthen . . . – . . . Gewährleistung . . . , der Festigung des Rufes . . . der Unterstützung . . .

(c2) Obligations

As stated earlier, both a Code of Practice and a *Satzung* of an association are (legally) binding for its members. A characteristic feature of legal documents and similar documents of a comparable function (see the reference to the requirements of legislation and to statutory requirements in the ST) is the expression of obligations (commissive speech acts, see Trosborg (1994) and introductory comments), both of the association as a whole and of the individual members (i.e. evidence of the nature of legal documents as being both descriptive and prescriptive). For English texts, modal verbs are characteristic to express obligations (typically 'shall, will, must' for strong obligations, 'should' for recommendations), whereas in German texts infinitive structures in the passive are the most frequently used structures to express obligations (see the examples from parallel texts: 'Eine Delegiertenversammlung ist einzuberufen.', 'Interessenten an einer Mitgliedschaft im Verein haben dies dem Vorstand schriftlich bekanntzugeben.'). In some cases, there is an explicit reference to the (legal) obligation, i.e. the use of the verb 'verpflichten' or the nouns 'Pflicht' or 'Verpflichtung', with present tense and indicative verb form (as in 'Die Mitglieder verpflichten sich, den Verband in der Verfolgung seiner Ziele zu unterstützen.'). These indicative verb forms stress the binding character and the general viability of a statement.

Based on these genre conventions, we have mostly opted for passive structures (frequently passive infinitives) in the TT in the cases of 'must, shall, will', see:
Must

Introduction 2:
Applicants for membership . . . must satisfy the Association that . . . – Jeder

Verein, der einen Antrag auf Mitgliedschaft . . . stellt, hat gegenüber dem
Verband zu gewährleisten, daß . . .

Introduction 3:
Applicants must also give an assurance that they conform to and will observe
the Code of Practice. – Jeder Verein, der einen Antrag auf Mitgliedschaft
stellt, hat sich zur Anerkennung und Einhaltung der Satzung zu verpflichten.

The combination of two propositions ('conform to and will observe') is also
common of legal documents. We have opted for a nominal structure in the TT.

Paragraph 6/1.1.
. . . must be over eighteen years of age in order to accept legal responsibilities
of office. – müssen das 18. Lebensjahr vollendet haben, um die mit einer
offiziellen Funktion verbundenen rechtlichen Verpflichtungen übernehmen
zu können.

Paragraph 7/2.1:
. . . there must be a written constitution, – . . . muß über schriftliche Statuten
verfügen.

Paragraph 11/6.1:
Association members must maintain the highest standards of operation and
must take adequate steps . . . – Die Mitgliedsvereine haben stets für höchste
Betriebsstandards zu sorgen und angemessene Sicherheitsmaßnahmen . . . zu
ergreifen.

Paragraph 11/6.3:
Operating Rules must be prepared . . . and must be adhered to . . . A copy . . .
must be deposited . . . – Betriebsvorschriften sind . . . zu formulieren und . . . zu
befolgen. Eine Ausfertigung . . . ist . . . zu hinterlegen.

Paragraph 11/6.4:
All staff . . . must be examined . . . Safety Critical Work Regulations must be
observed where necessary, . . . – Alle Angestellten sind . . . zu prüfen. . . . Die
Arbeitsschutzbestimmungen, . . . sind im erforderlichen Umfang zu
beachten.

Will and shall

Paragraph 6/1.2:
. . . they will agree to abide by the decision of three arbitrators . . . – . . .
verpflichten sie sich zur Anerkennung der Entscheidung von drei
Schlichtern, . . .

The obligation is part of the meaning of the verb 'verpflichten' (see previous
comments). In Paragraph 7, the obligation is the function of the paragraph as a
whole (i.e. as a macro-function). Therefore, the indicative verb forms and the
nominal structure we have opted for at the micro-level will be interpreted as
expressing obligations (supported by the reference to 'der Grundsatz' which we
have added in points (c) and (d)):

Paragraph 7/2.1:
(c) That all monies received shall be expended . . . , that proper books of accounts shall be kept and . . . there will be laid before members, . . . The requirements . . . will be observed at all times – . . . daß alle eingegangenen Gelder . . . verwendet werden, daß die Geschäftsbücher ordnungsgemäß geführt werden, und daß den Mitgliedern . . . vorgelegt wird. Die gesetzlichen Bestimmungen, . . . sind stets einzuhalten.

Paragraph 7/2.1:
(d) That the books of accounts will be examined by a . . . person (who will be independent of its members) . . . – . . . daß die Geschäftsbücher . . . von einer . . . Person (die nicht Mitglied des Vereins ist) geprüft werden.

Paragraph 7/2.1:
(e) That a General Meeting of members will be held . . . – Durchführung einer Hauptversammlung . . .

Paragraph 8/3.1:
. . . it shall: state . . . – . . . hat er: . . . anzugeben . . .

Paragraph 8/3.2:
. . . that member will legally limit the financial liability . . . – . . . hat es . . . dafür Sorge zu tragen, daß . . . finanziell nur beschränkt haftbar sind.

Paragraph 8/3.3:
All Association members shall comply with all Statutory Requirements . . . – Alle Mitgliedsvereine haben die gesetzlichen Vorschriften . . . einzuhalten.

Paragraph 9/4.1:
. . . any Insurance Policy will be taken out . . . – . . . hat . . . eine Versicherung abzuschließen, . . .

Paragraph 9/4.3:
. . . the body will take out . . . adequate insurance . . . – hat er . . . abzuschließen.

Paragraph 10/5.1:
All Association members shall comply with all appropriate Statutory Requirements and Codes of Practice. – Alle Mitgliedsvereine sind zur Einhaltung von Bestimmungen entsprechender Gesetze sowie von Richtlinien entsprechender Codes of Practice verpflichtet.

Paragraph 11/6.2:
Association members shall observe . . . – Die Mitgliedsvereine haben . . . zu beachten.

Paragraph 11 / 6.5:
The issuing . . . shall be carefully controlled. . . . They shall be given clear instructions . . . – Die Ausgabe . . . ist sorgfältig zu kontrollieren. . . . Ihnen sind . . . eindeutige Instruktionen zu erteilen.

Should
Paragraphs 4 and 5 provide information about the respective application of legislation, i.e. 'should', here, is part of this informative function (informing in a polite way). We have opted for a lexical specification (i.e. 'gelten' as belonging to a legislation frame) in the indicative form to convey this function:

Paragraph 4:
Organisations . . . should relate this legislation . . . – Für Vereine . . . gelten die . . . Gesetze.

Paragraph 5:
Organisations . . . should relate . . . References . . . should be related . . . – Für Vereine . . . gelten . . . Bei Bezugnahme . . . gilt . . .

Paragraph 11 refers to requirements and recommendations about a specific activity of the member associations, in other words, the propositions in this paragraph are not immediately related to the legal obligations of the functioning of the association as an association. The conditions for operating the railways specified in Paragraph 11, however, are nevertheless often of a legal nature. In other words, most of the requirements are also formulated in binding documents (see the references to Statutory Requirements, Codes of Practice, Work Regulations), whereas others are recommendation (see also the combination of 'must', 'shall' and 'should' throughout Paragraph 11). For the TT, we have decided to use a passive infinite again:

Paragraph 11 / 6.4:
All staff should have adequate training . . . – Alle Angestellten sind . . . einzuweisen . . . zu prüfen.

Paragraph 11 / 6.5:
All pass holders should be required to wear . . . – Alle Inhaber solcher Pässe haben . . . zu tragen, . . .

In Paragraph 7, we have introduced a passive infinitive structure as characteristic of the genre in German (translation strategy: transposition), see:

Paragraph 7 / 2.1:
. . . a written constitution, an up to date copy of which is lodged with the Association . . . – Die aktuelle Fassung dieses Dokuments ist dem Verband zu übergeben . . .

(c3) Conditions of application and/or validity

Another characteristic feature of (legally) binding documents is the specification of the conditions of application. Whenever there are exceptions or limited applicability, this needs to be explicitly stated; in other words; legal texts need to provide for any possible exceptions. Linguistic indicators of this are modal verbs, conditional sentences, and lexical expressions (such as 'if applicable, when necessary, where required, in the case of, in the event of'). In the German *Satzung*, there are also lexical and grammatical indicators to reflect a condition or limited applicability. In the parallel texts, we found mainly the following lexical indicators: 'entsprechend, gegebenenfalls, sofern, im Falle, ausgenommen, in der Regel, bei Bedarf' (see: ' . . . , sofern sie dem Vorstand bekannt sind', 'Die Delegiertenversammlung wird vom Vorsitzenden geleitet, im Falle seiner Verhinderung von einem Stellvertreter', 'zur Wahrnehmung bestimmter Aufgabenbereiche', ' . . . gilt Ziffer X entsprechend', 'gültige Beschlüsse, ausgenommen solche über . . . ', 'jedes Mitglied hat das Recht, auf einen entsprechenden Antrag hin . . . ', 'entsprechend der Satzung', 'in Ausnahme-fällen'). Characteristic syntactic indicators which we found in the German parallel texts are the initial sentence position of the verb, sometimes a modal verb (see: 'Sind die Mitgliedsbeiträge nicht gezahlt, ruhen die Rechte der Mitgliedschaft.', 'Sollten in diesem Falle noch Verpflichtungen gegenüber dem Verein bestehen, so entscheidet die Jahreshauptversammlung.') or conditional sentences (see: 'Falls die Mitgliedschaft im Laufe des Geschäftsjahres beginnt, ist die im Aufnahmeantrag angegebene Zahl der Vereinsmitglieder maßgebend.', 'Der Ausschluß kann erfolgen, wenn ein Mitglied den Interessen und dem Ansehen des BDEF in grober Weise zuwiderhandelt').

We have made use of these characteristic structures of the genre *Satzung* whenever possible in the TT. In the following examples, we have used a lexical indicator in the TT ('gegebenenfalls') for a grammatical indicator in the ST ('may') (translation strategy: transposition), see:

May

Paragraph 7/2.1:
(c) The requirements of any legislation to which a member may be subject . . . – Die gesetzlichen Bestimmungen, denen ein Mitgliedsverein gegebenenfalls unterliegt . . .

Paragraph 9/4.2:
. . . work for which . . . may be legally liable. – Tätigkeit, für welche . . . gegebenenfalls haftbar sind.

In the next example, we have opted for a specification, in conformity with conventions of the German genre:

Where necessary

Paragraph 11/6.4:
Safety Critical Work Regulations must be observed where necessary, . . . – Die Arbeitsschutzbestimmungen, . . . sind im erforderlichen Umfang zu beachten.

In the next examples, two options are presented, which are covered by 'oder' and 'bzw.', respectively, in the TT:

If applicable

Paragraph 7/2.1:
(c) . . . (. . . and, if applicable, the Charity Commissioners) . . . – (. . . oder die Bestimmungen für gemeinnützige britische Organisationen, Charity Commission)

Paragraph 7/2.1:
(d) . . . the Registrar of Companies or if applicable, the Charity Commissioners. – . . . des Registers des Company Act bzw. der Charity Commission . . .

In the following example we have followed the German conventions of using a conditional clause or a subordinate clause with front position of the verb:

In the case of

Paragraph 7/2.1:
In the case of . . . there must be . . . – Wenn . . . muß . . .

Paragraph 8/3.1:
In the case of . . . it shall: – Wenn sich ein Mitgliedsverein . . . hat er:

Paragraph 8/3.2:
In the case of . . . that member will . . . – Betreibt ein Mitgliedsverein . . . hat er . . .

Paragraph 9/4.3:
In the case of . . . the body will . . . – Wenn ein Mitgliedsverein . . . hat er . . .
'Ausgenommen' alone is sufficient in the following example:

Paragraph 7/2.2:
. . . right to suggest amendments . . . except in the case of: – . . . das Recht vor, . . . Änderungen vorzuschlagen. Ausgenommen davon sind: . . .

In the event of
Here we have opted for a conditional clause for the verbal structure (in 6/2.1) and for a nominal structure (in 7/2.1):

Paragraph 6/1.2:
In the event of two or more Association Members seeking . . . they will agree . . . – Wenn sich zwei oder mehr Mitgliedsvereine . . . verpflichten sie sich . . .

Paragraph 7/2.1:
(f) That in the event of a dissolution . . . provision has been made for . . . – Vorkehrungen . . . im Falle seiner Auflösung . . .

Appropriate
'Appropriate' denotes the suitability or the applicability of some activity, state of affairs, or legislation. In the TT, we have indicated this by lexical means (mostly by 'entsprechend'), see:

Mission Statement:
4. . . . such other help and assistance as may be appropriate. – gegebenenfalls Hilfe und Unterstützung in speziellen Angelegenheiten.

7. . . . advice and assistance in the obtaining of professional qualifications where appropriate. – . . . gegebenenfalls Beratung und Unterstützung beim Erwerb von beruflichen Qualifikationen . . .

8.... in all activities whenever it is appropriate to their organisation and operation. – ... Aktivitäten, wenn das mit der Organisation und der Arbeitsweise
der Mitgliedsvereine in Einklang steht.

Paragraph 4:
Organisations in Northern Ireland, Isle of Man and where appropriate, Scotland should relate this legislation to the appropriate regional equivalent. –
Für Vereine in Nordirland, auf der Isle of Man und gegebenenfalls in Schottland gelten die entsprechenden regionalen Gesetze.

Paragraph 5:
. . . the equivalent Irish legislation as appropriate. . . . the equivalent
Government Department as appropriate. – die entsprechenden irischen
Gesetze. . . . gilt dementsprechend die zuständige irische Regierungsbehörde.

Paragraph 11 / 6.4:
. . . including appropriate medical standards. – . . . einschließlich der entsprechenden Gesundheitsnormen, . . .

In the following two examples, 'appropriate' refers to certain aspects of the
text itself (as a text-internal cross-reference, so to speak). This is a characteristic
feature of (legally) binding documents, both in the source culture and in the
target culture (see, for example, from a German *Satzung*: 'Dem Vorstand obliegt
die Führung der Verbandsgeschäfte im Sinne dieser Satzung', 'Die Mittel des
Vereins dürfen nur für satzungsgemäße Zwecke verwendet werden.'). Our decision to use 'satzungsgemäß' in the TT has been motivated by these
considerations:

Paragraph 7 / 2.1:
(e) . . . which have been audited in accordance with the appropriate statutory
requirements. – . . . satzungsgemäß geprüfte . . .

Paragraph 10 / 5.1:
. . . comply with all appropriate Statutory Requirements . . . – zur Einhaltung
von Bestimmungen entsprechender Gesetze . . . verpflichtet.

(c4) *Extended verb phrases*

Another characteristic feature of legal documents is a rather complex syntactic structure (this is related to the requirement for precision and for specifying
any exception, as mentioned earlier). For example, an adverbial or a propositional phrase is placed between the verb and the accusative object:

Paragraph 7 / 2.1:
In the case of a member organisation whose own constituents are required as
a condition of membership to make an annual subscription, . . . – Wenn die
Angehörigen eines Mitgliedsvereins zur Zahlung eines Jahresbeitrages
verpflichtet sind, . . .

In the TT, 'as a condition of membership' is implied by 'zur Zahlung
verpflichtet'; in other words, specifically accounting for it would be redundant.

In the following case, the passive structure in the ST can be characterised as a typical example of 'legalese':

Paragraph 7/2.1:
(c)... that at regular intervals there will be laid before members, a Statement of Income and Expenditure and a current Balance Sheet. – daß den Mitgliedern in regelmäßigen Abständen eine Aufstellung über Einnahmen und Ausgaben sowie eine aktuelle Bilanz vorgelegt wird.

In German legal texts, syntactic structures in which the verb phrase is split are also common (as in the following example from parallel texts: 'Anträge von Mitgliedern zur ordentlichen Delegiertenversammlung müssen mit schriftlicher Begründung mindestens acht Wochen vor deren Zusammentritt beim Vorstand über die Geschäftsstelle eingegangen sein.').

Another characteristic feature are pre-modifications, i.e. extended attributes before the noun:

Paragraph 7/2.1:
(d) That the books of accounts will be examined by a suitably qualified and properly appointed person . . . – daß die Geschäftsbücher . . . von einer entsprechend qualifizierten und ordnungsgemäß ernannten Person . . . geprüft werden.

Such pre-modification structures are even more frequent in German legal documents (see the following examples of the genre *Satzung*: 'Die Hauptversammlung . . . hat einen Liquidator zu berufen und Beschluß darüber zu fassen, wem dieser das nach Abdeckung der Passiven verbleibende Vereinsvermögen zu übertragen hat.', 'jedes Mitglied ist verpflichtet, den Mitgliedsbeitrag gemäß den in der Beitragsordnung festgelegten Modalitäten pünktlich zu entrichten.', 'Beratung über sonstige auf der Tagesordnung stehende Fragen').

(d) Reference to the legal act

For legal documents it is a requirement to have an explicit reference to the act of adopting the text, as an act of legitimising the action (see Schäffner *et al.*, 1987). This is reflected in the first paragraph of the Introduction:

In order to ensure . . . and to enhance . . . and to strengthen . . . the Association has adopted the following Code of Practice as a condition of membership. – Die Association . . . hat zum Zwecke der Gewährleistung . . . , der Festigung . . . der Unterstützung . . . folgende Satzung als Voraussetzung für die Mitgliedschaft angenommen.

There is a conventional format for this act, which is especially found in contracts and treaties. In the English texts, a number of aims are listed first (usually verbal structures, infinitives), followed by naming the agent(s), and then the expression 'has/have adopted' (or similar), followed by the reference to the text itself (often using the label for the genre). Alternatively, the agent is mentioned first, then a list of aims and/or conditions, then 'has/have adopted' and the reference to the genre. This second structure is common in the case of international treaties, cf. the 1992 Maastricht Treaty:

- A, B, C … (i.e. references to heads of state)
- Resolved to …
- Recalling …
- Confirming … (and some more legitimating text actions)
- … have agreed as follows:

We have referred to this conventional structure for the production of the TT.

(e) Gender

The gender issue is explicit in one paragraph in the ST:

Paragraph 9/4.2:
When any person (paid or unpaid) is working on behalf of the Association member, he/she will be covered by an Insurance Policy . . . – Wenn ein Mitgliedsverein (angestellte oder freiwillige) Mitarbeiter beschäftigt, ist für diese Personen . . . eine Versicherung abzuschließen, . . .

We have opted for a plural form 'Personen', which covers both female and male employees. However, it is becoming more and more common in German legal and commercial texts to explicitly distinguish male and female genders, and/or to give both forms in the text (in order to ensure political correctness, see Hellinger, 1990). The parallel texts we analysed used mainly plural forms (but note the grammatical gender for specific functions, e.g. 'der Schatzmeister'). Uses of both male and female forms consistently next to each other could also be found (cf. the *Statuten* of the Verein Forum für Jugend und Kultur Spielboden: 'Den Vorsitz in der Hauptversammlung führt der Obmann bzw. die Obfrau, im Verhinderungsfalle der Stellvertreter bzw. die Stellvertreterin. Ist auch die Stellvertretung verhindert, . . . Bei Gefahr im Verzug ist er bzw. sie berechtigt, . . .').

In addition, we have opted for '(angestellte oder freiwillige) Mitarbeiter', i.e. focusing on the employment status, and not on the form of payment. Speaking of 'bezahlt oder unbezahlt' in the TT would cause confusion because it might presuppose that some of the employees get paid whereas others do not, for some reason or other. The TT, thus, makes a distinction between people having a regular work contract with the member (and who are paid for their work) and others who perform their duties on a voluntary basis (translation strategy: modulation). We have applied this phrase consistently (see 4.1, 4.2, see also the choice of 'Angestellte' and 'freiwillige Helfer' in 6.3 and 6.4. for 'staff and volunteers').

Text-specific translation problems

In conclusion, we only want to comment on terminological aspects as an example of text-specific translation problems.

(i) Terminology for railways

The ST is embedded in the context of railways and, therefore, also contains a number of terms from this field. We have already discussed some of the concepts that are related to the operational principles of the railways associations (e.g. independent and heritage railways, HM Railway Inspectorate). There are only a few technical terms that relate to the operation of railways (most of them occur in

Paragraph 11, e.g. 'operate a line or depot, steam locomotive, air receiver, lineside passes, high visibility vest'). For finding the German technical terms (e.g. 'Bahnstrecke, Eisenbahndepot, Dampflokomotive, Dampfsammler'), checking German texts about railways (again, for example, on the Internet) is usually more helpful than using bilingual dictionaries.

In the following paragraph we have opted for specifications in the TT:

Paragraph 11/6.5:
The issuing of lineside photographic passes . . . wear suitably identified high visibility vests when or near the operational railway. . . . importance of avoiding trespass. – Die Ausgabe von Streckenausweisen mit Paßfoto . . . deutlich gekennzeichnete Sicherheitswesten zu tragen, wenn sie sich an oder in der Nähe einer in Betrieb befindlichen Eisenbahnstrecke aufhalten. . . . Einhaltung der Zutrittsverbote . . .

The more specific 'Sicherheitswesten' (instead of 'Westen') was chosen because of the context of safety instructions which dominates the entire paragraph and because those vests belong to standard work clothes. 'In Betrieb befindliche Eisenbahnstrecke' reflects a lexical expansion, which is required because there is no commonly used compound noun or collocation in German (see 'einsatzfähig' oder 'betriebsbereit' which are used for machines). In the case of 'avoiding trespass' and 'Einhaltung der Zutrittsverbote' we have an example of antonymic translation (or of the semantic translation strategy of *converses* in Chesterman's (1997a) classification). It is also an example of German conventions to explicitly refer to the 'don'ts' (cf. the frequent use of 'Verbot' and/or 'verboten' in regulations and similar genres).

In section 6.5, there is also an error in the ST, i.e. a word is missing. It should say ' . . . when on or near the operational railway'. Since this is a minor error which can easily be spotted by the translator (it will probably not even be spotted by the average reader of the ST) it goes without saying that in conformity with the translation brief a grammatically correct TT version will be produced ('wenn sie sich an oder in der Nähe . . . aufhalten').

References

Álvarez, Román and Vidal, M. Carmen-África (eds) (1996) *Translation, Power, Subversion*. Clevedon: Multilingual Matters.

Arntz, Rainer (1992) Interlinguale Vergleiche von Terminologien und Fachtexten. In K.-D. Baumann and H. Kalverkämper (eds) *Kontrastive Fachsprachenforschung* (pp. 108–22). Tübingen: Narr.

Arrojo, Rosemary (1998) The revision of the traditional gap between theory and practice and the empowerment of translation in postmodern times. *The Translator* 4, 25–48.

Austin, John L. (1962) *How to Do Things with Words*. Oxford: Clarendon.

Baker, Mona (1995) Corpora in translation studies: An overview and suggestions for future research. *Target* 7, 223–43.

Baker, Mona (1996) Linguistics and cultural studies. In A. Lauer, H. Gerzymisch-Arbogast, J. Haller and E. Steiner (eds) *Übersetzungswissenschaft in Umbruch: Festschrift für Wolfram Wilss* (pp. 9–19). Tübingen: Narr.

Baker, Mona (ed.) (1998) *Routledge Encyclopedia of Translation Studies*. London and New York: Routledge.

Beard, Adrian (2000) *The Language of Politics*. London: Routledge.

Brinker, Klaus (1985) *Linguistische Textanalyse*. Berlin: Erich Schmidt.

Büchmann, Georg (1977) *Geflügelte Worte*. München: Knaur.

Catford, J.C. (1965) *A Linguistic Theory of Translation*. London: Oxford University Press.

Chesterman, Andrew (ed.) (1989) *Readings in Translation Theory*. Helsinki: Oy Finn Lectura Ab.

Chesterman, Andrew (1993) From 'Is' to 'Ought': Laws, norms and strategies in translation studies. *Target* 5, 1–20.

Chesterman, Andrew (1997a) *Memes of Translation*. Amsterdam and Philadelphia: Benjamins.

Chesterman, Andrew (1997b) Ethics of translation. In M. Snell-Hornby, Z. Jettmarova and K. Kaindl (eds) *Translation as Intercultural Communication. Selected Papers from the EST Congress, Prague 1995* (pp. 147–57). Amsterdam and Philadelphia: Benjamins.

Chesterman, Andrew (1998a) *Contrastive Functional Analysis*. Amsterdam and Philadelphia: Benjamins.

Chesterman, Andrew (1998b) Causes, translations, effects. *Target* 10, 201–30.

Chesterman, Andrew (2000) Teaching strategies for emancipatory translation. In C. Schäffner and B. Adab (eds) *Developing Translation Competence* (pp. 77–89). Amsterdam and Philadelphia: Benjamins.

Chesterman, Andrew and Arrojo, Rosemary (2000) Shared ground in translation studies. *Target* 12, 151–60.

Chilton, Paul and Lakoff, George (1995) Foreign policy by metaphor. In C.

Schäffner and A. Wenden (eds) *Language and Peace* (pp. 37–59). Aldershot: Dartmouth.

Chilton, Paul and Schäffner, Christina (1997) Discourse and politics. In T. van Dijk (ed.) *Discourse Studies: A Multidisciplinary Introduction, Vol. 2: Discourse as Social Interaction* (pp. 206–30). London: Sage.

Clark, Herbert H. and Marshall, Catherine R. (1981) Definite reference and mutual knowledge. In A. Joshi, B. Webber and I. Sag (eds) *Elements of Discourse Understanding* (pp. 10–63). Cambridge: Cambridge University Press.

Colina, Sonia (1997) Contrastive rhetoric and text-typological conventions in translation teaching. *Target* 9, 335–53.

Danks, Joseph H., Shreve G.M., Fountain S.B. and McBeatle M.K. (eds) (1997) *Cognitive Processes in Translation and Interpreting*. Thousand Oaks: Sage.

Darbelnet, Jean (1977) Niveaux de la traduction. *Babel* 23, 6–17.

de Beaugrande, Robert and Dressler, Wolfgang (1981) *Introduction to Text Linguistics*. London: Longman.

Delisle, Jean and Woodsworth, Judith (eds) (1995) *Translators through History*. Amsterdam and Philadelphia: Benjamins, UNESCO Publishing.

Doherty, Monika (1999) Clefts in translations between English and German. *Target* 11, 289–315.

Doherty, Monika and Angermüller, Hartmut (1983) Sprachliche Operationen beim Übersetzen. *Fremdsprachen* 27, 166–70.

Dollerup, Cay (1996) Language work at the European Union. In M. Gaddis Rose (ed.) *Translation Horizons Beyond the Boundaries of Translation Spectrum* (pp. 297–314). Binghamton: State University of New York.

Erdmann, Renate *et al.* (1994) *Perspectives on Pre-translational Text Analysis*. Duisburg. (L.A.U.D. Paper No. 343, Series A).

Even-Zohar, Itamar (1978) *Papers in Historical Poetics*. Tel Aviv: Porter Institute for Poetics and Semiotics.

Fillmore, Charles J. (1975) An alternative to checklists theories of meaning. *Proceedings of the First Annual Meeting of the Berkeley Linguistics Society* (pp. 123–31). Berkeley: Institute of Human Learning. University of California at Berkely.

Fillmore, Charles J. (1976) Frame semantics and the nature of understanding. *Annals of the New York Academy of Science* 280, 20–32.

Fillmore Charles J. (1985) Frames and the semantics of understanding. *Quaderni di Semantica* 6, 222–54.

Fleck, Klaus E.W. (1998) Urkundenübersetzung. In M. Snell-Hornby, H. G. Hönig, P. Kussmaul and B. A. Schmitt (eds) *Handbuch Translation* (pp. 230–34). Tübingen: Stauffenburg.

Frank, Armin P. *et al.* (eds) (in press) *Übersetzung – Translation – Traduction. Ein internationales Handbuch zur Übersetzungsforschung. An International Encyclopedia of Translation Studies. Encyclopédie internationale de la recherche sur la traduction.* Berlin and New York: de Gruyter.

Freigang, Karl-Heinz (1998) Machine-aided translation. In M. Baker (ed.) *Routledge Encyclopedia of Translation Studies* (pp. 134–36). London and New York: Routledge.

Friederich, Wolf (1969) *Technik des Übersetzens. Englisch und Deutsch.* München: Hueber.

Gentzler, Edwin (1993) *Contemporary Translation Theories*. London: Routledge.

Gilbert, Harriett (1999) Writing reviews. In W. Hicks with S. Adams and H. Gilbert (eds) *Writing for Journalists* (pp. 99–123). London: Routledge.

Gile, Daniel (1995) *Basic Concepts and Models for Interpreter and Translator Training*. Amsterdam and Philadelphia: Benjamins.

Gommlich, Klaus (1985) Textäquivalenz und Informationsverteilung (dargestellt an Beziehungen zwischen Satzäußerungen). *Linguistische Studien*, Reihe A, 135, 24–33.

Göpferich, Susanne (1995) *Textsorten in Naturwissenschaft und Technik. Pragmatische Typologie - Kontrastierung - Translation*. Tübingen: Narr.

Göpferich, Susanne (1998a) *Interkulturelles Technical Writing. Fachliches adressatengerecht vermitteln. Ein Lehr- und Arbeitsbuch*. Tübingen: Narr.

Göpferich, Susanne (1998b) Patentschriften. In M. Snell-Hornby, H. G. Hönig, P. Kussmaul and P.A. Schmitt (eds) *Handbuch Translation* (pp. 222–25). Tübingen: Stauffenburg.

Gorlee, Dinda L. (1997) Intercode translation: Words and music in opera. *Target* 9, 235–70.

Grice, Paul (1975) Logic and conversation. In P. Cole and J.J. Morgan (eds) *Syntax and Semantics, 3: Speech Acts* (pp. 41–58). New York: Academic Press.

Gutt, Ernst August (1991) *Translation and Relevance*. Oxford: Blackwell.

Hagen, Stephen (1998) Exporting today: Policy implications. *The Linguist* 37, 66–71.

Halverson, Sandra (1997) The concept of equivalence in translation studies: Much ado about something. *Target* 9, 207–33.

Hatim, Basil and Mason, Ian (1990) *Discourse and the Translator*. London: Longman.

Hatim, Basil and Mason, Ian (1997) *The Translator as Communicator*. London: Routledge.

Hellinger, Marlies (1990) *Kontrastive Feministische Linguistik. Mechanismen sprachlicher Diskriminierung im Englischen und Deutschen*. Ismaning: Hueber.

Hermans, Theo (ed.) (1985) *The Manipulation of Literature: Studies in Literary Translation*. London: Croom Helm.

Hermans, Theo (1998) Translation and normativity. *Current Issues in Language and Society* 5, 50–71.

Hermans, Theo (1999) *Translation in Systems. Descriptive and System-oriented Approaches Explained*. Manchester: St. Jerome.

Hervey, Sándor, Higgins, Ian and Loughridge, Michael (1995) *Thinking German Translation. A Course in Translation Method: German to English*. London and New York: Routledge.

Hickey, Leo (ed.) (1998) *The Pragmatics of Translation*. Clevedon: Multilingual Matters.

Hicks, Wynford with Adams, Sally and Gilbert, Harriett (1999) *Writing for Journalists*. London: Routledge.

Hohenadl, Christa and Will, Renate (1994) *Into German*. München: Hueber.

Holmes, James (1988) *Translated! Papers on Literary Translation and Translation Studies*. Amsterdam: Rodopi.

Holz-Mänttäri, Justa (1984) *Translatorisches Handeln. Theorie und Methode*. Helsinki: Suomalainen Tiedeakatemia.

Holz-Mänttäri, Justa (1993) Textdesign - verantwortlich und gehirngerecht. In J. Holz-Mänttäri and C. Nord (eds) *Traducere Navem. Festschrift für Katharina Reiss zum 70. Geburtstag* (pp. 301–20). Tampere: Tampereen Yliopisto (studia translatologica A 3).

Hönig, Hans G. (1995) *Konstruktives Übersetzen*. Tübingen: Stauffenburg.

Hönig, Hans G (1997) Positions, power and practice: Functionalist approaches and translation quality assessment. *Current Issues in Language and Society* 4, 6–34.

Hönig, Hans G. and Kussmaul, Paul (1982) *Strategie der Übersetzung. Ein Lehr- und Arbeitsbuch*. Tübingen: Narr.

Hönig, Hans G. and Kussmaul, Paul (1991) *Strategie der Übersetzung. Ein Lehr- und Arbeitsbuch*. Tübingen: Narr (4th edition).

House, Juliane (1977) *A Model for Translation Quality Assessment*. Tübingen: Narr.

House, J. (1997) *Translation Quality Assessment. A Model Revisited*. Tübingen: Narr.

Humboldt, Wilhelm von (1963) Einleitung zu Aeschylos Agamemnon metrisch übersetzt (1816). In H.J. Störig (ed.) *Das Problem des Übersetzens* (pp. 71–96). Darmstadt: Wissenschaftliche Buchgesellschaft. (Extracts translated into English by Douglas Robinson. In D. Robinson *Western Translation Theory from Herodotus to Nietzsche* (pp. 239–40)). Manchester: St. Jerome.)

Jäger, Gert and Müller, Dietrich (1982) Kommunikative und maximale Äquivalenz von Texten. In G. Jäger and A. Neubert (eds) *Äquivalenz bei der Translation* (pp. 42–57). Leipzig: Enzyklopädie (Übersetzungswissenschaftliche Beiträge 5).

Kade, Otto (1968) *Zufall und Gesetzmäßigkeit in der Übersetzung* (Beiheft I zur Zeitschrift *Fremdsprachen*). Leipzig: Enzyklopädie.

Kadric, Mira and Kaindl, Klaus (1997) Astérix – Vom Gallier zum Tschetnikjäger: Zur Problematik von Massenkommunikation und übersetzerischer Ethik. In M. Snell-Hornby, Z. Jettmarova and K. Kaindl (eds) *Translation as Intercultural Communication. Selected Papers from the EST Congress, Prague 1995* (pp. 135–46). Amsterdam and Philadelphia: Benjamins.

Kaindl, Klaus (1995) *Die Oper als Textgestalt. Perspektiven einer interdisziplinären Übersetzungswissenschaft*. Tübingen: Stauffenburg.

Kaindl, Klaus (1997) Die Übersetzung als Inszenierung: Ein interdisziplinärer Rahmen zur Analyse von Opernübersetzung. *Target* 9, 271–87.

Kirkpatrick, Betty (1996) *Dictionary of Clichés*. London: Bloomsbury.

Kohlmayer, Rainer (1988) Der Literaturübersetzer zwischen Original und Markt. Eine Kritik funktionalistischer Übersetzungstheorien. *Lebende Sprachen* 33, 145–56.

Koller, Werner (1979) *Einführung in die Übersetzungswissenschaft*. Heidelberg: Quelle & Meyer.

Koller, Werner (1992) *Einführung in die Übersetzungswissenschaft*. Heidelberg: Quelle & Meyer (2nd edition).

Koller, Werner (1993) Zum Begriff der 'eigentlichen' Übersetzung. In J. Holz-Mänttäri and C. Nord (eds) *Traducere Navem. Festschrift für Katharina Reiss zum 70. Geburtstag* (pp. 49–63). Tampere: Tampereen Yliopisto (studia translatologica A 3).

Königs, Karin (1998) Verbless clauses mit *with* und ihre Übersetzung. *Lebende Sprachen* 43, 106–12.

Koskinen, Kaisa (2000) Institutional illusions: Translating in the EU Commission. *The Translator* 6, 49–65.

Krings, Hans P. (1986) *Was in den Köpfen von Übersetzern vorgeht: Eine empirische Untersuchung zur Struktur des Übersetzungsprozesses an fortgeschrittenen Französischlernern.* Tübingen: Narr.

Kupsch-Losereit, Sigrid (1998) Vertragstexte. In M. Snell-Hornby, H.G. Hönig, P. Kussmaul and P.A. Schmitt (eds) *Handbuch Translation* (pp. 228–30). Tübingen: Stauffenburg.

Kussmaul, Paul (1990) Instruktionen in deutschen und englischen Bedienungsanleitungen. In R. Arntz and G. Thome (eds) *Übersetzungswissenschaft. Ergebnisse und Perspektiven* (pp. 369–79). Tübingen: Narr.

Kussmaul, Paul (1995) *Training the Translator.* Amsterdam and Philadelphia: Benjamins.

Kussmaul, Paul (1997) Text-type conventions and translating: Some methodological issues. In A. Trosborg (ed.) *Text Typology and Translation* (pp. 67–83). Amsterdam and Philadelphia: Benjamins.

Kussmaul, Paul (1998a) Die Erforschung von Übersetzungsprozessen: Resultate und Desiderate. *Lebende Sprachen* 43, 49–53.

Kussmaul, Paul (1998b) Kreativität. In M. Snell-Hornby, H.G. Hönig, P. Kussmaul and P.A. Schmitt (eds) *Handbuch Translation* (pp. 178–80). Tübingen: Stauffenburg.

Kussmaul, Paul (1998c) Philologische Texte. In M. Snell-Hornby, H.G. Hönig, P. Kussmaul and P.A. Schmitt (eds) *Handbuch Translation* (pp. 235–36). Tübingen: Stauffenburg.

Kussmaul, Paul (2000) *Kreatives Übersetzen.* Tübingen: Stauffenburg.

Lakoff, George and Johnson, Mark (1980) *Metaphors We Live By.* Chicago: University of Chicago Press.

Lambert, José (1994) The cultural component reconsidered. In M. Snell-Hornby, F. Pöchhacker and K. Kaindl (eds) *Translation Studies: An Interdiscipline* (pp. 17–26). Philadelphia/New York: Benjamins.

Laviosa, Sara (1997) How comparable can 'comparable corpora' be? *Target* 9, 289–319.

Lawson, Veronica (1983) The language of patents. *Lebende Sprachen* 28, 58–61.

Lefevere, André and Bassnett, Susan (1990) Introduction: Proust's grandmother and the Thousand and One Nights: The 'cultural turn' in translation studies. In S. Bassnett and A. Lefevere (eds) *Translation, History and Culture* (pp. 1–13). London: Pinter.

Liebert, Wolf-Andreas and Schmitt, Reinhold (1998) Texten als Dienstleistung. Sprachwissenschaftler schreiben die besseren Gebrauchsanweisungen. *Sprachreport* 14, 1–5.

Lörscher, Wolfgang (1991) *Translation Performance, Translation Process, and Translation Strategies.* Tübingen: Narr.

Luther, Martin (1997) Circular letter on translation (Sendbrief vom Dolmetschen, 1530). Extracts translated into English by Douglas Robinson. In

D. Robinson *Western Translation Theory from Herodotus to Nietzsche* (pp. 84–89). Manchester: St. Jerome.

Markstein, Elisabeth (1994) Sprache als Realie: Intertextualität und Übersetzung. Am Beispiel totalitärer Sprachen. In M. Snell-Hornby, F. Pöchhacker and K. Kaindl (eds) *Translation Studies: An Interdiscipline* (pp. 103–11). Philadelphia / New York: Benjamins.

Markstein, Elisabeth (1998) Realia. In M. Snell-Hornby, H.G. Hönig, P. Kussmaul and P.A. Schmitt (eds) *Handbuch Translation* (pp. 288–91). Tübingen: Stauffenburg.

Morris, Marshall (ed.) (1995) *Translation and the Law.* Amsterdam and Philadelphia: Benjamins. (= American Translators Association Scholarly Monograph, VIII).

Muzii, Luigi (1998) The quality wars. Qualifying quality: An Italian perspective. *Language International* 10, 18–21.

Neubert, Albrecht (1968) Pragmatische Aspekte der Übersetzung. *Grundfragen der Übersetzungswissenschaft. Beihefte zur Zeitschrift Fremdsprachen II*, 21–34.

Neubert, Albrecht (1985) *Text and Translation.* Leipzig: Enzyklopädie (Übersetzungswissenschaftliche Beiträge 8).

Neubert, Albrecht (2000) Competence in language, in languages, and in translation. In C. Schäffner and B. Adab (eds) *Developing Translation Competence* (pp. 3–18). Amsterdam and Philadelphia: Benjamins.

Neubert, Albrecht and Shreve, Gregory M. (1992) *Translation as Text.* Kent and London: Kent State University Press.

Newmark, Peter (1981) *Approaches to Translation.* Oxford: Pergamon

Newmark, Peter (1988) *A Textbook of Translation.* London: Prentice-Hall.

Newmark, Peter (1989) Communicative and semantic translation. In A. Chesterman (ed.) *Readings in Translation Theory* (pp. 116–40). Helsinki: Oy Finn Lectura Ab.

Newmark, Peter (1991a) *About Translation.* Clevedon: Multilingual Matters.

Newmark, Peter (1991b) The curse of dogma in translation studies. *Lebende Sprachen* 36, 105–08.

Nida, Eugene (1964) *Toward a Science of Translating: With Special Reference to Principles and Procedures Involved in Bible Translating.* Leiden: E.J. Brill.

Nida, Eugene and Taber, Ch. R. (1969) *The Theory and Practice of Translation.* Leiden: E.J. Brill.

Nord, Christiane (1988) *Textanalyse und Übersetzen.* Heidelberg: Groos.

Nord, Christiane (1991) *Text Analysis in Translation.* Amsterdam: Rodopi.

Nord, Christiane (1993) *Einführung in das funktionale Übersetzen. Am Beispiel von Titeln und Überschriften.* Tübingen und Basel: Francke (UTB).

Nord, Christiane (1997) *Translating as a Purposeful Activity. Functionalist Approaches Explained.* Manchester: St. Jerome.

Pavlovich, Henry (1999) Director's notes. *The Linguist* 38, 37.

Reiss, Katharina (1971) *Möglichkeiten und Grenzen der Übersetzungskritik.* München: Hueber.

Reiss, Katharina (1976) *Texttyp und Übersetzungsmethode. Der operative Text.* Kronberg: Scriptor.

Reiss, Katharina (2000) *Translation Criticism – The Potentials and Limitations.*

(translated by E.F. Rhodes). Manchester: St Jerome. New York: American Bible Society.

Reiss, Katharina and Vermeer, Hans (1984) *Grundlegung einer allgemeinen Translationstheorie*. Tübingen: Niemeyer.

Reiss, Katharina and Vermeer, Hans J. (1991) *Grundlegung einer allgemeinen Translationstheorie* (2nd edition). (= Linguistische Arbeiten 147). Tübingen: Niemeyer.

Robinson, Douglas (1997a) *Western Translation Theory from Herodotus to Nietzsche*. Manchester: St. Jerome.

Robinson, Douglas (1997b) *Translation and Empire: Postcolonial Theories Explained*. Manchester: St Jerome.

Rolf, Eckhard (1993) *Die Funktionen der Gebrauchstextsorten*. Berlin and New York: de Gruyter.

Rothkegel, Annely (1984) Sprachhandlungstypen in interaktionsregelnden Texten. In I. Rosengren (ed.) *Sprache und Pragmatik* (pp. 255–77). Lund: Almqvist and Wiksell (Lunder Symposium 1984).

Sager, Juan (1994) *Language Engineering and Translation: Consequences of Automation*. Amsterdam: Benjamins.

Sandford, John (1976) *The Mass Media of the German-speaking Countries*. London: Oswald Wolf.

Sandrini, Peter (ed.) (1999) *Übersetzen von Rechtstexten. Fachkommunikation im Spannungsfeld zwischen Rechtsordnung und Sprache*. Tübingen: Narr.

Sarcevic, Susan (1997) *New Approach to Legal Translation*. The Hague: Kluwer Law International.

Sauer, Christoph (1996) Echoes from abroad – Speeches for the domestic audience: Queen Beatrix' address to the Israeli Parliament. *Current Issues in Language and Society* 3, 233–67.

Schäffner, Christina (1992a) Translating governmental documents. In C. Mair and M. Markus (eds) *New Departures in Contrastive Linguistics/Neue Ansätze in der Kontrastiven Linguistik. Proceedings of the Conference held at the Leopold-Franzens-University of Innsbruck, Austria, 10–12 May 1991* (pp. 143–54). Innsbruck: University Press (Innsbrucker Beiträge zur Kulturwissenschaft, Anglistische Reihe Band 5, vol. II).

Schäffner, Christina (1992b) Sprache des Umbruchs und ihre Übersetzung. In A. Burkhardt and K.P. Fritzsche (eds) *Sprache im Umbruch. Politischer Sprachwandel im Zeichen von 'Wende' und 'Vereinigung'* (pp. 135–53). Berlin: de Gruyter.

Schäffner, Christina (1995a) Textsorten in der Übersetzung – Analyse eines Übersetzungsbeispiels. In I.-A. Busch-Lauer, S. Fiedler, M. Ruge (eds) *Texte als Gegenstand linguistischer Forschung und Vermittlung. Festschrift für Rosemarie Gläser* (pp. 47–56). Frankfurt: Lang (LFS = Leipziger Fachsprachenstudien, Band 10).

Schäffner, Christina (1995b) CSCE documents from the point of view of translation. In A. Neubert, G.M. Shreve and K. Gommlich (eds) *Basic Issues in Translation Studies. Proceedings of the Fifth International Conference, Leipzig 1991* (pp. 77–90). Kent: Kent State University Press (Kent Forum on Translation Studies, Vol. II).

Schäffner, Christina (1996) Building a European house? Or at two speeds into a dead end? Metaphors in the debate on the United Europe. In A. Musolff, C. Schäffner and M. Townson (eds) *Conceiving of Europe – Diversity in Unity* (pp. 31–59). Aldershot: Dartmouth.

Schäffner, Christina (1997a) Where is the source text? In H. Schmidt and G. Wotjak (eds) *Modelle der Translation. Models of Translation. Festschrift für Albrecht Neubert* (pp. 193–211). Frankfurt: Vervuert.

Schäffner, Christina (1997b) Metaphor and interdisciplinary analysis. *Journal of Area Studies* 11, 57–72.

Schäffner, Christina (1997c) Political texts as sensitive texts. In K. Simms (ed.) *Translating Sensitive Texts: Linguistic Aspects* (pp. 131–38). Amsterdam: Rodopi.

Schäffner, Christina (1997d) Strategies of translating political texts. In A. Trosborg (ed.) *Text Typology and Translation* (pp. 119–43). Amsterdam and Philadelphia: Benjamins.

Schäffner, Christina (1998a) Hedges in political texts: A translational perspective. In L. Hickey (ed.) *The Pragmatics of Translation* (pp. 185–202). Clevedon: Multilingual Matters.

Schäffner, Christina (1998b) Metaphern. In M. Snell-Hornby, H.G. Hönig, P. Kussmaul and P.A. Schmitt (eds) *Handbuch Translation* (pp. 280–85). Tübingen: Stauffenburg.

Schäffner, Christina (1998c) Parallel texts in translation. In L. Bowker, M. Cronin, D. Kenny and J. Pearson (eds) *Unity in Diversity? Current Trends in Translation Studies* (pp. 83–90). Manchester: St. Jerome.

Schäffner, Christina (2000a) The role of genre for translation. In A. Trosborg (ed.) *Analysing Professional Genres* (pp. 209–24). Amsterdam and Philadelphia: Benjamins.

Schäffner, Christina (2000b) Running before walking? Designing a translation programme at undergraduate level. In C. Schäffner and B. Adab (eds) *Developing Translation Competence* (pp. 143–56). Amsterdam and Philadelphia: Benjamins.

Schäffner, Christina (2000c) Translators as cosmopolitans? In S. Kirkbright (ed.) *Cosmopolitans in the Modern World* (pp. 96–110). München: iudicium.

Schäffner, Christina (in press a) Metaphor and translation: Some implications of a cognitive approach. *Journal of Pragmatics*.

Schäffner, Christina, Shreve, Gregory M. and Wiesemann, Uwe (1987) A procedural analysis of argumentative political texts. Case studies from *The Economist*. *Zeitschrift für Anglistik und Amerikanistik* 35, 105–17.

Schleiermacher, Friedrich (1963) Über die verschiedenen Methoden des Übersetzens. In H.J. Störig (ed.) *Das Problem des Übersetzens* (pp. 38–70). Darmstadt: Wissenschaftliche Buchgesellschaft. (On the different methods of translating. Translated into English by Douglas Robinson. In D. Robinson *Western Translation Theory from Herodotus to Nietzsche* (pp. 225–38). Manchester: St. Jerome.)

Schmidt, Heide (1977) Probleme der konfrontativen Beschreibung stilistischer Selektionsbeschränkunegn. In O. Kade (ed.) *Vermittelte Kommunikation, Sprachmittlung, Translation* (pp. 111–21). Leipzig: Enzyklopädie (Übersetzungwissenschaftliche Beiträge 1).

Schmidt, Paul (1998) Automatisches Übersetzen. In M. Snell-Hornby, H.G. Hönig, P. Kussmaul and P.A. Schmitt (eds) *Handbuch Translation* (pp. 133–37). Tübingen: Stauffenburg.

Schmitt, Peter A. (1990) Was übersetzen Übersetzer? Eine Umfrage. *Lebende Sprachen* 35, 97–106.

Schmitt, Peter A. (1996) Warnhinweise in deutschen und englischen Anleitungen. *Lebende Sprachen* 41, 49–57.

Schmitt, Peter A. (1998a) Marktsituation der Übersetzer. In M. Snell-Hornby, H.G. Hönig, P. Kussmaul and P.A. Schmitt (eds) *Handbuch Translation* (pp. 5–13). Tübingen: Stauffenburg.

Schmitt, Peter A. (1998b) Berufsbild. In M. Snell-Hornby, H.G. Hönig, P. Kussmaul and P.A. Schmitt (eds) *Handbuch Translation* (pp. 1–5). Tübingen: Stauffenburg.

Schmitt, Peter A. (1998c) Anleitungen/Benutzerhinweise. In M. Snell-Hornby, H.G. Hönig, P. Kussmaul and P.A. Schmitt (eds) *Handbuch Translation* (pp. 209–13). Tübingen: Stauffenburg.

Schmitt, Peter A. (1998d) Qualitätsmanagement. In M. Snell-Hornby, H.G. Hönig, P. Kussmaul and P.A. Schmitt (eds) *Handbuch Translation* (pp. 394–99). Tübingen: Stauffenburg.

Schmitt, Peter A. (1999) *Translation und Technik*. Tübingen: Stauffenburg.

Schmitz, Klaus-Dirk and Wahle, Kirsten (eds) (2000) *Softwarelokalisierung*. Tübingen: Stauffenburg.

Schopp, Jürgen F. (1998) Typographie und Layout. In M. Snell-Hornby, H.G. Hönig, P. Kussmaul and P.A. Schmitt (eds) *Handbuch Translation* (pp. 199–204). Tübingen: Stauffenburg.

Schreiber, Michael (1997) Übersetzungsverfahren: Klassifikation und didaktische Anwendung. In E. Fleischmann, W. Kutz and P.A. Schmitt (eds) *Translationsdidaktik. Grundfragen der Übersetzungswissenschaft* (pp. 219–26). Tübingen: Narr.

Schreitmüller, Andreas (1994) Interlinguale Relationen. *Lebende Sprachen* 39, 104–06.

Searle, John R. (1969) *Speech Acts: An Essay in the Philosophy of Language*. Cambridge: Cambridge University Press.

Séguinot, Candance (ed.) (1989) *The Translation Process*. Toronto: H.G. Publications, York University.

Séguinot, Candace (1994) Translation and advertising: Going global. *Current Issues in Language and Society* 1, 249–65.

Simeoni, Daniel (1998) The pivotal status of the translator's habitus. *Target* 10, 1–39.

Simon, Sherry (1996) *Gender in Translation. Cultural Identity and the Politics of Transmission*. London: Routledge.

Smith, Veronica (1998) Werbetexte. In M. Snell-Hornby, H.G. Hönig, P. Kussmaul and P.A. Schmitt (eds) *Handbuch Translation* (pp. 238–42). Tübingen: Stauffenburg.

Smith, Veronica and Klein-Braley, Christine (1997) Advertising: A five-stage strategy for translation. In M. Snell-Hornby, Z. Jettmarova and K. Kaindl (eds) *Translation as Intercultural Communication. Selected Papers from the EST Congress, Prague 1995* (pp. 173–84). Amsterdam and Philadelphia: Benjamins.

Snell-Hornby, Mary (1988) *Translation Studies: An Integrated Approach*. Amsterdam and Philadelphia: Benjamins.

Snell-Hornby, Mary (1999) Communicating in the global village. On language, translation and cultural identity. *Current Issues in Language and Society* 6, 103–20.

Snell-Hornby, Mary, Pöchhacker, Franz and Kaindl, Klaus (eds) (1992) *Translation Studies. An Interdiscipline*. Amsterdam and Philadelphia: Benjamins.

Snell-Hornby, Mary, Hönig, Hans G., Kussmaul, Paul and Schmitt, Peter A. (eds) (1998) *Handbuch Translation*. Tübingen: Stauffenburg.

Somers, Harold (1998) Machine translation. In M. Baker (ed.) *Routledge Encyclopedia of Translation Studies* (pp. 136–49). London and New York: Routledge.

Steiner, Erich (1998) A register-based translation evaluation: An advertisement as a case in point. *Target* 10, 291–318.

Stienstra, Nelly (1993) *YHWH is the Husband of His People. Analysis of a Biblical Metaphor with Special Reference to Translation*. Kampen: Kok Pharos.

Stoll, Karl-Heinz (2000) Zukunftsperspektiven der Translation. *Lebende Sprachen* 45, 49–59.

Stolze, Radegundis (1994) *Übersetzungstheorien. Eine Einführung*. Tübingen: Narr.

Stolze, Radegundis (1997) *Übersetzungstheorien. Eine Einführung*. Tübingen: Narr (2nd edition).

Stolze, Radegundis (1998) Stereotype – Bilder – Texte – Übersetzungen. Beobachtungen an Werbetexten in Brasilien und Deutschland. *Lebende Sprachen* 43, 97–104.

Stolze, Radegundis (1999) *Die Fachübersetzung. Eine Einführung*. Tübingen: Narr.

Störig, Hans J. (ed.) (1963) *Das Problem des Übersetzens*. Darmstadt: Wissenschaftliche Buchgesellschaft.

Suter, Hans-J. (1993) *The Wedding Report: A Prototypical Approach to the Study of Traditional Text Types*. Amsterdam and Philadelphia: Benjamins.

Swales, John (1990) *Genre Analysis. English in Academic and Research Settings*. Cambridge: Cambridge University Press.

Tannen, Deborah (1993) What's in a frame? Surface evidence for underlying expectations. In D. Tannen (ed.) *Framing in Discourse* (pp. 14–56). New York/Oxford: Oxford University Press.

The Economist Pocket Style Book (1986) London: The Economist Publications Ltd.

The Translator (1998), Special Issue on *Translation and Minority*. Guest Editor: L. Venuti, Vol. 4.

Thiel, Gisela and Thome, Gisela (1987) *Resolutionen. Ein empirisch entwickelter Beitrag zur Textanalyse*. Tübingen: Narr.

Toury, Gideon (1980) *In Search of a Theory of Translation*. Tel Aviv: The Porter Institute for Poetics and Semiotics.

Toury, Gideon (1995) *Descriptive Translation Studies and Beyond*. Amsterdam and Philadelphia: Benjamins.

Trosborg, Anna (1994) 'Acts' in contracts: Some guidelines for translation. In M.

Snell-Hornby, F. Pöchhacker and K. Kaindl (eds) *Translation Studies: An Interdiscipline* (pp. 309–18). Philadelphia/New York: Benjamins.

Trosborg, Anna (1997) Text typology: Register, genre and text type. In A. Trosborg (ed.) *Text Typology and Translation* (pp. 3–23). Amsterdam and Philadelphia: Benjamins.

Tymoczko, Maria (2000a) Translation and political engagement. *The Translator* 6, 23–47.

Tymoczko, Maria (2000b) Connecting the two infinite orders: Research methods in translation studies. Plenary paper delivered to the international conference 'Research Models in Translation Studies', Manchester, 28–30 April 2000.

van Dijk, Teun A. (1980) *Macrostructures. An Interdisciplinary Study of Global Structures in Discourse, Interaction, and Cognition.* Hillsdale, NJ: Erlbaum.

van Dijk, Teun A. (1985) Structures of news in the press. In T. van Dijk (ed.) *Discourse and Communication: New Approaches to the Analysis of Mass Media Discourse and Communication* (pp. 69–93). Berlin: de Gruyter.

Vannerem, Mia and Snell-Hornby, Mary (1986) Die Szene hinter dem Text: 'Scenes-and frames-semantics' in der Übersetzung. In M. Snell-Hornby (ed.) *Übersetzungswissenschaft. Eine Neuorientierung* (pp. 184–205). Tübingen: Francke (UTB).

Venuti, Lawrence (1995) *The Translator's Invisibility.* London: Routledge.

Venuti, Lawrence (1998) *The Scandals of Translation: Towards an Ethics of Difference.* London: Routledge.

Venuti, Lawrence (ed.) (2000) *The Translation Studies Reader.* London and New York: Routledge.

Vermeer, Hans J. (1978) Ein Rahmen für eine allgemeine Translationstheorie. *Lebende Sprachen* 23, 99–102.

Vermeer, Hans J. (1987) What does it mean to translate? *Indian Journal of Applied Linguistics* 13, 25–33.

Vermeer, Hans J. (1989) Skopos and commission in translational action. In A. Chesterman (ed.) *Readings in Translation Theory* (pp. 173–87). Helsinki: Oy Finn Lectura Ab.

Vermeer, Hans J. (1996) *A Skopos Theory of Translation (Some Arguments For and Against).* Heidelberg: TEXTconTEXT.

Vinay, Jean-Paul and Darbelnet, Jean (1958) *Stylistique comparée du français et de l'anglais. Méthode de traduction.* Paris: Didier.

Vuorinen, Erkka (1996) *Crossing Cultural Boundaries in International News Transmission: A Translational Approach.* University of Tampere, unpublished licentiate thesis.

Wilss, Wolfram (1977) *Übersetzungswissenschaft. Probleme und Methoden.* Stuttgart: Klett.

Wilss, Wolfram (1996) *Knowledge and Skills in Translator Behavior.* Amsterdam and Philadelphia: Benjamins.

Wotjak, Gerd (1985) Techniken der Übersetzung. *Fremdsprachen* 29, 24–34.

Yang, Wenliang (1990) *Anglizismen im Deutschen. Am Beispiel des Nachrichtenmagazins 'Der Spiegel'.* Tübingen: Niemeyer.